THE GLORIOUS MADNESS

. . .

TALES of THE IRISH and the GREAT WAR

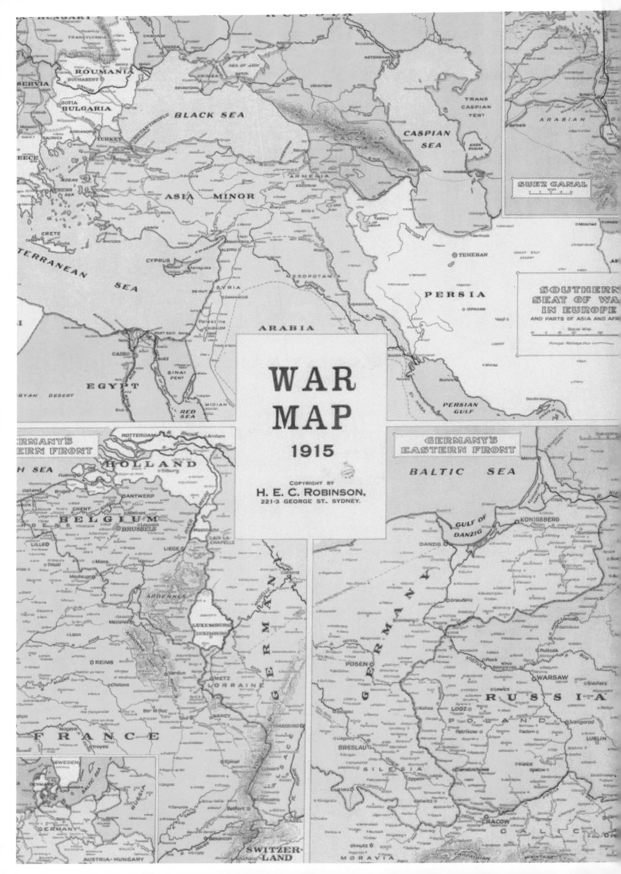

THE GLORIOUS MADNESS

...

TALES of the IRISH and the GREAT WAR

...

TURTLE BUNBURY

GILL & MACMILLAN

Gill & Macmillan
Hume Avenue, Park West, Dublin 12
www.gillmacmillanbooks.ie

© Turtle Bunbury 2014
978 07171 6234 5

Index compiled by Grainne Farren
Design and print origination by www.grahamthew.com
Printed by Printer Trento Srl, Italy

This book is typeset in 10.5pt Granjon on 12.5pt.

The paper used in this book comes from the wood pulp of managed forests.
For every tree felled, at least one tree is planted, thereby renewing natural
resources.

A CIP catalogue record for this book is available from the British Library.

1 3 5 4 2

DEDICATION

Every morning, as I set off to work on this book, my two small daughters would pounce upon me like clockwork and ask: 'Are you writing about dead people again, Daddy?' Such is the lot of a historian! But war is not an easy subject to share in a family home. Not unlike those who returned home from the front lines, I was inclined to keep my thoughts to myself for the most part. Therefore, I dedicate this book to those with whom I live — my beautiful wife Ally, my gorgeous daughters, Jemima and Bay — for keeping our home full of laughter and merriment and love while I wrote and dreamed of grim and ghastly war.

The book is also for Alan Appleby Drew, Guy Finlay, Bobby Finlay and all the other souls who lived and died during the time of the Great War.

'To every life that God hath given, he hath allotted a work — the fulfilment of that work comes naturally, and its proper accomplishment should form the sole ambition of that life.'

ALAN APPLEBY DREW (1884–1915)

WASTE

Waste of Muscle, waste of Brain,
Waste of Patience, waste of Pain,
Waste of Manhood, waste of Health,
Waste of Beauty, waste of Wealth,
Waste of Blood, and waste of Tears,
Waste of Youth's most precious years,
Waste of ways the Saints have trod,
Waste of Glory, waste of God — War!

REV GEOFFREY STUDDERT KENNEDY,
AKA WOODBINE WILLIE (1919)

CONTENTS

PART THREE: FORGOTTEN FRONTS

INTRODUCTION

My hairbrush once belonged to a man called Alan Appleby Drew, an uncle of my paternal grandmother, who was working as a teacher at Mostyn House School in Cheshire when the Great War broke out. Alan was a man who liked to sing and entertain. He had travelled a good deal and spent a few years in Shanghai. His father was on the Scottish team who took on England in the world's first rugby international. Alan evidently felt sufficiently Scottish to join the Cameronians, aka the Scottish Rifles. Lieutenant AA Drew arrived on the Western Front in February 1915 and lasted four weeks. The 31-year-old was killed at Neuve-Chapelle, alongside most of his fellow officers from the Cameronians. I found his grave in the Royal Irish Rifles cemetery at Laventie and I thanked him for his hairbrush. After his death, his distraught parents gifted a carillon of 31 bells to Mostyn House, one bell for every year of his life. When that school closed a few years ago, the bells were offered to Charterhouse in Surrey, where Alan had been at school. Considering that Alan was one of a staggering 687 past pupils from Charterhouse who died in the war, the school was very keen to take the bells. And so it was that on a sunny afternoon in May 2014, I stood beneath a belfry at Charterhouse, alongside my father and my oldest brother, listening to the clanging melodies as AA Drew's carillon rang anew.

My maternal grandmother also lost two uncles in the war. Guy Finlay and his younger brother Bobby grew up at Corkagh House near Clondalkin, County Dublin. Their father was Lieutenant Colonel of the 5th Battalion of the Royal Dublin Fusiliers and, not surprisingly, both sons joined the regiment. So too did their eldest brother, Harry, who succumbed to dysentery in the Anglo-Boer War. Bobby was killed in Flanders during a failed attempt to capture the German trenches at Aubers Ridge in May 1915. Fourteen months later, Guy fell at the Somme, caught out by the German counter-attack at Bazentin Ridge.

Three years ago, my brother and I went to find our great-great-uncles' graves on the Western Front. Before we left, I dashed into the woods of Corkagh Park on a whim, seeking something from the old family home that I might place on the Finlay brothers' graves, should we find them. Rather pathetically, the best I could come up with were two leaves from a majestic old horse chestnut tree that they had perhaps played beneath as boys. The bodies of Guy and Bobby were never found, so they had no graves. However, I found their names on the memorial walls at Ploegsteert and Pozières and I wedged the chestnut leaves alongside them.

It was exceptionally moving to find Alan Appleby Drew's grave and the names of the two Finlay brothers. But it was at the cemetery in Tyne Cot in Flanders that the immensity of the war overwhelmed me. I walked alone down a path through line after line of those proud white headstones, with a wall blocking the view to my left. I thought I might have become immune to all the death by then, but any jauntiness in my stride vanished and I found myself walking ever slower until I ground to a halt just at the point where the wall beside me ended. And then I turned my eyes to the left and I slumped. Behind the wall, the field of graves was replicated again and again as far as I could see, like the saddest dream ever dreamt. Endless rows of white upright slabs, 12,000 all told, framed at one end by the 'Memorial to the Missing' upon which were written the names of another 35,000 whose bodies were never identified.

Most veterans of the Great War felt compelled to submerge their experiences in grim silence, creating an emotional void that would torment their wives and their children to such an extent that I think the repercussions of that war will be felt by unknowing generations for many decades to come.

For those who returned to Ireland after the war, the horror of their experience was magnified by the realisation that everything they fought for amounted to naught and that anyone who thought otherwise was no longer welcome. Although many of those who won independence for the Irish Free State had formerly served in His Majesty's forces, there were powerful elements within the new order that would oblige the country at large to throw an unforgiving eye on ex-servicemen of the British Empire. In time, the hostility became amnesia and the Ireland of my youth in the late 20th century seemed to have a history in which the only war the Irish ever fought was for freedom from Britannia's rule.

Tom Kettle was one of Ireland's most brilliant nationalist politicians when the war erupted. He chose to fight because he believed the Kaiser's army would destroy the very fabric of Europe. And yet he was also intuitively aware of how the truth could coil upon itself. In the wake of the Easter Rising, he wrote: 'Pearse and the others will go down in history as heroes, and I will be just a bloody English officer.' When the Irish President Michael D Higgins addressed the Houses of Parliament in Westminster in the spring of 2014, he spoke of Kettle specifically, and acknowledged all of the other Irish men and women who served. It was another coming-of-age moment for Ireland, an end to decades of silent schizophrenia.

There are no clear-cut figures as to how many Irish actually fought. By the time you combine all the Irish or half-Irish who served in the British, Canadian, Australian, New Zealand and US armies, there was probably more than a quarter of a million. Tempers tend to rise during the guessing game of how many Irish-born actually died but a figure of between 35,000 and 40,000 seems to be increasingly accepted. The Irish war dead remain almost entirely forgotten in most of the towns and villages from whence they came. In the small town of Tullow, County Carlow, where I wrote this book, at least 63 men perished in the war but I suspect that very few people in the town have ever heard of those 63 dead men.

This is not a definitive book of Irish involvement in the war. It is simply a collection of Great War stories with an Irish twist. From the generals and field commanders through to the troopers and nurses on the front lines, the Irish served at every turn. They tore through the skies in flimsy biplanes. They soared across the seas in battleships. They charged across the tortured earth with bayonets fixed. They wrapped bandages and dabbed softly in the field hospitals. They prayed, they sang, they killed, they wept and they died.

The book explores the lives of some of these people — the Home Rule politicians who died for the Empire; the Anglo-Irish aristocrats and working-class Dubliners who fell side by side; the padres who tried to bring comfort and peace; the flying aces and sharp-shooting snipers; the dashing cavalry officers and their noble steeds; the future Irish rebel leaders who learned their military skills in British uniform; the luckless Benedictine nuns and white feather victims caught up in it all; the songwriters, poets and painters who tried to show people back home how it really was. Many of these men and women were unbelievably courageous. Others seem to have been pathologically designed for war. And there were some who loathed every second of it.

It has been an amazing privilege to spend such a concentrated time getting to grips with this tangled web of campaigns, battles, regiments, battalions and so many names, numbers, twists and deaths that it sometimes became hard to breathe. By night, I dreamt of giants shrouded in barbed wire cloaks upon the shattered shores of Gallipoli, of soldiers crying in the streets of Ypres, of cricketers catching hand grenades and nurses trudging through incessant snow.

My aim has been to look at war from the perspective of the people. When I walked the stark lines of Tyne Cot and all those other cemeteries, the war slowed down. Every headstone represented a human being; their names stared at me like eyes from another world. Their cheerless fate was decreed by the simple fact that their abbreviated lives coincided with one of the most brutal conflicts our world has ever known.

2ᵉ Année · Nᵒ 47.   Le numéro : 25 centimes   9 Septembre

LE PAYS DE FRANC

Fourneau de mine *sous une* tranchée allemande

rgane des
ÉTATS
NÉRAUX
DU
URISME

Éd
Le J
2
boulevard
PA

onnement pour la France....15 Frs   Abonnement pour l'Étrange

PART ONE

THE

WESTERN

FRONT

...

THE WESTERN FRONT

• • •

THE VAST MAJORITY OF THE IRISH MEN AND WOMEN WHO SERVED IN THE Great War did so on the Western Front. Running for approximately 400 miles from the North Sea through Belgium and northern France into the Swiss Alps, the front line was created when the British, French and Belgian armies combined forces to halt the German military advance. To consolidate their respective positions, the various armies dug trenches either side of the front line. Over the next four and a half years, the war for the Western Front would involve at least 50 different battles including the Somme and Ypres. Such offensives were characterised by the greatest artillery bombardments ever known, the ghastly introduction of poison gas and the increasingly fundamental role of aeroplanes to both observe and bomb enemy positions.

The Germans so nearly won the day when they launched their Spring Offensive in March 1918. However, the failure of that offensive spelled the end for the Kaiser's ambitions and finally brought the German Empire to its knees.

Upwards of four million people died on the Western Front. A further 11 million were wounded, captured or otherwise vanished. This section looks at some of the Irish who participated. The career soldiers and hapless civilians who marched side by side. The bold, godforsaken men who charged over the top. The holy men and medics who offered succour to the wounded and dying in No Man's Land. The audacious pilots who plunged through the lead-filled skies. The displaced octogenarian nuns scampering through the ruined city of Ypres. The artists who painted the carnage. The poets for whom the war became muse.

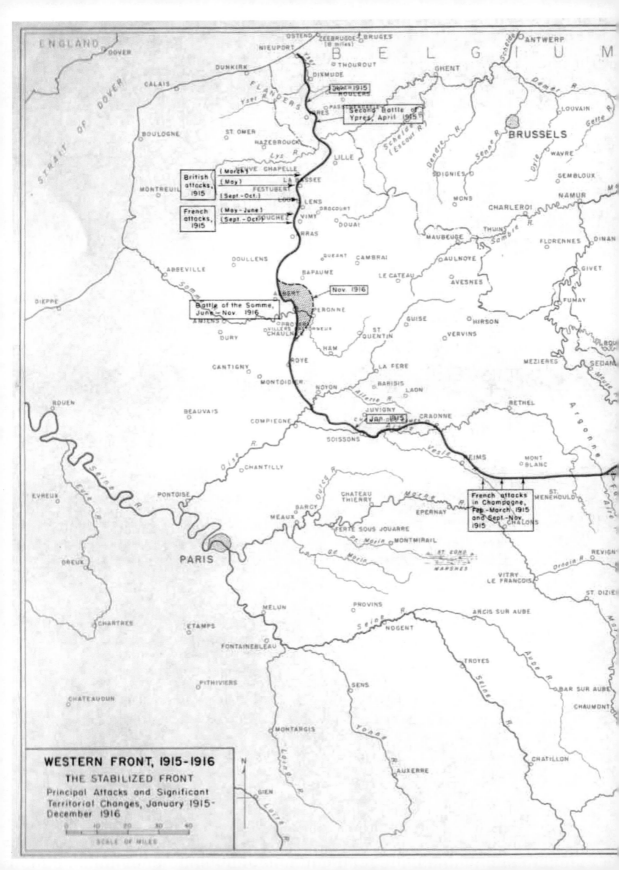

WESTERN FRONT, 1915-1916

THE STABILIZED FRONT

Principal Attacks and Significant
Territorial Changes, January 1915-
December 1916

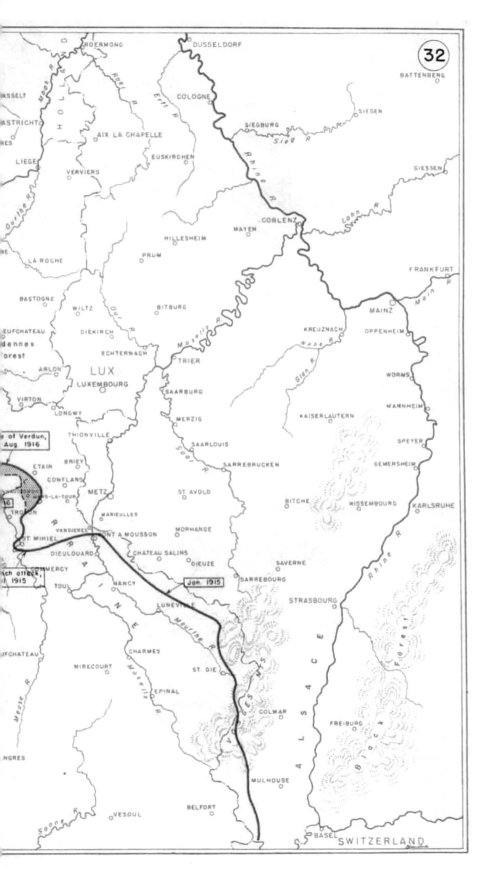

ROERMOND

DUSSELDORF

BATTENBERG

COLOGNE

HOLLAND

SIEGEN

ASSELT

Meuse R.

Roer R.

Erft R.

Eifel R.

AIX LA CHAPELLE

SIEGBURG

ASTRICHT

EUSKIRCHEN

Sieg R.

RES

LIEGE

VERVIERS

GIESSEN

Rhine R.

Ourthe R.

LA ROCHE

HILLESHEIM

MAYEN

COBLENZ

Lahn R.

RE

PRUM

FRANKFURT

dennes

orest

BASTOGNE

WILTZ

BITBURG

MAINZ

Main R.

UFCHATEAU

DIEKIRCH

KREUZNACH

OPPENHEIM

ARLON

ECHTERNACH

Moselle R.

TRIER

LUX.

LUXEMBOURG

Nahe R.

VIRTON

SAARBURG

WORMS

Glan R.

LONGWY

MERZIG

KAISERLAUTERN

MANNHEIM

THIONVILLE

SAARLOUIS

SPEYER

e of Verdun,

Aug. 1916

BRIEY

Saar R.

SARREBRUCKEN

GERMERSHEIM

ETAIN

CONFLANS

METZ

ST AVOLD

BITCHE

WISSEMBOURG

KARLSRUHE

16

S-LA-TOUR

TROON

MARIEULLES

VANDIERES

NT A MOUSSON

MORHANGE

Rhine R.

ST MIHIEL

DIEULOUARD

CHATEAU SALINS

DIEUZE

SAVERNE

ich attack,

1915

OMMERCY

NANCY

Jan. 1915

SARREBOURG

A

TOUL

LUNEVILLE

STRASBOURG

L

N

S

E

Meurthe R.

A

UFCHATEAU

CHARMES

C

MIRECOURT

ST DIE

Moselle R.

E

Meuse R.

EPINAL

COLMAR

FREIBURG

Black Forest

NGRES

VESOUL

MULHOUSE

Saône R.

BELFORT

BASEL

SWITZERLAND

D. Patrick.   D. Columban.   D. Bernard.   D. Teresa.   D. Walburge.

D. Placid.   Mother Prioress.   D. Aloysius.

THE IRISH DAMES OF YPRES.

THE
IRISH DAMES
OF
YPRES

...

THE GERMAN SHELLS WERE BLASTING INTO THE WALLS OF YPRES AS THE PRIORESS LED HER clutch of petrified nuns through the desecrated streets. Behind them, orange flames ripped through the corridors of the 17th century Irish convent which had been their home for so many years – over half a century in the case of Dame Josephine, the oldest of the Irish nuns.

It was not easy going as they stumbled through the rubble, their arms laden with packages of clothing and prized belongings. German shells shrieked through the skies. Every explosion was followed by the deafening crash of slates and bricks tumbling to the ground.

Through the haze, two men in British uniform appeared alongside the women, grabbed their packages and began to help them down the street.

'It is very kind of you to help us,' said a nun.

'It is our same religion,' replied one soldier.

'And our same country,' added the other.

The soldiers were Irish Catholics, one from Kerry, the other from Belfast. Their regiment is unknown, but together they helped the nuns reach the relative safety of the outskirts of the Belgian city. It must have been extraordinary for the two soldiers to find themselves lurching through the madness of Ypres with such an unlikely harem. Perhaps they wondered about escorting them all the way back to the Allied lines but, without authorisation from their superiors, they hesitated.

The Kerryman was the first to go, departing in haste, but the Belfast soldier remained until the nuns told him he really ought to rejoin his regiment. When Dame Columban later described their escape from Ypres, she told how the Ulsterman shook hands with each one of them while the nuns 'thanked him heartily, wishing him good luck and a safe return to dear old Ireland!'

Just before he left, the Prioress took him to one side and handed him a bag of pears. 'Here, take these pears and eat them, and we will pray for you.'

The Belfast man turned his head away abruptly, mumbled 'No, no, keep them for yourselves', and burst into tears. And then, just as suddenly, he ran back to the war, waving his hand and shouting 'God speed.'

The Prioress stood still with her bag of pears and wept as she watched him go. When Dame Columban arrived to comfort her, she said: 'I could keep up no longer when I saw that dear, kind, genuine, Irish-hearted man break down. How I wish I could know his name.'

'Come along,' said Dame Columban gently. 'Let us hope that one day we shall find it out, but don't cry any more or you'll have me joining in too.'

Ypres was once amongst the most affluent cities in medieval Europe. At its heart was an Irish convent, established in Rue St Jacques (now Sint Jacobstraat) in 1665. Twenty-one years later, the convent was officially dedicated as the Irish Benedictine Abbey of Our Lady of Grace. Dame Mary Joseph Butler of Callan, County Kilkenny, was elected its first Abbess.[1] Over the next quarter of a millennium, all bar two of its Lady Abbesses were Irish, carrying names such as O'Bryan, Ryan, Dalton, Lynch and Byrne. Amongst the best-known pupils to pass through its doors were Nano Nagle, who founded the Presentation Sisters in 1775, and Judith Wogan-Browne, who was entrusted with the leadership of the first Brigidine Sisters in 1807.

The convent at Ypres survived the French Revolution intact, largely thanks to the intervention of Jacques O'Moran, a Roscommon-born French General who was guillotined during the Reign of Terror. While Ypres itself was badly damaged during the ensuing Napoleonic Wars, the Benedictines discreetly continued about their business and, for several years, the Irish Abbey was the only convent of any order still existing in the Low Countries.

The convent's luck ran out 100 years later when Ypres — or 'Wipers' as the British pronounced it — became one of the most violently contested battlegrounds on the Western Front.

The Irish Dames, known in Ypres as De Iersche Damen or Les Dames Irlandaises, received a foretaste of the coming horror in early September 1914 when the Belgian Government ordered the expulsion of all German residents from the kingdom. Four of the Benedictine nuns were German; a choir dame and three lay sisters, one of whom was the cook. All four had been enclosed within the convent for at least 25 years. On 8 September, to the considerable shock of their community, a Belgian official arrived at the convent and ordered the four women to leave Belgium within 36 hours.

Scholastica Bergé, the Lady Abbess, was the first Belgian to lead the community. In her prime, she would have been able to put manners on King Leopold himself. However, she was now confined to her bed, having been paralysed by a stroke two years earlier. Dame Maura Ostyn, the 46-year-old Prioress, who was also Belgian, did what she could for the German Dames but to little avail. Amid scenes of much tearfulness, the four women left Ypres for a convent just over the frontier in Holland.

At least seven of the 15 Benedictine nuns who remained in Ypres after the departure of the German Dames were Irish. Dame Placid came from County Wexford, as did her cousin Kate Rossiter, aka Dame Aloysia. Dame Josephine, née Fletcher, may also have hailed from Wexford while Dame Patrick was certainly Irish, but from where is unknown. Sister Mary Winifred started life as Dublin-born Emma Hodges and may have been related to the well-known Dublin booksellers. Sister Romana King, who would join the group in their flight from Ypres, is also thought to have been Irish.

The two youngest Irish Benedictines were Dames Bernard and Teresa. Born in 1889 and christened Maureen Stewart, Dame Bernard was a granddaughter of James Stewart, a Catholic convert from England who moved to Dublin in 1851 to become Professor of Greek and Latin at Cardinal Newman's Catholic University.

Dame Teresa, aka Dora Howard, was 19 years old when she joined the Order in 1904.[2] She was a niece of John Redmond, the Irish Parliamentary Party leader, and his brother, Major Willie Redmond. The Redmond connection to the abbey at Ypres appears to have been strong for several generations, and it would soon play a fundamental role in the fate of the Benedictine nuns. It also explains why John Redmond sat down at his desk in April 1915 and penned the introduction to a 200-page memoir entitled *The Irish Nuns at Ypres: An Episode of the War*. Vividly written by Dame Columban, this manuscript offers a blow-by-blow account of how the Irish Dames coped with the destruction of everything around them, and chronicles their epic, but harrowing, escape.

Four weeks passed between the exodus of the German Dames and the first attack on the once sleepy city of Ypres. It was a hideously tense era during which the city did all it could to make itself seem unimportant. Any form of light by night was prohibited. So too were loud noises, and the belfry that normally summoned the nuns to prayer was replaced by a few discreet shakes of a handbell. All the while, the German Army edged ever closer.

At 1.30pm on 7 October, an enemy aeroplane flew overhead. Shortly afterwards, German long-range guns opened fire on Ypres and the convent began to shake. Enclosed within its walls, the women prayed fervently. Within half an hour of the German bombardment, the Prioress gathered her Dames and her Sisters and told them that the Germans had just overpowered the Belgian policemen defending the old city walls.

Over the next six hours, approximately 10,000 German cavalrymen trotted into the city from the Menin Road in the south-east and the Lille Gate in the south. Chanting victoriously, they were followed by convoys of armoured cars, carriages, carts and field guns. They quickly secured every building in the city, cut the telephone wires, destroyed the telegraph system and posted armed guards at every turn. Up above, German spotter planes circled the autumnal skies.

'It is all over with Ypres,' wrote Dame Teresa in her diary. 'The guns we heard all yesterday were the last defence of the Belgian Army "or rather police" and they were only a hundred against fifteen hundred. They are all over the town, and the Burgomaster is a prisoner. What is going to happen?'

Soldiers were billeted in the Cloth Hall, the schools, the army barracks and hundreds of private homes. The next morning, a washerwomen who worked for the Irish Dames

· · ·

One of the Irish Dames
wanders amid the ruins
of Ypres.

was obliged to give breakfast to 30 Germans, several of whom had slept in her house. Some had led their horses into her drawing-room and then, after jesting that she and her sons were now 'Belgo-Germans', they pilfered all her clean washing including, she added sadly, all the convent's towels.

But while the nuns prayed and prayed and waited for the Germans to smash their way into the convent, the only new arrival was Edmund, their elderly Falstaffian servant, who said the Germans were moving on already. When he asked a German where they were headed, the soldier brashly replied, 'To London!'

Amazingly, no Germans sought refuge in the abbey that night. In fact, during this first short occupation of Ypres by the Kaiser's army, the nuns' greatest concern was 'the want of bread'. Predictably the Germans relieved the nuns' baker of his loaves when he attempted to make a delivery to the convent. When the Prioress sent out for flour, she was informed that 'none was to be got', and so the nuns had to be content with their limited supply of rice, Quaker oats, coffee, butter and some tins of fish. 'The milk-woman, whose farm was a little way outside the town, was unable to come in,' wrote Dame Columban, 'and no meat could be got for love or money'. It was several days before a wily farmer managed to slip past the Germans and bring the nuns some potatoes.

One week later, 21,000 British and French troops arrived in Ypres. The first the Irish Dames knew of their arrival was when they heard the soldiers 'singing lustily' as they passed alongside the convent.

'We were actually engaged in the Litanies with the words, "From all evil, good Lord deliver us",' wrote Dame Teresa, 'when we suddenly heard the heavy tramp, tramp of soldiers, and the sound of singing. We trembled, thinking of the terrible Uhlans [a contemporary term for the German cavalry]… but judge of our surprise and amazement when we found out that it was an English song, and lo! mingled with our cries of supplication came as it were in answer: "Here we are! Here we are! Here we are, again!" We almost joined in, but, of course, we daren't.'

'But imagine the thrill of joy that went through our hearts. Then outside in the streets we heard the clamours of the populace joining in with "Alo, Alo!" and cries of joy. We were just wondering in our Irish hearts whether or not it was an Irish regiment that was the first to enter, thinking of the dear old standard with the harp on it, of the days of the Irish Brigade. Suddenly, we got our answer. In gruff brogue we heard the song which everyone seems to be singing everywhere else and always — "It's a long way to Tipperary, it's a long way to go."'

By the time Edmund arrived at the convent with eagerly awaited bread supplies, the Allies had taken up defensive positions around the east of the city, vowing that the Germans would never enter it again. Edmund added that much the greatest Belgian cheer had been for the 'petticoats' of the Scots Highlanders. Bread was still very much in demand, but the Prioress passed some of Edmund's precious loaves to a 'poor man, with tears in his eyes' who wanted to send them to his son on the front line.

For several weeks, Ypres became the British Army's chief headquarters on the Western Front. At the convent, the Irish Dames returned to the normal business of prayer, but the possibility of a German counter-attack was always on their mind, not

least when the octogenarian Dame Josephine prayed aloud to the Heavens, 'Dear St
Patrick, as you once chased the serpents and venomous reptiles out of Ireland, please
now chase the Germans out of Belgium!' Her words were all the more epic for her age.
Christened Josephine Fletcher, the Jubilarian was professed in 1851 and had been living
in Ypres since 1854. In her youth, she had known nuns who lived through the French
Revolution.

The Benedictines began making Sacred Heart badges for the Allied soldiers to wear,
particularly Irish Catholics in the British Army. Hélène, a poor woman who washed the
convent steps, distributed them amongst the troops. They proved so popular that the
convent was soon subject to 'the constant ringing of the bell' as more and more people
requested badges for loved ones on the front lines. One young girl literally brought
them by the dozen to St Peter's Church in the Rijselstraat, where an as yet unidenti-
fied Irish battalion was billeted. As she pinned the badge onto each man's uniform, she
solemnly announced that its makers were the Irish Dames of Ypres.

Dame Josephine was right to be fearful. While their daily news was full of conflicting
tales of neighbouring villages and towns lost and destroyed, there could be no doubt
that, as Dame Columban wrote, the 'ever-approaching sound' of gunfire meant that
'the danger was steadily increasing for the brave little town of Ypres'. The Germans
were staging a comeback.

With the rising noise came the first refugees. The Irish Dames soon found themselves feeding at least 40 such souls, serving up soup, boiled potatoes, bread, porridge
and beer. The Prioress put the nuns on standby to gather up emergency parcels in case
they had to flee suddenly. The very notion of leaving the convent was absolutely alien to
most of these women who had spent so much of their lives in peaceful solitude within
its walls.

From Edmund and the washerwomen they learned that the Germans now greatly
outnumbered the Allies and that a second assault on the city by the Kaiser's army
was imminent. Hearts sank when word arrived that Bruges had fallen. From their
upstairs windows, the Irish Dames could see smoke rising from distant battlefields. The
windows of the convent were starting to shake again.

On 21 October, the citizens of Ypres were advised that the city was about to be
shelled by the Germans. The Prioress arranged for all valuables to be taken down to
the cellar, including the bed-ridden Lady Abbess. Dame Columban was particularly
anxious about a large barrel of petrol in the garden. If it caught fire, she feared, 'we
should all be burned alive'. Armed with spades, Dames Teresa and Bernard dubbed
themselves the 'Royal Engineers' and spent an entire day digging a huge hole in the
garden. Unfortunately, when the hole was dug, the Dames did not have the strength to
either roll or tip the barrel into it but, on the plus side, they used all the freshly dug earth
to solidify the outer defences of their underground safe room.

Edmund reported on the brief wave of optimism that swept through Ypres when
nearly 40,000 khaki-clad troops from India and Nepal arrived into the city. However,
this was offset by the already commonplace sight of badly maimed and dying soldiers
being brought in by ambulance from the front.

· · ·

Officers and soldiers, thought to be
from the Cameronians (Scottish Rifles),
consider their situation amid the rubble
of Ypres following a major artillery
bombardment by German shellfire. The
luckless town was the site of three major
battles during the Great War and much
of its fine architecture was destroyed.

The Dames now spent their waking hours rolling bandages, cut from sheets and veils, fastening a Sacred Heart badge to each roll. It seemed likely that the convent would be requisitioned as a hospital. A French officer visited and declared it ideal. The nuns duly cleared out the rooms — the refectory, library, classrooms, children's dormitory, novitiate and workroom — only for the officer to return and tell them that he had found a better place.

Reports of German atrocities became ever more alarming. Two German aeroplanes were seen throwing petrol bombs on neighbouring villages. Women, including nuns, were reported to have been subjected to 'outrageous barbarities'. Dame Teresa wrote in her diary of how she 'trembled, thinking of the atrocities perpetrated on other convents like the one at Peck where they had torn clothes from the nun's backs.'

The second bombardment of the city of Ypres began on the afternoon of 28 October. Not everyone took it as seriously as they perhaps should have done. When a bomb blew out the windows of a house on Rue Notre-Dame, the owner gamely ordered the glazier to come and fit new ones.

That night, Dame Teresa found just enough light to scribble in her diary: 'The German shells fell on the town to-day. The first fell in the sleepy moat just outside the ramparts. We have now to live in our catacombs; even the sanctuary lamp is out, and the chapel no longer contains the Blessed Sacrament.'

The main concern for the Prioress was to remove the 84-year-old Lady Abbess from harm's way. She assigned this task to 38-year-old Dame Placid, aka Elizabeth Mary Druhan, who was born at Our Lady's Island in County Wexford, where the O'Druhans were territorial chiefs at the time of the Norman invasion. She took her name from her mother's uncle, Dom Placid Sinnott, OSB, one of the founders of the Benedictine monastery, Downside Abbey.

On 30 October, Dame Placid left the convent along with the three most vulnerable women: the paralysed Lady Abbess, the elderly Dame Josephine and 73-year-old Sister Magdalen Putte. The Lady Abbess did not want to go. As Dame Columban put it, the poor woman was so 'moved when the news was broken to her that it took four women to carry her downstairs'. With the aid of a carriage that the Prioress had managed to borrow, Dame Placid escorted her small party eight miles west to the small town of Poperinge — or 'Pops' as the British called it — where they were received into the convent of La Sainte-Union, together with several other refugee communities.

Meanwhile, as the bombing intensified in Ypres, the Prioress and the remaining Irish Dames dragged their carpets, armchairs and 'straw-sack' mattresses down to the cellars. As some priests were by now staying with them, the cellars were divided into male and female quarters.

It was miserable in the cellars, listening to the German guns growl 'like some caged lion'. Nobody had seen an egg or a drop of milk for weeks. Nor was there any fish or bread to be found. It was increasingly uncomfortable, with 57 people now sleeping in the cellars, including a Flemish workman who, panicked that his house was about to be blown up, had pleaded to join them with his wife and four children. By day, 'numberless poor' arrived at the door seeking food, 'for they could not find anything to eat in the town'.

. . .

A convoy of horses and wagons pass by
the ruins of St Martin's Church and the
Cloth Hall of Ypres.

In early November, the Prioress ordered the Dames to gather up their prized belongings and prepare to evacuate. Dames Columban and Bernard were given a quick blessing and then abruptly thrust into the mud and chaos of central Ypres with instructions to find a workman to carry their belongings.

'What a sensation!' marvelled Dame Columban. 'Happy prisoners for so many years, we now found ourselves in the streets. With a shudder, we started on our errand.' In a daze, the two women scampered from one doorway to the next. German shells and shrapnel bombs were once again whistling in from afar and exploding in the city. Allied guns responded with thunderous resolve. The abandoned grand houses of Ypres' once illustrious textile dynasties were collapsing. Men sloshed through the mud with bandaged bodies on makeshift stretchers, desperate to get the wounded out of the city. French cavalry trotted this way and that. Monoplanes and biplanes loomed above; some dropped bombs, others engaged in dogfights. And in between all this, the two nuns continued to dart with uncertainty until an officer finally persuaded them to return to their convent which was, as Edmund gallantly assured them, as fine a place to die as anywhere.

The Prioress became so determined to gauge the strength of the Allied defence of Ypres that she then decided to leave the convent and walk to a chateau in Brielen, two miles outside Ypres, where Sir Douglas Haig was based. She ambitiously sought an audience with Haig himself, but had to make do with his aide-de-camp who offered her some 'vague information' and a lift to Poperinge in his car. As she walked home, she met some British soldiers who assured her, 'Oh, it will soon be over… we'll be home for Christmas!' She no longer believed such upbeat remarks.

Back in Ypres, bombs were falling with increasing accuracy. On the Prioress's command, Les Dames Irlandaises assembled their packages and 'passed with a last farewell through the long-loved choir, which had known the joys and sorrows of our whole religious life'. Even as they were fastening the locks on the front door, the first shell struck the abbey, sending 'a shower of bricks and glass falling into the garden'. The Benedictines fled down the deserted street and then turned back to see the convent on fire. 'A cry of anguish arose from our hearts.' It was at this point that the two soldiers from Belfast and Kerry came to their aid and escorted them out of the ruined city.

There was some respite when, after the Belfast man left without his pears, their Flemish workman friend arrived with a 'stylish-looking hand-cart' onto which he roped their luggage. For decades the farthest any of these women had walked in a day had been six or seven perambulations around their little garden. Now, they found themselves on a heavy-hearted nine-mile trudge westwards to Poperinge, tramping alongside cavalry, infantry and scores of other refugees. The sisters followed behind the handcart, wading through 'thick slimy mire' so bad that 'we seemed to slide back two steps for every one that we made forward'. They walked through darkness and rain, the roadsides heaped with dead horses, a red moon glimmering through gaunt and leafless trees.

Finally, they came to Poperinge where they were reunited with the Lady Abbess and accommodated for two weeks in a refuge run by the Carmelites, along with 11 nuns from the Sacred Heart Chapel in Ypres.[3] The latter were particularly shook; six of their community were missing and at least one of them had been blown up.

The mood was sombre in Poperinge, but the Irish Dames did what they could to resume their normal routine, making badges, praying and reciting the Benedictine grace before and after meals. They began visiting the wounded, which gave them 'an insight into human misery which we should never have had'. Men laid out for amputation, men with missing jaws, men with broken eyes. They fed them pear slices and tried to raise their spirits. When they died, as so many did, they offered 'De Profundis' for the repose of their souls.

Dame Josephine did not survive. The 80-year-old Jubilarian, who had implored St Patrick to oust the Germans from Belgium, succumbed to a combination of shock and exhaustion.

A few days after her funeral — during which a German bomb exploded nearby — Dames Placid, Columban and Patrick ventured on a 'decidedly dangerous' mission back into Ypres to assess the damage to their convent. They passed the 13th century Cloth Hall of Ypres; one side of the great Gothic building was destroyed and most of its life-sized statues were maimed and mutilated. Their convent was badly damaged but still standing and Dame Patrick managed to salvage a 200-year-old silver crozier.

As the trio made their way back to Poperinge, a British cavalry regiment passed them by and asked who they were.

'We are English nuns from the Benedictine Convent of the Rue St Jacques,' answered Dame Columban.

'We are no such thing', interjected Dame Patrick. 'We are Irish Benedictines!'

'Irish!' laughed the soldiers. 'So are we!'

They were duly escorted back to Poperinge by what sounds like a detachment from the Connaught Rangers who sang 'Tipperary' as they marched.[4]

The British commandant at Poperinge had many things on his mind, one of which was a conviction that elderly Benedictine nuns should not be in a war zone. He placed three ambulances at their disposal, and so the 14-strong community, including their Lady Abbess, set off through heavy rains and bitterly cold winds for Boulogne, where they boarded a ship bound for England. Also in their convoy was Miss Keegan, a young Irish woman who had been trying to get home from Belgium ever since the war broke out.

On reaching Folkestone, the Irish Dames made their way to Euston Station in London. A train took them to Staffordshire, where the Benedictines of Oulton Abbey had offered temporary accommodation.

It had been their ambition to return to Ypres as soon as practical, but when it became apparent that the war was going to drag on indefinitely, John Redmond, Dame Teresa's uncle, launched a campaign to rehouse the Irish Dames. He established a benefit fund for them, which enabled the Prioress to purchase Merton House near Macmine in Redmond's home county of Wexford.

In 1915, the Irish Dames did their best to celebrate 250 years since the foundation of their order in Ypres. When Scholastica Bergé, the resilient Lady Abbess, passed away in 1916, Dame Maura Osytn, the Prioress, stepped into her place. She was invested with the same silver crozier that the nuns rescued from the convent during their return trip.

Further salvage was to come their way that same year when General Sir William Hickie, commander of the 16th (Irish) Division, presented the nuns with some black stone taken from the convent's ruins. The stone was a fragment of the original sacristy and the three men credited with its rescue were Monsignor James Ryan, Captain Maurice O'Connell and Major Willie Redmond, the latter being Dame Teresa's uncle.

According to a report cabled to *The New York Times* on 2 January 1915, Dame Teresa herself was responsible for bringing back a section of a flag that had hung in the Benedictine convent in Ypres since the battle of Ramillies in 1706. It was a British flag, reputedly captured during the battle by Lord Clare's Irish Brigade in the service of France.[5] Today, the flag hangs on the wall of the main hall in Kylemore Abbey, Connemara, County Galway.

In November 1920, the Lady Abbess negotiated the purchase of the 'silent and forlorn' Kylemore Castle from the Duke of Manchester. Under her watch, the Benedictine community expanded to 24 nuns, who ran a farm that bred prize cattle, as well as a boarding school that continued until 2010.

In thanksgiving for their safe delivery from Ypres to Kylemore, the Lady Abbess also recruited ten local men to erect a large statue of the Sacred Heart halfway up Dúchruach Mountain. It reminded the Benedictines of all the soldiers who had worn their badges along the Western Front.

At the time of her death in 1940, the Lady Abbess was the only nun in Ireland entitled to wear a jewelled ring and to carry a crozier.[6] She was succeeded by Dame Placid, who duly became the first Irishwoman to hold the office in 100 years. Dame Placid remained Lady Abbess until her death in 1953.

Bullet-holes in the walls
of the convent in Ypres.

JACK JUDGE –

THE **MAN** WHO

WROTE

'TIPPERARY'

...

WHEN THE BRITISH EXPEDITIONARY FORCE FIRST DISEMBARKED IN BOULOGNE, THE *DAILY Mail* correspondent George Curnock chanced to watch the 2nd Battalion of the Connaught Rangers marching by. 'Every man in the prime of life,' he wrote enviously, 'not a youth or a stripling among them'. As they passed, he heard them belting out a song he had not heard before.

'What is it they are singing?' a French woman beside him asked.

'I don't know, it is possibly a new song of our music-halls.'

'But the words, m'sieu?'

'Madame, they sing "It's a long way to Tipperary… it's a long way to go."'

By the time Curnock's report was published three days later, the song had spread like wildfire through the rank and file.[7] By 27 August, *The New York Times* was hailing 'Tipperary' as *the* marching song of the British Army; the newspaper also printed all the verses and chorus.

By the close of 1914, 'Tipperary' had sold over one and a half million records in the UK and sales were fast approaching the three million mark across the Atlantic in the neutral USA. And picking up a handsome royalty payment at the end of it all was Jack Judge, the son of an ironworker from County Mayo, and his wheelchair-bound neighbour, Harry Williams.

Jack Judge's great-grandfather Gilbert Judge was a carpenter from Carrowbeg near Ballyhaunis, County Mayo.[8] The area was badly hit during the Great Famine and many emigrated to the factories and mines of the English Midlands during that period. In 1870, Gilbert's son and grandson, both called John, moved to West Bromwich, near

• • •

Bert Feldman, music publisher, stands with his left hand on Jack Judge's shoulder with Harry Williams seated to his right. Judge and Williams were the composers and authors of 'It's a Long, Long Way to Tipperary', one of the most popular British marching songs of the Great War. By the time this photograph was released in 1915, the song had sold two million copies in Great Britain and nearly three million in the United States.

Birmingham, where they found work at the Bromford Iron Works. The following year, John junior married 18-year-old Mary McGuire whose parents had also emigrated from Ireland.[9] The couple moved into the McGuire family home in Oldbury, a few miles south of West Bromwich.

The music hall legend Jack Judge was the eldest of John and Mary's eight children. Born in Oldbury in 1872, his earliest memory was toppling into the ice-cold Birmingham Canal at the age of four. He would have drowned but for an older boy who saw him fall and came to his rescue.[10]

In 1885, John Judge took a bold step, acquired a loan and opened a fishmonger's stall in Oldbury. Three years later, tragedy struck when the Mayo man succumbed to tuberculosis aged 38. Desperate to avoid the workhouse, his widow and children took over the stall. Jack, then 16, had been working in the ironworks for four years. However, realising the need to earn more money, he purchased a barrow, which he filled with shellfish from the Birmingham market every morning. In the evenings he and his sister Jane Anne headed out to sell the shellfish to those gathered in the pubs and music halls of Oldbury.

Jack and Jane Anne could both sing, and soon began to compete in the talent shows staged at the music halls. Jack specialised in humorous songs, most of which he wrote himself, and he became a master at dismissing hecklers. By the mid-1890s, the sturdy, big-shouldered redhead was already an Oldbury legend. In June 1895, he married Jinny Carroll, a shy, diminutive Irish woman who worked as a laundress for the Judge family. For the next ten years they focused on the family fish business and raised three sons and a daughter.[11] The darkness was never far away. A measles epidemic killed two of Jack's siblings, while tuberculosis took his sister Nellie.

In 1903, Jack's life changed dramatically when Ben Williams took over the Malt Shovel Inn, close to the Judge family home in Oldbury. Ben introduced Jack to his twirly-moustached songwriter brother Harry, a whizz on both piano and mandolin, and sparks crackled in the world of music. For Jack, Harry Williams was a Godsend because, despite all the songs he had composed, he simply did not know how to read or write music.

The two became friends and Harry started writing down Jack's songs, occasionally adding his own harmonies and arrangements. A grateful Jack vowed that if he ever had any songs published, he would ensure that Harry's name was included as co-author.

In 1910, Jack had a major breakthrough when, clad in a bright check suit with a striped waistcoat, he came third with his song 'How are Yer?' at the Encore Variety Show in London. While the audience appeared to be as cold as his fish when he started, he quickly had them roaring out the chorus. His performance also garnered a positive response from the press and invitations were soon arriving from managers of music halls and theatres all over Britain. The 38-year-old took the plunge, delegating his fish business to his wife, and set off on a tour of Britain, performing the songs he had been working on since his teenage years.

He also crossed the Irish Sea to his parents' homeland to perform at the Tivoli and the Queen's Theatre in Dublin.[12] It is said that when he sang 'Tipperary' at the Queen's in 1912, the crowd included a number of officers and soldiers from the Connaught Rangers, who duly adopted the song as their anthem.

Jack maintained that he wrote 'Tipperary' during the course of a single night in January 1912, while staying at the now demolished New Market Tavern in Stalybridge, Cheshire, just east of Manchester. He certainly performed the song in the town's Grand Theatre the following night. It was written, he said, in response to a five-shilling bet wagered by Jack Newbury and Arthur Peel, trainers of performing seals, who reckoned he couldn't write a new song overnight. Jack replied: 'Well, if I head for my digs, I might have time to knock something up for tomorrow.'

Jack was something of a scoundrel on this front, frequently pretending to have just written songs that were already part of his repertoire. Indeed, many inhabitants of Oldbury, his own family included, claimed they heard versions of 'Tipperary' long before January 1912. One theory is that he simply reworked a ballad his mother taught him called 'It's a Long Way to Connemara'.

In any case, when he performed 'Tipperary' at Stalybridge's Grand Theatre on 31 January 1912, it went down a storm with the artistes, cleaners, handymen, bill posters and animal trainers who comprised his audience. The buzz caught the ear of London-based music publisher Bert Feldman who subsequently spotted an advertisement placed in the stage press by Jack stating that his song was for sale. Feldman proposed turning the song into a gramophone record. Jack agreed, insisting that Harry Williams was co-author, and Feldman signed a royalty deal with the two men, as well as offering an upfront payment of £5. The deal was signed on 18 September 1912, and included another of Jack's compositions 'Mona from Barcelona' on the B-side.

By Christmas 1912, 'Tipperary' was available as a record, sung in a resonant baritone by Ted Yorke.[13] The following year, Florrie Forde, Britain's Queen of the Music Hall, sang it in the Isle of Man, propelling the song to best-selling status. It was a massive coup for Feldman who, sensing an appetite for Irish songs, followed it up by releasing other popular melodies such as 'When Irish Eyes Are Smiling' and 'It Takes an Irish Heart to Sing an Irish Song', all of which fed into the growing sense of patriotism amongst Irish émigrés and their descendants in Britain and America.

Jack was performing with a comedy troupe at the Tivoli in Dublin on the evening of 27 August 1914 when word came back from the Western Front confirming that 'Tipperary' was now the British Army's most popular song.[14] When John McCormack recorded his outstanding version two months later, it became a huge hit all over again. The London correspondent of *The Irish Times* astutely predicted that the original manuscript on which the words were written 'may some day find its way into a museum as a relic of the great war'.

One reason why 'Tipperary' stood out is because, unlike most marching songs, it wasn't about the great and glorious havoc the soldiers were about to wreak on their dastardly enemy. It reflected a yearning for home that was simultaneously poignant and fortifying. And that is why it was sung with such gusto by both Irish and British troops in Egypt, the Dardanelles, Mesopotamia and Palestine, as well as France and Flanders. It wasn't just English speakers who sang it. There were versions sung by the French, the Germans and the Russians. And, of course, it wasn't long before the soldiers were conjuring up bawdier versions:

That's the wrong way to tickle Mary,
That's the wrong way to kiss.
Don't you know that over here, lad
They like it best like this.
Hooray pour Les Français
Farewell Angleterre.
We didn't know how to tickle Mary,
But we learnt how over there.

The Judges wholeheartedly backed the Allied cause. Jack's eldest son Jackie and two of his brothers were amongst those on the Western Front. Despite his Irish ancestry, Jack considered himself a loyal British subject. He would have gone to war himself except the government deemed that his foremost skill was boosting morale back home with his music.

As co-author of the war's most popular song, Jack was by now a wealthy man. He sold another 17 songs to Feldman and concentrated on the war effort. He became a regular performer at recruiting offices and events organised to raise money for the wounded, war widows and poor working-class families where the breadwinner had enlisted.

He also did his bit to spur the Irish to join up, recording two songs in 1915, namely 'Michael O'Leary, V.C.', about an Irish Guardsman who won the Victoria Cross, and 'Paddy Maloney's Aeroplane', about a magical plane.[15] A whopping 8,000 copies of the latter record were dispatched to the army and navy free of charge.

In February 1917, Private Jackie Judge of the Royal Welsh Fusiliers was killed by Ottoman shells during the capture of the Dahra Bend in Mesopotamia (present-day Iraq). Before he died, the 20-year-old sent his father a song of his own composition, 'Everybody's Proud of Their Own', which Jack later published.

Jack was furious at the way in which the 'returning heroes' were treated after the war. In 1920 he performed a song called 'Where is Peaceland?' expressing his anger at the lack of jobs and pay, but Feldman deemed it too controversial to publish.

Meanwhile, Jack's family took a hard knock when the tuberculosis that killed his father came back with a vengeance in 1921, taking his wife, his mother and his second son, as well as his writing partner Harry Williams within less than a year.[16] His third son was also destined to die of the same illness, while his only daughter Cissie died from heart complications after giving birth to what would be his only grandson.

Devastated by so many deaths, Jack ceased touring and resumed his business as a fishmonger in Oldbury. He married again, a war widow, with whom he started a new family and had three more daughters. His brother Ted brought in some extra money by singing Jack's songs, including 'Paddyland' about young Patrick John Molloy who sails away to America and dreams of his sweetheart back in Ireland.

After he was diagnosed with cancer in 1930, Jack continued recording for three more years. His football song 'Down Old Wembley Way' undoubtedly helped his team West Bromwich Albion win the 1931 FA Cup Final. Two years later, he scored a double hit when 'I Go to Monte Carlo' and 'Snooze the Blues Away', his final song, were recorded by the same Florrie Forde who sang 'Tipperary' to such great effect two decades earlier.

The 65-year-old songwriter died in a West Bromwich hospital in 1938, and was buried in Oldbury. King George VI sent a telegram to express his condolences. A headline in *The New York Times* applauded the man 'Famed for the Ballad to Which Doughboys and Tommies Marched Off to War', while *The Times* reckoned that 'Tipperary' was a song which could 'still recall more immediately than anything else the spirit and excitement of the early days of the War'.[17]

Today, a bronze statue of Jack Judge stands in Stalybridge, while the library in Oldbury also bears his name. 'Tipperary' regularly pops up in war movies too but, arguably, the most moving version is that played by the carillon of St Nicholas' Church in Mesen, Belgium, close to the Messines Ridge battlefield where, in the summer of 1917, Irishmen from the 16th (Irish) and 36th (Ulster) Divisions fought alongside one another for the first time. The song also stands as a rather otherworldly ode to the singing voices of the Connaught Rangers, of whom over 2,500 died during the war.

• • •

The Irish-Australian music hall star Florrie Forde (née Flanagan), who sang one of the most popular versions of 'Tipperary' for Jack Judge in 1912, again featured as the singer on his final hit 'Snooze the Blues Away', released in 1933.

• • •

Jocelyn Lee Hardy's photograph as it appeared
in the frontispiece of his book *I Escape!* Taken in
February 1918, he is clad in the uniform of the
Connaught Rangers.

HOPPY HARDY —

THE

MULTIPLE ESCAPER

...

Bloody Sunday, 21 November 1920. The assassins assigned to execute Captain Jocelyn Lee Hardy, MC, DSO, slipped quietly into the hotel on Harcourt Street where he had lived since his arrival in Dublin. The brief from Michael Collins had not been complex. They were to kill the man and then vanish. They duly made their way to his bedroom and burst in with their loaded guns. The room was empty. Hoppy Hardy had escaped again.

There were many men who performed remarkable feats of escape during the First World War, but Hoppy Hardy stands at the head of the pack — in part because he was involved in at least eight escape attempts from various German prisoner-of-war (POW) camps, and in part because he continued to pull off similar dramatic stunts during the Irish War of Independence, when he became one of the most notorious British Intelligence operatives in Dublin. His latter-day escapades were all the more remarkable given that one of his legs was blown off in the last six weeks of the Great War.

The Hardy family were long established in the north of Ireland. Hoppy's great-grandfather Thomas Hardy was the proprietor of a large and well-known firm of woollen-drapers, haberdashers, silk mercers, hosiers and house furnishers based at 33–37 High Street, Belfast, for much of the Victorian period.[18] Howard Hardy, Hoppy's father, was born in Holywood, County Down, in 1854 and worked as a wool merchant, later settling in London.[19]

Hoppy, or Jocelyn Lee Hardy, as he was christened in 1894, was not yet 20 years old when he was commissioned as a Second Lieutenant in the 2nd Battalion of the Connaught Rangers in January 1914.[20] He was assigned to D Company which, together with C Company, was commanded by Major William Stopford Sarsfield, scion of a well-known Cork family. In the middle of August, the Rangers sailed for France on board the SS *Herschel*. As they marched through Boulogne the next day, *Daily Mail* journalist George Curnock heard them singing 'It's a Long, Long Way to Tipperary'.

During their first ten days in France, the Connaught Rangers engaged in endless drilling and marching until 23 August, when they found themselves subject to intense

German shellfire as they waited in a trench by a crossroads just north of Bougnies. It became apparent that, despite inflicting heavy casualties on the Germans, the British Expeditionary Force was beating a hasty retreat from Mons, with the Germans in hot pursuit.

Fast forward three days and Hoppy and 19 of his fellow men were crouched low in the hospital where they were now hidden. The soldiers were part of a group commanded by Captain Walter Roche, who had been cut off from the main body of the army. Two days earlier, the unit had been ordered to provide covering fire while the 5th Infantry Brigade retreated through the fields from Le Grand Fayt under heavy fire. When the Germans upped the volume of air-bursting shrapnel shells overhead, the Rangers were forced to backstep. As darkness fell on 26 August, they slipped into the French village of Maroilles and billeted themselves in two houses that had been commandeered as hospitals for the British wounded. They slept secure in the knowledge that British rein-forcements would relieve them in the morning. To their immense dismay, it was not British troops who swarmed into the town but Germans. They came in quickly, from two sides, which is why Hoppy and his friends were trying, unsuccessfully, to hide. At approximately seven o'clock on the morning of 27 August, Captain Roche, Lieutenant Hardy and the other 18 Connaught Rangers put their hands in the air and surrendered to the Germans who were pointing guns at them.

Taken prisoner just four days after the British Expeditionary Force fired its first shot at a German, Hoppy Hardy and his fellow prisoners glumly trudged through Belgium to the Germany-bound transport trains. One wonders whether they realised just how bad things were. The battle of Le Grand Fayt was an utter disaster for the Connaught Rangers. Worse would follow, later in the war, but on that day six officers and nearly 300 soldiers were either killed or captured, including their commanding officer who, like Hoppy, was now bound for a POW camp in Germany. Major Sarsfield, who managed to avoid capture, penned a note to his superiors later in the week, asserting that 'all ranks behaved with perfect coolness, and even at the last there were no signs of panic'. Major Sarsfield was fated to die at the Aisne on 20 September.

Hardy's first prison was an Offizierslager, or officers' camp, at Torgau in north-west Saxony. Amongst those incarcerated with him was Major Charles Yate, who had endured a monstrous time at the battle of Le Cateau, culminating in a fearless charge at the German lines when his ammunition ran out. Major Yate — who could speak French, German, Japanese, Hindustani and Persian — had no intention of remaining captive and escaped from Torgau almost as soon as they arrived. However, when he was captured the following day, he decided enough was enough and cut his own throat. He was subsequently awarded the Victoria Cross for his courage at Le Cateau.

Hoppy Hardy must have mused on the fate of Major Yate as he commenced a seven-month sojourn at Halle Camp shortly before Christmas 1915.[21] The camp was in a dirty, ugly, derelict machine factory some 21 miles from Leipzig. In a clear sign of what would follow, Hoppy began patiently scraping one of the camp's brick walls with a view to one day breaking through it. After five months of scraping, he deduced that his plan was impracticable. However, he had simultaneously put his young mind to work and, taking a leaf from the late Major Yate, he learned how to speak fluent German. If you plan to escape from a particular place, he reasoned, it's probably essential that you master the language of the locals.

In the summer of 1915 he was moved to a new camp at Augustabad, a converted hotel on the outskirts of the medieval city of Neubrandenburg.[22] Ten days after his arrival, he grabbed his first real shot at freedom when a dozy guard allowed him and a Russian officer called Wasilief to slip away while the prisoners were having a bath outside the camp. With just 50 miles separating them from the Baltic coast, the Ulsterman and the Russian ran across fields, swam a river, slept in haystacks and narrowly avoided capture several times before they finally reached the port city of Stralsund. After five days of freedom, they were all set to stow away on a Swedish schooner when they were rumbled and arrested at the last moment.

Hardy was whisked back to Halle Camp where he joined an unsuccessful attempt by a group of Russian officers to pull down a prison wall in March 1916. Next he had a crack at escaping on his lonesome, craftily using the stiffening wire from the peak of his officer's cap to pick a series of locks. He then popped up through a skylight, lowered himself down onto the street with a rope of plaited leather straps and vanished into the rain and darkness with nothing but a compass, a bad map, a bag of food and some civilian clothes. Soaked to the skin, he made his way to the railway station and boarded the first train he could find. 'My father has died and I'm going to his funeral', he mumbled to the ticket clerk, half closing one eye and holding the other in a glassy stare in a bid to look like a madman.

His approximate endgame was to somehow cross the marshes into Holland. After a litany of mishaps, he reached the town of Delmenhorst at midnight and set off west on foot. However, the temperature plummeted to such an extent that he was unable to think straight. Struggling with pneumonia and hunger, he returned to Delmenhorst. As he passed the telegraph office, he spotted a roaring fire through the window. The room seemed to be empty. Hoppy took a gamble that it would stay empty long enough for him to at least defrost his hands. 'But it was surrender really,' he later wrote. 'And in my heart of hearts I knew it. I threw my chances away because I hadn't the guts to stand the cold that soldiers on every front were putting up with — and because I was alone.' He had not been in the room for long when a railway official returned and the game was up.

After three weeks of solitary confinement, he was forwarded to Camp Scharnhorst at Magdeburg. The prison consisted of a citadel on an island in the River Elbe surrounded by barbed wire, blazing arc lamps and approximately 30 sentry posts. Security was assumed to be airtight until Hoppy Hardy and a stocky, moustachioed Belgian officer called Baschwitz managed to combine 'elaborate subterfuge, audacity and good fortune' to bolt free again. They took a train to Berlin and then made for Stralsund, the same cobbled Baltic city where Hardy had been in 1915. This time he got a little further, crossing to the island of Rügen, but the duo were intercepted by a suspicious, red-bearded German unteroffizier (a junior officer) while searching for a fishing boat to bring them to Sweden. He took them to his guardroom for questioning and decided to keep them overnight.

• • •

A sketch of the entrance to the
prison camp in Magdeburg
where Hardy spent much of 1915,
drawn by Lieutenant Colonel
Reginald Copleston Bond, DSO.

• • •

The map from Hardy's book
I Escape! shows the miscellaneous
escape routes he pursued.

To their astonishment, they awoke to find the three men assigned to watch over them fast asleep, including the unteroffizier. They quickly grabbed their belongings and legged it. When the unteroffizier realised what had occurred on his watch, he calmly pulled off his boot, stuck the muzzle of his rifle in his mouth and pulled the trigger with his toe. At least that's what Hoppy Hardy maintained when he and Bachwitz were later rounded up by an irate search posse and tried for the unteroffizier's murder. It seems extraordinary that the Germans would even bother to try them but they did and, moreover, the two escapers were acquitted seven days later.

But, of course, they weren't exactly free to waltz off home. Instead, it was back to Magdeburg, where Hoppy spent ten weeks of solitary confinement in a 12-foot by 4-foot cell. He was then transferred to Fort Zorndorf, a damp, miserable and utterly impregnable prison some 70 miles east of Berlin where he was held for 18 months, living underground in the ramparts. During his daily exercise, he managed to befriend the air ace Duncan Grinnell-Milne. On a cold January afternoon in 1917, the German Commandant at Fort Zorndorf invited Hardy, Grinnell-Milne and another officer to his house which stood just outside the fort on the edge of a forest. As the sentry notified the Commandant of their arrival, the trio strolled casually around the corner, took a running jump over a fence and then sprinted at full speed into the forest. The third man couldn't keep up, but Hardy and Grinnell-Milne got away and, traversing swamps, dense forests, streams in flood, villages and farms, they covered 45 miles in 15 hours. Alas, this 'wild dash for freedom' came asunder and they were recaptured on the train to Berlin. As Grinnell-Milne put it, they were bought back 'for a little solitary confinement'.

On another occasion, Grinnell-Milne, Hardy and some others tried to slip out at night wearing white women's nightgowns. They nearly managed to climb a wall to freedom but the ladder they brought along was too short. That scored them another three months in the cooler.

At the end of February 1918, Hoppy was transferred to Schweidnitz (now Świdnica) in what was then Silesia, eastern Germany. He almost immediately seized an opportunity to escape, teaming up with Captain Willie Loder-Symonds, a friend of Arthur Conan Doyle, author of the Sherlock Holmes stories. In a nutshell, they managed to forge passports, purchase travel permits and don civilian clothes before clambering over a wire fence and a wall topped in broken glass. They took a train to Berlin from where another train took them all the way across Germany via Dresden, Leipzig, Cologne and Aachen. Within two days of busting out of Schweidnitz, they took a tram from Richterich and that night, glory hallelujah, they snuck into the safety of Holland.[23]

Free at last, Hoppy Hardy and Loder-Symonds were presented to the King within days of their return to England. Hoppy would later be awarded a Distinguished Service Order 'in recognition of gallant conduct and determination displayed in escaping or attempting to escape from captivity'. On 6 April 1918, Hoppy was in the church to watch Loder-Symonds marry his girlfriend Melloney Waring. Sadly, the groom was killed in a flying accident just seven weeks later. He was the fourth Loder-Symonds brother to die in the war.

Meanwhile, Hoppy was given three months' leave but, itching to get back into the action, he transferred to the 2nd Battalion of the Royal Inniskilling Fusiliers, with whom he saw out the rest of his war.[24]

On 1 August 1918, five months after his escape from Schweidnitz, Captain Hardy led a patrol out from their trenches on the Ypres front and ran into a group of Germans who were trying to shift their line a little closer to the British one. Two German machine-guns opened fire at close range. Hoppy managed to silence one but was knocked side-ways by a bomb, which seriously wounded his sergeant. Barking at his men to retreat, he then dragged the sergeant across 200 metres of broken ground to safety, simultaneously noting with his eagle eyes just how and where the new enemy line was shaping up. For showing 'conspicuous gallantry and cool work in command of an offensive patrol' he was awarded a Military Cross. A gazetted Bar was added after the war.

He nearly made it through with his ligaments intact. However, on 2 October 1918, the 24-year-old was leading a counter attack against the Germans at a farm near Dadizeele when a series of lead bullets shot into his stomach and leg. He was so surprised that as he sank to the ground, he apparently shouted, 'Stop the war! I've been hurt!' He was sent back to England where his leg was taken off. However, he became so adept at using the wooden prosthesis fitted in its place that if he walked at speed, it was almost impos-sible to discern. Henceforth, he would be known by many as 'Hoppy'.

'A man with such inventive power and desperate energy will surely make his mark in peace as well as in war', predicted Arthur Conan Doyle. He made his mark, for sure, but Hoppy Hardy's post-war activities also cast a severe blot on his *Boy's Own* reputa-tion, particularly in Ireland, where he emerged as one of the most ruthless members of British Intelligence at Dublin Castle. Although he continued to wear his Connaught Rangers uniform, he was seconded to the Royal Irish Constabulary's Auxiliary Division. His subsequent service with F Company led Michael Noyk, Arthur Griffith's personal solicitor, to refer to him as the head of the 'Murder Gang', while Michael Collins simi-larly spoke of him as 'a notorious murderer'.[25]

Captain Hardy's role during the Irish War of Independence was to interrogate Republican suspects, a task which he seems to have relished. Tony Woods, an IRA staff captain, recalled him as 'a brave but desperate person who never spared himself or others. He was responsible for the shootings, tortures and beatings which took place in the Castle, but he reserved himself only for the most important fish.'[26] Other senior Republicans marked him as 'very vicious'.[27] Amongst those whom Hardy interro-gated were Kevin Barry and Ernie O'Malley; there were allegations of torture in both instances. According to some reports, he simulated executions to extract information. The results were dispatched to Sir Ormonde Winter, deputy chief of police and director of intelligence, from whom it went on to Scotland Yard. Such information also enabled Hardy to mastermind several raids on IRA hotspots, while Tony Woods maintained that Hardy was 'responsible' for the Talbot Street shootout in which the IRA's Seán Treacy was killed in October 1920.

In the 2014 series of 'Who Do You Think You Are?' (UK), Hardy was also named as the man who murdered Peter O'Carroll, grandfather of the comedian Brendan O'Carroll, again in October 1920. The elder O'Carroll was apparently killed because two of his sons, serving as Irish Volunteers, had refused to surrender to the authorities.

As Michael Noyk remarked, 'needless to say, [Hardy] was very much sought after by Michael Collins, not exactly for "social reasons".' The closest they came to assassinating him was in London when Joe Dolan, one of Collins's infamous Squad, had him in his sights until Hardy, a master of disguise, gave him the slip at King's Cross. On another occasion, not long before Bloody Sunday, Liam Tobin and Ned Kelleher were waiting to ambush him as he cycled down Wicklow Street on his way to work at the Castle, but again he managed to get away.[28]

Captain Hardy's darkest hour involved the killing of Peadar Clancy and Dick McKee, two senior members of the Dublin IRA, along with Conor Clune, a Gaelic League member. The men were arrested on the eve of Bloody Sunday in November 1920. Hardy personally commanded the raid on Vaughn's Hotel on Parnell Square in which Conor Clune was captured. The three Republicans were brought to the Detective Office in Exchange Court, off Dame Street, where all three would die in extremely controversial circumstances the following morning. The official report claimed the trio were killed when they grabbed some hand grenades from a box and threw it at their sentries. One of them also allegedly got hold of a rifle. Other accounts suggest the men were badly tortured and then killed in direct response to the murder of 13 British intelligence officers by Collins's Squad that morning. Hardy was in the building when the three men were shot, but it is not clear what role he played. Some have diagnosed a veritable confession to the killing in his 1938 novel *Never in Vain* but he is, unsurprisingly, not named in any official document.

Hoppy Hardy was one of 35 people on Collins's hit list for Bloody Sunday. The reason he wasn't in his bedroom when his would-be assassins burst in is because he was in Exchange Court interrogating Clancy, McKee and Clune at the time. Remarkably, he survived the rest of the War of Independence.

He retired from the army in 1925 owing to 'ill health caused by wounds' and, after a stint with Lloyds Bank in London, he took up farming in Norfolk, cultivating 600 acres at Washpit Farm, Rougham, near King's Lynn. He also became a fascist convert and in March 1934 he gave a talk to the King's Lynn branch of the British Union of Fascists on his wartime experiences. During the 1930s and 1940s, he was frequently to be seen motoring around the English countryside in his Rolls-Royce Phantom II.[29] He maintained his fitness by playing polo, notwithstanding his wooden leg, and he commanded an anti-aircraft gun during the Second World War. A lucid writer, his work as a playwright and novelist stood him in good stead when two of his books became movies. He also wrote two novels based on his time in Ireland, *Never in Vain* and *Recoil*.[30]

Hardy's most successful book was his auto biography *I Escape*, for which Sir Arthur Conan Doyle penned the introduction. 'There are some wild birds who settle down in captivity,' wrote Doyle. 'There are others who alternate between brooding on their perch and dashing themselves against the bars. Of the latter breed is Captain Hardy, once of the Connaught Rangers. Many times he dashed himself against the bars, and then at last on one glorious day he slipped between the bars and was free once more.'

In 1919, Captain Jocelyn Lee Hardy, MC, married Kathleen Hutton-Potts, the 22-year-old daughter of a Hong Kong stockbroker; they had two children.[31] Hoppy Hardy died in Hammersmith, London, in 1958, at the age of 63.

Charles FitzClarence, VC, of County Kildare is credited with holding the British line during one of the most crucial moments of 1914. His grandson Anthony Fitz-Clarence was the 7th and last Earl of Munster.

CHARLES FITZCLARENCE – KILDARE'S ROYAL VC WINNER

...

CHARLES FITZCLARENCE WAS BORN AT BISHOPSCOURT, COUNTY KILDARE IN 1865. HIS grandfather was an illegitimate son of William IV, the British monarch, and thus a first cousin of Queen Victoria. During the Anglo-Boer War, FitzClarence was awarded the Victoria Cross (VC) for his efforts in 1899 when he rode alongside Bryan Mahon to relieve the siege of Mafeking. He went on to command the 1st Battalion of the Irish Guards in 1909, achieving the rank of Brigadier General.

In September 1914, he was appointed commander of the 1st Guards Brigade of the British Expeditionary Force, managing to rally his men to hold the British line at Ypres despite crushing losses. On 11 November, 13 battalions of the Prussian Guard attacked the British along the Menin Road, breaking through at three places. If the Germans had pressed home their advantage, they could have decimated the British front line at this point.

Enter FitzClarence. Early the next morning, the 49-year-old Kildare man launched a counter-attack at Polygon Wood, which utterly stunned the Germans and gave the British enough breathing space to rebuild the line. Sir John French declared it 'the most critical moment in the whole of this great battle' (i.e. the first battle of Ypres). Fitz-Clarence was killed during the attack.

He is the highest-ranking officer commemorated on the Menin Gate Memorial to the Missing in Ypres, which lists the names of 54,896 Commonwealth officers and soldiers whose bodies were never found or identified.

. . .

Lord Desmond
FitzGerald was the
second son of the
Duke of Leinster.

LORD

DESMOND FITZGERALD
AND THE MICKS

...

Lord Desmond FitzGerald stood alongside the padre on the sandy beach at Calais watching the Irish Guards throw their hand grenades with all the strength they could muster. Lieutenant Hanbury stood nearby, guiding the men through the motions.

Britain's munitions factories were producing hundreds of thousands of No 5 Mills grenades every week but it was by no means a perfect bomb. It was essential that the 600-gram missile detonated at least 100 feet from the thrower because if it fell short, there was every chance he'd be caught in the blast. Achieving such a distance wasn't likely to be a problem for an old Etonian cricketer like Desmond FitzGerald, but it was the accuracy of one's throw that would ultimately determine the effectiveness of each bomb.

'Now Father,' said Lord Desmond, turning to the Irish Guards' 36-year-old chaplain. 'You can have a try.'

Father Richard Lane-Fox duly gripped a grenade and pulled out the pin.

Lord Desmond FitzGerald was born on 21 September 1888, the second son of the 5th Duke of Leinster, the premier duke in the Irish peerage. Headquartered between the County Kildare strongholds of Kilkea Castle and Carton House, the Leinsters claimed descent from Maurice FitzGerald, one of the first Cambro-Norman warriors to participate in the late 12th century conquest of Ireland. Over the ensuing centuries, the FitzGeralds became one of the most powerful families in Ireland and Desmond's colourful ancestors included Silken Thomas, the 16th century rebel who defied Henry VIII, and the doomed 1798 icon Lord Edward FitzGerald.

In 1890, his mother Hermione, a society beauty, joyously described how 'little Desmond laughs and jumps and tumbles & shouts all day.' However, immense tragedy was soon to befall the family. Desmond was five years old when his father died of typhoid fever. Hermione succumbed to tuberculosis just 15 months later. The premature demise of the Duke and Duchess of Leinster inevitably turned the spotlight on Desmond and his two brothers — Maurice, his senior by a year, who was now the 6th Duke, and Edward, three years his junior. Tittle-tattle was already doing the rounds that young Edward's real father was not the 5th Duke of Leinster but Lord Wemys, one of the leading lights of an intellectual elite called 'The Souls'.

One of 'The Souls' favourite haunts was Taplow Court, the Thames-side home of Lord and Lady Desborough. Desmond certainly spent much of his childhood at Taplow, where he became a favourite of Ettie Desborough, one of the most glamorous women of Edwardian England.[32] Her sons Julian and Billy Grenfell were close friends of Desmond, and the Irish aristocrat was mooted as a possible husband for her daughter Monica.[33] Another youngster in this circle was the Prince of Wales (later Edward VII) who regarded Desmond as his 'greatest friend'. In later life, Desmond would be one of the few people permitted to call the Prince 'Eddie'.

In November 1903, when Desmond was a 15-year-old schoolboy at Eton, the trustees of the ancient FitzGerald estate in Ireland sold over 45,000 acres, primarily in County Kildare, to 506 tenant farmers through the Land Commission. It was one of the biggest land sales in Ireland in the wake of Wyndham's Land Purchase (Ireland) Act. The sale may have been partly connected to the warning bells that were now starting to sound about the mental status of Desmond's older brother Maurice.

On the eve of the 6th Duke's 21st birthday in 1908, *The New York Times* observed that, 'Owing to the careful way in which he has been obliged to live, the Duke is little known in London, where mammas with eligible daughters are keen in their desire to catch him before any American girls can enter the running.'[34] In fact, poor Maurice, an epileptic, had become so obsessed by his late mother that he was soon to be confined to a private bungalow at Craig House, a psychiatric institution outside Edinburgh. He would remain there, attended by a butler, until his death in 1922.

Maurice's mental illness was tragic. Few believed he would live long and many eyes now turned on Desmond as heir apparent to the dukedom. Desmond had gone on from Eton through the Royal Military College, Sandhurst, to join the Irish Guards in 1909.[35] The regiment was formed in 1900 by a special proclamation of Queen Victoria to commemorate the bravery of all those Irishmen who fought for the British Empire in the Anglo-Boer War. The first 200 Micks, as the Irish Guards became known, were given a uniform that included a black bearskin and a scarlet tunic with shamrock emblems on the collar. The regimental mascot was an Irish wolfhound called Brian Boru. Prior to the war, the Irish Guards' main role comprised ceremonial duties in London.

Desmond rapidly rose through their ranks. By June 1913, he was Adjutant to Lieutenant Colonel George Morris, commanding officer of the 1st Battalion of the Irish Guards. Colonel Morris was a highly regarded Anglo-Boer War veteran and military tactician from Spiddal, County Galway. A measure of the man can be gleaned from an anecdote concerning John Redmond and John Dillon, the two most influential men in the Irish Parliamentary Party, who happened to be strolling down Birdcage Walk alongside the Wellington Barracks in London just as the Irish Guards began forming a ceremonial square. As more and more Micks became aware of the identity of the two men passing them, their enthusiasm grew into such a loud cheer that the incident was reported in newspapers as far away as New Zealand and Tasmania.[36] When order was finally restored, Colonel Morris delivered a sharp rebuke to the Irish Guards: 'You are all, or nearly all, racing men and like a good bet from time to time. Back what horse you like — but keep your tips to yourself.'

LT. COLONEL GEORGE MORRIS

LIEUTENANT ROBERT
BLACKER-DOUGLASS

VALENTINE BROWNE,
VISCOUNT CASTLEROSSE

FATHER JOHN GWYNN,
CHAPLAIN TO THE IRISH GUARDS

THE 'RETIREMENT' FROM MONS

The Irish Guards were mobilised on the declaration of war on 4 August. One week later, Desmond was one of nearly 1,000 Micks who gathered for a farewell inspection at the Wellington Barracks by Field Marshal Lord Roberts, aka 'Old Bobs', Colonel of the Regiment. 'Bring back baskets full of medals,' he exhorted them. The following evening the 1st Battalion steamed out of Southampton, ready for battle. Rudyard Kipling, who was to write such an authoritative history of the regiment's wartime activities, noted how 'many of the officers at that moment were sincerely afraid that they might be late for the war!' These officers included Valentine Browne, Viscount Castlerosse, the 23-year-old heir of the Earl of Kenmare. A man with no military experience, Lord Castlerosse came along for the ride simply because his father was a friend of Colonel Morris.

The Irish Guards arrived in Belgium just in time to play a vital role during the Retreat from Mons as the British Expeditionary Force back-pedalled in the face of the vastly superior numbers of the advancing Imperial Germany Army. The Irish Guards formed part of the 4th (Guards) Brigade assigned to cover the exodus of 18,000 men of the 2nd Division. Their job was to blockade towns along the 200-mile retreat from Mons to the Marne and to entrench themselves in villages, hills and woods. By 23 August, they had their first experience of being under fire, as well as digging a trench of such precision that a seasoned veteran who saw it years later hailed it as a classic example of 'the valour of ignorance'.

They marched for days on end in the high August heat, taking a ten-minute break every hour. Intense weariness quickly set in. They slept it off as best they could in the orchards, woods and fields they passed. By day, some were so 'drunk with fatigue', as Kipling put it, they began to hallucinate. Three exhausted men literally sleepwalked southwards by clinging to Desmond FitzGerald's belt.[37] Others became so exhausted, or their feet so sore, that they just couldn't march any more. They were left by the roadside to make their own way back as and when they could.

By 31 August, the 2nd Division had reached the beech forests of Retz, which surrounded the village of Villers-Cotterêts in Picardy. The Micks were instructed to defend the woods and delay the German III Corps that was giving chase. At 10 o'clock on the rainy morning of 1 September, they found themselves being heavily shelled and machine-gunned, while large numbers of German infantry and cavalry piled into the woods. The Micks were told to hold their position. Colonel Morris did his best to maintain morale as the shells began to fall, shouting, 'D'you hear that? They're only doing that to frighten us.' Aubrey Herbert, standing nearby, replied, 'If that is their object, they have succeeded as far as I am concerned.'[38]

The Irishmen were soon obliged to fall back, retiring through the dense brambles and the briars, firing as they did, but the German response was horrifically effective. Colonel Morris was last seen urging his men on from the saddle of his horse, blood dripping from his field boot.[39] Major Hubert Crichton, his Kildare-born second-in-command, was also killed, as was Captain Charles Tisdall of Charlesfort, County Meath, who as a youth had been taught how to play the violin by the English composer Elgar.

Four other Micks were killed and 64 were missing. In all, the 4th (Guards) Brigade lost some 300 of its 4,000 men in that confused battle in the beeches, but somehow their combined efforts managed to check the German advance on Paris.

Desmond FitzGerald and Valentine Castlerosse were amongst the 41 wounded Irish Guards.[40] Castlerosse's arm had been shattered by a German bullet as he lifted it to fend off a wasp. He passed out unconscious and awoke to find himself surrounded by German soldiers. He feared the worst when one of them began jabbing him with a bayonet. His unlikely saviour was Burghard Freiherr von Cramm, a Prussian officer of the Death's Head Hussars, who ordered the soldier to leave the wounded Viscount alone and then sent word for a medical orderly to be brought to the scene. Before he left, von Cramm wrote his name in Castlerosse's field notebook along with the message, 'If ever a German should fall into your hands, be kind to him as I have been to you.' Castlerosse never had an opportunity because he was sent back home, but if it wasn't for von Cramm's intervention, we would never have been blessed with his lordship's wonderful riposte, delivered later in life, to a woman who pointed at his midriff and said, 'Lord Castlerosse, if that stomach was on a woman I would say she was pregnant.' To which he replied, 'Madame, half an hour ago it was, and she is!' A close friend of Lord Beaverbrook, Castlerosse penned the famous 'Londoner's Log' gossip column for the *Sunday Express* between the wars. As for von Cramm, he survived the war to witness his tennis-playing son Gottfried win the French Open on two occasions.

While the men buried the dead at Villers-Cotterêts, Desmond FitzGerald was carted off in a field ambulance alongside Lieutenant Blacker-Douglass of Bellevue Park, Killiney, County Dublin, who had been wounded in one of his thighs.[41] Desmond was eventually shipped back to Grosvenor Street hospital in London, from where he went home to Carton House in County Kildare to recuperate.[42] He did not rejoin the battalion until 21 November, when he found them at the village of Meteren, near Bailleul. In the meantime, the Micks had gone through the horrors of the Aisne, and the battalion had been practically wiped out during the first month-long battle of Ypres. Over 700 of those with whom Desmond had marched through Southampton ten weeks earlier were dead, disabled or missing. The eight surviving officers and 380 men whom Desmond found at Meteren were battered and 'desperately tired'. Many were suffering considerable emotional turmoil after such devastation on the front line. The solitary plus was that the enemy had still not broken through the Allied line.

Two days later, the battalion welcomed a new chaplain in the shape of Father John Gwynn, a 50-year-old Jesuit from County Galway, of whom Desmond became particularly fond. Father Gwynn, one of Ireland's most eloquent preachers, was a professor at Clongowes Wood College in County Kildare, which stood just 10 miles from the FitzGerald stronghold of Carton House. He served on the governing body of University College Dublin and was well known for his efforts to relieve distress amongst the poor in Dublin's inner-city tenements. As chaplain to the 1st Battalion he quickly set to work, bringing such comfort and cheer to each and every Guardsman that, as Desmond remarked, 'it is certainly no exaggeration to say that he was loved by every officer,

N.C.O. and man in the battalion'. He organised the men into sports teams and put on concerts for them. He set up a choir who would sing whenever he said Mass. It was all about keeping the men busy and lifting their spirits.

Also in the convoy of newcomers who arrived with Father Gwynn was Mick O'Leary, an Irish-speaking farmer's son from Inchigeela near Macroom, County Cork. At the age of 16, O'Leary left home to join the Royal Navy. He subsequently served three years in the Irish Guards, arriving not long after Desmond, but left the regiment in August 1913 for a new life in Canada. In 1914, Constable O'Leary of the Royal North-West Mounted Police earned a gold medal when he took part in a two-hour gun battle that culminated in the capture of two outlaws at Regina, Saskatchewan. Following the outbreak of hostilities with Germany, O'Leary had successfully requested permission to rejoin his old regiment.

By mid-December, the 1st Battalion's strength had been re-boosted to 800 men, although the regimental diarist gravely noted that over half of their new officers had no pre-war experience of soldiering. At least their new commanding officer had experience. The Hon John Trefusis, better known as 'Jack Tre', was the son of one of Benjamin Disraeli's intimate allies and had served as a trooper in the Imperial Yeomanry during the Anglo-Boer War.

Meanwhile, Desmond FitzGerald was with the men when they lined out on 3 December for a visitation from no less a soul than King George V, who arrived with Sir Douglas Haig. Having walked the lines of the 4th (Guards) Brigade and shaken hands with each of the four Commanding Officers, the King said: 'I am very proud of my Guards and am full of admiration for their bravery, endurance, and fine spirit. I wish I could have addressed them all, but that is impossible, so you must tell them what I say to you. You are fighting a brave and determined enemy, but if you go on as you have been doing and show the same fine spirit, there can be only one end, please God, and that is victory. I wish you all good luck.'

Further grounds for optimism came with the arrival of new cardigan waistcoats, goatskin coats and American hard-toe boots for each man, although the Battalion diarist glumly predicted that the American boots might 'not stand the wear of the old ammunition-boot.' By day the men practised bomb-throwing, bayoneting, marching and crafting what the diarist called 'blocks of wood made in the form of a platform at the bottom of the trenches'.

THE TRENCHES OF CUINCHY AND LA BASSÉE

By 22 December, it was back to the front for the 1st Battalion as they marched out from Meteren to relieve the beleaguered Indian troops entrenched by the Cuinchy Brick-stacks on the Canal d'Aire. There was a degree of humour when the Micks first moved into the cold, dank Indian trenches and discovered that the 9th Gurkhas who dug them were clearly rather shorter than the Irishmen. The Micks duly grabbed their spades and dug down a further two feet.

The landscape where Desmond FitzGerald was to spend much of the next two months was not a place where causes for hilarity were readily found. The clay in which the labyrinth of trenches had been dug could not compete with the heavy winter rains. Instead, the trenches filled with water, leading Rudyard Kipling to describe the soil as being 'no stiffer than porridge'. The rain turned the earth into a muddy glue that stuck to the soldiers' clothes, their rifles and their spades whenever they tried to clear it out of the trenches. The only hope was to line the base with logs and bundles of straw, and then lay planks of wood on top. Inevitably, the trenches teemed with rats and lice. As Robert Graves recalled in his memoir *Goodbye to All That*, the rats 'came up from the canal, fed on the plentiful corpses, and multiplied exceedingly'. In contrast, the soldiers' sole source of nutrition was tea and chunks of canned Maconochie stew, which they heated up on their braziers.

The Germans were so close that the Micks could hear them singing and playing harmonicas. However, for all the talk of a softening of aggression during the Christmas Truce of 1914, it had little effect on this section of the front line. German artillery continued to pound away and eight Micks were wounded on Christmas Day. In fact, there was hardly a day when one of the regiment's men wasn't killed or disabled. On 30 December, Captain Eric Gough fell victim to a stray bullet. As Transport Officer, the 26-year-old had been a vital member of the battalion ever since their departure from England.

• • •

The brickstacks of Cuinchy beneath which the Micks were entrenched over Christmas 1914.

The Micks harassed and attacked the enemy where they could, especially when the first trench mortars were delivered shortly after Christmas. The battalion also benefited from a telescopic-sighted Holland & Holland sporting rifle, a gift from the Earl of Kingston which Drill Serjeant Bracken, the regimental sniper, used to lethal effect.[43]

On 3 January 1915, the Micks retired to billets near Vieille-Chapelle for five days' rest. During that time, they were taught how to throw bombs and operate a machine-gun, while Father Gwynn conducted Mass in a roofless, shell-wrecked church. Without question, the highlight of their stay in Vieille-Chapelle was the hot tubs where they could rub off the clay and soothe their swollen feet.

All too soon they were back in the trenches which, following incessant rain, increasingly resembled canals. The trench water frequently rose to a height of two to three feet. In one of the trenches, seven men literally got stuck in the mud, and it took six hours to get one of them out.

Trench foot and rheumatism were rampant. In a particular 48-hour period, 50 Micks were sent to hospital. An indication of just how bad things got was an order, issued on 12 January, which stated that men were 'not to stand in the water for more than twelve hours at a time'. Captain McCarthy, the Medical Officer, worked out that the men could greatly protect themselves against trench foot if they basted a mustard and lard paste onto their feet.

The battalion was continually reinforced by new drafts — 100 men here, 100 men there — as well as by young moustachioed officers with public school accents and haphazard Irish connections. Daylight hours were spent repairing and improving the trench system. During their breaks at the reserve billets, there was little if any let-up; their time was taken up with rifle exercises, kit inspection, route marches and bombing practice. The latter was always hazardous. Thirty-year-old Harry Sheehy Keating, a well-known Irish sportsman, was the regiment's Bombing Instructor.[44] He had been in Germany when the war broke out, but escaped and, after initial training with the Royal Flying Corps, he joined the Irish Guards as a Second Lieutenant. On 20 January, he was showing the men how to use a bomb when it exploded prematurely, killing him and wounding 13 others. The same fate befell his successor while he was schooling some Coldstream Guardsmen with live grenades.

By February 1915, the Micks had been shifted further up the trench line to the famous La Bassée Road. It was a landscape so flat that, as Kipling wrote, 'a bullet once started had no reason to stop'. The trenches lay close to a canal that the Germans were relentlessly trying to destroy in an attempt to flood the British lines.

On 1 February, the Irish Guards were in the act of plotting an attack on their assailants when a company of Coldstreamers holding a nearby line were unexpectedly bombed and rushed by the Germans. Lieutenant Robert Blacker-Douglass, who had been wounded alongside Desmond FitzGerald in the forest of Retz, had only just rejoined the regiment. The 22-year-old Dubliner was ordered to bring a Company of Micks to assist the Coldstreamers. He was felled by a bomb just shy of the German line, stumbled back on his feet to renew the charge, but was shot through the head a moment later. The German machine-guns opened up and suddenly another nine Guardsmen lay dead with a further 26 men wounded.

• • •

A recruitment poster showing a portrait of the Irish Guards war hero Michael O'Leary.

It was at about this moment that Lance Corporal Mick O'Leary, the farmer's son from Macroom, performed one of the most astonishing solo charges of the First World War. He began by sprinting along a railway embankment that ran above the trenches, with ten rounds stuffed into his rifle's magazine. He landed in on five startled German soldiers hiding behind a barricade and, quick as a whippet, he shot them all. Next, his eyes fell on a group of Germans attempting to remount a machine-gun behind a nest of sandbags. He realised that if the machine-gun kicked into gear, it would wreak havoc on his fellow Guardsmen who were now following behind him. He reloaded his rifle and calmly made his way towards them, half-hidden in the shadows of the embankment. He arrived just as the machine-gunner was about to pull the trigger. The German hesitated when he saw O'Leary. Moments later he and two others were dead. Two more Germans sensibly flung their arms in the air and surrendered. O'Leary concluded his solo run with a tally of eight kills and two captured prisoners, returning to his comrades 'as cool as if he had been for a walk in the park'.

In peacetime, that sort of carry-on would earn you a very long spell in prison. In war, it made you a hero. O'Leary's mad dash enabled the Micks not only to burst back through the German lines but also to grab 60 yards of enemy trench, including two complete machine-gun units. At a time when every square inch of territory gained counted, these achievements were an almighty morale booster for the Micks.

As well as these gains, they also captured 32 German prisoners, including O'Leary's two. Kipling claimed that, with one exception, all 32 wept aloud.

O'Leary was subsequently honoured with a Victoria Cross from the King and was immortalised in a song written by Jack Judge. Asked about his son's exploits some time later, his father Daniel, a fervent nationalist, replied: 'I am surprised he didn't do more. I often laid out twenty men myself with a stick coming from Macroom Fair, and it is a bad trial of Mick that he could kill only eight, and he having a rifle and bayonet.' Mick O'Leary later fetched up as a doorman at Harrod's department store in London.

Father Gwynn very nearly lost his life six days after O'Leary's charge. The Galway priest had been a pillar of fortitude throughout the winter. Whenever he saw or heard men fall wounded or dying, he would seek them out, irrespective of bullets and shell-fire, often wading through chest-high waters until he found them. During times of action, he worked alongside the Medical Officer at the Regimental Aid Post, helping to bandage up the wounded and administering Extreme Unction (the last rites) when necessary. After each death came the burial, over which he presided with tremendous courage, standing throughout the service while German lead ripped up the ground around him. On 6 February, he was close at hand when the Micks once again rushed the German lines and, after brutal hand-to-hand fighting, secured a further 70 feet of enemy trench. Second Lieutenant Tommy Musgrave and six other Micks died in the attack. Father Gwynn was badly wounded by a piece of shrapnel as he watched. He recovered and insisted on remaining on duty until a bout of lumbago in his lower back threatened to cripple him and he was taken to hospital in mid-May.[45]

NEUVE-CHAPELLE AND FESTUBERT

By early March 1915, the stalemate on the Western Front was becoming ever more depressing, as increasingly complex trench systems and barbed wire entanglements unfurled across the friendless land. For Desmond FitzGerald and his fellow officers, all eyes were now focused on Neuve-Chapelle, a village in the Artois region that had been in German hands since October. The plan was to launch a massive assault that would rip the German line apart and allow the Allies to seize Aubers Ridge and maybe even push on to the German-occupied city of Lille. As Jack Trefusis was on leave, command of the Irish Guards was entrusted to William Parsons, the 41-year-old 5th Earl of Rosse.

The battle of Neuve-Chapelle began at 7.30 on the foggy morning of 10 March, when over 300 British guns began a gigantic bombardment of the village and its defences, confident that the artillery would destroy the huge swathes of barbed wire that marked the German lines. In conjunction with the bombardment, 40,000 British, Irish and Indian troops charged through the fog at the German lines, with the 1st Battalion of the Irish Guards amongst them. Just as their comrades would discover in Gallipoli six weeks later, the intense artillery bombardment had failed to destroy the enemy defences. As battalion after battalion tried to work out what to do, hidden nests of German machine-guns and rifles opened fire. Running between the German trenches that day was a young dispatch rider called Adolf Hitler, who bounded between shell holes delivering messages for his Bavarian comrades with an enthusiasm that was noted by one of his officers in their regimental diary.

It took five days for Field Marshal Sir John French to concede that the offensive was not working, by which time 22,000 Allied and German soldiers had been killed or wounded.

The trenches at Givenchy, where the Irish Guards were next posted, were the worst they had yet encountered — filthy, insecure and subject to continual bombardment. Now numbering over 1,000 men, the battalion was still there on St Patrick's Day when Queen Alexandra sent shamrock and a good luck telegram. Similar messages arrived from Lord Kitchener, who had succeeded Lord Roberts as Colonel of the Regiment. Father Gwynn, not yet crippled, held an open-air service in the early morning, every man was given a hot bath at Béthune and there was free beer for all come dinner time.

The war was intensifying daily. More and more planes were appearing in the skies above. Activity was also much heightened below ground where Allied tunnellers, mostly volunteers from coal-mining communities, dug a vast warren of subways, cable trenches and subterranean chambers, while German tunnellers were equally busy digging the other way. Chlorine gas had also now reared it is malevolent head while men from both sides were continually subject to random sniper and shell fire.

Terence Nugent was lucky to survive a shot in the back of his neck, but the life of 19-year-old John Maurice Stewart came to an abrupt end when a sniper slammed a bullet between his eyes as he peeked over the parapet on 1 April. His older brother Gerald was killed at Ypres six weeks later. Desmond FitzGerald wrote to the boy's father who lived in County Donegal:[46] 'As Adjutant of this Battalion I can quite honestly

• • •

Irish Guardsmen knuckle
down in the trenches at
Loos.

tell you that your son was a most keen and efficient soldier, and never once during the whole time he was out here has he been heard to grumble. In addition to this he had made himself so popular, not only with his brother-officers, but also with the men of his Company; so not only has the Regiment lost a promising Officer, but a real friend. We had only a few days before I put in a special recommendation that he should become a regular Officer of the Regiment.'

In the middle of May, the Micks were plunged into the battle of Festubert, which almost replicated the battle of Neuve-Chapelle. It took the form of an immense artillery bombardment — 100,000 shells designed to smash the defences of the German Sixth Army — followed by a massive charge along a three-mile length of the front. The big difference was that this attack took place in the dark. Once again, the plan failed because the artillery had not destroyed the barbed wire defences sufficiently to enable the men to get through. On 18 May alone, the Irish Guards lost two officers and 22 soldiers, with a further 11 officers and 284 soldiers wounded. Amongst the wounded was Lord Rosse, who was struck in the head by a piece of shell. So severe was his injury that he never fully recovered, and in the summer of 1918 he died at Birr Castle. After ten days of intense warfare, the Allies had gained 1.8 miles of land and had captured 800 German prisoners. The cost was immense — nearly 17,000 British casualties and 5,000 German ones. And yet, how many people today have ever heard of the battle of Festubert?

For Desmond FitzGerald, the impact of so much death amongst his comrades was compounded by the loss of the Grenfell brothers. Julian succumbed to shellfire near Boulogne at the end of May 1915; Billy went down two months later. Another friend, Ernest Brabazon, youngest son of the Earl of Meath, was killed during a visit to the Micks at Nœux-les-Mines, when a shell fell on top of a machine-gun post while he was inside.[47]

On 24 June, the Micks received a visit from the Prince of Wales, who was celebrating his 21st birthday. This caused a degree of angst, as the Germans understandably tended to up the tempo of the shelling activity if they got wind of a senior British Royal in the neighbourhood. Desmond wrote to the Prince afterwards, apologising for not giving him a birthday present and, displaying considerable insight into the mind of the man who would later abdicate the throne, he added: 'The only thing I know of that you would really like, I cannot give you, and that is that you would become an ordinary person.'[48]

THE BATTLE OF LOOS

The Irish Guards spent July and August back in the trenches at Cuinchy, where Father Gwynn rejoined them following electrical treatment for his lumbago in Paris. On 15 August, Jack Trefusis was promoted to command the 20th Brigade, and leadership of the Micks passed to Colonel Gerald Madden, a scion of the Maddens of Hilton Park, Clones, County Monaghan.

COLONEL MADDEN,
SOMETIME COMMANDER
OF THE IRISH GUARDS

JOHN KIPLING,
SON OF THE AUTHOR
RUDYARD KIPLING

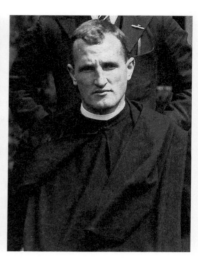

FATHER RICHARD LANE-FOX,
CHAPLAIN TO THE
IRISH GUARDS

Six weeks after Colonel Madden took command, the regiment was ordered to take part in the battle of Loos, the largest British offensive of 1915. The three-week battle was fought in a heavily tunnelled landscape, described by Kipling as 'a jagged, scarred, and mutilated sweep of mining-villages, factories, quarries, slag-dumps, pitheads, chalk-pits, and railway embankments'. It was an unmitigated disaster for humanity, with over 60,000 casualties on the two sides. It also marked the first time that the British Army resorted to poison, pumping some 150 tons of chlorine gas at the German lines on the morning of 25 September. Seven British soldiers died and over 2,500 were gassed when the wind changed direction.

The battle of Loos was a time of considerable morbidity for the Irish Guards who lost many good men to random bombs, aerial torpedoes and snipers. One early casualty was 18-year-old Second Lieutenant John Kipling, aka 'My Boy Jack', only son of Rudyard Kipling, who had spoofed his way into the regiment despite being virtually blind without his glasses. He was posted as missing and his body was never found in the lifetime of his grieving parents. It is assumed he was killed by shellfire.[49]

On 3 October the Guards Division was sent in as relief to the Hohenzollern Redoubt and the Hulluch quarries. Desmond, wounded again during the battle, was subsequently awarded the Military Cross, the third-level decoration awarded to officers 'for an act or acts of exemplary gallantry', and mentioned twice in despatches.[50]

The Micks bivouacked in misery in the rain-sodden trenches west of the railway line just outside Vermelles. On the morning of 10 October, Lieutenant Gore-Langton — one of the battalion's best officers — was shot through the head by a German sniper. Just hours later, a fresh disaster befell the battalion. Lord Desmond had just finished lunch with Father Gwynn, Colonel Madden and two other officers in their makeshift headquarters when a German shell smashed into the door and exploded. Part of the shell tore through Father Gwynn's lung and lodged in his back; other shards ripped into his legs. Both of Colonel Madden's legs were broken and another piece of shrapnel embedded itself in Desmond's foot. Father Gwynn was taken to the hospital at Béthune, but the combination of shock and his injuries proved too much and he passed away at eight o'clock the following morning.

With Colonel Madden felled, Desmond was now the battalion's most senior officer. According to Dr McCarthy, the Irish Guards medical officer, 'although wounded, he endeavoured for days in extreme pain to carry out the duties of Commanding Officer.' On 14 October, the heavy rains and overpowering German defence obliged General Haig to call a halt to the British offensive at Loos. The Irish Guards were relieved and gradually made their way to the old coal mining town of Verquin, where Desmond and Colonel Madden finally had their wounds seen to by a proper doctor. They were both sent back to England where Colonel Madden died four weeks later. The 1st Battalion was to lose five of its Commanding Officers in the first 15 months of the war.[51] By the end of October, command had passed to Colonel Robert McCalmont who, as Ulster Unionist MP for Antrim East, was one of the strongest advocates for arming the Ulster Volunteer Force during the Home Rule crisis in Ireland before the war.

Desmond FitzGerald was out of the war for the next three months. He spent a good deal of time in Ireland, primarily staying at Carton House. He also visited Taplow Court where he found Ettie Desborough mourning for her two sons. She recalled how he tried to cheer her up with a beaming smile, saying: 'If I see Julian and Billy before you do, I shall take them your love.' In February 1916, shortly before he returned to the war, he and Ettie took a walk through the winter woods at Taplow. She expressed great concern because his battalion was now bound for the Ypres Salient, a notorious death trap for officers. Desmond gently replied: 'If it is me, you must never mind.' He later wrote a thank-you letter to Ettie. 'You have always been so kind to me & we have had so many happy days together in the past. I cannot express how much I admire your pluck & faith in looking on the brighter side of things for I know how terrible your loss has been. But our religion & very existence are worth nothing unless death means passing into happiness & life is given us to use for the helping of others to that happiness.'

Desmond rejoined the 1st Battalion as second-in-command to Colonel McCalmont shortly before the men, who had been back on the front lines, were ordered to march through bitter cold and snow to a rest camp at Calais. During the journey, Desmond wrote: 'Things change so quickly nowadays, it is impossible to see ahead.'

Those were perhaps the last words the 28-year-old wrote before Father Lane-Fox pulled the pin on the Mills bomb on the beach in Calais on 3 March 1916. The five-second time fuse was supposed to be activated when the grenade left the hand, but it turned out to be defective. The bomb exploded immediately, blew out Father Lane-Fox's right eye and chopped off several of his fingers. Lieutenant Hanbury, standing nearby, caught the blast in his hand and leg.[52] Terence Nugent was also dangerously wounded in the liver but, unaware of the seriousness of his predicament, calmly took control of the situation until help arrived. Unfortunately, the grenade wreaked its worst mischief on Lord Desmond FitzGerald. Struck directly in the head, he was rushed to the wooden huts on the Calais sand dunes where the nurses of Millicent Sutherland's No 9 Red Cross Hospital did what they could. He died within an hour of the blast.

Although everyone insisted that the grenade was at fault, Father Lane-Fox blamed himself for Desmond's death. He transferred to the 2nd London Irish, with whom he was awarded the Military Cross and the French Médaille Militaire. His successor as chaplain to the Irish Guards was Father Francis Browne, a Jesuit from Cork with a remarkable talent for photography. Before the war, Father Browne was on board the *Titanic* for her maiden voyage from Southampton to Queenstown, County Cork. When a rich American couple on board offered to pay for him to go all the way to New York first class, he sent an optimistic telegram to his Provincial Superior seeking permission. 'Get Off That Ship' came the stern reply. He glumly disembarked at Queenstown and watched the liner steam off to her doom. In 1986, over a quarter of a century after his death, a Jesuit colleague discovered a metal trunk that had belonged to Father Browne. It was full of negatives of thousands of photographs, including 159 excellent and invaluable shots of passengers, crew and various rooms taken during his short time on the *Titanic*. Father Browne was wounded on five occasions during his time with the Irish Guards, including a gas attack that nearly finished him. He was awarded the Military Cross and Bar for his valour in combat.

Lord Desmond FitzGerald was buried in the public cemetery at Calais two days after his death.[53] The entire battalion lined the road to his grave.[54] Ettie Desbrough, who had walked with him just three weeks earlier, declared 'surely no one can ever have been so ready to go into the presence of God, that wonderful natural goodness & innocence, & he had envisaged this from the first so quietly & calmly'.[55]

'All are very sad about Desmond Fitzgerald's death,' wrote Aubrey Herbert. 'There was no one quite like him. He would have played a great part. He was extraordinarily fine, too fine to be a type, though he was a type, but not of these times. I shall never forget him during the Retreat, always calm and always cheerful.'[56]

Dr McCarthy likewise praised him as an officer of 'splendid character' and 'wonderful pluck … brave, steadfast, loyal and courteous, he was a great example of the chivalrous knight of history.'[57]

Desmond's death made news headlines across the world. 'Bomb Kills Duke's Heir', declared *The New York Times* while *The Times* of London solemnly noted that he was 'the 48th heir to a peerage to fall in the present war'. With his death, his younger brother Edward became heir presumptive to the dukedom. At the time, Edward was probably best known for having married pretty May Etheridge, one of the Pink Pyjama Girls of the Shaftesbury Theatre. Edward also served in the war, but was invalided out in August 1915. He subsequently ran up such massive gambling debts that he was compelled to strike a deal with the Tory millionaire Sir Harry Mallaby-Deeley. As part of the deal, he sold his reversionary interest in the FitzGeralds' Irish estates for a relatively small sum of £67,500 — enough to clear his debts — plus a tax-free allowance of £1,000 a year for life. In return, Sir Harry was to be given the income from the Duchy's Irish estates, but only if Lord Edward should succeed as Duke. In 1922, that's exactly what happened when the 6th Duke died in Edinburgh aged 35 and Edward succeeded as the 7th Duke. Sir Harry henceforth raked in over £50,000 a year from the FitzGeralds' Irish estates for the remainder of his life.

There was a bizarre addendum to the saga when a wealthy American called Leonard FitzGerald put himself forward as a contender for the Duchy. One of the theories advanced during this long and complex case was that Desmond FitzGerald was not killed by the Mills bomb at all. Having apparently decided to throw his lot in with the Irish Republican cause, Desmond was said to have faked his death and emigrated to Canada, where he promoted Ireland's revolutionary cause in Manitoba, Winnipeg. It was alleged that he later moved to California where he died in 1967, having had one son, the aforementioned Leonard. If it all sounds unlikely, Leonard's son Paul Maurice FitzGerald spent over £1.3 million advancing his claim in the House of Lords before the Lord Chancellor finally dismissed the case in 2009.

LA BASSÉE ROAD BY PATRICK MACGILL

You'll see from the La Bassée Road, on any summer's day,
The children herding nanny-goats, the women making hay.
You'll see the soldiers, khaki clad, in column and platoon,
Come swinging up La Bassée Road from billets in Béthune.
There's hay to save and corn to cut, but harder work by far
Awaits the soldier boys who reap the harvest fields of war.
You'll see them swinging up the road where women work at hay,
The straight long road, La Bassée Road, on any summer's day.
The night breeze sweeps La Bassée Road, the night-dews wet the hay,
The boys are coming back again, a straggling crowd are they.
The column's lines are broken, there are gaps in the platoon,
They'll not need many billets, now, for soldiers in Béthune.
For many boys, good lusty boys, who marched away so fine,
Have now got little homes of clay beside the firing line.
Good luck to them, God speed to them, the boys who march away,
A-singing up La Bassée road each sunny summer day.

Written during the summer of 1915 at Cuinchy by
Rifleman Patrick MacGill, London Irish Rifles.

• • •

Lieutenant Fred Harvey was twice capped
for the Irish rugby team before the war.

IRISH RUGBY PLAYERS
ON THE WESTERN FRONT

...

FRED HARVEY'S
VC-WINNING SUPER-JUMP

...

ONE OF IRELAND'S MOST COURAGEOUS RUGBY ICONS TO SERVE IN THE GREAT WAR WAS Fred Harvey of Athboy, County Meath. The Wanderers fly-half was twice capped for Ireland, making his debut in the 1907 team that also starred Cecil Parke and Basil Maclear. Harvey was just 20 when he emigrated to Canada to work as a surveyor in northern Alberta, but he returned to Ireland for the Five Nations Championship in 1911, lining out as full-back in the team that triumphed over France by 25-5.

On 27 March 1917, Lieutenant Harvey of Lord Strathcona's Horse — part of the Canadian Cavalry Brigade — was taking part in an attack on the German-held village of Guyencourt-Saulcourt when things began to go horribly wrong. A party of Germans unexpectedly seized control of a low-lying machine-gun post during the attack, and opened fire on the assailants with devastating effect.

The German post was surrounded by three rows of barbed wire entanglements, but that didn't stop Harvey from charging at it, leaping over all three rows, shooting the gunner stone dead and capturing the machine-gun. Inspired by his gusto, the Canadian cavalrymen swept onwards and won the day.

Fred Harvey was awarded the Distinguished Service Order (DSO), but this was later upped to a Victoria Cross. He remained an army man ever after, becoming commanding officer of Lord Strathcona's Horse in 1938 and Brigadier General of the 13th Alberta Military District on the eve of the Second World War. He died in Calgary in 1980 aged 91. Today, his Victoria Cross is displayed in Calgary's Museum of the Regiments.

Dave Gallaher, first
captain of the New
Zealand All Blacks,
pictured during the
1905 tour.

DAVE GALLAHER —
THE DONEGAL MAN WHO CAPTAINED
THE ALL BLACKS

. . .

DAVE GALLAHER, THE FIRST CAPTAIN OF THE NEW ZEALAND ALL BLACKS, WAS BORN IN Ramelton, County Donegal in 1873. His father James was a linen draper and haberdasher; his mother Maria was a schoolteacher. In 1878, James upped sticks with his family and emigrated to New Zealand. Having served in the Anglo-Boer War, Dave Gallaher turned to rugby with considerable fervour, playing in the new position of Wing Forward. He won his first international cap for New Zealand in 1903 and, two years later, captained the All Blacks when they toured Britain and Ireland.

Gallaher joined the New Zealand Division in February 1917, enlisting in the 2nd Battalion of the Auckland Regiment. On 4 October 1917, Sergeant Major Gallaher led his men over the top at the battle of Passchendaele. During the assault, a shell exploded right in front of him. The 44-year-old was rushed to a makeshift hospital, where he was given the last rites by an Irish priest who recognised the dying man as the former captain of the All Blacks.

IRISH RUGBY INTERNATIONALS
WHO FELL IN THE GREAT WAR

BASIL MacLEAR,
died on 24 May 1915, aged 34

JASPER BRETT
died on 4 February 1917, aged 21

ERNEST COTTON DEANE MC,
died on 25 September 1915, aged 28

ALBERT LEWIS STEWART DSO,
died on 4 October 1917, aged 28

ALFRED SQUIRE TAYLOR,
died on 31 July 1917, aged 29

VINCENT McNAMARA,
died on 29 November 1915, aged 24

WILLIAM VICTOR EDWARDS,
died on 29 December 1917, aged 30

ROBERT BALDERSTONE BURGESS,
died on 9 December 1915, aged 25

WILLIAM HALLARAN,
died on 23 January 1917, aged 56

CAPTAIN DD SHEEHAN, MP FOR MID-CORK

...

It occurred to Captain Daniel Desmond Sheehan that making any meaningful progress down the trench was going to be pretty tricky — what with the pitch-black night, the weighty equipment on his back, and trying to squeeze past all the men who were already crammed into the trench. Behind him, the captain of the London Scottish was having much the same thought. And yet, both captains needed to be at the head of their companies as quickly as possible.

'There was nothing for it,' wrote Sheehan, 'but to get over the parapet and walk along in front.' And so the two men popped up from the trench and began hightailing it towards their respective companies. German flares shot into the sky and a machine-gun was soon pumping bullets into the air around them. At the age of 42, DD Sheehan, the Member of Parliament for Mid-Cork, had never been under fire before. He described the experience as 'decidedly unpleasant.' But somehow his luck held and he dived into the trench alongside his own men just as a hail of bullets ploughed into the parapet upon which he had been running only a few seconds earlier.

'I thought myself lucky at the time,' he wrote. 'And so I was, but further experience has shown me that the number of escapes a man may have out here and still live are marvellous, when they are not miraculous.'[58]

DD Sheehan was one of five Irish nationalist MPs who served in Kitchener's New Army during the First World War.[59] He was also perhaps the most unlikely of the five, being from a family of a strong Fenian persuasion. Born in 1873, his early years were spent in the Duhallow farmlands of Kanturk in north-west County Cork. In 1880, at the height of the Land War, his family was evicted from their homestead because his father refused to pay what he considered an unfair and disproportionate rent. Two days before the eviction, 7-year-old DD was placed in a cart alongside some of his parents' belongings, and taken to temporary shelter with friends. Meanwhile, his father watched with silent bitterness as his farm was taken over by a "land-grabber" who paid the family's rent arrears.

• • •

Captain Daniel Desmond Sheehan was
Member of Parliament for Mid-Cork
from 1901 to 1918. He enlisted with the
Royal Munster Fusiliers in 1914.

As a teenager, DD pinned his loyalty on Charles Stewart Parnell, and was one of those who regarded the nationalist leader as the "Uncrowned King of Ireland". In 1891, Parnell visited Tralee and DD set off to meet his hero with a deputation from Killarney. They duly presented an address, written by DD, declaring their loyalty and confidence in a man who was then in the throes of his downfall. DD recalled Parnell as 'a broken and a hunted man... the pallor of death was upon his cheeks, but even then I was impressed by the majesty of his bearing, the dignity of his poise, the indescribably magnetic glance of his wondrous eyes, and the lineaments of power in every gesture, every tone and every movement'.[60]

After a stint as a schoolteacher, DD became a journalist, working with the *Kerry Sentinel* and the *Cork Daily Herald*, as well as editing the *Catholic News* in England for a year. In February 1894, he married Mary O'Connor, the pretty daughter of a Tralee merchant who was known as the 'Rose of Tralee'. Over the next eighteen years, the Sheehans would have five sons and five daughters.

Even at this early stage, DD described his raison d'être as a desire 'to lead the labourers out of the bondage and misery that encompassed them'. Six months after his marriage, he co-founded the Irish Land and Labour Association (ILLA), primarily to establish tenant rights for small farmers and also to redress the extreme poverty that compelled so many agricultural labourers 'to live in hovels not fit to house the brute beast of the field' as he later put it in a speech to the House of Commons in Westminster. Under his leadership, the ILLA mushroomed across Munster and Connaught, and by 1904 it had 144 branches.

DD Sheehan was clearly a force to be reckoned with. At a by-election for the Mid-Cork seat in 1901, the 28-year-old stood as an ILLA candidate and triumphed to become the youngest and arguably the most candid of the Irish nationalists then sitting in Westminster. He was to remain MP for Mid-Cork until 1918. However, his hope of providing greater welfare for the rural poor was thwarted by the larger farmers and middle-class shopkeepers who dominated Ireland's county councils. Eager to keep the labouring classes in check, they threw their weight behind the less radical option of John Redmond's Irish Parliamentary Party (IPP). To DD's dismay, Redmond refused to countenance the ILLA as an ally.

In 1898, the administration of the Irish countryside underwent a massive revolution when locally elected county councils replaced the Ascendancy-based Grand Juries that had run the show for countless generations. Of every bit as much significance, Wyndham's Land Purchase Act of 1903 virtually abolished landlordism in Ireland overnight when the government offered landowners exceptionally generous bonus subsidies in return for land sales. By 1910, more than 200,000 Irish tenant farmers had purchased their own holdings, representing over 50 per cent of farmers. Forty years earlier, just 3 per cent of Ireland's farmers owned their land.

DD Sheehan was intimately involved with these reforms, either personally or indirectly negotiating an astonishing 16,159 land purchases in Munster. Having helped to secure this victory for small farmers, he then turned his attention to the impoverished rural peasantry and his dream to 'root the labourers in the soil'. He duly teamed up with

William O'Brien, a flamboyant newspaper proprietor and MP for Cork City who had abandoned the IPP when Redmond's party rejected the Wyndham Act as too conciliatory to landlords.[61]

Sheehan and O'Brien were hugely influential in persuading the relevant powers at Westminster to pass the 1906 Labourers (Ireland) Act, by which over 40,000 'commodious cottage homes' were constructed in Ireland, each on an acre of land, to replace the mud hovels and single-room cabins of the past. Such a massive public housing scheme was unprecedented in Europe, and it prompted a veritable social revolution in the Irish countryside, not least with the rapid decline in outbreaks of tuberculosis, typhoid and other contagious diseases that followed. The 7,560 cottages erected in County Cork became known as 'Sheehan's Cottages' after DD himself. On New Year's Eve 1906, DD became Ireland's first Independent Nationalist Labour MP when he was elected to Westminister unopposed.[62]

A series of attempts by Sheehan and O'Brien to team up with the IPP failed. The final straw came during a nationalist convention at Dublin's Mansion House in February 1909 when Sheehan was bloodied during a baton charge orchestrated by 'Little Joe' Devlin, Redmond's Belfast-born sidekick. Less than a month later, Sheehan and O'Brien co-founded the All-for-Ireland League (AFIL), which sought to win Home Rule by dint of 'the Three C's', namely Conference, Conciliation and Consent, and by working much closer with Ireland's Protestant Unionist minority than the IPP would allow.[63]

At the two general elections of 1910, DD managed to retain his seat in the face of a massive campaign mounted against him by the IPP in cahoots with the clergy. The second election was particularly heated — there were riots and a revolver was fired during one of his orations — but the AFIL successfully returned eight MPs for the nine Cork constituencies. Sheehan's party was now the main nationalist rival to the IPP. A song called 'The Ballad of D. D. Sheehan' was fast ensuring DD's status as a household name across southern Ireland. He was also by now a qualified barrister on the Munster circuit.

DD advocated that the island of Ireland be given full 'dominion status' within the British Empire, on a par with the dominions of Canada, New Zealand and South Africa. By 1913, he was vice Chairman of the Imperial Federation League, which hoped to replace the British Empire with something akin to the United States of America.

In May 1914, Sheehan and his fellow MPs from the AFIL abstained from voting when the Third Home Rule Bill was enacted, abhorrent of what they prophetically deemed to be the irreversible partition of the six north-eastern counties.[64]

Both Sheehan and O'Brien saw the outbreak of war in August 1914 as a last-gasp opportunity to avert a civil war with Ulster by potentially unifying all strands of Ireland in the common cause. O'Brien was the first nationalist leader to call on his countrymen to enlist in Irish regiments. In a speech frequently interrupted by loud cheers, he declared, 'I am convinced to the heart's core that we are fighting the most effective battle in all the ages for Ireland's liberty [against] the most appalling horde of brutes in human shape that ever cursed this earth since Atilla met his doom at the hands of eternal justice.'[65]

In late August 1914, O'Brien met with Lord Kitchener and proposed the creation of an Irish Army Corps to embrace volunteers from all creeds and classes. Kitchener agreed and, with a government guarantee that 'it would be manned by Irishmen and officered by Irishmen', the 16th (Irish) Division was born.[66]

Sheehan, who fully complied with O'Brien's sentiments, believed it was imperative that Europe be free of all German belligerence if Home Rule in Ireland was ever to flourish. In November 1914, to show the depth of his convictions, the 41-year-old father of ten joined the Royal Munster Fusiliers.

'True, I was no longer a young man,' he wrote in a piece for the *Daily Express* called 'Why I joined the Army', published in February 1916. 'I had reached what is known as the prime of life. True, also, I had a wife and a large family, to whom I am deeply attached… But, after all, when I came to examine my position by the cold light of logic and reason, I found that these were only the flimsiest of pretexts and excuses, and that so long as I could serve, so long as no physical bar or impediment existed, so long as no overwhelming private or public claims barred the way, there was only one thing for me to do — unless I was for ever to stand condemned as a coward before my own conscience — and that was to offer myself to the Army, so that I might share the same perils, endure the same hardships, undergo the same training, equip myself in the same way as the thousands of other married men who were bravely leaving home and family and affection behind to give their all for the causes most dear to mankind — liberty and justice and the right to live under a free flag and a generous Constitution.'[67]

After training at Kilworth Camp near Buttevant in County Cork, the freshly gazetted Lieutenant DD Sheehan received a personal request from General Sir Laurence Parsons, the commander of the 16th (Irish) Division, to lead a recruitment campaign across Cork, Limerick and Clare. He proved such a powerful voice that he is credited with having convinced 5,000 recruits to enlist over the course of 1915. He almost single-handedly raised the 1,200 Munster volunteers who formed the 9th (Service) Battalion of the Royal Munster Fusiliers.[68]

DD's wife Mary and daughter Eileen also threw their weight into the recruitment drive and became active members of the Cork City Irishwomen's Recruiting Committee when it was established in March 1916.[69] The consequence of the Easter Rising the following month would ultimately change Irish attitudes towards the war effort dramatically, with unpleasant long-term consequences for the Sheehan family.

Seven members of the Sheehan family served on the Western Front during the Great War. DD's two oldest sons, Daniel and Martin, started in the Royal Navy and the Canadian Expeditionary Force (CEF), respectively, but both would later die fighting the war in the sky. Michael, his third son, was 15 years old and just shy of six feet tall when he ran away from school to enlist at the Crinkill Barracks near Birr, where the Prince of Wales's Leinster Regiment was garrisoned. Robert O'Connor, DD's brother-in-law, was a sergeant in the regiment. In September 1915, Michael Sheehan had the extraordinary distinction of being the youngest commissioned officer on the Western Front when, aged 16, he was transferred to the Royal Munster Fusiliers as a Second Lieutenant. He survived the war, despite being wounded twice, and as Brigadier Sheehan, earned considerable praise, a CBE and an OBE for his service as Director of Supplies and Transport during the successful Burma campaign at the end of the Second World War.[70]

• • •

A recruitment rally on Shandon Street in Cork City on 15 September 1915. The man addressing the crowd is William Archer Redmond (1886–1932), MP for East Tyrone and a son of John Redmond, the leader of the Irish Parliamentary Party. During the war, he served on the Western Front, first in the Royal Dublin Fusiliers and then with the Irish Guards. He rose to the rank of captain and was awarded the DSO.

Meanwhile, shortly after Christmas 1915, Captain Sheehan and the 9th Battalion made their way to the wintry trenches of northern France to serve in the 16th (Irish) Division. The division was now under the command of the Tipperary-born Major General William Hickie, one of the few senior British Army officers who were both Catholic and Irish.

Captain Sheehan was entrusted with the command of four platoons and instructed to hold a section of the line near Aire-sur-la-Lys. This was where he was based when he and the London Scottish captain experienced such a close encounter with death during their hasty gallop along the parapet in February 1916. From these trenches, he penned a series of articles for London's *Daily Express*, *The Irish Times* and *The Cork Constitution,* offering a stirring insight into the experiences of the Munsters on the front lines.

The 9th Battalion was only destined to fight as a unit for five months. A relentless German mortar and bombing campaign during March 1916, combined with horrific weather, shocking trench conditions and the devastating chlorine attack at Hulluch village in April, greatly depleted their strength. Despite this, Captain Sheehan wrote, 'the men cracked jokes at one another as they endeavoured to negotiate some particularly deep pool, and, as is their way, treated the worst side of life in the most good humoured manner'.[71] On 30 May, the battalion was disbanded and its personnel were scattered amongst the 1st, 2nd and 8th Battalions of the Royal Munster Fusiliers, all of which had suffered severely during the previous months.

In the wake of the Easter Rising, Captain Sheehan briefly returned to his constituency and, on 18 May 1916, he was amongst those who met Asquith in Cork when the Prime Minister came to assess the gravity of the situation in the aftermath of the Irish rebellion.[72]

By June, Captain Sheehan had been reassigned as an instructor to the 2nd Battalion of the Munsters, teaching the men how to handle gas attacks and how to operate a Lewis gun. He was to spend the rest of the summer and most of the autumn in the trenches of the Somme, where the battalion suffered high losses. DD was so badly deafened by shellfire that it ended his career as a barrister. Some believe he also suffered shell-shock and post-traumatic stress disorder. In October 1916, his condition was so poor that, on doctor's orders, he was moved back to the Royal Munster Fusiliers' Reserve depot in County Cork.[73] He was hospitalised several times, both in Cork and London, before he applied to be decommissioned. He was honourably discharged in January 1918 with the permanent honorary rank of Captain, and, for the remainder of his days, he would insist on being addressed as Captain Sheehan.[74]

Captain and Mary Sheehan were to experience much personal sorrow over the next two years, with the death of their sons, Daniel and Martin, as well as Mary's 37-year-old brother, Robert.

Born in Tralee, Robert O'Connor had served in the Anglo-Boer War, after which he and his wife settled in Youghal, County Cork. During the battle of Passchendaele, he was with the 2nd Battalion of the Leinster Regiment when they were ordered to capture a section of the German front line just north of Mont Sorrel. The battalion achieved its mission, but a combination of machine-gun fire, aerial bombing and intense hand-to-

• • •

A sketched portrait of
Robert O'Connor, DD
Sheehan's brother-in-law,
from 1914.

hand combat left 34 dead and a further 53 missing. Robert O'Connor's body was never identified. Eighteen days after his death, his young widow gave birth to their only son, whom she christened Robert; he would go on to serve as a Sergeant in the Irish Army at Collins Barracks in Cork.[75]

The Sheehan family were also hard hit with injury. Their son, Michael, was wounded twice and DD's brother Jack, a tug-of-war champion who served as a Private in the Irish Guards, was severely disabled. However, perhaps the saddest fate was to befall the Sheehans' eldest daughter, Eileen, a nurse and ambulance driver with the Voluntary Aid Detachment in north-east France. In 1916, the 19-year-old was badly wounded in a bombing raid on the General Hospital at Wimereux, where she was based. She was hospitalised in Boulogne before returning to her family home in Cork; while there she became utterly traumatised by the intimidation her family was subjected to by hardline Irish Republicans after the war. She spent her last years in a sanatorium in Epsom, Surrey, convinced 'they are outside waiting to get me'.

When Britain attempted to impose conscription on Ireland in 1918, DD was amongst the most vocal in opposition, dramatically warning the House of Commons that the Irish would 'fight you if you enforce conscription on us'. He had hoped to resume his legal and parliamentary work in Ireland, but the political map had changed so much since 1914 that when the election of December 1918 approached, he and O'Brien recognised the pointlessness of putting any AFIL candidates forward. They threw their support behind Sinn Féin, which duly took all of the eight seats previously held by the AFIL. DD's Mid-Cork seat was won by the playwright and poet Terence MacSwiney who, as Mayor of Cork, was fated to die on hunger strike less than two years later.

In that same election, Captain Sheehan actually stood unsuccessfully as a Labour candidate for London-Stepney. His campaign slogan "Land for Fighters" was instrumental in persuading Lloyd George's government to provide cottages for thousands of ex-servicemen, under the Irish Land (Provision for Soldiers and Sailors) Act 1919.

DD's move to London was in part a response to the manner in which the tide had turned so sharply against the Sheehan family in post-war Ireland. They were ostracised not simply because so many had served in the King's forces but because Captain Sheehan, his wife Mary and his daughter Eileen had played such an active role in the recruitment of the Munster volunteers.

Shortly after the December 1918 election, gunshots were fired into the Sheehan family home on the Victoria Road in Cork, most likely by radical militant Republican elements, forcing them to abandon their home and belongings and leave Cork. Mary moved to Kingstown (Dún Laoghaire) in south County Dublin while DD remained in London. Not wishing to have his children educated in England, he arranged for Loreto Abbey in Dalkey to take in their three younger daughters, where they were nicknamed 'the charity girls'. His two younger sons Patrick (later Pádraig) and John were taken in by Rochestown College and Blackrock College, respectively. The children repaid their school fees on their own account in the 1930s.

When DD returned to Ireland to visit Mary in 1919, things turned darker still. 'I was recognised,' he later recalled, 'stopped in Kingstown Main Street by two young men who stated they were members of the Republican Army. They ordered me out of the country. I promptly left. Shortly afterwards the room my wife was sitting in at 1 Windsor Terrace, Kingstown, was fired into at night, making her further residence in the country impossible.'[76]

Unable to live or work in the country he had devoted his life to, DD and his family took refuge in England, where he returned to his career of journalism, becoming publisher and editor of *The Stadium*, a daily newspaper for sportsmen. During this time, he wrote his seminal history *Ireland Since Parnell* in which he offered a further insight into his motives for joining the army. 'I was actuated by one desire and one only — to advance, humbly as may be, in myself the cause of Irish freedom. For the rest, I served and I suffered, and I sacrificed, and if the results were not all that we intended, let this credit at least be given to those of us who joined up then, that we enlisted for worthy and honourable motives and that we sought, and sought alone, the ultimate good of Ireland in doing so.'[77]

Shortly before Mary's death in 1926, DD returned to Dublin to take up the post of managing director and editor of the *South Dublin Chronicle*. The paper did much to highlight the appalling living conditions of slum-dwellers across Ireland. Amongst other issues, he decried the manner in which the Republican newspaper *An Phoblacht* slated Great War veterans for serving "England", expostulating in a November 1929 editorial:

'*An Phoblacht* writes: "Mislead by lying promises and faked propaganda, you fought for England." Nothing of the kind! There were no lying promises and no faked propaganda; and the Irishmen who fought in the Great War did not fight for England. They fought for liberty, they fought for the freedom of humanity, and against the spirit of Prussianism, which if it had prevailed would put the whole world under the sway of an atrocious tyranny. As well say that the Americans, the Italians, the Belgians, the Canadians, the Anzacs and all the others who rallied to the standard of the Allied cause, fought for England. The thing is too absurd and ridiculous for words.'[78]

In 1930, he was defeated when he stood for election as a Labour Party candidate for Dublin City Council. He went on to become one of the strongest advocates of the 'Buy Irish Goods' campaign. He continued to offer legal advice to his former constituents, defending them from attacks on their right to 'security of tenure' and other land owner-ship entitlements which had been granted under pre-war legislation.[79] He also worked closely with the Old Comrades Association, which had one eye on ex-servicemen who were unemployed or otherwise distressed. In 1946, he penned 'A Tribute and a Claim', a lengthy ode to the Irish men and women who served in both world wars.[80]

Captain DD Sheehan died on 28 November 1948 at the age of 75 while visiting his daughter Mona in Queen Anne Street, London. He was buried alongside his wife in Glasnevin Cemetery, Dublin. Amongst his surviving children was his fourth son, Pádraig Augustine Ó Síocháin SC, a journalist and author who later became a passionate Irish language activist and did much to boost the international sale of Aran knitwear in the 1950s and 1960s.

• • •

Daniel Joseph Sheehan,
DD and Mary's eldest
son, who served with
No 66 Squadron and
was fated to do battle
with Manfred von
Richthofen, brother
of the Red Baron.

• • •

Martin Sheehan, DD
and Mary's second son,
who served as an
observer and gunner
in northern France
with the Royal Air
Force's No 13
Squadron.

THE SHEEHAN BROTHERS
WHO TOOK TO THE SKIES

On the morning of 2 October 1918, Mary Sheehan arrived downstairs in floods of tears. 'I saw him coming down in flames,' she explained to her family, over and over again. She was referring to her second son, 21-year-old Martin, who was then serving as an observer and gunner in northern France with the Royal Air Force's No 13 Squadron. A few days later, an official telegram arrived at Captain Sheehan's home to say that Martin and his pilot had been killed on 1 October when their reconnaissance biplane crashed near Cambrai. Although the exact circumstances of what happened are unknown, it is believed their aeroplane was felled by ground fire.

As a schoolboy at Christian Brothers' College, Cork, Martin Sheehan represented Munster in the Rugby Inter-Provincial Senior College Championships and was described in the Dublin press as 'the most brilliant three-quarter back the College had produced for years'. In 1913, he emigrated to Canada and was working at the Union Bank of Bellevue, Alberta when the war broke out. He enlisted in the Canadian Expeditionary Force and continued to show his sporting prowess by winning the all-round Athletic Championship of his Division in Nova Scotia. In 1916, his battalion arrived in Europe and he transferred to the Royal Munster Fusiliers, with whom he served at Passchendaele. He then transferred to the No 13 Squadron, with whom he served on the battlefields of both France and Italy until his death.

In perhaps his last letter to his father in July 1918, he wrote: 'Well father you need not worry about me. You say the Bosche has got better and braver than me. Perhaps. But that was in the days when we were not superior in the air. Now we have them licked upside down, and I am a damn good shot and my gun fires 600 rounds a minute. And it is a better gun and is better mounted than the Bosche Gun. A year ago was different from today. I have not been brought down yet, and I have flown a decent amount over the Lines. I am quite sure of coming Home alright. Yesterday we brought a Bosche down in flames. He dared to come over the Lines. He never went Home.'[81]

Martin's oldest brother Daniel, another star player of the Christian Brothers' College rugby team, had initially joined the Royal Navy, serving as a Midshipman on board the battleship HMS *Hibernia*. He later transferred to the Royal Flying Corps. By 14 April 1917, he was serving with No 66 Squadron, based at Vert-Galant aerodrome north of Amiens. Morale was particularly low amongst Allied aviators that month, later known as 'Bloody April', with the superior German Jasta fighter squadrons eliminating 298 British aircraft. Over 200 aircrew were dead or missing and a further 108 had been captured.

Daniel met his end early on the morning of 10 May 1917, when his Sopwith Pup biplane was ambushed during a routine patrol. The 23-year-old Irishman was fated to become the 22nd kill of German air ace Lothar von Richthofen, the gung-ho younger brother of the top-scoring ace Manfred von Richthofen, aka the Red Baron.[82] Daniel managed to land his severely damaged plane near Noyelles, but died in his cockpit soon after. 'He was loved by all,' wrote one of his superiors, 'and was, by nature, absolutely devoid of fear'.

THE
SHORT ARMY CAREER
OF PRIVATE KIT CONWAY

...

ONE OF THE MORE UNLIKELY MEN TO ENLIST AND TRAIN AT KILWORTH CAMP, COUNTY Cork, in DD Sheehan's time was the future Republican, Communist and Spanish Civil War fighter, Kit Conway. Orphaned as a boy, Conway grew up in a poorhouse in Clogheen, County Tipperary, before going to work on a farm, where he earned two shillings a week. He joined the British Army in 1915 but, after a few weeks' training, he decided army life wasn't for him. In order to convince his superiors to discharge him, he performed a sequence of acts of elaborate madness, pretending to eat his cap, beating himself with his rifle and pouring buckets of water over himself, until he was eventually booted out.[83] Kit Conway made his name as a guerrilla during the Troubles, fighting both the Black and Tans and later the National Army of the Irish Free State. He died defending the Spanish Republic in 1937 at the head of the Irish unit known as the Connolly Column.

MAJOR GENERAL

LOUIS LIPSETT, CBE, MC

(1874-1918)

...

As he crawled along the banks of the River Selle on the afternoon of his death in October 1918, Louis Lipsett could not have known that the war would be over within less than a month. The Donegal-born officer had been assigned to attack the small French town of Saulzoir. Two thousand years earlier this was where the Nervian tribesmen so nearly routed the Roman army, only for the legionaries, with Julius Caesar himself at their head, to rally and all but annihilate the Nervii.

Like Caesar, Major General Louis Lipsett was a man who liked to lead by example, commanding the 3rd Division of the Canadian Expeditionary Force (CEF) during their most successful era of the war. A man of considerable initiative, he was amongst the first to work out that urine-soaked handkerchiefs and cotton bandoliers could counteract the effects of poison gas.

The forefathers of the Lipsetts are believed to be either Dutch or German Protestants who settled in County Donegal in the 17th century. In 1724, a branch of the family took a lease from William 'Speaker' Conolly on a farm overlooking Donegal Bay at Cashel, near Rossnowlagh. During the 1870s, Louis's father, Richard, and his uncle, Robert, established the biggest general store in Ballyshannon, four miles from Cashel. As auctioneers, they also acquired considerable property in the Ballyshannon and Bundoran area; Richard served as Chairman of the Ballyshannon Town Commissioners.[84]

Louis's mother, Esther Plews, was living at Prospect House in Enniskillen at the time of her marriage to Richard Lipsett in 1872. Her father, Henry Plews, was Traffic Manager for the Great Northern Railway of Ireland, later becoming its General Manager.

The Lipsett marriage was plagued by tragedy; two small daughters died young and Richard himself passed away in 1880 at just 48 years of age. Esther then took her two surviving children, William, aged seven, and Louis, aged six, to live with her mother's family in Masham, Yorkshire.

...

Louis Lipsett's portrait by Sir William Orpen. The Donegal-born Lipsett was the last British general to command a Canadian division in the field. Orpen recalled him as 'a thoughtful, clever, quiet man, [who] was greatly respected.'

"FAITH, THERE'S NO WAN COULD BE BOLDER"

Come on Boys!

JOIN THE

IRISH CANADIAN

OVERSEAS
BATTALION RANGERS

Headquarters·
91 STANLEY ST..
MONTREAL.

Under
Lt. Col. H. J. TRIHEY.

· · ·

Following the outbreak of the war, a group of senior Irish citizens in Montreal were granted permission to form the 55th Regiment, Irish Canadian Rangers, comprising 475 men of Irish descent, complete with a forty piece band. 'Faith, there's no wan could be bolder . . . Come on Boys!' was the begorrah-esque rallying call. Harry Trihey, a former captain of the Montreal Shamrocks ice hockey team, became the principal organiser and the first commanding officer. He raised considerable funds for the regiment from a St Patrick's Day concert in Montreal and also secured the Duke of Connaught's wife as a patron. Thereafter they became known as the Duchess of Connaught's Own Irish-Canadian Rangers.

From Bedford School, where he excelled at rugby, Louis went on to the Royal Military College at Sandhurst. In 1894, the 20-year-old was commissioned as a second lieutenant in the Royal Irish Regiment. For the next five years, he served on the North-West Frontier (present-day Pakistan) where he narrowly survived a bout of cholera.

By 1911, his track record as a staff officer in South Africa and as a sometime aide-de-camp was sufficient to secure him an appointment from the Colonial Office to go to Canada, where he was to help improve military training in the Dominion. Many of the staff officers and generals who served with the CEF in the Great War were trained by Major Lipsett. Renowned for his sparkly humour, sporting passion and general efficiency, he also set up a series of schools and training courses that were closely affiliated with the Canadian military.[85]

When war broke out, the Canadians were fearful of an attack on their Pacific coast by Admiral Maximilian von Spee, commander of the German East Asian Cruiser Squadron, who had effectively been given free rein by the German Admiralty to cause as much mayhem in the Pacific Ocean as he saw fit. Louis Lipsett was sent to strengthen defences along the vulnerable coastline of British Columbia, working in conjunction with Richard McBride, the provincial Premier whose parents both hailed from Ireland.[86] While Lipsett organised the local militia, McBride seized an opportunity to expend $1,150,000 of provincial funds on two shiny new submarines built at a shipyard in Seattle.

Although von Spee's fleet managed to destroy two British cruisers off Chile on 1 November 1914, Lipsett correctly doubted its long-term capabilities. Five weeks later, von Spee's fleet was destroyed in the Falkland Islands; the Admiral went down with his flagship.

With von Spee dead, Lipsett took command of the Winnipeg-based 8th Battalion, aka the 'Little Black Devils'. The battalion was destined to experience some of the heaviest fighting of the war in Europe, earning three Victoria Crosses in the process.

In 1915, Lipsett led the 8th Battalion across the Atlantic Ocean, where they joined the British Army in France as part of the 3rd Canadian Division. His men must have still been acclimatising when they were thrust into the horrific second battle of Ypres. The first gas attack in modern warfare took place on 22 April when the Germans attached hoses to 5,730 gas canisters and unleashed 160 tons of chlorine gas on the French lines. Over 6,000 Moroccan and Algerian troops of the French army were killed, blinded or maimed within ten minutes. Hundreds of Canadian soldiers also died in the attack, including Lipsett's Ballyshannon-born first cousin, the barrister William Alfred Lipsett.

The German High Command had not anticipated such devastation and were slow to exploit the opportunity. In the confusion, the 8th Battalion was amongst those sent to plug the gap in the Allied line. As such, they were in an unenviable position when the Germans released a second deadly cloud of poison gas at 4am on 24 April. When the 15-foot high green haze rolled into the Canadian lines, it immediately began to suffocate Lipsett's men in a manner of indescribable awfulness. In the ominous words of one observer, the men had 'no place to run'.[87]

There was, however, an unlikely remedy. After the initial attack on 22 April, Dr George Nasmith, a 26-year-old bacteriologist serving with the Canadian Army Medical Corps quickly diagnosed the German gas as chlorine. Perhaps because he had been listening attentively when his chemistry teacher at Bedford was discussing the propensities of chlorine, Lipsett was amongst the first to deduce that if a man peed on a handkerchief and tied it around his face or, better still, stuffed it in his mouth, then the ammonia in the urine would at least partially neutralise the chlorine. He quickly ordered all his men to do just that. Those unable to piss, or too petrified to react, or who simply found the concept too embarrassing, were invariably choked by the gas. The 8th Battalion just about managed to hold the line, for which Lipsett was roundly acclaimed by his superiors and his men alike.[88]

Lipsett was soon commanding the Canadian 2nd Brigade, with whom he planned and supervised the first of a series of major raids on the German trench lines in the

THE SPHERE

AN ILLUSTRATED NEWSPAPER FOR THE HOME

With which is incorporated "BLACK & WHITE"

Volume LXI. No. 801. | REGISTERED AT THE GENERAL POST OFFICE AS A NEWSPAPER | London, May 29, 1915 | Price Sixpence.

DRAWN BY F. MATANIA, SPECIAL ARTIST OF "THE SPHERE" IN FRANCE, 1915

HOW THE GAS DEVIL COMES—"THE THICK GREEN MIST CAME ROLLING TOWARDS THE PARAPET"

autumn of 1915. The following June, he was given command of the shattered 3rd Canadian Division when Malcolm Mercer, the original commander, was killed by shellfire at Mont Sorrel. Major General Lipsett duly converted the 3rd Canadian Division into one of the most efficient in the Canadian Corps, leading his men through the carnage of the Somme, Vimy Ridge and Passchendaele, each of which extracted a huge loss of life from the division.

In August 1918, Lipsett played an instrumental role in organising the morale-boosting victory over the Germans in the battle of Amiens, the opening phase of the Hundred Days Offensive that concluded the war.

Lipsett was frequently hailed as 'a wonderful soldier and a wonderful man'. As one of his men recalled, his gift as a leader was that he was 'always accessible and charming in manner, yet there was that about him which made him respected and no one ever presumed on his kindness, except the few old soldiers, who with their war ribbons up, and uncanny intuition, never failed to touch a soft spot in his heart'.

Ernest Davis, another of his men, recalled an episode when Lipsett's staff car appeared alongside another car that had been derailed behind the lines. 'This general got out of his car, organised everyone within reach into a rescue squad, all of us heaving at the derailed car, including the general himself. As I recall it, his chauffeur gave visible evidence of hating to put his spotless shoulder to the load but he had to... That one encounter told me that here was a general one could follow, knowing he was not one of the remote kind, far above his men.'

It was also no surprise to those who knew the fun-loving Irishman that the Dumbells, the best-known Canadian concert troupe of the war, wore the badge of Lipsett's division with pride. He even managed some time off in Paris, where he was captured on canvas by the Dublin-born artist William Orpen.

Lipsett was highly regarded by both General Currie, commander of the CEF, and Douglas Haig, commander of the British Expeditionary Force. The only problem, as far as General Currie was concerned, was that Lipsett wasn't Canadian. Currie wanted his entire Canadian Corps to be commanded by Canadians. Therefore, Currie did not object when Haig sought to transfer Lipsett's command to the British 4th Division.

Although reluctant to say goodbye to his Canadian troops, Lipsett had little option but to comply and he subsequently led the 4th Division during the long-drawn-out final offensive. On 14 October 1918, the fearless 44-year-old embarked on a reconnaissance expedition along the left bank of the River Selle to examine ways to attack Saulzoir. An alert German machine-gunner on the opposite side of the river spotted the scouting party and opened fire. Everyone ducked except Lipsett, who was hit in the face by a solitary bullet. He managed to make it back to his men in the Bois de Vordon, where he collapsed from the huge loss of blood. He never regained consciousness and so became the 59th — and last — British officer of Brigadier General rank or above to be killed during the war. The Great War ended 29 days later.

The Prince of Wales joined the scores of British and Canadian officers who attended Louis Lipsett's funeral in Quéant Communal Cemetery the day after his death. An unmarried man, he is also recalled by a memorial on his family gravestone in St Anne's Churchyard, Ballyshannon, Co Donegal.[89]

COLONEL HART-McHARG AND PRIVATE O'ROURKE, VC

The 11th Regiment (Irish Fusiliers of Canada) was one of five militia regiments raised in Greater Vancouver in 1913, and ultimately sent 4,308 men to serve on the Western Front. In September 1914, eight officers and 350 men from the Irish Fusiliers were drafted into Canada's 7th Battalion under the command of Lieutenant Colonel William Hart-McHarg. Born in Kilkenny Barracks in 1869, Hart-McHarg emigrated to Canada at the age of 15 and went on to become one of Vancouver's most prominent lawyers. An outstanding marksman, he represented Canada in several international shooting competitions. He was fatally wounded outside the village of Keerselaere during the second battle of Ypres.

One of the 7th Battalion's three Victoria Cross winners was Private Michael James O'Rourke, a Limerick-born stretcher-bearer, who impressed his superiors when, in the face of heavy machine-gun fire, he 'worked unceasingly in bringing the wounded into safety, dressing them, and getting them food and water' during the fight for Hill 70, near Lens, in August 1917. O'Rourke survived the war and died in Vancouver in 1957.

BOB HANNA, VC – THE LUMBERJACK FROM COUNTY DOWN

Two hundred and fifty men from the 11th Regiment (Irish Fusiliers of Canada) were drafted into the 29th Battalion which became known as Tobin's Tigers after its commander, Lieutenant Colonel Henry Seymour Tobin, a Catholic barrister and Anglo-Boer War veteran from Vancouver. Amongst their ranks was Bob Hanna, a happy-faced lumberjack from Aughnahoory, Kilkeel, County Down who had emigrated to British Columbia aged 18. He won a Victoria Cross for his actions at the battle of Lens in 1917 when, after an ambush decimated his company and either killed or wounded every one of its officers, he had arisen 'under heavy machine-gun and rifle fire, coolly collected and led a party against the strong point, rushed through the wire and personally killed four of the enemy, capturing the position and silencing the machine-gun'. When Bob Hanna visited Kilkeel after the war, 3,000 people packed the town square to congratulate him. He then returned to Vancouver where he ran a logging camp, had a family and passed away in 1967.[90]

Known to millions as 'Woodbine Willie', the Anglican priest and poet Geoffrey Anketell Studdert Kennedy was deeply proud of his Irish origins.

WOODBINE WILLIE –
THE **SOLDIERS'** POET

...

They gave me this name like their nature,
Compacted of laughter and tears,
A sweet that was born of the bitter,
A joke that was torn from the years.

Of their travail and torture, Christ's fools,
Atoning my sins with their blood.
Who grinned in their agony, sharing
The glorious madness of God.

Their name! Let me hear it — the symbol
Of unpaid — unpayable debt,
For the men to whom I owed God's Peace,
I put off with a cigarette.

WOODBINE WILLIE BY GA STUDDERT KENNEDY

And then came the awful silence. Or a sort of silence. The whistling train was gone, the cheering men departed, the canteen empty. But the whistles and cheers continued to echo through Woodbine Willie's mind long into the night.

Nearly every time it was the same. One day the fresh recruits would arrive into the old Gare de Rouen Saint-Sever, flooding the canteen with their giddy innocence. Within one sunset, or at most two, they were gone again. Before the troop trains left the station, the young Irish clergyman would clamber on board and slowly make his way down the aisles, carriage after carriage, distributing his wares to every private and officer he passed. From one sack came the pocket-sized New Testaments. From the other, the five-packs of Woodbine cigarettes from which he acquired his moniker. And

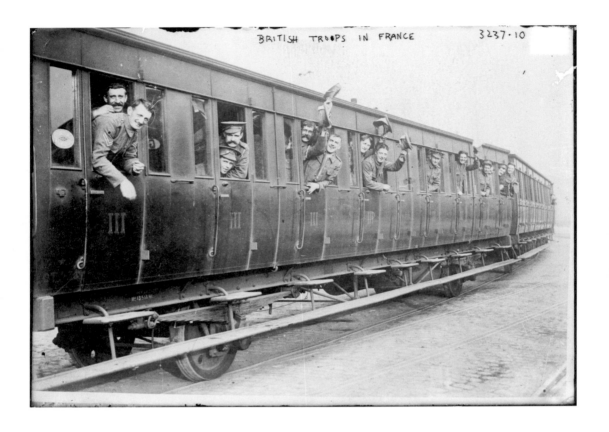

British soldiers en route to the
Western Front in the early days of
the Great War.

then he would stand on the platform and watch the train chug away, across the River Seine, leading its cargo of men to whatever lay in store for them at the Western Front.

The Rev Geoffrey Studdert Kennedy was born in Yorkshire but always maintained that he was an Irishmen, and his powerful voice was imbued with the rich Irish brogue of his forefathers. The church was in his genes. His paternal grandfather was Dean of Clonfert in County Galway from 1850 until his death in 1864. His mother Jeanette also came from a family closely associated with the Church of Ireland, the Anketells of Dungillick House, Emyvale, County Monaghan.[91]

William Studdert Kennedy, his father, was born in Blackrock, County Dublin, in 1826, and spent 35 years of his life as Vicar of St Mary's in Quarry Hill, outside Leeds. Regarded as one of the worst inner-city slums in northern England, this was where Geoffrey was born in 1883. Most people worked in the eponymous quarry and either lived in squalid back-to-back tenements or the workhouse. Life was so bleak that the local pub was called the Cemetery Tavern. Geoffrey's health was always precarious, almost certainly because of the intense Quarry Hill smog; he suffered the first of many asthma attacks at the age of six.

The seventh of nine children, he grew into a scruffy boy who read copiously at all times. When his head wasn't buried in a book, he was to be found either daydreaming or chattering incessantly with his eight siblings. He was considered rather absent-minded and the words 'I must've been thinking of something entirely different' became a family catch phrase. His siblings would later speak of his 'gentle, forgiving, loving nature' and 'his extraordinary laugh', although his brother Maurice recalled how 'he would blaze with fierce indignation at anything nasty, mean, unmanly, treacherous or unkind'.

Educated privately in his younger years, he advanced from Leeds Grammar School in 1901 to the cobblestones of Trinity College, Dublin, where his father and two of his older brothers also studied. Four years later, he graduated with a First Class degree in Classics and Divinity, winning a Silver medal for his efforts.

He didn't choose the church straight away but instead had a stint as a grammar school teacher in Lancashire. However, the calling was strong and by the summer of 1908 he was a deacon in the Anglican Church. Two years later, he was dispatched as curate to the industrial slums of Rugby on the River Avon. He found a community deeply disheartened by the church; its laborious messages and old-world pomposity seemed so utterly irrelevant to the grim realities of daily life in Rugby.

He immediately began to impress upon his flock that he was rather different from the traditional curates they might have known. He took to venturing into the town's pubs and mingling with the men as if he were a normal punter. When he listened to their tales of woe, he was frequently so moved that he would give all his money and clothes away until, eventually, his landlady felt obliged to take charge of his relatively meagre income and ration it.

Although just five feet six inches in height and rather thin, Geoffrey rarely failed to make an impression on those who met him. In part this was due to his jug-handle ears, of which he made light, but it was primarily his sense of humour, his boisterous laugh and his extraordinary eloquence that captured people's attention. Imploring them to give Christianity another chance, he held his listeners spellbound with a combination of his heartfelt words and his curious Irish lilt. Such exhortations would pave the way to make him one of the finest soapbox orators of his generation.

In 1912, he returned to Quarry Hill to help his father, by then an ailing widower in his late eighties. In April 1914, he married Emily Catlow, the daughter of a Leeds coal merchant. By the time his father died soon afterwards, Geoffrey had been offered a choice of three parishes. He was inclined towards a Vicarage amid the impoverished community of St Paul's Parish in the Blockhouse at Worcester. However, he wanted to be sure his new bride was up for it. 'St Paul's has the smallest income and the poorest people', he said to her. 'Go and look at the house, and if you think you can manage it, I will accept the offer.'

Emily declared that she was game and so, on 9 June 1914, Geoffrey took charge of a parish of 4,000 people, mostly workers from the various glove, porcelain, vinegar, tin plate and iron factories and foundries around the town. He threw himself into the role with vigour and started by going from door to door through the poorest parts of his parish. Within weeks he was electrifying his new congregation with his sermons. He was also stimulating both morale and the local economy by organising boot and clothing drives, as well as soup kitchens. The Studdert Kennedys offered hope, and soon the vicarage was awash with people afflicted by depression, alcoholism, loneliness and other such miseries, who sought their counsel. Geoffrey was particularly good with children, often slipping them a penny so that they could watch a film or buy some fruit or nuts. When he officiated at a child's funeral, contagious tears welled up in his big, sad brown eyes.

When the Great War broke out, Geoffrey was all for the Allied cause. He turned his oratorical skills into rallying the young men of his parish to enlist. 'I cannot say too strongly that I believe every able-bodied man ought to volunteer for service anywhere. There ought to be no shirking of that duty.' Much to his later horror, many took him at his word and sallied forth for death and glory.

Over the next year, Geoffrey became appalled by the relentlessly grim stories that came back from the Western Front and Gallipoli. Having urged so many others to join up, he felt compelled to enlist as an army chaplain and by Christmas Day 1915 he was ankle-deep in cold French mud.

One week later he received his first assignment to a canteen shed next to the railway station in Rouen, where he remained until Easter 1916. Rouen was a staging post where the new troops who arrived into Le Havre could pause for a quick prayer and some food en route to the front. The soldiers were soon besotted by the big-eared, shoddily dressed cleric who presided over the canteen. He certainly knew how to make his presence felt. He would stand up on a box, gather the men around and then belt out a hat trick of songs in a fine baritone voice. For those who missed their mothers, he sang 'Mother Machree', which had been a great hit for the Irish tenor, John McCormack, before the war. For husbands, he sang 'Little Grey Home in the West' and for young lovers there was 'The Sunshine of your Smile'.

It was at Rouen that he became famous as the man who distributed Woodbine cigarettes and New Testaments to the departing troops. As he later advised a padre bound for the thick of the fighting, 'Take a box of fags in your haversack and a great deal of love in your heart.' The New Testaments were the brainchild of a daughter of the Cadbury chocolate family. An extraordinary number of soldiers would later claim that a bullet bound for their heart had been halted by a copy of these pocket-sized tomes which they had kept over their left-side breast. One wonders how many of these life-saving books passed through the hands of Geoffrey Studdert Kennedy.

He received his first taste of the front line when he was sent up to the trenches of the Somme in June 1916. He spent the next four months doing his bit to maintain morale, helping to bring in the wounded from the battlefields, offering solace to the dying. He was often to be found penning letters to loved ones on behalf of those who could not write.

'What did you do before the war, Padre?' a soldier asked him.

'I was a revolutionary agnostic socialist who used to stand on a tub and talk in public places in the Midlands.'

One of the reasons why the men loved him was because, for all his fancy education, he seemed to

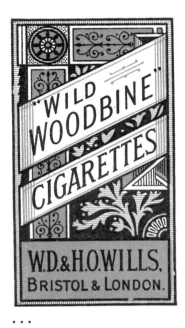

...

Woodbine Willie derived his name from distributing five-packs of 'Wild Woodbine' cigarettes to soldiers bound for the killing fields of Ypres and the Somme.

acutely understand the ways of the working class. As one contemporary put it, he mastered the 'soldier's vernacular'. By entering that mindset, he was able to provide them with a degree of comfort in that alien, shell-blitzed world around them. He was also not afraid to confront the immense doubts that so many of these ostensibly Christian soldiers now felt. They had seen enough of war to believe in Hell, but their faith in Heaven and a benevolent God was by no means so assured. Describing one of the front line bombardments in his book *The Hardest Part*, he summed up such thoughts: 'But, by George, it's a glorious barrage, and English girls made 'em. We're all in it — sweethearts, mothers and wives. The hand that rocks the cradle wrecks the world. There are no non-combatants. We're all in it, and God, God Almighty, the loving father who takes count of every sparrow's fall, what is He doing? It is hard to fathom.'

In October 1916, he returned to England where the Anglican Church recruited him to tour the country's army training camps on behalf of the new National Mission for Repentance and Hope. His mission was to reignite waning interest in the messages of the Church and to speak out against what they perceived as declining moral standards brought about by the war. Over the next five months, he visited every single army base in Britain, despite being laid low for three weeks by a severe asthma attack.

In June 1917, he returned to the front and he served through the first weeks of the gruesome battle of Passchendaele. He was serving with the 24th Division under

General Gough when he was awarded a Military Cross. His citation told how he had stomped across No Man's Land under heavy fire, searching shell holes for wounded soldiers, Allied and German alike — so that he could bring them back to the dressing station. 'His cheerfulness and endurance had a splendid effect upon all ranks in the front line trenches, which he constantly visited,' concluded his citation. What that blurb did not say was that his initial trot across No Man's Land was to fetch some urgently needed morphine for a dying soldier. Nor did it say that one of the three wounded men he sought to bring in was blown to pieces during the attempt.

Fortunately, he was given ten days' leave along with his Military Cross, enabling him to return to Worcester, where he was reunited with his beloved Emily and met their newborn son Patrick. On account of his resurgent asthma, his leave was extended and, ultimately, the fighting parson's next assignment was not the front line but a farm near Saint-Pol, where he was to serve as chaplain at the School for Physical and Bayonet Training, dubbed the 'School of Courage'. Run by Colonel Ronald Campbell, the school's aim was to reignite the zest for life in men who had been sent back from the trenches — 'dazed, sullen, stupid, dismal, broken'. Geoffrey, who had by now earned the moniker of 'Woodbine Willie', formed part of a bizarre team assigned to oversee this spiritual renaissance. His teammates included former world featherweight boxing champion Jimmy Driscoll, two wrestlers, a violinist, a tame bear called Flanagan, miscellaneous pigs and a sergeant who claimed to have killed 18 Germans with a bayonet. Woodbine Willie referred to them as 'the travelling circus'.

Certainly, humour and entertainment was a large part of the project. Gathering all the shell-shocked men into one place, Colonel Campbell would establish the running theme with lines such as, 'You may meet a German who says, "Mercy! I have ten children." Kill him! He might have ten more.' And then, after an evening of mock bayonet jousting, boxing fights and rousing music, it fell to Woodbine Willie to wrap it all up. As the London journalist Philip Gibbs put it, he 'stepped up and talked of God, and war, and the weakness of men, and the meaning of courage. He held all those fellows in his hand, put a spell on them, kept them excited by a new revelation, gave them, poor devils, an extra touch of courage to face the menace that was ahead of them when they went to the trenches again.'[92]

Such words belied his true feelings, because by now Woodbine Willie was well on the road to becoming an ardent pacifist. He was appalled by 'the glorious madness of God', as he described it in a poem, and, while at the School of Courage, he began his book *The Hardest Part* in which he wrote, 'The brutality of war is literally unutterable. There are no words foul and filthy enough to describe it.'

In March 1918, the German Spring Offensive got under way, and he was once again sent to the front line, joining the 42nd Division. He remained in France long after the war ended and was finally reunited with Emily and Patrick in March 1919. In the interim he produced his first anthology of poetry, *Rough Rhymes of a Padre*, giving all proceeds to a charity for the blind. Like his sermons and his daily banter, these poems weren't complex refrains that one needed a Classics degree to understand. They were written in the same jerky vernacular that had made him so popular in the inner-city

The canteen in a camp-hospital at Rouen, France, October 1914. Woodbine Willie spent the first three months of 1916 in Rouen, singing and praying with the troops before they moved onwards to the front lines.

slums and the front-line trenches. The book was such a massive hit that he published a second volume, *More Rough Rhymes* in 1919.

Over the course of the 1920s, he went on to become one of Britain's most outspoken pacifists. 'When I went to the war, I believed that the war would end to the benefit of mankind,' he declared. 'I believed that a better order was coming for the ordinary man, and, God help me, I believe it still. But it is not through war that this order will be brought about. There are no fruits of victory, no such thing as victory in modern war. War is a universal disaster and, as far as I am concerned, I'm through.'

Always a champion of the downtrodden, he emerged as a hugely influential social reformer, throwing his support behind Christian Socialism and castigating capitalism as the source of much evil. 'This post-war world is black with lies,' he growled, 'biting and buzzing round everything There's a bad smell about, a very bad smell, it is like the smell of the Dead... it is the smell of dead souls.'

In 1922, he was appointed Rector of St Edmund, King and Martyr in Lombard Street in the financial district of London. This at least offered financial security at a time when he and Emily were parents of three small boys. His sermons became so legendary that he was invited to deliver one to George V at the Royal Chapel, a brave move given his growing propensity to startle his congregation with his radical thoughts. During one of his Lombard Street sermons, for instance, the chain-smoking war veteran expressed an urge to smash every stained glass window in the church with a sledgehammer and bring everyone to celebrate the Eucharist in a field instead.

• • •

Crowds line Worcester's High Street to watch the funeral procession bearing the coffin of the Rev Geoffrey Studdert Kennedy. The vicar preached at a church in the city's slum district.

Nonetheless, the King was impressed with his oratory and duly appointed him a Royal Chaplain. Woodbine Willie behaved himself when in front of the Royal family, although there was one occasion when he forgot to bring any clothes to the chapel, and so found himself delivering a sermon to half the House of Windsor wearing nothing but rugby shorts beneath his red cassock.

In fact, the absent-mindedness that his siblings had teased him for in his childhood had never really gone away. He was constantly failing to get off at the right train station and leaving things behind. Even on the front line he had been famous for his forgetfulness.

Nonetheless, he piled his energies into writing anything that would help expound his beliefs: poems, essays, pamphlets, articles — sometimes dictated as he paced around his office. He even published a novel called *I Pronounce Them* in 1927, tackling sexual matters such as birth control, desire and fidelity.

However, it was as an orator that he was best known. In 1927, the Industrial Christian Fellowship (ICF) recruited him to go on the road and tell people how labour and capitalism could work together with the Christian faith. He spent many long hours carefully honing and memorising each talk so that he could deliver every line as if it were spontaneous. To some it must have seemed that hidden spirits were channelling their messages through him. He became one of the ICF's most sought-after speakers and tens of thousands came to hear him.[93] On one occasion, after he received an invitation from Trinity College, Dublin, to deliver a Sunday sermon to the students at the College Chapel, he apologised that his Sundays were 'booked up' for the following two years, but proposed that he might be able to give a weekday address instead.

Unfortunately, his end came before he had that opportunity. In March 1929, his wife and sons were taken ill with a flu epidemic that swept across England. Geoffrey was also feeling unwell, but he had been asked to give a talk in Liverpool on behalf of the ICF and he was unwilling to let them down. Emily said she could manage the children on her own, so he duly took a train to Liverpool. By the time he arrived, he was seriously ill. He managed to reach St Catherine's Vicarage, where he was sent straight to bed. It transpired that he had pneumonia. Combined with his asthma, his cigarette smoking and the mustard gas he had inhaled on the Western Front, it proved too much. Emily arrived shortly after midnight to find him sunk into a coma. His heart gave out at 1.30am on 8 March. He was 45 years old.

Woodbine Willie's death was greeted with widespread sorrow amongst the working class, but when the head of the ICF proposed to the Dean of Westminster that he be buried in Westminster Cathedral, the latter responded, 'What!? Studdert Kennedy!? He was a socialist!' In the end, he was buried in Worcester Cathedral. Tributes poured in from the King and Queen, as well as countless soldiers whom he had served alongside. Thousands lined the two-mile route between the cathedral and the cemetery where he was buried. As his coffin was lowered into its grave, a number of his old comrades stepped forward and solemnly showered it with packets of Woodbines.[94]

His will was made on a sheet torn from a notebook at the British General Headquarters in France on 18 April 1916. In it, he left everything to Emily.[95] When she died in 1964, her last words were 'Geoffrey is here! Geoffrey is here!'

A mine explodes during the battle of Messines Ridge in June 1917 following the biggest underground tunnelling operation in recorded history.

HILL 16 —
LEGENDS OF THE RUBBLE

...

ONE OF THE LONGEST-RUNNING URBAN LEGENDS TO CIRCULATE THROUGH THE ANNALS OF the Gaelic Athletic Association is that the famous Croke Park terrace 'Hill 16' was built on the rubble of the Easter Rising of 1916. The items reputedly buried beneath the Hill ranged from the bricks of the General Post Office to a De Dion-Bouton motorcar belonging to Michael O'Rahilly, one of the Rising's slain leaders. Sadly, when the Hill was redeveloped in 1988, archaeologists supervising the works discovered that the base of 'Hill 16' was not the blood-stained debris of the Irish revolution. It was plain old earth.

In fact, the embankment was largely completed the year before the Easter Rising began and was originally christened 'Hill 60'. It is generally believed that the name was a nod to 'Hill 60' on the Gallipoli Peninsula. Together with Scimitar Hill, this low rise at the northern end of the Sari Bair range was considered a vital cog in the doomed plan to link the Allied forces at Anzac Cove and Suvla Bay. During the last week of August 1915, a force of 5,000 Irish, Indian, Australian and New Zealand soldiers tried repeatedly to take the hill, with devastating consequences. Nearly half the men were killed or wounded by Turkish shells and machine-guns, including large numbers from the 5th Battalion of the Connaught Rangers. The eight-day battle was the penultimate act of the hopeless Dardanelles campaign.

However, this author is inclined to think that the Croke Park embankment was actually named for another 'Hill 60', a spoil heap thrown up on the Western Front when the Ypres-Comines Railway was under construction. This man-made hill, which lay just three miles south-east of Ypres, became a warren of underground tunnels and was the scene of intense fighting throughout the war. In April and May 1915, for example, it was central to a major battle in which the 2nd Battalion of the Royal Dublin Fusiliers took part.

Most of the 'Hill 60' at Ypres was destroyed when, following the biggest underground tunnelling operation in history, 19 mines, stuffed with 450,000 kilograms

(990,000 lb) of explosives, were detonated along the Messines Ridge at 3.10am on 7 June 1917. It was the largest planned explosion the world had yet known and it blew a crater 60 feet deep and 260 feet wide. David Lloyd George, the British Prime Minister, was awoken moments before it went off and heard it from his home at Walton Heath in Surrey.[96] Approximately 10,000 German soldiers are said to have died directly because of the detonation of the Messines mines, making it the deadliest non-nuclear man-made explosion in history. As General Harington remarked to some Allied war correspondents on the eve of the attack, 'Gentlemen, I don't know whether we are going to make history tomorrow, but at any rate we shall change geography.'[97]

The name of the Croke Park terrace was altered to 'Hill 16' during the 1930s in a move by the GAA to eliminate such blatant reminders of an age when Irishmen served in British uniform. The myth was later propagated that the Hill had been constructed from the rubble and relics of the 1916 Rising.

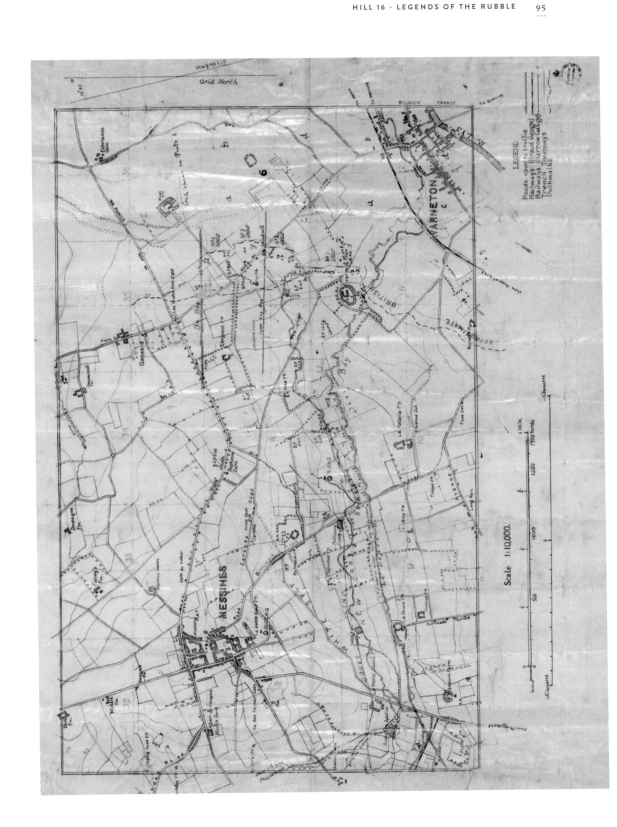

• • •

Tom MacGreevy in his Royal Field
Artillery uniform, pictured alongside
his sister Nora Phelan. This was taken
either during home leave in March
1917, or before his demobilisation in
January 1919.

TOM MacGREEVY –
MODERNIST POET

...

'DAA, DA-DAH, DAH', WENT THE BRITISH MACHINE-GUN.

'Dah, Dah', replied the German one.

Nothing like a bit of rhythmical tennis to whittle away the hours on the Western Front.

That was one of Tom MacGreevy's outstanding memories of his time on the front lines. The tempo of the machine-guns had a certain appeal to the Kerryman who, born in 1896, is regarded as one of Ireland's first modernist poets.

Born in Tarbert, north Kerry, he grew up in a Catholic family of farmers and school-teachers. At the age of 16, he went to work with the Irish Land Commission in Upper Merrion Street in Dublin. He arrived in the city just in time to witness John Redmond unveil the Parnell monument in Sackville (now O'Connell) Street.

When war broke out, his exceptional intellect saw him swiftly transferred to London where he became a Second Division Clerk under Rear Admiral Sir William 'Blinker' Hall, Britain's Director of Naval Intelligence. Primarily working night shifts for the Marine Section — 12 hours on, 24 hours off — he spent much of the next 18 months organising the miscellaneous diplomatic and military updates and telegrams that came in for the day staff. He was also frequently assigned to personally deliver confidential messages to Admirals based in and around the ports of Britain and Ireland.

On one occasion he was asked to deliver a message to the Royal Navy's code-breakers, a part of the Intelligence Division, who operated out of the top secret 'Room 40'. In April 1916, this team intercepted a number of missives between John Devoy of Clan na Gael and the German General Staff. These led directly to the capture of a German ship carrying arms to the Irish Volunteers in County Kerry on the eve of the Easter Rising, as well as the arrest of Sir Roger Casement. The press coverage of Casement's subsequent trial and execution inspired MacGreevy to write his first work of fiction — a dialogue between the imprisoned Casement and a senior British politician.

Perhaps discomfited by such close proximity to the heart of British Intelligence, MacGreevy changed tack. In March 1916, with universal conscription on the way, he enlisted in the Royal Field Artillery. By the summer he had embarked upon a gruelling 12-month stint of hard graft training in artillery and gunnery.

On 1 January 1918, Second Lieutenant Thomas MacGreevy arrived on the Ypres Salient to begin front-line service with a Battery of the Royal Field Artillery's 148th Brigade. In his unpublished memoirs, he describes his first night:

'We were being shot at, being shot at steadily and accurately. The "stuff", heavy "stuff", was coming down on us hard and fast. Twice the sandbagged roof of the dug-out was hit with "five-nines", German high-explosive shells. The light went out both times; the whole dug-out shook. Still it did not fall in on us. We were able to light up again. If this was war it was not a battle. To the Germans it was only a routine "shoot". We would send them back their ration of shells when the scheduled hour came round. Meantime we had to take what was coming to us for the half-hour or forty minutes the bombardment lasted.'

Tom MacGreevy was enjoying leave in Kerry when the Germans launched their Spring Offensive in 1918. He was subsequently among the thousands who defended the Allied lines and survived intact until 3 October when shellfire caught him so badly that he was transferred back to a hospital in Manchester. Shortly after the Armistice, he moved to the artillery depot at Athlone. He resigned his commission on 22 January 1919 and left the army with the rank of Lieutenant. He later became a friend of James Joyce, Samuel Beckett and TS Eliot, and served as Director of the National Gallery of Ireland from 1950 to 1963.

Coming to terms with his experiences of war would form the core of much of his poetry and essays. Amongst his most epic poems was 'Nocturne', a quatrain published in 1934, which recalled his time on the front line:

> I labour in a barren place,
> Alone, self-conscious, frightened, blundering,
> Far away, stars wheeling in space,
> About my feet, earth voices whispering.

TOM KETTLE
AND EMMET DALTON—
MAD GUNS AND
INVISIBLE WANDS

...

'SOMEWHERE', WROTE TOM KETTLE TO HIS BROTHER ON THE DAY OF HIS DEATH, 'THE Choosers of the Slain are touching … with invisible wands those who are to die.'[98] The 36-year-old Dubliner was not ready to die. In that same letter, he avowed that he was 'calm and happy but desperately anxious to live'. And yet he must have had an inkling that the Choosers were coming for him. In another letter, penned in those same moments, he wrote to his friend Joe Devlin, expressing a yearning to return to Ireland, yet reasoning that, should he be killed in the war, 'to sleep here in the France that I have loved is no harsh fate'.[99]

On the afternoon of 9 September 1916, Captain TJ Kettle, commander of D Company in the 9th Battalion of the Royal Dublin Fusiliers, received absolution from his padre. He then summoned his batman, an 18-year-old orphan called Robert Bingham. Private Bingham was heading home on leave to Belfast after the coming action; Tom Kettle quietly unstrapped his watch and presented it to the young man.

As the dusk began to settle that autumn evening, he rejoined his men in the stinking trench. Perhaps he exchanged some words with Captain Bill Murphy, who had taken command of the 9th Battalion less than 48 hours earlier. Born in 1880, Bill Murphy hailed from Tullow, County Carlow, where his parents ran a grocery. His father Edward, a nationalist, was elected to the first Carlow County Council in 1899 but died of pneumonia soon afterwards. Bill, an only son, emigrated to Australia some time later but was back visiting his family in Carlow when the war broke out. He initially joined the Leinster Regiment, later transferring to the 9th Battalion of the aforementioned Dubs.

Having won a Victoria Prize at the King's Inns, Tom Kettle was called to the Irish Bar in 1905, the year this photograph was taken. Musing upon the reasons why his subsequent career as a barrister did not last long, his wife Mary wrote: 'He had that uncanny gift of seeing everybody's point of view with equal intensity of vision. Such a gift makes for a very lovable personality, but a lawyer should only see the point of view for which he is briefed.'

Captain William Edward
Murphy grew up in Tullow,
County Carlow, where his
father was a grocer and nation-
alist councillor. Bill Murphy
would later command the 9th
Battalion of the Royal Dublin
Fusiliers at the battle of Ginchy.

Standing close by was Second Lieutenant William Hatchell Boyd, Kettle's second-in-command. The 29-year-old son of a Methodist minister, Boyd had worked as an accountant in Londonderry before the war.[100]

Also nearby was 18-year-old Emmet Dalton, a second lieutenant, who had just been made second-in-command of the battalion's C Company. Tom Kettle was a close friend of Emmet's father, a second-generation Irish-American called James Francis Dalton. Born in Fall River, Massachusetts, Emmet was still a toddler when his parents settled back in Ireland in about 1901, running a laundry enterprise in Drumcondra, Dublin. Emmet's father also became a major fundraiser for the Irish Parliamentary Party. Like Tom Kettle, Emmet was educated at the Christian Brothers' School in North Richmond Street, Dublin.

By the time Tom Kettle and young Dalton met again, on the banks of the Somme in those strange September days, they had much in common.[101] Emmet was just behind Tom Kettle when, at approximately five o'clock, Captain Murphy blew his whistle and the first wave of the 9th Battalion sallied over the top.

Thomas Michael Kettle was born in Artane, Dublin, on 9 February 1880. His father Andrew 'Andy' Kettle probably had other things on his mind when the boy — the seventh of 12 children — arrived. Just three months before Tom's birth, Andy Kettle co-founded the Irish Land League in Castlebar, Co Mayo. A close ally of both Isaac Butt and Michael Davitt, he went on to become Parnell's right-hand man, sticking by the formidable nationalist leader during his fall from power. After Parnell's death, the elder Kettle bowed out of politics and focused instead on his farm at St Margaret's in Finglas, Dublin. The farm where Tom Kettle spent his childhood was one of the most progressive in Ireland.

Tom was an attentive schoolboy, quick-witted and game for a laugh. For decades after his death, both the Christian Brothers of North Richmond Street and the Jesuits of Clongowes Wood College in County Kildare would hail him as a model pupil. An enthusiastic athlete, cricketer and cyclist, he also impressed his peers at University College, Dublin, where he won a gold medal for oratory and became auditor of the Literary and Historical Society in the last years of the 19th century.[102]

The columnist William Dawson would later recall him as '… a genial cynic, a pleasant pessimist, an earnest trifler, he was made up of contradictions … a fellow of infinite jest, and infinite sadness'. Magnetically intellectual, his circle included the Home Rule journalist Frank Cruise O'Brien and the pacifist Francis Sheehy Skeffington, both of whom were to become his brothers-in-law. James Joyce was another friend, while Oliver St John Gogarty, immortalised as 'Stately, plump Buck Mulligan' in Joyce's *Ulysses*, was one of Kettle's cycling and drinking comrades.

Kettle was at UCD when the Anglo-Boer War began in 1899. Echoing the anti-war stance taken by so many students in modern times, he protested vehemently against British motives for invading the Boer lands. He was among those who distributed pro-Boer pamphlets on behalf of the Irish Transvaal Committee which, founded by Maud Gonne and Arthur Griffith in 1899, boasted a high-calibre membership list that included WB Yeats, James Connolly, Willie Redmond, the veteran Fenian John O'Leary and Andy Kettle's old friend Michael Davitt.

For those at UCD who heard Tom Kettle speak, it must have seemed likely that this young man, the prodigy of one of the Land League's co-founders, would one day make a sizeable impression on the Irish political scene. His biggest obstacle was himself. Highly strung and prone to melancholy, he drank too much, not least when his favourite brother died in 1903. Shortly afterwards, the 24-year-old suffered some form of a nervous breakdown that led him overseas. He spent a year at Innsbruck University where he studied history and philosophy.[103] He also used this time to devour every European literary classic he could find, as well as mastering the German and French languages.

By the time he returned, a securer soul, it seemed certain that he would pursue a career as a barrister, not least when he won the Victoria Prize at the King's Inns and was called to the Bar. However, that sort of bar just didn't grab him and political journalism was fast becoming his raison d'être. He started by writing for newspapers and magazines until the newspaper proprietors took fright at his broad-minded but controversial views on topics such as the Gaelic League, women's rights and university education.

He then established his own weekly journal, *The Nationist*, combining his opinions with some of the more extreme views held by John Redmond's IPP. Redmond had known of Kettle since at least 1904 when the young man co-founded the Young Ireland Branch of the United Irish League and became its first president. The 'Yibs', as they became known, injected a welcome dollop of youth culture into the aging IPP. Redmond was particularly enchanted by Kettle, even tolerating *The Nationist*'s dreamy notions of an alliance between the IPP and Sinn Féin. Redmond asked Kettle if he'd like to stand for Parliament as an IPP candidate. Kettle initially declined, preferring to stay focused on his journalism, but in 1906 he conceded that perhaps politics was for him. That summer, the 26-year-old defeated the Unionist candidate by 19 votes in a by-election, and so began his four years in Westminster as MP for East Tyrone.

Tall, slight, youthful and exuberant, he cut a dash in the House of Commons from the moment he made his maiden speech, arguing that it should be the British War Office rather than Dublin ratepayers who footed the bill for the Dublin Metropolitan Police. He also put his oratorical skills to good use, memorably lambasting Britain's two biggest political parties with the observation that, 'When in office, the Liberals forget their principles, and the Tories remember their friends.'[104] Not surprisingly, many considered him a shoo-in to succeed John Redmond as and when the older man stepped down.

Emmet Dalton's father was presumably closely involved when John Redmond sent his bright young star on a six-month trip to the US to raise funds for the IPP and to push home the party's message. At Carnegie Hall in New York, Tom Kettle shared a platform with the old Fenian 'dynamitard' Jeremiah O'Donovan Rossa.[105]

But while he undoubtedly paid close heed to Irish-American politics, Tom Kettle's mindset was always more closely entwined with Europe. 'My only programme for Ireland,' he declared, 'consists in equal parts of Home Rule and the Ten Commandments. My only counsel to Ireland is, that to become deeply Irish, she must become European.'[106] Ever since his European adventure, he had considered Ireland's future as intrinsically bound up with Europe, predicting something not dissimilar to the European Union. His European vision would play a major role in sending him to the trenches in 1916.

His personal life took a bold step forward when he married Mary Sheehy on 8 September 1909. Her father was also an MP for Redmond's party but the newlyweds had manifold other connections. She too had studied at UCD, where James Joyce developed a crush on her, and she not only shared Tom's beliefs in suffrage and nationalism but she was also closely related to two of his best friends. Her sister Hannah married Francis Skeffington in 1903; he duly bucked the trend and attached her name to his, thereby becoming Francis Sheehy Skeffington. Another of Mary's sisters, Kathleen, married Frank Cruise O'Brien and was mother of the future government minister, writer and historian, Conor Cruise O'Brien. Also into the mix was Father Eugene Sheehy, Mary's uncle, a co-founder of the GAA who oversaw young Éamon de Valera's education in Limerick.

Tom Kettle was by now such a good speaker that everyone wanted him. This became rather problematic from 1908, when he was appointed first Professor of National Economics at UCD. The post meant a lot to him; he was fascinated with economics as a means of creating the society he believed Ireland and Europe could become. In the first of the two General Elections of 1910, he was re-elected for East Tyrone. However, when the second election was called, he took the opportunity to stand down. He subsequently teamed up with the Protestant Home Ruler Swift MacNeill and others to co-found UCD's Legal and Economic Society (now the Law Society).

While he was no longer at Westminster, Professor Kettle continued to make his voice heard, applauding the Home Rule Bill in 1912, pushing for a united Ireland and scoffing at Unionist fears of 'Rome Rule'. Unlike most middle-class Dubliners, he also threw his support behind the strikers during the 1913 Lock Out, serving on the Peace Committee that was formed to broker a deal between the strikers and the employers. He published a series of articles highlighting the appalling working conditions and the state of the slums where so many people lived.

In 1913, the year his daughter Betty was born, Tom became so fed up with Unionist resistance to Home Rule that he co-founded the Irish Volunteers. On account of his impressive German, he was dispatched by the Volunteers to raise arms in Europe. The guns were successfully procured, but they were never to reach Ireland because the cargo was still being considered by Belgian Customs when the German Army invaded the neutral kingdom in August 1914. The guns were subsequently gifted to the Belgians to assist their defence against the Germans.[107]

Thus Tom Kettle found himself in Brussels when the Great War broke out. He was soon tapping out stories on his typewriter as a war correspondent for the *Daily News*, the London newspaper founded by Charles Dickens in 1846. As the conflict exploded across Europe, he counselled his readers that this was a war of 'civilization against barbarians'. He was to remain in Brussels for two months, during which time he witnessed the infamous 'Rape of Belgium'. Like many Irish Catholics, he regarded Belgium as one of Ireland's closest spiritual soulmates and he was appalled by the horrific manner

"THE DAILY NEWS & LEADER"
Football Annual
NOW READY.
1d. everywhere.

Daily News & Leader

No 21,343.　　LONDON & MANCHESTER, WEDNESDAY, AUGUST 5, 1914.　　ONE HALF-PENNY.

GREAT BRITAIN AT WAR WITH GERMANY.

WAR WITH GERMANY.

Reported Sinking of a British Ship.

OUR ULTIMATUM.

Demand for Withdrawal from Belgium.

KING'S MESSAGE TO NAVY.

AT 11.17 LAST NIGHT IT WAS ANNOUNCED THAT A STATE OF WAR EXISTS BETWEEN GREAT BRITAIN AND GERMANY

Late last night it was reported that the Government had received news of the sinking of a British mine-laying vessel by the German navy. The destroyer Pathfinder was chased, but eluded her pursuers.

Great Britain delivered an ultimatum to Germany yesterday, and demanded a reply by midnight. This action followed Germany's declaration of war on France and Belgium and the receipt of official news during the forenoon of the invasion of Belgian territory.

The Premier, in announcing the Government's momentous action in the House of Commons, stated that early yesterday morning Germany was asked for an assurance that her demand upon Belgium would not be proceeded with, and that her neutrality should be respected.

An immediate reply was asked for, and a message was received from the German Foreign Secretary to the effect that no Belgian territory would be consumed, but that Germany was compelled to disregard Belgian neutrality owing to fears of a French attack through that country

News also reached London that the German Army was marching into Belgium.

To enquire the British Government repeated its request for an assurance of Belgian neutrality on the same lines as that given by France, demanding that a satisfactory reply should reach London before midnight.

This grave announcement was received with loud cheers

First news of Germany's declaration of war on Belgium reached London yesterday in a telegram from Mr. Ernest W. Smith, the special correspondent of "The Daily News" at Brussels. The German action was a reply to Belgium's firm refusal to allow the Kaiser's troops to cross her frontiers.

Great Britain is prepared for war. The Navy is mobilised and at sea; the Army is being mobilised. Men and youths are flocking to the colours, and crowds besiege the recruiting offices.

Admiral Jellicoe has been appointed to the supreme command of the Home Fleet, with Rear-Admiral Madden as his Chief of Staff. Sir John French has been reappointed to his former post as Inspector-General of the Forces.

The Lobby Correspondent of "The Daily News" says that Lord Haldane, the Lord Chancellor, is acting as Assistant Secretary for War. Mr. Asquith retaining the office of Secretary. Lord Kitchener's services, it is believed, will be available in this country

The British railways have been taken over by the Government for military purposes, and it is notified that the ordinary services may be dislocated for some time.

A scheme for the distribution of food is under the consideration of the Government, and yesterday Mr. Lloyd George announced details of an important scheme to insure our merchant ships against war risks, so that foodstuffs for the people and raw material for our industries may continue to come to our shores.

There has been panic buying of foodstuffs in large centres, and many shops have been compelled to close temporarily. Municipalities are beginning to take action to conserve the supplies.

Our military correspondent deals (on Page Three) with the question of invasion and the methods in which the fleet would oppose the transports of an enemy.

There is a division in the Cabinet on the question of British intervention. Lord Morley, Mr. John Burns, and Mr. C. P. Trevelyan have tendered their resignations to the Prime Minister.

News of Britain's promise to guard the northern and western coasts of France has been received with enthusiasm in Paris. French papers denounce Germany for "committing an outrage not simply against Belgium, France, England, and Russia, but the civilised world"

GERMAN ADVANCE.

Reported Entry into Belgium at Three Points.

BRUSSELS, Tuesday.
The Germans have entered Belgium at three places—Dolhain, Francorchamps, and Stavelot—and represented to patrol late last Thirteen, Liege—Exchange Telegraph Co.

"Of these three places Dolhain stands nearest Prussian territory, a village south of Aix-la-Chapelle, near the eastern corner of Belgian Liege. The others are nearer the Prussian frontier, and lead from the latter place to Liège."

BRIDGES DESTROYED.

BRUSSELS, Tuesday.
The newspaper "Le Peuple" announces that Belgian engineers have blown up rail-bridges and tunnels throughout the valleys of the Vesdre. The river rises in Prussia and flows into Belgium north of Verviers.—Central News.

MOVING INTO FRANCE.

Three Columns Pressing Forward from Luxemburg.

BRUSSELS, Tuesday 9.30 a.m.
The Germans forces are advancing through Luxemburg in three columns, one towards Longwy, another towards Villerupt, and the third towards Thionville.
A telegram from Givet states that the French and German troops are advancing on the French and German frontier stations.—Central News.
(Villerupt is a French village situated eight miles east-north-east of Longwy. Thionville (German Diedenhofen) is situated in Alsace-Lorraine, 18 miles north of Metz on the Moselle.)

NEAR MARS-LA-TOUR.

PARIS, Tuesday.
A German company is reported to be in French territory near Mars-la-Tour, the scene of one of the most sanguinary battles of the war of 1870.—Reuter.
(Mars-la-Tour lies close to the German frontier, south-west of Metz.)

GERMANS SINK BRITISH SHIP.

Reported Loss of a Mine-Layer.

A DESTROYER'S ESCAPE.

Late last night we received the following:
The Press Association learns that there is no truth in the report of a naval engagement in the North Sea.
It is understood that the British Government has received intimation of the sinking of a British mine-layer by the German Fleet, and also that the Pathfinder, a destroyer, was chased, but managed to elude the pursuers.

CALL TO DOCTORS.

It was reported yesterday afternoon at Aberdeen that a naval engagement had taken place off the North of Scotland, and that the wounded had been landed at Cromarty.
It was impossible to obtain any confirmation of the report, but it was definitely ascertained that a telegram had been received at Aberdeen asking that surgeons and nurses should be sent at once to Invergordon and Cromarty. Aberdeen medical men on special service were also ordered to hold themselves in readiness.
During the afternoon special trains were made up at Aberdeen to take contingents of nurses and surgeons to Invergordon.
The doctors were naturally declined to discuss the matters of the submarines they had received, but it was stated in Aberdeen that the step was merely a precautionary measure in view of possible contingencies.
The prospect of Cromarty is about 100 miles north-east of Aberdeen and 20 north-east of Inverness, with a population of 8,000. Cromarty Firth, on one of the North Sea, penetrates inland for 18 miles, and is thus open to the sea in width, with complete shelter for shipping—natural advantages not enjoyed by any harbour in the kingdom.

KING'S MESSAGE TO ADMIRAL JELLICOE.

The Navy, the Sure Shield of the Empire.

The following message has been addressed by his Majesty the King to Admiral Sir John Jellicoe:—
At the grave moment in our national history I send to you, and through you to the officers and men of the fleet of which you have assumed command, the assurance of my confidence that under your direction they will revive and renew the old glories of the Royal Navy, and prove once again the sure shield of Britain and of her Empire in the hour of trial

　　　　　　　　GEORGE, R.I.
(This signal message has been communicated to the several naval officers on all stations outside of home waters.)

THE GERMAN FLEET.

Bombardments in Baltic and Mediterranean.

An official message issued by the French Embassy quotes Reuter that the German Baltic bombarded the town of Berlin, in Algeria, at four o'clock yesterday morning and afterwards steamed off at full speed in a westerly direction.
(Bona, or Béne, is a fortified town of some 4,000 inhabitants, on the coast of Algeria, near the frontier of Tunis, with the capital of which it is connected by rail. It is a French territory.)
A Central News message from Flushing received yesterday by an indirect route, declares the statement that several of the German warships were fired at near Brussels.

IN THE BALTIC SEA.

A German cruiser has bombarded the Russian port Libau. According to a Russian official communiqué cabled by Reuter, one shot hit the naval hospital, and two struck private houses. The material damage was very small and there were no casualties.
There is no confirmation of the report that German warships have entered the Åland Islands.

TAMPERING WITH THE MINES.

BOULOGNE-SUR-MER, Tuesday.
A small sailing ship which had been observed tugging the coast in a suspicious manner was challenged by the authorities at Alprecht, and hoisted the German flag, but pulled it down immediately afterwards and substituted the Spanish colours.
Other guns were being prepared to fire upon her when she put on all sail and disappeared in the gathering night. It was believed that she had endeavoured to tamper with the mines.—Central News.

GERMAN LINER'S PLIGHT.

The Hamburg-America liner Belgia, from Bremen to Hamburg, called off Alprecht early yesterday, and anchored off the port. The captain found himself unable to get into communication with the German Consul at Newport, but up to last night had been unable to do so.
He stated that he has run short of bunker coal. It is believed that he is apprehensive of proceeding up the English Channel in case of capture by the French. It is stated that the Belgia has a large amount of specie aboard.

NEW HEADS OF ARMY AND NAVY.

Admiral Jellicoe to Command the Fleet.

It was announced officially yesterday that Vice-Admiral Sir John Jellicoe has been appointed to the supreme command of the Home Fleet.
Rear-Admiral Sir Jack French has been reappointed to his former position of Inspector-General of the Forces, which he resigned some time ago in connection with the General Court incident in Ulster.
Sir John Jellicoe has been second Sea lord since December, 1911, and it was known several months ago that he had been selected to succeed Admiral Callaghan when such succession became necessary. The latter officer was appointed Commander-in-Chief of the Home Fleets on Dec. 4, 1911, so that in the ordinary course the tenure of the command expired last December; but with the distinction with which he discharged the duties of his command, however, and so great the confidence reposed in him by the Admiralty, that his appointment was extended until December of the present year.
Sir John Jellicoe was made rear-admiral in February 1907 and has since been —
Second in command of the Atlantic Fleet (August, 1907)
Third Sea Lord (October, 1908);
Vice-Admiral commanding Atlantic Fleet (December, 1910);
Second Sea Lord (December, 1911)
He has not a most distinguished career, having served in the Egyptian war and in China. He was wounded in 1900 in the Victoria, but was cured after sinking, and severely wounded at Peking. Among his many adventures is the rescue from the Kaiser. He is it, and his men described by the Burdock and of his country and the Empire on the hour of trial

---

WAR DECLARED ON BELGIUM.

German Army Enters Her Territory.

KING'S SPEECH IN THE BELGIAN CHAMBER.

From Our Own Correspondent
ERNEST W SMITH
　　　　　　　BRUSSELS, Tuesday
I learn officially at the Ministry of War that Germany has declared war upon Belgium this morning
M. de Broqueville, the Prime Minister, has announced in the Chamber that Belgian territory has been invaded at Verviers. He read the German reply to the Belgian Note, which said that Germany would take by force of arms the measures of security demanded by the situation
I feel in my duty to pay a tribute to the splendid calm and restraint of the popular, as on the days which preceded German's ultimatum, with its tragic sequel—a state of war. Their attitude has been a provocative and tried by the sole desire to defend the independence of the country. This little people has resolutely upheld calm refusing to France up to the time I left them
I wired last night that events were moving quickly, but I confess I was unprepared for the dramatic turn which things took this morning. Thousands of people collected around the Royal Palace to cheer the King on his way to open Parliament, and when the news that Germany was at war with Belgium was known it spread like wildfire I called at the Ministry of War, where I received confirmation, and thence to the Chamber, where M. de Broqueville the Premier and Minister of War was making a long declaration
M. de Broqueville read almost instantly the Edward Grey's statement made in the House last night describing Germany's demand and Belgium's answer. We have waited till the necessary reply to Germany's reply to the Belgian Note, and the Minister Germany has replied that she will take the measures which the situation imposes by force of arms. A message of immediate admonishment ran through the Chamber. "This copy is beyond comment," added M. de Broqueville. "La parole est donnée aux armes."
We will do our duty our whole duty. We may be beaten but we shall never be cast down. The Belgian people will not fail to do their duty. So that I say continued
Later the Premier announced that Belgian territory had been violated. Great cheering greeted the announcement that M. Vandervelde, the Socialist leader, had been nominated Minister of State. Immense crowds cheered King Albert on his return to the Palace, and then promenaded the centre of the city amid tremendous scenes of enthusiasm and cries of "Vive Belgique, France, Angleterre."
This afternoon the aspect is almost normal except that many groups are discussing the situation

KING ALBERT'S CALL.

Every Citizen Required to Do His Duty.

　　　　　　　BRUSSELS, Tuesday.
The King addressed the following speech to the deputies:
"Never since 1839 has a graver hour sounded for Belgium. The strength of our right and the tried of Europe for our autonomous existence make us still keep that the dreaded events will not occur. But if it is necessary for us to resist an army

The "Daily News" - War Telegrams arriving during the day will be published in "The Star."

WAR DECLARED ON BELGIUM.

KING'S SPEECH IN THE BELGIAN CHAMBER.

(continued)

GERMAN WIRELESS SEIZED.

BRUSSELS, Tuesday
The "Chronegue" announces that The authorities yesterday seized the wireless installation at the German school here.—Reuter

BELGIAN AVIATORS ARRESTED.

AMSTERDAM, Tuesday
Two Belgian aviator officers have descended at Emmerich, near Borrosend (Limburg), and have been placed under arrest by Dutch Frontier Guards.—Central News.

NO REPLY EXPECTED TO ULTIMATUM.

Lord Haldane Assisting at War Office.

(By Our Lobby Correspondent.)
It was not expected in official circles last night that a reply would be made by Germany to the British ultimatum, and the German Ambassador (Prince Lichnowsky) it is expected, will call at the Foreign Office at 10.30 this morning, presumably as a preliminary to leaving the country. In such case it has already been arranged that the United States will take charge of the German Embassy in this country.
Lord Haldane is acting as Assistant Secretary of State at the War Office, and is to daily attendance there. The Lord Chancellor, it is obvious, could not be called upon to undertake the whole duties of the War Office, and Lord Haldane as one who has filled that post with personal success, has come forward to undertake, in addition to his own, the duties of Secretary of State.
Lord Kitchener's invaluable services will, there is reason to believe, be available to this country but his suggestion which has been put forward in irresponsible quarters that he should be appointed Secretary of State was not very likely Parliamentary experience is peculiarly necessary in a Minister of State at the juncture

LIBERAL AND LABOUR FEELING.

The feeling among the Liberal rank and file yesterday was more rigidly behind the Government in the course which events have inevitably thrust upon them. The German declaration of war against Belgium is resented by the Liberal Members who attended the meeting at which Mr. Ponsonby presided on Monday.
The Labour Party are now divided in feeling. Some hold that the Government must be supported in view of the unscrupulous behaviour of Germany. It is an attitude of silent antagonism to the Government once inclined the party would not have a united support from the Labour Party in the country.
The Labour Conference which has been summoned for to-day will probably give the chief consideration to the steps which must be taken for the relief of distress if unemployment results. But there will also be a peace propaganda.

CABINET RESIGNATIONS

Lord Morley and Mr John Burns have tendered their resignations. It is not believed that Lord Morley will withdraw his resignation, but whether Mr. Burns will reconsider his position was a doubt last night. Mr Trevelyan, Secretary to the Board of Education, has also tendered his resignation. No official announcements have yet been made, but neither Lord Morley nor Mr. Burns attended the Cabinet meeting yesterday.

WAR ON FRANCE.

German Ambassador Leaves Paris.

From Our Own Correspondent.
H. COZENS-HARDY
　　　　　　　PARIS, Tuesday
Germany has declared war against France, and Baron von Schoen, the German Ambassador, left for a special train from the Gare du Boulogne station at 10.52 last night. The departure was very quiet. The Chief of the Protocol which hands off with the departing Ambassador. Baron von Schoen was accompanied by his wife and daughter, who have been very popular and very Parisian.
The staff, two motor-cars, and the luggage also left by the same special.
All the cafés were closed early, and the streets were almost deserted when the party left.
The French interpretation of Sir E. Grey's statement has given profound satisfaction to Paris. The hesitating and wavering altar in the British Fleet are a serious discussion — the part of the mobilisation of the British Navy.

ULTIMATUM

PREMIER INFORMS THE COMMONS.

MIDNIGHT FIXED FOR A SATISFACTORY REPLY.

Mr. Asquith in the House of Commons yesterday made the momentous announcement that an ultimatum, expiring at midnight, had been presented to Germany in respect to the neutrality of Belgium. Received with general cheers, the Premier said:
"In conformity with the statement of policy which was made by my right hon friend the Foreign Secretary yesterday, telegram was sent early this morning by him to our Ambassador in Berlin. It was to this effect
The King of the Belgians has made an appeal to his Majesty the King for diplomatic intervention on behalf of Belgium. His Majesty's Government are also informed that the German Government has delivered to the Belgian Government a Note proposing friendly neutrality for maintaining a free passage through Belgium and promising to maintain the independence and integrity of the kingdom and its possessions at the conclusion of peace but threatening in case of refusal to treat Belgium as an enemy. An answer was requested within twelve hours. We also understand that Belgium has categorically refused this as a flagrant violation of the law of nations. His Majesty's Government are bound to protest against this violation of a treaty to which Germany is a party in common with us, and must request an assurance that the demand made upon Belgium will not be proceeded with and that her neutrality will be respected by Germany.—Reuter
We asked for an immediate reply—
(Renewed cheers)

BELGIUM INVADED

We received this morning from our Minister at Brussels the following telegram:
The German Minister has this morning addressed a Note to the Belgian Minister for Foreign Affairs stating that, as the Belgian Government had declined the well-intentioned proposals submitted to them by the Imperial Government, the latter would, to their deep regret, be compelled to carry out, if necessary by force of arms, the measures considered indispensable in view of the French menace.
Simultaneously or almost immediately afterwards we received from the Belgian Legation here a London the following telegram from our Belgian Minister for Foreign Affairs

General Staff announced that territory has been violated at Gemmenich near Aix-la-Chapelle Subsequent information tends to show the German Army has penetrated still farther into Belgian territory

THE GERMAN REPLY

We also received this morning from the German Ambassador here a telegram sent to him by the German Foreign Secretary and communicated by the Ambassador to us which is in these terms
Please dispel any distrust that may subsist on the part of the British Government with regard to our intention by repeating most positively the formal assurance that even in the case of armed conflict with Belgium Germany will under no pretence whatever annex Belgian territory (Laughter). The sincerity of this declaration is borne out by the fact that we have solemnly pledged our word to Holland strictly to respect her neutrality. It is obvious we could not profitably annex Belgian territory without coming at the same time into territorial acquisitions at the expense of Holland. (Laughter)
Please impress upon Sir Edward Grey that the German army could not be exposed to French attack across Belgium, which was in the plan, according to absolutely unimpeachable information. Germany has consequently to disregard Belgian neutrality it being for her a question of life and death to prevent the French advance

That is the end of the communication then. I have to add that on behalf of his Majesty's Government:
We cannot regard this as in any sense a satisfactory communication (Cheers). We have in reply to it repeated the request we made to the German Ambassador. But we have also repeated it to him in a comprehensive form and have asked that a reply to this most satisfactory answer to the telegram this morning which I read to the House—should be given before midnight. (Loud cheers.)

A MAP OF THE NORTH SEA, SHOWING THE GERMAN NAVAL BASES.

NEW HEADS OF ARMY AND NAVY. (continued)

THE BRITISH DEMAND

Sir Edward Grey's Request to German Ambassador

Reuter's Agency is informed that the British Note to Germany was sent direct to Sir Edward Grey's demand, made being of the same lines heralded to the German Embassy
Sir Edward Grey has asked Prince Lichnowsky, the German Ambassador, to call at the Foreign Office this morning

It should reach a narrow becoming necessary, it has been arranged that the United States will take over the affairs of the German Embassy

100,000 GERMAN TROOPS

Preparing to Advance from Luxemburg.

From Our Own Correspondent.
HUGH MARTIN
　　　　ROTTERDAM, Tuesday
Messages received from Brussels confirm, on the authority of the Belgian Government, the general statement that the German Minister has already left Brussels.
It is impossible to verify from here the latter statement; but a prominent journal prints a declaration of a member of the German Legation at Brussels to the effect that Germany must at all costs cross Belgian territory and would be prepared to pay for all the damage done, she only asks that the bridges and railway may not be destroyed.
According to trustworthy information here the German army in Luxemburg, concentrating upon Longwy and Liege, is about 100,000 strong.
A military censorship on all messages has been established here

The "Daily News" - War Telegrams arriving during the day will be published in "The Star."

in which the Germans overran the country, killing 6,000 civilians and destroying over 25,000 buildings.[108] When he visited the smouldering ruins of the University of Louvain, including its celebrated Irish seminary, he became so incensed that his further writings were unhesitatingly vitriolic against the Germans. He condemned Germany as 'guilty of a systematic campaign of murder, pillage, outrage, and destruction, planned and ordered by her military and intellectual leaders'.

He had no doubt that it was Ireland's sacred duty to take up arms against Germany. 'This war is without parallel,' he wrote. 'Britain, France, Russia enter it purged from their past sins of domination. France is right now as she was wrong in 1870. England is right now as she was wrong in the Boer War. Russia is right now as she was wrong on Bloody Sunday.'[109]

He instantly sided with John Redmond's call to join what he hailed as 'the Army of Freedom' and was commissioned as an officer with the Royal Dublin Fusiliers in November 1914.[110] The army were quick to pounce on such a fine orator, and Lieutenant TM Kettle was soon touring Ireland on a massive recruitment drive, apparently addressing some 200 rallies in his army uniform.

Having witnessed what happened in Belgium first-hand, he was desperate to convey to his fellow Irishmen that if 'Prussian barbarity' won the war, all talk of home rule would be canned. 'It is a confession to make and I make it,' he said in 1915. 'I care for liberty more than I care for Ireland.'[111] By no means everyone was convinced. When he showed up at an anti-recruitment meeting in Dublin wearing that same uniform, he was heckled and booed by the audience.

Like many moderate nationalists, he also believed that a united effort by the National Volunteers and the Ulster Volunteers to defeat Germany would bond the two sides and stem the dreaded civil war that seemed to be coming down the line.

The Easter Rising was a blow for him on many levels, not least because he was close to many of the rebel leaders. He had served on the board of the Theatre of Ireland with both Thomas MacDonagh and Patrick Pearse, while Joseph Plunkett had been one of the secretaries on the Peace Committee during the Lock Out. Kettle's brother Lawrence also took part in the Rising.

Tom Kettle was livid with the rebels for destroying what he saw as the best chance for reconciliation between Protestant Ulster and the rest of Ireland. However, as his wife later said, 'what really seared his heart was the fearful retribution that fell on the leaders of the rebellion'. As he himself astutely forecast, 'Pearse and the others will go down in history as heroes, and I will be just a bloody English officer.'[112] From a personal perspective, he was also profoundly shaken by the murder of his brother-in-law and college friend Francis Sheehy Skeffington, killed by an insane British officer during the course of the Rising.[113] It didn't help when he went to console his bereaved sister-in-law and her children clad in the same uniform that Francis's killer had worn. 'The Sinn Féin nightmare upset me a little,' he wrote later, 'but then if you tickle the ear of an elephant with a pop-gun, and he walks on you, that is a natural concatenation of events.'[114]

Perhaps because of all this he urged his superiors to send him to Europe so that he could fight the good fight. They finally relented and he sailed for France on Bastille

Day 1916. On 24 July, five days after he found his battalion near Béthune, he went into the trenches for the first time. About a week later, a Dublin City postman arrived at 3 Belgrave Park, Rathmines, and delivered a letter to Mary Kettle. 'My ears are becoming a little more accustomed to the diabolism of sound,' her husband wrote, 'but it remains terrible beyond belief. This morning, as I was shaving, the enemy began to find us and dropped aerial torpedoes, shells and a mine right on top of our dug-out. The strain is terrible. It continues from hour to hour and minute to minute. It is indeed an ordeal to which human nature is hardly equal.'[115]

In another letter to Mary, written nearly three weeks later, he expressed his abhorrence of war. 'I want to live, too, to use all my powers of thinking, writing and working to drive out of civilization this foul thing called war and to put in its place understanding and comradeship.'[116]

Among those he teamed up with during this time was Major Willie Redmond, his fellow Nationalist MP and brother of John Redmond, who was serving on the divisional staff. Willie Redmond would later tell Sir Arthur Conan Doyle of their front-line friendship. 'I saw a good deal of Kettle,' he wrote, 'and we had many talks of the Unity we both hoped would come out of the War.'[117]

Within weeks of his arrival, the hot summer, the constant death and the drudgery of trench life were taking a toll on Tom Kettle. 'Physically I am having a heavy time,' he admitted to his wife. 'I am doing my best, but I see better men than me dropping out day by day and wonder if I shall ever have the luck or grace to come home … The heat is bad, as are the insects and rats, but the moral strain is positively terrible. It is not that I am not happy in a way — a poor way — but my heart does long for a chance to come home.' To offset his melancholy, Tom Kettle began writing a history of the 16th (Irish) Division.

On 29 August, the 9th Battalion marched from Longueau to billets at Corbie on the River Somme. It was at about this time that he became reacquainted with Emmet Dalton. The American-born officer was only 18 years old, but he had already lived an interesting life. In November 1913, aged 15, he had signed up with the Irish Volunteers and while Tom Kettle was gunrunning in Belgium, the youngster was helping his father dispatch a small cargo of rifles to County Mayo for Patrick Moylett, a future President of the Irish Republican Brotherhood. Encouraged by Joe Devlin, Emmet opted to join the 7th Service (Dublin Pals) Battalion of the Royal Dublin Fusiliers in 1915. Moylett tried to talk him out of it, but to no avail.[118] His father was likewise appalled. 'The first he knew was when I'd walked into my home dressed as a second lieutenant,' Dalton recalled. 'He told me to get out, that no bloody redcoat would enter his home.'

On 5 September, the men marched through heavy rains for three hours to the Sherwood and Pagan trenches at Trônes Wood from where they took part in the attack on Guillemont two mornings later. On the eve of Guillemont, Tom Kettle found the time to pen the poem he is best known for, a sonnet entitled 'To My Daughter Betty, the Gift of God', written in a field near Guillemont. The final line inspired the title of Sebastian Barry's award-winning novel, *The Secret Scripture*.

To My Daughter Betty, the Gift of God

In wiser days, my darling rosebud, blown
To beauty proud as was your mother's prime,
In that desired, delayed, incredible time,
You'll ask why I abandoned you, my own,
And the dear heart that was your baby throne,
To dice with death. And oh! they'll give you rhyme
And reason: some will call the thing sublime,
And some decry it in a knowing tone.
So here, while the mad guns curse overhead,
And tired men sigh with mud for couch and floor,
Know that we fools, now with the foolish dead,
Died not for flag, nor King, nor Emperor,
But for a dream, born in a herdsman's shed,
And for the secret Scripture of the poor.

Tom Kettle came through Guillemont unscathed, leading some to briefly wonder if he had a charmed life. However, as Emmet Dalton later wrote, the 9th Battalion had lost seven officers and 200 men to 'the Bosch shell fire' during the battle. As they raced to refill the upper ranks, Captain Murphy took command of the battalion, Tom Kettle took over B Company and Emmet Dalton became second in command of A Company.

On 8 September, Captain Murphy received his orders. The Dubs were to advance on Ginchy the following day, not at dawn, as was the norm, but when the twilight came. Their mission was to clear out the Bavarians who occupied the western side of the village. There had been many Allied attempts to conquer Ginchy during the war; none had succeeded.

Tom Kettle wrote his last letter to his brother. 'If I live I mean to spend the rest of my life working for perpetual peace. I have seen the war and faced modern artillery, and know what an outrage it is against simple men… We are moving up tonight into the battle of the Somme. The bombardment, destruction and bloodshed are beyond all imagination, nor did I ever think the valour of simple men could be quite as beautiful as that of my Dublin Fusiliers. I have had two chances of leaving them — one on sick leave and one to take a staff job. I have chosen to stay with my comrades… The big guns are coughing and smacking their shells, which sound for all the world like overhead express trains, at anything from 10 to 100 per minute on this sector.'

That was also the letter in which he referred to 'the Choosers of the Slain' and their 'invisible wand'.

As they made their way out of Trônes Wood, Emmet Dalton recalled how 'the stench of the dead that covered our road was so awful that we both [i.e. he and Tom] used some foot powder on our faces.'

On the outskirts of Ginchy, the Dubs dug in for the day. Professor Kettle received his absolution, wrote his final letters and gave Private Bingham his watch.[119] And then,

Supplement Gratis with the WEEKLY FREEMAN, NATIONAL PRESS & IRISH AGRICULTURIST Xmas No., Dec. 16th, 1916.

Price 3d.

Drawn by W. C. MILLS.   Printed by JAMES WALKER (Dublin) Ltd.

THE NIGHT BEFORE THE BATTLE: THE IRISH BRIGADE ON THE EVE OF GUILLEMONT, SEPT. 2nd, 1916.

. . .

'The Night Before the Battle' is an unusual depiction of the soldiers of the 16th (Irish) Division on the eve of the battle of Guillemont, 3 September 1916. Major Willie Redmond later recalled how the soldiers were all set for some shut-eye when the Catholic chaplain arrived into their midst. 'In a moment he was surrounded by the men. They came to him without orders — they came gladly and willingly, and they hailed his visit with plain delight. He spoke to them in the simple, homely language which they liked. He spoke of the sacrifice which they had made in freely and promptly leaving their homes to fight for a cause which was the cause of religion, freedom and civilisation. He reminded them that in this struggle they were most certainly defending the homes and the relations and friends they had left behind them in Ireland. It was a simple, yet most moving address, and deeply affected the soldiers . . . When the chaplain had finished his address he signed to the men to kneel, and administered to them the General Absolution given in times of emergency. The vast majority of the men present knelt, and those of other faith stood by in attitudes of reverent respect. The chaplain then asked the men to recite with him the Rosary. It was most wonderful the effect produced as hundreds and hundreds of voices repeated the prayers and recited the words, "Pray for us now and at the hour of our death. Amen."'

• • •

The bodies of the fallen line the road
through Guillemont in the last days of
the battle of the Somme, 1916.

upon the sound of the whistle, he and his men went over the top. A staff captain who knew Kettle claimed that he threw himself into the ensuing charge with a degree of relish. 'He was enjoying it like any veteran, though it cannot be denied that the trade of war, and the horrible business of killing one's fellows was distasteful to a man with his sensitive mind and kindly disposition.'[120]

German bullets and bombs slashed through the rain-sodden skies and the Dubs began dropping left and right. Sixty-seven of them would die that day. Many weeks later, Emmet Dalton found the strength to write to Mary Kettle and explain what happened to her husband.

'I was just behind Tom when we went over the top. He was in a bent position and a bullet got over a steel waistcoat that he wore and entered his heart. Well, he only lasted about one minute, and he had my crucifix in his hands. He also said, "This is the seventh anniversary of my wedding."'[121]

When it became apparent that Tom Kettle was dead, Emmet Dalton quickly removed all his papers and personal items from his pocket. He then handed them to Second Lieutenant Boyd, the Londonderry accountant, with instructions to send them back to Mary. Just minutes later, William H Boyd was atomised by a howitzer shell, and all Tom's belongings with him.

Bill Murphy, the grocer's son from Tullow, was also now dead; his body was last seen crumpled in a trench.[122] It was left to 18-year-old Emmet Dalton to take command of both A and B Companies for the final push. With night falling fast, he led the men onwards, under intense fire. He positioned a series of machine-gunners in the most commanding spots he could find and instructed them on how to protect their flank. While he and a sergeant were on a mission to check these positions, they ran into an enemy patrol. Amazingly, the two Irishmen managed to stun the officer commanding the patrol into surrender and they returned to their trench line with 21 German prisoners. The following year Dalton would be presented with a Military Cross at Buckingham Palace for having displayed 'great bravery and leadership in action'.[123]

The Irish conquest of Ginchy turned out to be one of the few victories the Allies could claim in the terrible year of 1916. It gave them control of a series of vital observation posts overlooking much of the Somme region, and that would prove to be a game changer of a sort in the inch-by-inch battle for the Western Front. That the Bavarians had been ousted from the village was almost entirely thanks to the 16th (Irish) Division. 'The wild rush of our Irish lads swept the Germans away like chaff,' applauded Father Willie Doyle, Chaplain of the 8th Royal Irish Fusiliers, who also won a Military Cross for his service during the battle. 'The first line went clean through the village and out the other side, and were it not for the officers, acting under orders, would certainly be in Berlin by this time!'

The cost to the Irish was immense. Tom Kettle was one of over 4,350 casualties recorded by the 16th (Irish) Division between 7 and 12 September, compared with a tally of 884 casualties for the village's Bavarian defenders. The Dubs were so badly hit that Emmet Dalton and Second Lieutenant ER Hurst were the only two of their eight officers to leave the battlefield alive. Amongst the 61 others from the battalion who died were Tullow-born Sergeant Edward Wall and Private James Rathband, the 16-year-old son of an auction porter from Gardiner Street in Dublin. The Royal Munster Fusiliers, who also took part in the battle of Ginchy, suffered worse still, losing eight officers and 220 men.

Tom Kettle's body was buried by the Welsh Guards who took over the ground where he died after the Irish had pushed on. Despite extensive searches initiated by his widow, its location remains unknown. His name would be carved upon the Thiepval Monument to the Missing of the Somme along with 72,194 others whose remains were never identified.

'Kettle was one of the finest officers we had with us,' wrote an unnamed staff officer in the coming weeks. 'The men worshipped him, and would have followed him to the ends of the earth... When the battle was over, his men came back to camp with sore hearts. They seemed to feel his loss more than that of any of the others. The men would talk of nothing else but the loss of their 'own Captain Tom,' and his brother officers were quite as sincere, if less effusive, in the display of their grief.'

'Tom's death has been a big blow to the Regiment', agreed Emmet Dalton in a letter he wrote to Mary Kettle five weeks later, 'and I'm afraid that I could not put in words my feelings on the subject.' The orphan Robert Bingham also took a moment to write to Mary. 'He was a brave officer and was like a father to me... I was awfully sorry when God called such a brave man away.' Mary would do her best to take Private Bingham under her wing, sending him cake and other parcels in the coming years. He survived the war, but died in Belfast at the age of 21 in October 1919, possibly a victim of the Spanish Flu.

News of Tom Kettle's death, just 52 days after he arrived on the Western Front, shocked his political and intellectual colleagues in Ireland. As the columnist William Dawson put it in an introduction to *Poems and Parodies*, a book of Tom's poetry published later that year, 'it is not the death of the Professor nor of the soldier, nor of the politician, nor even of the poet and the essayist that causes the heart-ache we feel. It is the loss of that rare, charming, wondrous personality summed up in those two simple words, Tom Kettle.'[124]

Reports on his death and extracts from his letters home regularly featured in *The Irish Times* for the rest of the year, while the *Freeman's Journal* of 23 October published an extraordinary letter which he wrote on the eve of Ginchy with directions that it was to be sent to Mary in the event of his death.

'Had I lived, I had meant to call my next book on the relations of Ireland and England: *The Two Fools: A Tragedy of Errors*. It has needed all the folly of England and all the folly of Ireland to produce the situation in which our unhappy country is now involved. I have mixed much with Englishmen and with Protestant Ulstermen and I know that there is no real or abiding reason for the gulfs, saltier than the sea, that now dismember the natural alliance of both of them with us Irish Nationalists. It needs only a Fiat Lux [i.e. 'let there be light'], of a kind very easily compassed, to replace the unnatural with the natural. In the name, and by the seal of the blood given in the last two years, I ask for Colonial Home Rule for Ireland — a thing essential in itself and essential as a prologue to the reconstruction of the Empire. Ulster will agree. And I ask for the immediate withdrawal of martial law in Ireland and an amnesty for all Sinn Féin prisoners. If this war has taught us anything it is that great things can be done only in a great way.'

Those who knew him must have imagined that the name of Tom Kettle would be enshrined forever, with perhaps a city street or a train station named in his honour. As it happened, on account of his allegiance to the Crown and his massive support for the recruitment drive, he was largely purged from memory when the new Irish Free State took shape. There was a considerable rumpus when his supporters commissioned a commemorative bust by the sculptor Albert Power. Cast in Brussels, the bust now stands discreetly in St Stephen's Green, Dublin, and hails him as a 'Poet, Essayist, Patriot'. He is also recalled by a bronze plaque in the Four Courts in Dublin along with the 25 other Irish barristers who died in the war, including Major Willie Redmond.

Tom's heartbroken father died at home in Finglas less than two weeks after the battle of Ginchy.[125] Tom's widow, Mary, continued to play a leading role in the emancipation of women, as well as in Dublin's municipal affairs, and lived until 1967. She had made her last public appearance three months earlier at a Mass in St Francis Xavier Church to mark the fiftieth anniversary of Tom's death. Their daughter, Betty Dooley, also studied at UCD and became a solicitor. She died at a nursing home in Clontarf in 1996 and is buried in the family plot in Swords.

Emmet Dalton was destined to have a particularly remarkable life after Ginchy. Promoted to the rank of Major, the Military Cross winner was wounded in the chest and knee and would go through the rest of his life with a bullet scar on his face. He served out the remainder of the war in Germany, Palestine and France. Demobbed in 1919, he then reverted to his pre-war empathies, re-joined the Irish Volunteers as a training officer and rapidly rose to become the organisation's Director of Training and Munitions during the War of Independence. In his spare time, he played for Bohemian Football Club during the 1919-1920 season.[126]

In the wake of the Anglo-Irish Treaty, Dalton supported Michael Collins and the pro-Treaty side and was one of the leading military brains involved with the National Army's subsequent campaigns. On 28 June 1922, he commanded the Free State troops assigned to dislodge the rebel 'Provisional Executive' from the Four Courts in Dublin, an event generally considered to be the start of the Irish Civil War. The following month, he led the army south, driving the Irregulars out of towns such as Tullow, the home of the late Captain Bill Murphy, his commander at Ginchy. Depending on one's convictions, Major General Dalton is to be either credited with, or blamed for, breaking the back of the Anti-Treaty forces in the 'Munster Republic' during the summer of 1922, including a dramatic amphibious attack on Cork. Tom Kettle's 'invisible wand' passed close to him once again that August when, as General Officer Commanding the Southern Command, he was with Michael Collins when the latter was gunned down at Béal na Bláth.

Emmet Dalton resigned his army commission in December 1922, having marked his card as an opponent of the Free State government's policy of executing anti-Treaty IRA prisoners without trial. After a short stint as Clerk of the Senate, he quit politics to try

· · ·

July 1922: Major General Emmet Dalton stands alongside Michael
Collins, Commander in Chief of the Irish Free State Army, at the
Curragh camp in County Kildare. Dalton was in the convoy with
Collins when the latter was killed at Béal na Bláth.

and rescue his father's ailing wholesale goods business. A fan of the silver screen, he then moved to London to work as a film distributor and producer. In 1958 he co-founded Ardmore Studios in Bray, County Wicklow. Its first production was an adaptation of Walter Macken's play, *Home is the Hero*, starring Macken himself and Joan O'Hara, mother of the novelist Sebastian Barry. Ardmore went on to produce films such as *The Blue Max*, *The Spy Who Came in from the Cold* and *The Lion in Winter*, all filmed in Ireland. In more recent years, Ardmore has been the base for movies such as *Braveheart*, *My Left Foot*, *The Commitments* and *Veronica Guerin*, as well as *The Tudors*, *Moone Boy* and *Penny Dreadful*.

Emmet Dalton died in 1978, over 60 years after Ginchy. He was survived by his daughter, the actress Audrey Dalton.

Orpen painted this self-portrait on 10
June 1917, shortly after his arrival in
France. He called it 'Ready to Start'.

SIR WILLIAM ORPEN

...

MAJOR WILLIAM ORPEN MOPPED HIS MUDDY BROW AND CLENCHED HIS PAINTBRUSH
The 29-year-old artist from Dublin was feeling distinctly uncomfortable. Earlier on
that hot July day in 1917 he had pitched his easel amid the trenches of Ypres and
commenced work on a painting. His subject, as he later explained in a letter to his
father, was 'the remains of a Boche [German] and an Englishman – just skulls, bones,
clothes, rifles, water bottles etc.'

However, after a couple of hours, he began to feel 'sort of strange.'

'I did not know if I was lonely or afraid — so I put down my palette and went a few
yards back and sat down — when suddenly a huge puff of wind came and blew over
my heavy easel, canvas and all, tearing the canvas to bits on the stump of a shelled tree.
This did not make me feel any better and it was as much as I could do to sit down and
start on a fresh canvas'.

William Orpen was arguably the finest war artist of the Great War and amongst the
most talented men ever to project the brutality of conflict onto canvas. During his time
on the Western Front, he produced an extraordinary collection of works that continue
to stir feelings of immense compassion, disquiet and admiration amongst those who
behold them.

William Newenham Montague Orpen was born in the wet autumn of 1878 and
grew up on Grove Avenue in the bustling south Dublin village of Stillorgan. His Protestant forebears had settled in Kenmare, County Kerry in the late 17th century, but
later moved to Dublin.[127]

Orpen's artistic genius was apparent from an early age. In 1891, the 13-year-old
was accepted at the Dublin Metropolitan School of Art where he excelled in figurative
drawing and painting. At the age of 18, he entered London's Slade School, where he
befriended the artists Augustus John and Albert Rutherston; they became known as
'The Three Musketeers'.

In 1900, the 22-year-old Orpen was briefly engaged to Emily Scobel, the Slade School model and aspiring architect featured in his painting 'The Mirror'. Later that same year, he fell head over heels in love with Grace Knewstub, whose father had been studio assistant to Ford Madox Brown. When Orpen's father refused to warm to Grace, the artist lamented, 'I suppose it is the lot of all men to fall in love... but not always with the right person.'

Whether his father approved or not, Orpen married Grace in 1901. They had three daughters, but the marriage was ultimately an unhappy one. Orpen was away for long periods, sometimes on assignment with canvas and brush, sometimes carousing with Rutherston and John.

In 1906, Orpen met Mrs Evelyn St George, the leggy, fun-loving American wife of one of his distant cousins. He subsequently produced three paintings of her father, George F Baker, the president of the National Bank of America, who was known to his contemporaries as "The Sphinx of Wall Street".

The chemistry between Orpen and Evelyn was powerful, fuelled by a mutual delight in mischief, merriment and creativity. By 1908, their friendship had became romantic. She became his patron, his counsellor, his muse and the procurer of many useful commissions.

As Evelyn was a slender six feet tall and Orpen measured just over five feet, some dubbed them "Jack and the Beanstalk". They tried to keep their affair discreet, often meeting at Screebe Lodge, Evelyn's Connemara hideaway near Maam Cross. Maintaining secrecy became increasingly difficult after 1912 when Evelyn bore Orpen's fourth daughter, Vivien.

Orpen was teaching at the Metropolitan School of Art in Dublin when the Great War broke out. One of the reasons why he subsequently enlisted in the British Army was that George Baker had by now learned of the affair with Evelyn from one of her daughters. On Baker's command, the romance between Orpen and Evelyn was terminated.

In April 1917, the War Propaganda Bureau promoted Orpen to Major and sent him to the Western Front as an official British war artist. He would later publish his frontline experiences in 'An Onlooker in France', an illustrated war diary which he described as 'merely an attempt to record some certain little incidents that occurred in my own life there.' In the preface, he also noted his 'sincere thanks for the wonderful opportunity that was given me to look on and see the fighting man, and to learn to revere and worship him'. The book makes no reference to one of his earliest adventures on the front line when he smuggled the beautiful Sybil Sassoon out to the Somme battlefield by hiding her on the floor of his Rolls-Royce; women were not allowed into the war zone.

Assigned to paint portraits of the top brass, he began with Field Marshal Haig, who suggested he would be better employed concentrating his brush on the ordinary soldiers at the front. Orpen took him at his word and made his way to the Ypres Salient. The next few months were to considerably dampen Orpen's sense of humour. He was shocked by the endless bodies and limbs strewn across battlefields, of the lunar landscapes created by the incessant bombing, of zombie-eyed faces ravaged by poison gas. The canvas was an outlet for his torment and certainly he used his genius to tremendous advantage, creating some of the most gripping, poignant and disturbing depictions of war ever painted.

Not long after his canvas was ripped by the tree stump in Ypres, he met Yvonne Aubicq, a young French woman with whom he had a ten-year-long romance.[128] However, his wife Grace was to become Lady Orpen when he was knighted in 1918 for his work as a war artist.

138 of his wartime works went on exhibition at the Imperial War Museum in London after the war. The same museum then commissioned him to go to the Hall of Mirrors at Versailles in 1919 and produce three paintings of the Paris Peace Conference. The third of his Versailles paintings was originally supposed to depict forty of the 'politicians and generals and admirals who had won the war'. However, Orpen found himself unable to complete the work and instead converted it into 'To the Unknown British Soldier Killed in France', a grim masterpiece that portrayed a flag-draped coffin flanked by two skeletal soldiers clad in tattered blankets. Explaining his motive to the *London Evening Standard*, he said: 'And then, you know, I couldn't go on. It all seemed so unimportant somehow, beside the reality as I had seen it, and felt it, when I was working with the armies. In spite of all these eminent men, I kept thinking of the soldiers who remain in France for ever …. So I painted all the statesmen and commanders out.' Many critics were appalled but the public voted it 'Picture of the Year' at the Royal Academy's 1923 summer exhibition.[129] Unfortunately the Imperial War Museum was less accommodating and they refused to accept the work until Orpen reluctantly painted out the two wraith-like soldiers.

Orpen continued to be one of the most sought-after society portrait artists in London throughout the 1920s. Winston Churchill, Woodrow Wilson and Count John McCormack all sat for him, although he is probably better known for his exquisite portraits of beauties like Vera Hone, Lady Evelyn Herbert and Lady Idina Wallace.

Like so many others, Orpen never got over his wartime experience. Haunted by the memory of those who died, he became increasingly morose and drank heavily. Failure of both liver and heart brought about his death, aged 52, in September 1931. He was survived by Lady Orpen, their three daughters Christine, Diana and Mary, and also by his daughter Vivien.

Orpen's desolate 1918 painting 'Zonnebeke' shows the apocalyptic devastation wrought on the Belgian landscape around Passchendaele, with a dead soldier sprawled beside a flooded shell crater.

• • •

The Irish novelist Liam O'Flaherty
was photographed by the German-born
portrait photographer Emil Otto Hoppé
in 1925.

LIAM O'FLAHERTY –
AN ARAN ISLANDER AT WAR

...

'I WAS BORN ON A STORM-SWEPT ROCK AND HATE THE SOFT GROWTH OF SUN-BAKED LANDS where there is no frost in men's bones.' So wrote Liam O'Flaherty of the Aran island of Inis Mór, County Galway, where he was born in 1896.

From the age of 11 he was educated by the Holy Ghost Fathers at Rockwell College, County Tipperary, where the Irish-speaking farmer's son initially trained as a missionary with a view to going to Africa. He then changed his mind and went to study at a diocesan seminary in Dublin. He was still all set to become a priest when he abruptly changed tack again and entered University College, Dublin, where he became increasingly impressed by Marxist thought and joined the college corps of the Irish Volunteers.

In 1915 the 19-year-old enlisted in the Irish Guards under the name 'Bill Ganly' employing the name of his maternal grandfather, a member of the Plymouth Brethren from Portadown. He described his motives for joining up as 'what an adventurous youth felt impelled to do, not through idealism, but with the selfish desire to take part in a world drama'. Trained at Caterham, he soon realised the importance of fitness. 'I who had until then worshipped the mind to the extent of neglecting the body, now worshipped the body to the neglect of the mind.'

At the Western Front, he was thrown into the devastating monotony of trench life until September 1917 when he was comatosed and badly injured by an artillery shell at Langemarck. He spent several months in a variety of neurological hospitals, the last being the King George V at Arbour Hill in Dublin. Released in early 1918, he was subsequently diagnosed with *melancholia acuta,* acute depression, and discharged from the army.

During the 1920s he travelled widely between North and South America, evolving his beliefs on atheism, communism and how an independent Ireland ought to function. As a founder-member of the Communist Party of Ireland, he became something of a household name in January 1922 when he led a group of 120 unemployed workers who briefly seized the Rotunda Concert Hall (now the Gate Theatre) in Dublin, in protest against the Free State government's apparent apathy towards unemployment. On O'Flaherty's command, a red flag flew on the concert hall roof until Free State troops forced their surrender.

He subsequently moved to England where, penniless and forsaken, he took to writing. In 1925, he hit the literary jackpot with his best-selling novel, *The Informer*, which tells the story of a man who, confused by his ideals and short of a few bob, betrays his friends during the Irish War of Independence. Four years later, his short novel *Return of the Brute* proved another success, grimly following the fate of nine soldiers living on the muddy front line of Arras during the Great War.

O'Flaherty was handsome and well built, with steely blue eyes that, as one writer put it, reflected the 'ocean that encircled his boyhood'. Not surprisingly, the young Aran Islander caught the gaze of film director Brian Desmond Hurst, a fellow Irish war veteran. Hurst introduced O'Flaherty to the Irish-American director John Ford who, recalling how one of his grandmothers was an O'Flaherty from Inis Mór, ecstatically declared a long-lost kinship. O'Flaherty duly fetched up in Hollywood writing a screenplay for *The Informer*, which Ford converted into an Oscar-winning film, with Victor McLaglen delivering a sublime performance as Gypo Nolan.

O'Flaherty became one of Ireland's most prolific writers during the 1930s and 1940s and is often regarded as the finest novelist of his generation. It seems likely that the shell-shock he suffered in Langemarck caused the mental illness that plagued him in later life. He died in Dublin in 1984, aged 88.

• • •

A film poster for *The Informer*, the 1935 film based on Liam O'Flaherty's book which was set during the Irish War of Independence. The film won four Academy Awards including Best Actor for Victor McLagen and Best Director for John Ford.

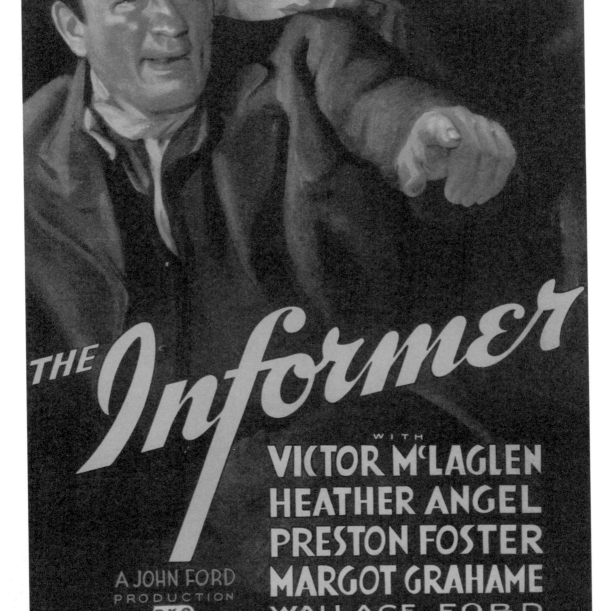

THE *Informer*

WITH

VICTOR McLAGLEN
HEATHER ANGEL
PRESTON FOSTER
MARGOT GRAHAME
WALLACE FORD
UNA O'CONNOR

A JOHN FORD
PRODUCTION

RKO
Radio
Pictures

FROM THE STORY BY LIAM O'FLAHERTY
ASSOCIATE PRODUCER CLIFF REID

A dogfight between
British and German
aircraft during the
latter years of the
Great War.

THE

IRISH AIR ACES

...

EDWARD 'MICK' MANNOCK, VC

IT WAS DURING THE FAREWELL DINNER FOR GWILYM (Gwil) 'Noisy' Lewis in July 1918 that Mick Mannock pulled George McElroy aside and gave his protégé an earful. 'Don't throw yourself away,' he barked. 'I hear you're going down to the deck. Don't do that. You'll get shot down from the ground.' Within ten days of that dinner, both pilots were dead, killed in two separate incidents, victims of the very ground fire Mannock had spoken of.[130]

Precise figures for which pilots won more aerial victories in the sky are often a matter of considerable dispute, but it is generally agreed that the top three World War One air aces from Britain and Ireland were Edward 'Mick' Mannock with at least 61 kills, James McCudden with 57 and George 'McIrish' McElroy with 47. All three were destined to die in the war. A rather lesser known fact is that all three had strong Irish connections.

Mannock was born in Ireland to a mother from Cork. McCudden's father was born in County Carlow. McElroy, who was born and raised in Dublin, was the son of a Roscommon man and his Westmeath-born wife.

Mick Mannock, the eldest of the three, was born at Ballincollig Barracks in County Cork on 24 May

...

Born in County Cork in 1887, Major Edward 'Mick' Mannock, VC, became the highest scoring British air ace of the war.

'Irish by birth, he displayed all the impetuosity of the Irish. He was, of course, a fearless fighter. He was also a brilliant leader and exponent of the air combat tactics of his time.'

Captain WE Johns, author of the *Biggles* novels

1887. His mother, Julia O'Sullivan, grew up in the nearby village. In the summer of 1881, Julia befriended Edward Mannock, the son of a Fleet Street editor, who was serving as a corporal in the Royal Scots Greys, then stationed at Ballincollig. The couple, both Catholics, married the following spring. Five years later, after postings in Glasgow and Aldershot, the Mannocks returned to Ballincollig with two small children, Patrick and Jessica. Edward ('Mick'), their third and youngest child, was born soon afterwards.

Mick's father then left the army but, having drunk his way through his army gratuity, he re-enlisted in 1893, becoming a trooper in the 5th Dragoon Guards. His family, including young Mick, accompanied him to India when the regiment was posted to Meerut. During his six years in India, Mick was nearly blinded in his left eye by an amoebic infestation. His father had a violent temper and a drink problem that worsened after his service in the South African War. Shortly after his return from the war in 1901, Edward Mannock deserted his family and vanished.

While Julia moved to Canterbury, young Mick Mannock headed for the old Saxon town of Wellingborough in Northamptonshire, where he found work in a grocery and then in a post office. By 1911, he was a skilled telephone engineer. Always outspoken, he became a passionate socialist and was elected secretary of the Wellingborough branch of the Independent Labour Party. Proud of his Irish ancestry, he supported the ILP's call for Home Rule for Ireland.

When the war broke out, Mick Mannock was 1,500 miles from London, laying cables in Constantinople (present-day Istanbul) for the National Telephone Company. Shortly after the Ottoman Empire formally joined the Central Powers of Germany and the Austro-Hungarian Empire, he was arrested by the Turkish authorities. After several failed escape attempts, he was sent to a concentration camp at Stamboul in the heart of Constantinople. He remained there until April 1915, when he was repatriated in an exchange of prisoners.

Inspired by the exploits of air ace Albert Ball, he joined the Royal Flying Corps (RFC) in August 1916. Life expectancy for wartime pilots was never great. Of 14,000 airmen killed in the war, more than half died while training. Mannock swiftly mastered the rudiments of flying, but his convoluted background did not immediately win him friends amongst the public-school educated elite who dominated the RFC. Lionel Blaxland, one of his fellow pilots, recalled Mannock as 'a boorish know-all and we all felt that the quicker he got amongst the Huns, the better that would show him how little he knew'.

In the spring of 1917, Mannock was assigned to the RFC's No 40 Squadron and given a Nieuport 17, a nimble French biplane fighter. Considered superior to any British plane of the time, it was particularly well suited to bursting observation balloons and low-level, hedge-hopping attacks on enemy spotters.

It took him several weeks to adjust to his new life. April 1917 was the most devastating month in the RFC's short history. Two hundred and eleven aircrew were dead or missing and a further 108 had been taken prisoner. Such statistics inevitably played on pilots' nerves and when Mannock repeatedly held back in flight patrols, some began to question the courage of a man who, at 29, was much older than most men in the squadron.

He was, by his own admission, frightened. At length, he took hold of his fear. On

7 May he scored his first hit when he shot down a German balloon. He would go on to become one of the most deadly fighter pilots on the Western Front. There is still considerable debate about just how many enemy aircraft he shot down, but the figure is at least 61 and could be as high as 75.

The War Office in London warmly welcomed him to the fray, bedecking him with not one but three Distinguished Service Orders as well as a Military Cross and, ultimately, a posthumous Victoria Cross.

Mannock's tally soon earned him the absolute respect of 'Forty' Squadron and he excelled as a patrol leader. He was one of the finest mentors in the RFC, which was to be a major plus for a curly-headed young Dubliner called George McElroy who arrived at 'Forty' in August 1917.

GEORGE 'McIRISH' McELROY, MC

The McElroys were Protestant farmers from Kiltycreaghtan, just outside Boyle, County Roscommon. George Edward Henry McElroy was born in a Protestant school at Beaver Row on the banks of the River Dodder in Donnybrook, south Dublin, on 14 May 1893; his parents Samuel and Ellen had established the school shortly before his birth.[131] George, the eldest of eight, grew up to be a particularly bright boy. From Beaver Row he went to the Educational Institute in Dundalk in 1906. Three years later he went to Mountjoy School, where he excelled at rugby and showed himself to be of a mathematical, mechanical mindset.

In 1912, he went to Rosse College, the Dublin business school on St Stephen's Green, after which he went to work as a clerk in the civil service. Most of his summers were spent in Roscommon, where his uncle kept a large rowing boat for George and his siblings to indulge their passion for fly-fishing. Aged 21 when war broke out, he volunteered as a Despatch Rider on 13 September.[132] He almost certainly brought his own motorcycle to the service, for which the army would have paid him. Just over two weeks later, he was one of 34 Despatch Riders who landed in France with the British Expeditionary Force, serving in the latter days of the Great Retreat from Mons.

On 8 April 1915, he was sent to the Cadet School at Bailleul to train as an officer and, just over four weeks later, Second Lieutenant McElroy went to the front line to join the 1st Battalion of the Royal Irish Regiment (RIR). During the ensuing battle of Ypres, he was nearly choked to death by one of the deadly clouds of chlorine gas unleashed by the Germans.

McElroy was recuperating with his family in the Irish capital when the Easter Rising broke out. As a soldier, he was drafted in to help put an end to the rebellion. Eight men from the Royal Irish Regiment were killed and 16 more were wounded, but McElroy apparently refused to fire on his fellow Irishmen. Fortunate to escape serious punishment, he was assigned to menial garrison duty for a short period.

. . .

What goes up . . .

. . . must come down.
George 'McIrish' McElroy
excelled at destroying
German observation
balloons like this.

• • •

George McElroy was born and raised between
Donnybrook and Roscommon before going on
to become one of the leading air aces of the war.
He achieved a record 47 victories in 40 weeks of
service.

'McElroy also got a Hun — he gets Huns most days.
He specialises in two-seaters, and sits up by himself
and stalks them. He is a pupil of Mannock's.'

Gwilym 'Noisy' Lewis, *Wings Over the Somme*

• • •

The British air ace Captain James McCudden,
VC, became one of Mick Mannock's closest
friends.

On 1 June 1916, he gained entry as a Gentleman Cadet to the Royal Military Academy
at Woolwich and relinquished his commission in the RIR. He graduated from Woolwich in February 1917 and joined the Royal Garrison Artillery as a Second Lieutenant.
By this time he had developed an infatuation with flight and, the same month, he began
training at the Central Flying School in Upavon on the River Avon in Wiltshire.[133]

In August 1917, just six weeks after he became a flying officer, McElroy joined the
10th Wing of 'Forty' Squadron at Bruay, west of Lens, where he was to be instructed by
the now legendary Mick Mannock.[134]

It is not known how Mannock reacted to the 1916 Rising. It seems likely that he would have sympathised with the rebels and that he would have been duly impressed by McElroy's refusal to fire upon them. In any event, the two Irishmen became friends. Mannock already had one 'Mac' in his squadron — a Scot called George McLanachan — so to simplify things, he rechristened McLanachan "McScottish" and McElroy became "McIrish".[135]

The rugby-loving, song-singing McElroy would go on to become the star of the mess, according to Gwil Lewis. However, his initial outings in the Nieuport biplane so beloved by Mannock did not suit. After wrecking two of these valuable fighters while landing, he was on the point of being sent home as a failure. Mannock intervened on his behalf and McElroy was given a single-seat SE5a fighter shortly before Christmas 1917. It was one of the fastest aircraft of the war; its top speed of 138 mph (222 km/h) was faster than any of its German rivals.[136] This was the plane in which McElroy came into his own and racked up all 47 of his aerial victories.

On 28 December 1917, McElroy claimed his first victory at Drocourt-Vitry, while two other pilots from 'Forty' also scored hits. That night, the men stayed up late, with McElroy singing Irish ballads, accompanied by Mannock on his violin, while everyone knocked back the squadron's signature cocktail, the 'Ladykiller', a concoction of whiskey, brandy, port and grenadine.

By January 1918, McElroy was soaring through the skies like 'a terrier let loose in a rat-infested barn'. He shot down two German planes and, the following month, knocked out three enemy observation balloons in a 72-hour period.

January was also the month in which Mick Mannock was given eight weeks' leave. He went to find his family in England but, to his horror, his mother had become an alcoholic and his sister Jessie was working as a prostitute. Unable to handle this situation, he persuaded the RFC to take him back early. In February, he was appointed Flight Commander of the newly formed No 74 (Training) Squadron in London, which he then took to France.

Mannock still had his sense of humour. He once took his squadron on a mission to bomb the Mess of the RFC's No 1 Squadron at the Clairmarais aerodrome near Ypres. The bombs comprised 200 oranges. The pilots of No 1 retaliated with a banana attack soon afterwards. The two squadrons then joined forces at the George Robey café in St Omer for 'a memorable evening'.

However, Mannock also had a hard edge that sometimes stunned his men. In April 1918, Manfred von Richthofen — the notorious Red Baron — was shot down. When some English pilots raised their glasses to salute their deadliest foe, Mannock growled, 'I hope the bastard burnt all the way down.'[137]

The following month, Mannock ruthlessly downed 20 German planes, sometimes zoning his guns on the stricken crew with a terrifying callousness. On a single day he claimed four kills, bursting into the mess afterwards with the words 'Flamerinoes boys! Sizzle sizzle wonk.' Thereafter, any German aircraft that went spiralling down in flames became known to the men of 'Forty' as a 'flamerino'.

In fact, Mick Mannock's greatest nightmare was to finish up as a 'flamerino'. When he flew, he kept a revolver in the cockpit so that, as he told McScottish, he could 'finish

Manfred von Richthofen, better known as the Red Baron, prepares his squadron for another battle in the skies. His own red-painted aircraft is second in line, with the boarding step-ladder in place.

myself as soon as I see the first signs of flames.'[138] Behind his bravado, he was suffering intense trauma, tormented by the apparent cheapness of life and haunted by the memory of so many dead faces, friend and enemy alike. His diary suggests a fragile mind. 'I felt exactly like a murderer,' he wrote after seeing the body of a German airman he killed. On another occasion, he wrote: 'Feeling nervy and ill during the last week. Afraid I'm breaking up.'

By the time Mannock went on leave to London in June 1918, some of his closest friends feared that he was indeed breaking up. There was some respite in London when he became close friends with Jimmy McCudden, the most decorated British airman of the war, who was also on leave.[139] The two men had much in common. Unlike most pilots, neither had been to public school. They were also both sons of military men of Irish stock; McCudden's father was born in County Carlow.[140] A good deal of their time in London centred around a West End dancer called Teddie O'Neill whom McCudden, a Victoria Cross winner, took out for a joy ride. Mannock's new-found friendship ended on 9 July when Jimmy McCudden's plane stalled after take-off and crash-landed near a small RAF airfield at Auxi-le-Château. Mannock was greatly upset when he heard the news.

Meanwhile, George McElroy, his old protégé, was fast becoming the leading light of the RFC. In March and April, the pipe-smoking Dubliner spent eight weeks as Flight Commander of No 24 Squadron at Matigny on the Somme. One of his pupils was the future American air ace Bill Lambert who later recalled: 'George McElroy, without a doubt, was one of the most fearless men I have ever met. He was also most considerate of the pilots under him and at all times tried to keep his pilots out of trouble. He would not allow me to go out until he felt I was ready and I think I owe my survival to his teaching.'[141]

During his time with No 24 Squadron, McElroy claimed 16 of his 47 victories and was awarded the Military Cross.[142] By now a highly skilled dogfighter, he established himself as a master of the SE5a's dual gun system. The biplane was equipped with a Vickers machine-gun up front, synchronised to fire through the propellers, while he also had a Lewis machine-gun pitched up on the top wing. The Lewis was set upon a sliding rail, so that he could yank its breech back down to the cockpit and load fresh ammunition, or clear stoppages, while he was flying. Between the two guns, he could either fire both guns forward, or use one to attack an enemy aircraft from behind and below. At all times, he made sure his guns were meticulously oiled and clean.

As one colleague observed, an analysis of his flights 'reveals the hallmark of the high-class fighter, low expenditure of ammunition… he would only fire a few short bursts and the trick was done. Unlike most great fighters, however, he used frequently to open fire at comparatively long range, and being a wonderful shot, the fight was sometimes over before the victim had time to realise it had begun.'

McElroy prowled the skies with terrifying belligerence, repeatedly risking his life and barging into scenes where the odds were stacked against him. The only thing he could not handle was the cold, particularly when he had to fly high. Much to the amusement of his fellow pilots, he endeavoured to counter this problem by purchasing a 'pocket warmer', a small cylindrical tin containing a chunk of smouldering charcoal. He stuffed this into his trouser pocket, so that he could keep at least one part of himself warm during such flights. Unfortunately, it overheated while he was flying and, unable to reach the pesky thing through his heavy, fur-lined coat, he fetched up with a burn the size of a chicken egg.

On 1 April, the day the Royal Flying Corps was reborn as the Royal Air Force, McElroy was awarded a Bar to his Military Cross for showing 'skill and determination… most praiseworthy'.[143] One week later, he claimed three victories on a single patrol but, as he came into land, his plane clipped a treetop and he spent the next two months recovering on the sidelines.[144]

When his convalescence was complete in June, McElroy rejoined his old pals at 'Forty' Squadron in Bryas, shortly after the squadron leader, Australian air ace Stan Dallas, was shot down. In his first eight days back with 'Forty', he took out eight planes, as well as bombing several key German strongpoints along the front. By the end of June, McElroy had taken his tally to 30. In July, he went ballistic and, during the first three weeks, there was hardly a day in which he did not return to base having shot or destroyed some form of enemy aircraft. His score of 17 new victims in that time was one of the most remarkable in the history of fighter aviation and put him on a par with the Red Baron.

On 20 July, McElroy again crash-landed his plane, but despite being left shaken and bruised, he made it to Gwil Lewis's farewell dinner that same evening. This was the occasion on which Mannock accosted him for flying too low. The two men had known each other less than a year and strong words between them were by no means unknown. 'Each was convinced that the other was rash, and took risks,' recalled fellow squadron member FT Gilbert. 'Each reproved the other and issued solemn warnings. To hear them on this was amazing. But McElroy was less *berserk* than Mannock and … his nerves showed little sign of being on edge, except in a new petulance when he could not get combats.'

Mannock, now commanding 85 Squadron, was still in deep depression after Jimmy McCudden's death. Those who knew him said the 31-year-old should never have been allowed to fly. His nerves were shot, his wit and sparkle depleted and, as Gwil Lewis remarked, he had been 'kept out on the battlefront too long and he'd suffered in losing his judgment'. When Mannock shot down yet another German aircraft two days after Gwil's farewell, a fellow pilot said: 'They'll have the red carpet out for you after the war, Mick'. Mannock grimly replied, 'There won't be any "after the war" for me.'[145]

He was correct. On 26 July, Mick Mannock set off alongside a young New Zealand pilot, Donald Inglis, crossing the German front line. Ignoring his own wise words, he flew too close to the ground, apparently to view the wreckage of an enemy two-seater they had shot down near Robecq. A German machine-gun opened up and, in moments, his plane was engulfed in a bluish white flame. He never used his revolver but instead jumped from the blazing plane. His body was found 250 yards from the wreck but, bizarrely, it was never formally recovered by the Commonwealth War Graves Commission so the precise whereabouts of his remains are unknown.

After intensive lobbying by friends, Mannock was awarded a posthumous Victoria Cross in July 1919. It was presented to his father, Edward, at Buckingham Palace.

Contrary to the explicit terms of Mick's will, his father also secured his other medals. He sold the whole lot for £5 soon afterwards. They have since been recovered and, having been on display at the RAF Museum in Hendon, they are now displayed on rotation in the 'Extraordinary Heroes' exhibition at the Lord Ashcroft Gallery in the Imperial War Museum, London.

On the day Mannock died, McElroy received the second Bar to his Military Cross for his 'most enterprising work in attacking enemy troops and transport'.[146] It was his greatest ambition to be awarded the DSO, which would have given him equal status to Mannock. After Mannock's death, the DSO became a fixation for him, more powerful even than his competitive urge to beat Mannock's victory tally.

Early on the morning of 31 July, McElroy set off in a new SE5, a plane so crisp that it had only logged 11 hours' flying time. When he didn't return, the squadron feared the worst. At length, the Germans dropped a note to say that the 25-year-old Dubliner had been killed and buried. Precise details as to how he died remain a mystery but it is thought he was shot down over Laventie by anti-aircraft guns shortly after he had taken out a German two-seater.[147]

'We took [the news of his death] very quietly', recalled FT Gilbert. 'There did not seem much to say. And somehow, he doesn't seem dead even now for we all drew something from him, to become a part of us. We worshipped him for his prowess, and loved him for himself. 40 Squadron thought there was no one like him, and we shall never forget him.'[148]

On 3 August, McElroy received the posthumous Distinguished Flying Cross for 'his dashing and skilful leadership'.[149] A Bar followed six weeks later.[150] He never received the DSO he had so desperately sought.

George McElroy was buried in the Laventie Military Cemetary, 12 miles west of Lille. Whilst it is unlikely ever to be proved, there is an extraordinary possibility that the nearby grave of an 'Unknown British Aviator' is that of Mick Mannock.

PART TWO

THE

DARDANELLES

. . .

Where the LANDING took place of the AUSTRALIAN & NEW ZEALAND TROOPS here 12,000 men drove the TURKS from shore back into the hills, and securing the slopes of SARIBAIR MT. held successfully 24,000 TURKS and TEUTONS at bay

Where a temporary LANDING was made at BEACH Y by SCOTTISH BORDERERS, Plymouth Marine Battn. & Royal Naval Division; after holding the TURKS at bay for 30 hours while the TROOPS at BEACH X were able to entrench, they re-embarked, having lost about half their men in the desperate struggle against overwhelming numbers & artillery

Position at BEACH Y2 so strongly defended by the TURKS that a landing was not attempted

Where the LANDING at BEACH X was made by the ROYAL FUSILIERS on a narrow strip of sand at base of cliff, here covered by the Guns of the IMPLACABLE; they drove the TURKS before them, scaled HILL 114 & entrenched

Where the LANDING on BEACH W was effected by the LANCASHIRE FUSILIERS by storming the BEACH and 3 Lines of TRENCHES on the HEIGHTS above, afterwards taking Hill 114 & uniting with BEACH X; the WORCESTERS stormed HILL 138 and REDOUBT in face of enormous obstacles & endeavoured to reach V. BEACH

Where the LANDING at BEACH V was made by the DUBLIN FUSILIERS the MUNSTER FUSILIERS and the HAMPSHIRES in spite of terrible losses from a ceaseless fire poured down upon them as they endeavoured to cross the gangway of Lighters to the slight shelter of the shelving beach shown at A.A.A. After 24 hours of frightful ordeal on this fire-swept BEACH they made the magnificent onslaught that cleared the TRENCHES above them, captured the GUNS, No.1 Fort, the Village & old Fort of SEDD el BAHR & HILL 141

BEACH S, where the SOUTH WALES BORDERERS LANDED and secured the high ground near DeTOTT'S Battery

Turkish Trenches with 4 pom-poms & machine Guns on cliffs 100 feet high

G.F. MORRELL.

BATTERING AT THE GATE TO CONSTANTINOPLE: THE PROGRESS OF

This pictorial presentation of the Dardanelles campaign is specially designed to illustrate the joint naval and military operations in the Gallipoli Peninsula, and to enable the Public to follow the movements of the Allies in their progress to Constantinople. Mr. Morrell's drawing illustrates very clearly what Sir Ian Hamilton calls the three dominating features in this section—(1) Saribair Mountain, running up in a succession of almost perpendicular escarpments to 970 feet, and consisting of a network of ravines covered with thick jungle; (2) Kilid Bahr Plateau, which rises, a natural fortification artificially fortified, to a height of 700 feet, to cover the forts of the Narrows

DARDANELLES OPERATIONS

Karachali, the scene of the landing of British troops on August 7.

GULF of XEROS

840ft · 1322ft · 1478ft · 1060ft · 932ft · 450ft · 550ft · BULAIR
BULAIR LINE
Gallipoli Strait
Gallipoli to CONSTANTINOPLE 130 Miles
Burges · Chaltankeui · Kavakli · Ak Yerlar Dagh 1050ft · Chardak Burnu · CHARDAK 500
Chinar Dagh 970ft · Karanlia · Hurtumus Dere
rchen Keui · Uveik Dagh 1160ft · Ulgar Keui · 991ft · GALLIPOLI · GALATA · LAMPSAKI
Karsilar Dagh 820ft · Usunderleh · Kum Keui · YATLOVA · Ak Bashi Ova · Sarair Tepe 1000ft
Mal Tépé 520 · BOKALI · 680ft · Bakajak 820ft · Bergaz Chai · BERGAZ
Khelia Tepe 450 · Bokali Kalessi Fort · Batteries · CHANAK to GALLIPOLI 25 Miles · Kangarli Tépé 720ft
CROSS · ELEC · NAGARA Fort Z · B... · British...
KELKMAZ DAGH (Mts) · Maidos Tépé 400ft Fort DD · Tekeh · Fort KOSSE KALE · Fort MEDJIDIEH · Barracks
Kilid Bahr Plateau · Cham Kalessi Fort Battery · KILID BAHR · CHANAK · Rhodius River
617ft Jisoi · Fort C · Dermaburnu · Fort O · FLK · Fort T · ONE SMILE · SULTANIEH Fort V · Corn Fields
RAM · 610ft · Ft L · Fort R · Fort S · HAMIDIEH Fort
Fort N · Fort Q · THE NARROWS
Fort I · Soghan Dere · 518 ft · Fort F · SARI SIGLAR BAY
344ft · Kephez Point Fort H · Kalabakli
STEM · KEPHEZ BAY Fort DARDANUS · Ruins of DARDANUS
SEDD el BAHR to CHANAK 15 Miles · Fort G · Kuz Keui
arlik Point · 1107ft
AREN KEUI
AREN KEUI BAY

There the FRENCH TROOPS first LANDED on Apr.25(!), capturing 500 prisoners, after causing a diversion of the TURKISH GUNS from shelling the European shore. On the 26th they re-embarked & LANDED to the right of V BEACH where they joined the general advance.

KUM KALE

[Design registered.]

THE ALLIED NAVAL AND MILITARY FORCES AT THE DARDANELLES

from an attack from the Ægean; and (3) Achi Baba, a hill 600 feet in height, dominating at long field-gun range the toe of the peninsula. Gallipoli is an ideal place to defend, and the Turks have made the most of their opportunities, the whole peninsula being converted into a network of trenches and small redoubts, well supplied with guns of all calibres and protected by elaborate entanglements. Here is being fought out what Mr. Churchill has well called "the last and finest crusade," and slowly but surely the heroic troops of France and Great Britain are overcoming all the obstacles with which both man and nature have beset the road to Constantinople.

THE DARDANELLES

• • •

THE GALLIPOLI PENINSULA IS APPROXIMATELY 400 SQUARE MILES — ABOUT the same size as County Longford, or a little bigger than County Dublin. Most of the fighting took place in a region about twice the size of Achill Island. It was a minuscule area in terms of the wider conflict and yet, for nine terrible months, this luckless landscape was the second greatest war zone in the world after the Western Front.

Concocted by Winston Churchill, the Allied campaign at Gallipoli was based on a plan to force the surrender of Constantinople, the capital of the Ottoman Empire. The Irish were involved from the outset, when two Admirals from Tipperary and Kildare led the initial naval attack on the Dardanelles Straits in the spring of 1915.

When that failed, the British tried again with a combined naval and ground assault. A hideous fate awaited most of the 2,000 men from the Royal Dublin Fusiliers and Royal Munster Fusiliers who took part in the ground invasion at Seddelbahr. Many were professional soldiers who had enlisted long before the war broke out.

One feels still greater sympathy for civilian volunteers like the Dublin Pals who arrived on the peninsula via Suvla Bay in August. During a month when they would ordinarily have been swanning around the Dublin Horse Show, they were hurled into the lethal mayhem of Kiretch Tepe and Chunuk Bahr.

Several of the military commanders were Irish, including General Godley whose large army of Australians and New Zealanders also contained large numbers from Ireland. Among those whose stories are profiled in this section are a curious array of sporting legends, Hollywood icons, exemplary botanists and plucky aristocrats. All had the misfortune to serve during the debacle that was Gallipoli.

• • •

Vice Admiral Sackville Carden, the first commander of the
British fleet during the Gallipoli campaign, is pictured in front of
Admiralty House, Malta, shortly before he was ordered to force the
Dardanelles. To his left stands Lionel Ormsby-Johnson, his Flag
Lieutenant, who played a key role in the evacuation of Gallipoli.
Ormsby-Johnson was fated to die in Cork Military Hospital in 1920
following a hunting accident. Originally printed in the *Illustrated War
News* for 16 March 1915.

SACKVILLE CARDEN

AND THE

NAVAL ATTACK

ON THE

DARDANELLES

...

The Admiralty could never admit that Vice Admiral Sackville Carden, the commander of the biggest naval operation since Trafalgar, had suffered a nervous breakdown. That his collapse occurred just 48 hours before his fleet entered the Dardanelles Straits was unfortunate and understandable in equal measure. Rear Admiral Jack de Robeck, his Kildare-born second-in-command, duly led the ensuing attack of 18 March 1915 which would leave one-third of the Allied fleet at the bottom of the Aegean Sea and 700 men dead. The failure of the navy was the first in the litany of catastrophes that marked the Gallipoli campaign.

'Who expected Carden to be in command of a big fleet?' scoffed Jacky Fisher, Britain's elderly and eccentric First Sea Lord, in a letter to Admiral Jellicoe written on the day of Carden's collapse.[1] 'He was made Admiral Superintendent of Malta to shelve him!'

Sackville Carden had indeed been living a relatively quiet life on the island of Malta when the war broke out. As Admiral Superintendent, his role was simply to oversee the Malta Dockyard in Valletta and the 58-year-old was looking forward to a quiet retirement with plenty of yachting.

Perhaps he had set his sights on Ireland, where the Cardens had been living since the 17th century. Their stronghold was Barnane House at the foot of the Devil's Bit Mountain near Templemore in North Tipperary. Once the centrepiece of a 3,000-acre estate, the Barnane of Sackville's childhood belonged to his uncle, John 'Woodcock' Carden, so called because of the number of times he had avoided being shot by his own tenants.[2] Shortly before Sackville's birth, Woodcock was sentenced to two years' hard labour for his scandalous attempt to abduct Miss Eleanor Arbuthnot.[3]

Sackville was born at 44 Harley Street in London in 1857. He spent the first nine years of his life at Stradone House in County Cavan, where his father Andrew was agent to his brother-in-law Robert Burrowes. Following Woodcock's death in 1866, Andrew succeeded to Barnane and moved his family of seven sons and two daughters south from Cavan. When Andrew died a decade later, Barnane passed to Sackville's older brother, also Andrew, who sold much of the estate to the Irish Land Commission in 1908.

Sackville was just 12 years old when his father sent him to *Conway*, a private training ship established in Liverpool to supply merchant shipping officers.[4] The following year he joined the Royal Navy and by 1876 he was known as 'the hairy midshipman' on account of a robust beard on his teenage chin. Appointed a lieutenant in 1881, he rose steadily through the ranks and was awarded the Légion d'Honneur in 1903. He commanded a squadron in the Atlantic Fleet before he was given the Maltese job in August 1912.

Two years later, he was promoted to Vice Admiral and unexpectedly given command of the Eastern Mediterranean fleet. His first brief was to keep an eye out for two German ships, *Goeben* and *Breslau*, which the Kaiser had lately gifted to the bankrupt Ottoman Empire in a bid to woo the Turks into an alliance with the German Empire.[5] The ships had caused considerable embarrassment to the Royal Navy when they slipped past Carden's predecessor and successfully sailed up the 38-mile-long Dardanelles Straits to the Ottoman capital of Constantinople.

By the time Turkey joined the Germans at the end of October 1914, the war on the Western Front was in a state of bleak deadlock. Something had to give. Winston Churchill, First Lord of the Admiralty, studied the maps. Germany had enemies on two sides — France and Britain to the west, Russia to the east. The problem was that Russia was now cut off from its allies by the Ottoman Turks who controlled the all-important Dardanelles, which linked the Russian ports on the Black Sea via the Sea of Marmara to the Aegean Sea, the Mediterranean and the Suez Canal.

Unimpressed by the Turks' decision to join the Germans, a fleet of French and British warships under Carden's command arrived at the southern entrance to the Dardanelles Straits on 5 November 1914 and let rip with a preliminary bombardment of the forts at Cape Helles and Kum Kale.

Churchill's naval advisers generally rejected his ideas. However, in the autumn of 1914, he hit upon one that they agreed on. The key to victory, he deduced, would be to knock the Turks out of the war and re-establish the direct link with Russia. In January 1915, he sent a message to Carden asking for his thoughts on an expedition 'by ships alone' to smash through the Dardanelles Straits and lay siege to Constantinople.

Churchill had his doubts about Carden. 'I am not aware of anything that he has done which is in any way remarkable,' he wrote in December 1914. However, to his surprise, Carden's reply indicated that the straits might indeed be breached. They must not be 'rushed', said Carden, but a squadron could feasibly advance slowly up the Dardanelles, systematically destroying the numerous Turkish fortifications along the way.[6]

Winston Churchill
served as First Lord
of the Admiralty from
1911 until May 1915
when he was removed
from the post because
of his promotion of the
catastrophic Gallipoli
campaign.

Weather permitting, Carden reckoned that he 'might do it all in a month about' but that he would need a sizeable fleet, including at least two battlecruisers to take on the *Goeben*, which was now at large in the Sea of Marmara at the northern end of the straits. He would also require a large amount of ammunition and some seaplanes to show the ships' gunners where the Turkish guns lay.

Churchill enthusiastically presented Carden's plan to the British War Council, making much of the concept that this was a 'ships only' project, so that Lord Kitchener, the Secretary of War, couldn't complain about losing vital soldiers from the Western Front.

Swamped by the massiveness of its task, the War Council was constantly beset with so much new information and opinion about how the war should be fought that their conclusions were invariably vague and they had a propensity to change their minds as regularly as their socks. If any of them thought Carden's plan was a non-runner, nobody said so at the time. It seemed relatively risk-free and, if all went according to schedule, the considerable prize would be the conquest of Constantinople and the submission of the Ottoman Empire by the spring. On the other hand, if it looked as if Carden's fleet couldn't hack it, the Vice Admiral could simply about turn and retreat to the Aegean. 'It was a gamble', admitted Churchill later, 'but a perfectly legitimate gamble'.[7]

On 15 January, the War Office endorsed Sackville Carden's plan. The Admiralty also supported it although Jacky Fisher took a curious stance, objecting in private yet simultaneously approving it and adding the *Queen Elizabeth*, the world's most powerful battleship, to Carden's squadron.

Over the ensuing four weeks, Carden's plan was inevitably amended. Of particular relevance was a growing acceptance that if the Allies wanted to secure unimpeded access to the Dardanelles, it was imperative that they also control the Gallipoli Peninsula which ran along the western side of the straits. This would require 'strong military landing parties with strong covering forces' or, in other words, the army.[8] Churchill, who had sold the plan to the War Council on the grounds that it was a 'ships only' project, had to proceed cautiously. If he admitted to the War Council that a large number of experienced soldiers were also now required, they might panic at the prospect of a large-scale land war with the Turks and call the whole thing off.

Churchill took a deep breath and requested the support of the 29th Division — the last of the pre-war Regular divisions — which was then in training in England. In his mind, these 50,000 soldiers would initially secure Gallipoli and then, after its conquest, occupy Constantinople. However, Kitchener declined, having earmarked the 29th for the Western Front. Instead, he offered Churchill the use of 39,000 raw but eager Australian and New Zealand troops who were then based in Egypt, protecting the Suez Canal.

Meanwhile, sticking to schedule, Vice Admiral Carden kicked off the battle for Gallipoli at 7.30am on 19 February, when two of his destroyers gingerly advanced into the Dardanelles. Twenty-eight minutes later, the Turkish guns of Kum Kale at the eastern entrance to the straits opened fire.

Phase one of the Carden plan involved the piecemeal destruction of the 27 guns that guarded the entrance to the straits at Cape Helles and Kum Kale. This was to be achieved by a long-range bombardment from the French and British battleships, despite Carden's gnawing doubts that such forts could actually be destroyed by shellfire. The Italian Navy had fired 180 projectiles at the forts during their war with the Turks in 1912 and yet, despite the fact that each one was apparently a direct hit, the forts ostensibly remained intact.[9]

As well as the *Queen Elizabeth*, Carden's fleet included another dreadnought battlecruiser called the *Inflexible*, 16 destroyers, 12 battleships, four light cruisers, six submarines, 21 minesweepers and an early form of aircraft carrier which carried six seaplanes.[10] Jack de Robeck was to be his second-in-command while Roger Keyes, a friend of Churchill, would serve as his Chief of Staff.

It looked so good on paper. In reality, Carden's fleet was dangerously below par. Put simply, the Royal Navy had not been prepared to send its best ships south to the Turkish theatre, insisting that they were needed in order to keep a watchful eye on Germany in the North Sea.[11] As a result, the battleships in Carden's squadron were doddering pre-dreadnought relics, incapable of supporting the new big guns or modern firing systems. Most were fitted with gun barrels too old and worn to handle the shelling that was shortly to be asked of them. If the ships and guns were creaky, so too were the crews whom Jack de Robeck referred to as 'grandfathers', adding that they 'should hardly have been sent out during a "show" of this sort'.[12]

The 21 minesweepers assigned to Carden were, in fact, rickety North Sea trawlers, manned by civilians. This was unforgivably slack planning by the Admiralty, which seems to have assumed that 'little Johnny Turk' had little or no comprehension as to how to even set a mine. In fact, the network of minefields that Carden's ships would encounter in the straits was incredibly complex. Nine lines of contact mines, containing 271 mines, had already been set by the time the battle began. These minefields were protected by some 87 guns, mostly howitzers, which were guided at night by 12 powerful searchlights. The Turkish gunners were perfectly poised to pour their shells into any vessels that sought to clear the mines. Moreover, each gun battery was so carefully and ingeniously concealed between ridges of earth as to make them virtually invincible.

The most farcical aspect of all this was that the North Sea trawlers were unable to reach the minefields. The problem was that the water of the Dardanelles Straits flows both ways; the surface current runs south from the Sea of Marmara into the Aegean while the undercurrent runs in the opposite direction. There is also a strong and regular northerly wind that causes much turbulence at the entrance to the straits. Carden's trawlers were barely strong enough to break into the straits, never mind break out the other end. Many a Turk must have chortled as he watched these vessels trying, largely in vain, to reach the minefields.

Carden would also face difficulties with the spotter planes assigned to tell his ships where the Turkish guns were. In order to transmit this vital information, the planes carried radios. However, the radios were so heavy that the puny seaplanes couldn't gain sufficient altitude to make accurate observations. Obliged to fly so low, they were also in constant danger of being zapped by the Turkish guns.[13]

The elephants in the corner were stacking up. The majority of Carden's battleships unfit for purpose. Guns so worn they couldn't possibly fire with efficiency. Minesweepers that couldn't sweep. Spotter planes that couldn't spot.

HMS *Triumph* follows another battleship up the Dardanelles Straits under heavy shellfire from Turkish land forts on 18 March 1915. Undetected Turkish mines and artillery sank several British ships before the armada withdrew. Nine weeks later, the *Triumph* was torpedoed and sunk off Gaba Tepe on the west coast of Gallipoli by the German submarine *U-21*.

Worse was to come. At 9.51am on 19 February, Carden's fleet launched a five-hour, high-velocity bombardment of the gun batteries at Cape Helles and Kum Kale. They fired from various ranges of between 2.17 and six miles, so the strike rate was presumably something of a guessing game.[14] By the early afternoon Carden was sufficiently satisfied that all 27 guns had been silenced to order his ships to close in. To his eternal dismay, the Turkish guns opened fire. Carden realised that the Turks still had a full complement of guns. The naval bombardment had resulted in the destruction of precisely no Turkish guns, although six Ottoman soldiers were killed.

The complete failure to knock out the forts should not have been such a surprise. The customary difficulties of firing accurately from the sea were augmented by the strong Dardanelles currents, which meant that Carden's battleships were constantly pitching and shifting position, irrespective of anchors fore and aft. Add in the fact that so many of the gun barrels were worn, and that his gunners were firing without the guidance of spotter planes, and the odds of a long-range British shell actually hitting its mark began entering the realm of mere fantasy.

The anticlimax of the first day deepened as foul weather put the campaign on hold for nearly a week. Carden warned anyone who would listen about 'the futility of bombardment to destroy guns and forts'.[15] Jack de Robeck likewise telegrammed Churchill his opinion that the 'permanent disablement' of the forts would require 'an excessive expenditure of ammunition at point-blank range'.[16] He advocated the use of demolition parties instead, a concept supported by Carden who advised the War Office on 24 February that he now believed a combined naval and military attack was the best way forward.

Although the War Office threw 'cold water' on Carden's proposal, this was the plan the military men would adopt four weeks later. In the meantime, Kitchener dourly told the War Council 'there could be no going back'. So much for the notion that Carden would be allowed to about turn and skedaddle if things got too hot in the Dardanelles.

Carden had better news on 25 February when the *Queen Elizabeth* and the *Irresistible*, one of the pre-dreadnought battleships, hit upon a winning streak and took out four Turkish guns. There was also considerable success when the requested demolition parties landed at Seddelbahr and Kum Kale, and destroyed or disabled a further 43 guns and howitzers over the next week, including the heavy guns at Cape Helles and Kum Kale.[17]

Three days later, Churchill telegrammed the Admiral from London, asking 'What is your latest estimate of number of days required excluding bad weather days, to the Sea of Marmora.' Carden ambitiously but succinctly replied, '14 days'. The Admiralty seems to have interpreted this as cause for celebration, speculating that the fleet would reach Constantinople within a fortnight.[18] London was euphoric. The War Council began drawing up the peace terms they would impose on the Ottomans. This developed into a considerable crisis when word leaked out that the British were planning to give Constantinople to the Russians, infuriating the Balkan states of Bulgaria, Romania and Greece, which were as yet undeclared about which side they were on.

Meanwhile, in the Dardanelles, nothing happened. And then nothing continued to happen. Vice Admiral Carden's grand advance on Constantinople was at a virtual standstill, save for a daily visitation by two or three of his battleships into the straits,

• • •

The superdreadnought HMS *Queen Elizabeth*, then
the world's most powerful battleship, was photographed by Ernest Brooks as she left Mudros Harbour
to bomb the forts at the Dardanelles with her eight
15-inch guns. Her bow was painted white to simulate
the water thrown up when moving rapidly, thus
deceiving the Turkish shore batteries as to her actual
speed.

where they would fire a few token shells at the inner forts and then retire. The reasons for Carden's unexpected timidity are still unclear. The traditional theory is that he was worried that his ammunition was running low. However, it also seems likely that he had finally sized up all that was wrong with his fleet and concluded that it would be sheer madness to send it into the Dardanelles.[19]

He had a valid point. Such a narrow waterway — between three-quarters of a mile and 4 miles in width — made it child's play for the Turkish gunners to hit any enemy ships passing through. Roger Keyes found that out on 13 March when he brazenly powered into the straits on board the Royal Navy cruiser *Amethyst* with six of the so-called minesweepers. The Turkish artillerymen had a field day. Keyes' squadron limped home with heavy damage to the *Amethyst* and four trawlers, leaving Carden to ruminate on the fact that, after 17 attempts, the Royal Navy had managed to sweep just two mines. It transpired that there were at least 385 more waiting for them.

Irrespective of the damage that had been wrought on the Turkish forts at the entrance, there were still over 200 Ottoman guns of varying sizes positioned along the two shorelines. And even as Carden wavered, the Turks were busy rebuilding the defences destroyed before 2 March. At the southern end of the straits, below Achi Baba, Jack de Robeck unhappily noted how the Turks were 'continuously making new entrenchments and improving their position'. Under the guidance of the ever-methodical German officers now managing the Turkish Army, the Turks were establishing new machine-gun and sniper posts all along the Gallipoli coast. More and more minefields and torpedo tubes were also springing up across the straits. The Ottoman Empire clearly had no intention of rolling over and submitting to the forces of George V.

London had not yet twigged that Carden had ground to a halt. Indeed, much to Churchill's relief, Kitchener had now relented and announced that at least 80,000 soldiers were available for action in Gallipoli. However, when the First Lord got wind that Carden's fleet had not budged, he ordered the Irishman to immediately prepare for a full-scale attack on the Turkish forts. 'The results to be gained', stated Churchill, 'are great enough to justify loss of ships and men if success cannot be obtained without it.'

Carden's staff glumly drew up a plan in which all his main ships, spread over three lines, would unleash their firepower on the Turkish positions while the North Sea trawlers dashed out to sweep the mines. The attack was scheduled for 18 March.

On 16 March, Vice Admiral Carden collapsed. The official diagnosis was nervous dyspepsia. He had also developed an ulcer. Rumours abounded that he simply found the operation too stressful and broke down. There may have been other factors, such as news from Ireland that his brother Arnold had been involved in a serious car accident in Bray, County Wicklow, a week earlier.[20]

As Carden headed off to sick bay, Churchill ordered Rear Admiral de Robeck to proceed with the attack as ordered. The ensuing naval attack was a grim and predictable failure. The Turks saw the whole thing coming. The first of de Robeck's ships to go was the French battleship *Bouvet*. She took a direct hit in her magazine store, blew up and sank inside two minutes, with the loss of 640 men. The minesweepers then launched another futile attempt to push out into the straits, but were rapidly driven back by Turkish fire. In the late afternoon the *Inflexible*, the dreadnought, was forced to withdraw when she ran into a mine.[21] *Irresistible*, the hero of 25 February, was also disabled by a mine and, while her crew were rescued, the ship was utterly obliterated when she drifted into a chain of mines during the night. Two more Allied battleships were also lost.

It was a tremendous morale booster for the Turks, who had lost just one of their heavy guns, whereas one-third of de Robeck's fleet was either sunk or seriously damaged, with 700 men dead. In the heat of the moment, de Robeck assured Churchill 'we are all getting ready for another "go" & not in the least beaten or down-hearted'. Convinced that Turkish ammunition supplies were running low, Roger Keyes was also adamant that the fleet recommence the attack as soon as possible.

However, just days later, de Robeck declared that there would be no further naval attacks on the Dardanelles until ground troops had captured the high ground on Gallipoli and neutralised the Turkish guns.[22] Outraged by this apparent change of mind, Churchill urged the Admiralty War Group to telegram an order to renew the attack. The War Group declined, reasoning that de Robeck, as a man on the spot, was better placed than Churchill to understand the situation. One of the big 'What ifs' of the Great War is what if de Robeck *had* renewed the attack as Churchill wanted, broken through the Turkish defences and advanced on Constantinople?

By 27 March, Churchill conceded that the Dardanelles could not be won 'by ship alone' and that a combined operation with the army was 'essential'.[23] When Jack de Robeck opined that 'the assistance of all naval forces available will... be needed to land an army of the size contemplated in the face of strenuous opposition', Churchill arranged for another battleship, eight destroyers, three cruisers and 'three of our best submarines' to join his fleet. The First Lord added: 'Irrespective of Admiral Carden's recovery, it is my intention that you retain command.'

From the moment Sackville Carden took ill, he was removed from the scene and rushed to Bighi Hospital in Malta where the Deputy Surgeon General diagnosed that he 'appears to be suffering from atonic dyspepsia with painful acerbations'.[24] Although very run down, he recovered within days and was soon clamouring to be reinstated. However, a telegram from the Admiralty on 27 March put an end to his immediate ambitions. 'Inform Admiral Carden that Admiralty sympathises with his desire to resume command of the operations at earliest possible moment but this is a matter that must be governed by medical advice. He should therefore return to England for survey.' He tried again from London, but the final blow to the old seadog was delivered in a hand-written letter by the First Lord himself which arrived at Carden's London address on 16 April 1915.[25]

> *My dear Admiral,*
> *I quite understand your wish to resume active duty, but at the present time you must concentrate upon a full recovery of your health & strength. After your hard service a good rest is necessary and deserved.*
> *Yours very truly,*
> *Winston S. Churchill*

Sir Sackville Carden was knighted in 1916 and retired with the rank of full Admiral the following year.[26] He spent his final years yachting around the Isle of Wight and Lymington, Hampshire, where he passed away in 1930, three days after his 73rd birthday. Married twice, he was survived by a daughter Anne, born in Malta in 1913.

Perhaps the naval attack on the Dardanelles might have worked, but nearly every aspect of the campaign was flawed. Like the coming horrors of Gallipoli, much of the failure came down to the indolence, ineptitude, arrogance and short-sightedness of the planners, primarily the Admiralty and the War Office. Undoubtedly there were opportunities for those in high command to blow the whistle and call off the operation. And yet nobody was prepared to do so. On the contrary, they were now about to dig themselves into a vastly deeper hole.

The Bouvet, pre-Dreadnought, completed 1898, cost £1,100,770.

The Irresistible, a pre-Dreadnought battleship, completed 1902, cost £989,116.

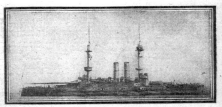

The Ocean, pre-Dreadnought, completed 1900, cost £883,778.

The price of Admiralty has again been paid. In the attack on the forts of the Narrows of the Dardanelles three battleships of the Allied Fleet have been sunk. The Irresistible and the Ocean, of the British squadron, and the French battleship Bouvet, which advanced after mine-sweeping operations, were struck by drifting mines. The British losses were slight, but practically the whole of the crew of the Bouvet was lost.

• • •

Admiral Jack de Robeck, who succeeded
to the command of the Eastern Mediterranean fleet, with General Sir Ian Hamilton,
commander of the Mediterranean Expeditionary Force, on board de Robeck's yacht
HMS *Triad*.

ADMIRAL
JACK DE ROBECK

(1862-1928)

. . .

Jack de Robeck, who commanded the Eastern Mediterranean fleet through most of the Gallipoli campaign, was born in 1862 at Gowran Grange, a Gothic Revival house which his father built near Punchestown in County Kildare.

The de Robecks had always been fighting men. Their ancestors were one of the most powerful families in Estonia and Sweden during the 17th and 18th centuries. In 1778, Jakob Constantin Fock of Råbäck was made a friherre (or baron) by King Gustav III. During the American War of Independence, his son Johann Fock rode out against the British with a cavalry regiment of multilingual volunteers, considered the finest riders in Europe, led by the Duc de Lauzun, a favourite of Marie-Antoinette. Johann later became a British citizen and, following his father's death in 1803, he succeeded as 2nd Baron de Robeck.

The 2nd Baron's wife, Anne Fitzpatrick, was the sole heiress of the Galway land-owner Richard Fitzpatrick from whom the de Robecks acquired most of their land-holdings in counties Kildare, Wicklow and Dublin. Their son Henry — the Admiral's grandfather — fought in the Napoleonic Wars during his youth and married a daughter of Lord Cloncurry, one of the few aristocrats to support Wolfe Tone's ill-fated rebellion in 1798.

When Henry drowned in the River Liffey in 1856, Jack's father, John Henry Edward Fock, succeeded as 4th Baron, inheriting the 9,000-acre family estate at Punchestown. He was one of Ireland's greatest hunting men, famed for his 'good hands', nerves of steel and 'a quick, cool head'. Together with Lord Naas, the 4th Baron turned the Kildare Hunt into the undisputed premier pack in Ireland.

Jack, the 4th Baron's second son, entered the Royal Navy at the age of 13 and gradu-ally rose through the ranks, becoming a Rear Admiral in 1911. In 1899, he was the second of 11 officers listed as potential commanders for the Discovery Expedition to Antarctica. Sir Clements Markham, who compiled the list, described him as 'hard as nails, lots of nerve, an excellent messmate.' Ultimately the command of that epic assignment would instead fall to Captain Robert Falcon Scott who set sail in 1901 with Ernest Shackleton and Tom Crean among the crew.

Recalled from half-pay at the beginning of the war, Jack de Robeck was initially placed in charge of the 9th Cruiser Squadron which, based in Gibraltar, kept watch over the mid-Atlantic. He was then given command of a new squadron formed to guard the British and French colonies on the West African coast against the possibility of attack from the notorious German Admiral von Spee. Jack flew his flag from the powerful battleship *Warrior*, but when the squadron was disbanded on 19 November he resumed command of the 9th Cruiser Squadron.[27]

The first months of 1915 must have been inordinately stressful as he and Vice Admiral Carden grappled with the logistical nightmare of trying to break through the Dardanelles. His mind may also have been startled by reports from Ireland where his older brother Harry, now the 5th Baron, was facing potential bankruptcy as the family estate was placed under a receiving order. As it happens, the family managed to hold on and the de Robecks continue to live at Gowran Grange to this day.

Harry de Robeck, a former Master of the Kildare Hunt, spent the first part of the war looking after horses with the Remount Service. As a Lieutenant Colonel with the Royal Field Artillery, he then commanded an ammunition column in France for three years. His wife Nanny, youngest daughter of Lorenzo Alexander of Straw Hall, County Carlow, played a prominent role as a fundraiser throughout the war and frequently sent packages of hot water bottles and cigarettes to the wounded soldiers of the Western Front.

Having taken command of the hard-pressed Eastern Mediterranean fleet after Admiral Carden's collapse, Jack de Robeck earned much praise from certain quarters for refusing to send the fleet to almost certain doom in the Dardanelles. During the ensuing Gallipoli campaign, his ships provided the covering fire during the major ground offensives, including those at Seddelbahr and Suvla Bay.[28]

In November 1914, he returned home on leave to recover from chronic insomnia and neuralgia. Prior to his departure, he devised much of the plan on which the extraordinarily successful evacuation of Gallipoli was based. In his absence, Roger Keyes and Rear Admiral Sir Rosslyn Wemyss oversaw the evacuation of the troops from Suvla Bay and Anzac Cove in December 1915. De Robeck returned in time to evacuate the final bridgehead at Cape Helles on the night of 8–9 January 1916, which marked the end of the campaign. Roger Keyes would later claim much of the credit for this operation, prompting a falling out between the two men.

Promoted to Vice Admiral in May 1917, Jack de Robeck saw out the remainder of the war commanding the Grand Fleet's Second Battle Squadron. In 1919, he was created 1st Baronet de Robeck of Naas in the County of Kildare and received the thanks of Parliament, along with a grant of £10,000.

In July 1919, as commander in chief in the Mediterranean, he was sent to Constantinople to serve as British High Commissioner. Amongst his principal tasks was a review of the position of 100 Turks being held in Malta on charges of mass murder in Armenia. He showed considerable tact in this role, realising that while the Turkish Government was locked in political negotiations with the rapidly rising Turkish National Party of his old foe Mustafa Kemal Atatürk, Britain would be ill-advised to intervene. That said, he was careful to stress that many of the prisoners in Malta had been arrested on the strength of nothing more than statements made by informers and intriguers.

In July 1922, Sir John de Robeck married a Scottish widow called Hilda Lockhart. The following month he was given command of the Atlantic Fleet. In 1925, he was promoted to the top rank of Admiral of the Fleet.

He was involved in a serious car accident in 1923, which considerably impaired his health. He died aged 64 at his home in Hyde Park, London, three years later. Earl Jellicoe, his former Commander in Chief, was amongst the pall-bearers at his funeral on the Isle of Wight.

• • •

Admiral de Robeck's staff in the Eastern Mediterranean. Back row l-r: Commander James Sommerville (Wireless Officer); Commander Hood (Naval Secretary); Lieutenant Bowlby (Flag Lieutenant); Lieutenant Ormsby Johnson (Flag Lieutenant); Flag Commander Ramsay; Major Godfrey, RMA. Front row l-r: Captain Lambart; Commodore Roger Keyes; Vice Admiral Jack de Robeck; Captain John William Leopold McClintock; Commander Millot (French Naval Attaché).

• • •

Admiral Francis William Kennedy, the
son of a Home Rule supporter from
County Kildare, participated in the chase
for the *Goeben* and *Breslau*, two German
ships gifted by the Kaiser to the Ottomans
to woo the Turks into an alliance with
the German Empire.

ADMIRAL
FRANCIS KENNEDY, CB

(1862–1939)

...

AMONG THE SHIPS THAT TOOK PART IN THE CHASE OF THE *GOEBEN* AND *BRESLAU*, AND THE subsequent bombardment of the Dardanelles forts in November 1914, was the battlecruiser HMS *Indomitable*, commanded by Admiral Francis William Kennedy.

Born in Straffan, County Kildare, in 1862, 'Frank' Kennedy descended from a colourful 18th century gentleman called Darby O'Kennedy who lived at Ballikerogue Castle, near Campile, County Wexford. Like the de Robecks, the Kennedys were well-known fox hunters in County Kildare, where the Admiral's grandfather Sir John Kennedy was hailed as the father of the Kildare Hunt.

At the time of Queen Victoria's visit to Ireland in April 1900, the Admiral's father, Robert Kennedy, was Lord Lieutenant of County Kildare. Robert, an ardent supporter of Home Rule, caused considerable controversy when he refused to present an address to the Queen. The Admiral's brother Edward 'Cub' Kennedy (1860–1925) was one of Ireland's foremost thoroughbred breeders, best known for breeding The Tetrarch, one of the greatest two-year-olds of all time.

In January 1915, the *Indomitable*, under Kennedy's command, served at the battle of Dogger Bank in the North Sea. During the engagement, the German squadron managed to disable Vice Admiral Sir David Beatty's flagship HMS *Lion*, which was thereafter exposed to the considerable threat of submarine attack. *Indomitable* was assigned to tow the *Lion* back to the Forth, a potentially fatal voyage for both battlecruisers had the German submarines struck. To screen their slow progress home, over 50 ships were assigned to guard them.

Admiral Kennedy also captained the *Indomitable* as part of the Third Battlecruiser Squadron under Rear Admiral Hood at the battle of Jutland on 31 May 1916. When Hood's ship *Invincible* was blown up, killing all but six of the 1,026 men on board, Frank Kennedy took command of the squadron. The dispatches of the battle record that he fought his ship 'with great skill and gallantry'. He was promoted to Rear Admiral the following day and was subsequently made a Companion of the Most Honourable Order of the Bath in direct consequence of his actions at Jutland.

In June 1917, he went to Peterhead off the east coast of Scotland where he was based for the remainder of the war. He was promoted to Vice Admiral in 1920 and Admiral in 1925, and passed away in 1939.

• • •

The Turkish fortress of Seddelbahr at
Cape Helles was built in 1659 to guard
the entrance to the Dardanelles Straits.
This was a landscape through which the
mighty armies of men such as Agamemnon and Alexander the Great marched
in distant ages. In 1915, Seddelbahr was
subjected to a massive attack by 2,000
men from the Royal Dublin Fusiliers and
Royal Munster Fusiliers.

THE
BATTLE
OF
SEDDELBAHR

...

Captain Guy Geddes of the Royal Munster Fusiliers was feeling under-standably edgy as the requisitioned collier creaked ever closer to the southern shore of the Gallipoli Peninsula. Squeezed alongside him in the *River Clyde*'s hull were upwards of 2,000 men, mostly Irish, all bracing themselves for the impending fight. Inspired by Homer's tale of the Trojan Horse, the plan was to beach the collier beneath the Turkish fort at Seddelbahr as innocently as possible and then to unleash the Irishmen in a surprise attack. The men would spring out from two holes cut through the steel plates in the collier's sides and then gallop ashore over a jetty made up of gangways and barges.

Nearly 1,000 of the men were from the 1st Battalion of the Munsters, including the ginger-haired Captain Geddes and his men from X Company. For the previous three weeks, they had been training intensively on the Greek island of Lemnos, simulating the precise manner in which they would clamber out of the *River Clyde* and storm the Turkish defences.

Across the main deck on the starboard side stood Captain Eric Henderson, the hand-some 34-year-old commander of Z Company. Geddes had known Henderson since the Boer War days, when they had fought side by side for the Munsters.[29] The two men had enlisted as teenagers and progressed steadily through the ranks, spending the years immediately before the war in Burma (Myanmar) where Lieutenant Colonel Henry Tizard — the man now leading them to Gallipoli — became the battalion's commander.

Back in 1881, when Geddes and Henderson were babies, the regiment was known as the Royal Bengal Fusiliers, a legacy of its initial foundation by the East India Company.[30] And yet it was very much an Irish outfit; its headquarters were in Tralee, County Kerry, the regimental cap badges were adorned with shamrock and the regimental mascot was an Irish wolfhound called Gary.

As it happened, both Geddes and Henderson knew a good deal about Bengal.[31] Geddes was actually born there, while Henderson's father was a surgeon with the Indian Medical Service. Henderson grew up at 13 Hume Street in Dublin, close to the Royal College of Surgeons where his father had studied. The war had already brought sorrow to the Henderson family; his younger brother Raymond perished while defending the trenches on the Aisne Heights in September 1914.[32]

Amongst the other Munsters awaiting the call to exit the ship was one man whom nobody could miss. Standing six feet six inches in height and weighing in at 16 stone, Corporal Willie Cosgrove was the biggest man in the battalion. Born and reared on the eastern shore of Cork Harbour, Cosgrove had previously worked as an apprentice butcher in the fishing port of Whitegate. One of his daily assignments was to bring meat to the British soldiers who were garrisoned at Fort Carlisle (now Fort Davis) at the entrance to Cork Harbour. By 1909, he had decided that army life was for him and, aged 21, he said cheerio to the butcher and joined up.[33]

Like Geddes and Henderson, Cosgrove had been in Burma when the war broke out. Towards the end of November 1914, the battalion was summoned back to Blighty, arriving into ice-cold Avonmouth seven weeks later, still clad in their Indian khaki drill shorts. An intense training period followed before they were assigned to the 86th Brigade of Lord Kitchener's 29th Division and dispatched south to the Dardanelles.

Dr Peter Burrowes Kelly, one of at least three doctors on board the *River Clyde*, was working at Charing Cross Hospital in Hammersmith, London, when the war erupted. He was one of the Kellys of Ballintubbert, County Laois, whose forebears included the Rev Thomas Kelly, the evangelist who penned the hymn, 'The Head that Once was Crowned with Thorns' and founded his own religious sect, the short-lived 'Kellyites'. Educated at St Vincent's College, Castleknock, Dr Burrowes Kelly had served with the Royal Naval Air Service during the siege of Antwerp in October 1914. He was the only medical man to escape when the Germans swept into the Belgian city.[34]

The *River Clyde* creaked closer still. Few on board had managed any sleep, despite the cocoa sent around to steady nerves. Geddes was one of the exceptions. He'd chanced upon his friend Commander Josiah Wedgwood, who offered him 'a shake down on his cabin floor'. Wedgwood, a kinsman of Charles Darwin, was in charge of the 11 Maxim machine-guns mounted on the *River Clyde* that were due to be gainfully employed when the attack began. Perhaps Geddes and Wedgwood took a moment to consider what the attack was all about.

By 27 March 1915, Winston Churchill, First Lord of the Admiralty, had accepted that his dream of laying siege to Constantinople was as nothing unless the army captured the Gallipoli Peninsula and made it safe for the Royal Navy to power up the Dardanelles Straits. Lord Kitchener offered 52,000 men, combining the 18,000-strong 29th Division and 34,000 ANZACs, while the French added a further 18,000 colonial troops. The Mediterranean Expeditionary Force was to be commanded by Sir Ian Hamilton, an energetic 61-year-old who had been Kitchener's Chief of Staff during the Anglo-Boer

War. Hamilton was a cheery soul of the old school, but it was to emerge that he was largely unsuited to the challenges of modern warfare.

Having little previous knowledge of the Dardanelles region, Hamilton was dispatched south with a large survey map, a 1912 handbook on the Turkish army and instructions from Kitchener that he could do what he liked with the 80,000 men so long as he conquered Gallipoli.

Hamilton duly summoned his staff, unfurled his map and devised a plan.[35] Although the British and French armies had camped along Gallipoli's shoreline during the Crimean War in the 1850s, the topography of the peninsula was largely unknown to the Allies. It had, after all, been Ottoman territory for five and a half centuries. Such a lack of knowledge about the Gallipoli interior would have devastating consequences.

Hamilton's plan was based upon a four-pronged amphibious assault. First there would be a diversion; some of Admiral de Robeck's warships were to head for the north of the peninsula and pretend that they were about to land a lot of men there. Secondly, to foment further confusion amongst the Turks, the French were to pounce on the eastern or Asian shore of the Dardanelles. Thirdly, the ANZAC forces were to land at Gaba Tepe, a headland about halfway up Gallipoli's Aegean shore. Finally, the 29th Division would roll into Cape Helles at the southern tip of the peninsula and, following a massive 30-minute bombardment by His Majesty's fleet, disembark on five beaches which were to be henceforth named S, V, W, X and Y. From the points at which they landed, the ANZACs would advance east and the 29th Division north, driving the Ottomans back and securing control of the various hills and forts they passed along the way.

All of this was to kick off at pretty much the same time which, Hamilton proposed, ought to be at the break of dawn on the morning of 23 April. With luck, the peninsula would be in Allied hands by the middle of May and Constantinople's surrender would surely follow soon afterwards.

While Hamilton was initially rather gung-ho about the prospects of success, he had his concerns. Anyone aboard a ship with a pair of binoculars could see the barbed wire entanglements sprawling across the beaches of Cape Helles, a sizeable deterrent for those planning to land there. Admiral de Robeck's ships had been instructed to bomb the wire but even when the gunners actually hit the target there was, Hamilton dourly observed, 'no visible effect whatever'.

Hamilton was also unnerved by the increasing reports of Turkish soldiers 'tucked away in the folds of the ground' all along the coast. The Ottoman Government had entrusted the defence of Gallipoli to General Otto Liman von Sanders, a Prussian aristocrat who had been instrumental in persuading the Turks to side with the Kaiser. At his disposal was the Fifth Army, comprising 80,000 soldiers, including the III Corps, battle-hardened veterans of the Balkan Wars of 1912–1913 and arguably the best outfit in the Turkish Army. Utterly committed to defending their homeland from an Allied invasion, many of these Turks were now entrenched in compact, carefully hidden outposts, overlooking all of the obvious beaches where the Allies mighty try to land, such as, say, the beaches around Cape Helles.

Hamilton wasn't about to let his plan be scuppered by the threat of Turkish marksmen and indestructible wire. In sync with his old friend Kitchener, he was clearly

General Sir Ian Hamilton, photographed by Ernest Brooks as he prepared to return to his headquarters after an inspection of the Royal Navy Division, which had been assigned to row the Royal Dublin Fusiliers to the beach at Seddelbahr.

of the view that the show must go on. The only major alteration he conceded was to postpone the invasion by 48 hours when an ominous storm crackled from the sky on 21 April.

And so it was that at 5.30pm on Friday 23 April 1915, the 1st Battalion of the Royal Munster Fusiliers, together with the 1st Battalion of the Royal Dublin Fusiliers and two companies of the Hampshire Regiment, sailed out from Lemnos, destination Gallipoli.[36]

The Munsters voyaged upon the SS *Caledonia*, once the premier passenger liner on the Glasgow to New York run. The Dubs and the two Hampshire companies sailed on the *Ausonia* and the *Alaunia*, two Cunard liners. They steamed slowly through the night with the lights out.

Just six days earlier, *The Weekly Irish Times* had applauded 'a new patriotic song' called 'The Fighting Fusiliers' dedicated to the Munsters' commanding officer, Colonel Tizard.[37] However, while there was much cheering from the shoreline as they steamed out of Lemnos, Captain Geddes was surprised at the quietness of the battalion's 28 officers and 1,002 men. 'What struck me most forcibly was the demeanour of our own men, from whom not a sound, and this from the light hearted, devil may care men from the South of Ireland. Even they were filled with a sense of something impending which was quite beyond their ken.'[38]

Early the following morning, the three ships anchored at Tenedos Island, halfway between Lemnos and the tip of the Gallipoli peninsula, where a forward base had been established for the troops bound for Cape Helles. Amongst the destroyers, torpedo boats, mine sweepers, tugs and other small boats anchored at Tenedos was the collier *River Clyde*, which had been converted to carry troops.

The Munsters, with two companies of Hampshire and one company of the Royal Dublin Fusiliers, were duly transferred to the *River Clyde*, while the other three companies of Dubs were put on board a minesweeper.

The objective for the men on the *River Clyde* was to take what was designated as V Beach, including the fortress and village of Seddelbahr to the east of Cape Helles. An Allied naval bombardment six months earlier, combined with a daring raid by a demolition team in February 1915, had done much to undermine the 17th century fortress at Seddelbahr. Nevertheless, this was still a heavily prized Turkish possession and the beaches beneath it were the most heavily defended of all southern beaches. Watching from the Aegean, Admiral de Robeck had cautioned that any attempt to land troops at Seddelbahr would be 'extremely costly'.

Irrespective of such stark warnings, the men on the *River Clyde* were instructed that they would be advancing on V Beach where, by dint of their numerical superiority, they would quickly overpower the Turks, and Seddelbahr would fall.

V Beach was an open strand measuring just over 1,500 feet, a little longer than Dublin's Grafton Street. Framed between steep cliffs on the west and the village of Seddelbahr on the east, the beach was dominated by a thick line of barbed wire entanglements, secured by steel posts that ran from one end to the other. Two further lines of barbed wire mesh were strewn upon the cultivated terraces that rolled upwards towards the old fortress. From within this fearsome amphitheatre, four Maxim guns and miscellaneous pom-poms discreetly poked their barrels out from walls of both cliff and fort. It was, as a Turkish historian put it, 'a sloping arena designed by nature and arranged by the Turks for a butchery.'[39]

The early morning of Sunday 25 April was calm and beautiful, recalled Captain Geddes. 'Not a breath of wind and a slight haze which rapidly disappeared... My nerves were tense and strung up. And yet, I never doubted that we would not win through, because I knew the splendid fellows at my back, highly trained, strictly disciplined, and they would follow me anywhere.'

At Seddelbahr, the Turkish snipers must have rubbed their eyes and watched with mounting disbelief as the Allied invasion began. Although the Royal Navy's bombardment had managed to knock out the big guns overlooking the beach, it is reckoned that there were still at least 200 Turks waiting with their fingers ready on the triggers of their machine-guns and rifles.

The Dubs were first up. Like the Munsters, the 1st Battalion of the Royal Dublin Fusiliers had returned to England at the start of the war, sailing home from Madras where the regiment had actually been formed some 270 years earlier. Billeted first at Torquay on the Devon coast, and later at Nuneaton in Warwickshire, the Blue Caps, as they were nicknamed, departed for the Dardanelles on St Patrick's Day 1915.

When the 1,100-strong battalion left Torquay for Nuneaton, Lieutenant Colonel Richard Rooth, the commanding officer, presented the regimental colours to the town's Mayor for safekeeping. By the time the Dubs got their colours back three years later, just 40 of those 1,100 men were still in the regiment. Hundreds of them were to die in Gallipoli, many upon the approaching shores of V Beach.

In the dark of night, three companies of Dubs disembarked from de Robeck's minesweepers and boarded a flotilla of 24 cutter boats, organised into six 'tows', four boats a-tow. Each boat had a crew from the Royal Naval Division comprising of a midshipman and six seamen. Each of the Dubs carried a rifle, 200 rounds of ammunition, a heavy coat, a waterproof sheet and a back-pack with three days' rations.

Colonel Rooth took his place in one of these boats, alongside the battalion adjutant Captain William Higginson and Father William Finn, a 40-year-old Carmelite priest who had been chaplain to the Dubs for the previous four months. Colonel Rooth had been keen to leave the chaplain behind but Father Finn was insistent: 'The priest's place is beside the dying soldier; I must go.'

And so, as the rosy-fingered dawn began to illuminate Gallipoli, the Dubs and their tows made their way towards V Beach. The original concept was for them to arrive on shore under the cover of a ferocious naval bombardment that would quell the Turkish gunners. This ought to have given the Dubs just long enough to establish a superior foothold on the beach. Unfortunately, just like the trawlers assigned to sweep mines for poor Admiral Carden earlier in the year, the cutters struggled against the swirling Dardanelles current.

By the time the hapless oarsmen paddled within range at 5.30am, the bombardment was over and the Turks had fully regained their composure.[40] One tow managed to break away from the others and reached a point called Camber, just north-east of the

• • •

This photograph of the officers of the Royal Dublin Fusiliers, aka the 'Blue Caps', was taken immediately prior to their departure for Gallipoli on 17 March 1915. Back row l-r: Lieut. J Hosford, Lieut. JP Walters, Lieut. RH de Lusignan, Lieut. Corbet, Lieut. HD O'Hara, Lieut. W Andrews, Lieut. CW Maffett, Lieut. & Quarter Master J Kennedy, **REV FATHER WILLIAM FINN**, CF, Lieut. H de Boer, RAMC, Capt. GM Dunlop, Lieut. FS Lanigan-O'Keeffe, **LIEUT. ROBERT BERNARD**, Lieut. CG Carruthers, **LIEUT. LAWRENCE C BOUSTEAD**. Front row l-r: Capt. D French, Capt. JRW Grove, Capt. JM Mood, Capt. AM Johnson, **CAPT. WILLIAM F HIGGINSON**, Major E Fetherstonhaugh, **LIEUT.-COL. RICHARD A ROOTH, CAPT. CECIL TW GRIMSHAW**, DSO, Capt. EA Molesworth, Capt. HC Crozier, Capt. AW Molony, Capt. DVF Anderson, Lieut. HM Floyd. The men whose names appear in capitals are referred to in this chapter.

fort at Seddelbahr. The Irishmen managed to crawl ashore and would later reach the village of Seddelbahr where they were destined to be 'overwhelmed' by a 'crowd of snipers'.

Meanwhile, with less than 70 feet to go before the first of the other tows reached the beach, the Turkish guns let rip and suddenly the sky was filled with the screams of lead and shells and dying men. Many of the Dubliners were killed in the first 60 seconds. All their years of training in Madras and Devon amounted to nothing. Some fell or dived into the water where, weighed down by their ammunition and great-coats, they simply sank and drowned. Most died in their boats, riddled with bullets. 'One fellow's brains were shot into my mouth as I was shouting to them to jump for it', remarked Sergeant McColgan afterwards. Of the 32 men in his barge, all but six were killed.

Colonel Rooth, the Dubs' 48-year-old commanding officer, was killed on the water's edge. Father Finn had leapt from his boat the instant the first men were hit. The first bullet caught him in the chest. He somehow made it to the shore where he was shot in the arm and leg. Despite the immense pain he must have been suffering, he scrambled upon the sands, offering consolation and absolution to the dying. He was in the act of blessing one of the men when a piece of shrapnel tore into his skull. He was the first British chaplain of any denomination to be killed in the Great War. There would be 178 more, 16 of whom were Irish.[41]

Watching horror-struck from the *River Clyde*, Dr Burrowes Kelly would be haunted by the sight for the rest of his life. 'Our men were simply butchered and the water was red with blood and the air boiling with bullets.'[42] As Captain Geddes remarked, 'they were literally slaughtered like rats in a trap'. Amongst those killed were 17-year-old Alfie Verrent, the son of the Kinnitty Castle gamekeeper, and 21-year-old Sam Mallaghan from County Down. Sam and his younger brother Jack had once worked as gardeners and general labourers for a solicitor on the outskirts of their home town, Newry. They had been serving with the battalion in India when the war broke out. Their younger brothers Herbie and Willie were serving with the Royal Irish Fusiliers. In December 1914, their father, John, received a letter from Buckingham Palace commending him for having four sons serving with the colours. It was indicative of the times that the boys' mother, Annie, was not mentioned in the letter. Jack Mallaghan was also on a Gallipoli-bound cutter that awful April morning; aged 19, he was killed just days later.[43]

One of the luckier men to make it ashore was Private William Harris from Athy, County Kildare, who later wrote to his mother. 'It was only by chance anyone got out, for whichever way you swam that day you faced death'.[44] Soaked and utterly shocked, Harris and the other survivors found a brief respite beneath an eight-foot-high sand-bank that ran just over 30 feet from the shoreline.

Meanwhile, as Private Harris dug in for dear life, the *River Clyde* was unloading its cargo of 2,000 men. The collier had beached on a rocky spit about 25 feet off the eastern end of V Beach. It was a little further out than planned, but she had landed so softly that Guy Geddes hadn't even noticed. While the Dubs were being annihilated to the west, two large holes in each side of the collier were prised open so that the men of

Munster could join the fray. The first to open was on the starboard side. With Captain Henderson to the fore, the soldiers of Z Company popped out, one by one, and dropped onto the wooden gangway below.

Once again the Turks bided their time before opening fire with what Dr Burrowes Kelly recalled as 'such a din of pom-poms and bullets I never want to be in again'. The Turkish machine-guns were capable of firing over 1,200 bullets a minute and these horrific instruments now swept along the gangway, splaying hot lead into scores of men who crashed down in agony, one after the other. Of the first 200 men who left the collier, it is reckoned that 149 were immediately killed and 30 wounded. Many tumbled into the water where, if not already dead, they soon drowned because there was no chance of rescuing them.[45]

• • •

Loaded with over 2,000 troops, mostly Irish, the collier *River Clyde* was deliberately run ashore at V Beach by Seddelbahr. She was known as 'The Wooden Horse', an allusion to the famous and somewhat similar expedient employed by the Greeks on this very same terrain during the Trojan Wars.

Guy Geddes had planned to lead X Company out of the port-side hole in perfect synchronicity with Henderson's men, but the damned thing jammed. Once they got it open, he led his men into the madness. One of the first to fall was Lieutenant John Watts who, wounded in five places, lay on the gangway and shouted at the men to 'follow the Captain'. And follow him they did. 'Man after man behind me was shot down but they never wavered,' wrote Geddes. 'I think no finer episode could be found of the men's bravery and discipline than this — of leaving the safety of the *River Clyde* to go to what was practically certain death.'

One of the two gangways had by now been destroyed by shellfire. The second gangway was submerged in so many dead bodies that the only option for the survivors was to roll their fallen comrades into the sea. And then, 'like gladiators', they roared and charged.

The only problem was that there was nowhere they could really charge. There was supposed to be a causeway of barges and planks connecting the *River Clyde* to the shore. However, amid the chaos of the Turkish artillery attack, the steam vessel assigned to connect the barges had broken loose and there was no such causeway. Captain Raymond Lane of the Munsters quickly ascertained that his only option was to plunge into the reddening waters. The sea came up to his shoulders but at least he could stand and try to wade ashore.

Edward Unwin, commander of the *River Clyde*, realised that the causeway was imperative. Accompanied by Able Seaman Williams, he dived into the water, manhandled two barges into position and lashed them into a bridge. Chunks of Turkish lead continued to whistle and whip through the air, slamming into flesh and bones, clanking off the collier's side. Unwin and Williams would both win Victoria Crosses for their valour, but the latter was killed as he earned it.

Lieutenant Colonel Carrington Smith, the officer commanding the troops aboard the *River Clyde*, was watching all this from the ship's bridge when a Turkish sniper struck gold and shot him dead.[46] Soon afterwards, Brigadier General Henry Napier, who was to take command of the operation once ashore, arrived into this unhappy scene on a small boat, only to be killed by a hail of bullets, alongside his Brigade Major.

Like Captain Lane, Guy Geddes realised his best chance was to jump into the sea and swim for the shore. Despite carrying his equipment, he reached it in a dozen lengths and scampered to the sandbank where many of his fellow soldiers, Munsters and Dubs alike, were hiding beneath this meagre shelter, wounded and dying, including Eric Henderson, the first officer to reach the shore. Henderson was badly hit and one of his arms was shattered. He would die on a hospital bed in the Egyptian city of Alexandria five weeks later.[47]

With Henderson down, command of the Munsters' Z Company passed to Captain Lane, who had miraculously reached the sandbank with his platoon unscathed. During their approach, Lane noted the barbed wire strewn across the beach, just 65 feet from where he and his men were huddled. Directly in front of the wire lay the bodies of five soldiers. Unperturbed, Lane made a dash at full pelt. A sniper spotted him and the same bullet that sliced through his right ankle went on to smash his left leg to pieces. One of his men zipped out and 'very pluckily' pulled him back behind the ridge. 'I had only been on the beach five minutes and never saw a Turk,' said Lane.[48]

• • •

The amphibious attack on the Dardanelles commenced on 25 April 1915 when thousands
of seaborne troops landed along the southern and western shores of the Gallipoli peninsula. This photo shows V Beach beneath the fort of Seddelbahr, where almost 2,000 men
serving with the Royal Munster Fusiliers and the Royal Dublin Fusiliers were greeted
with a horrific onslaught of Turkish shell and gunfire. You can see the surviving soldiers
huddled beneath an eight-foot-high sandbank that ran just over 30 feet from the shoreline. In the foreground, behold the barges and fallen planks of the broken causeway that
was attempting to connect the *River Clyde* to the shore.

Dr Burrowes Kelly was on the gangplank trying to rescue the wounded when he
was hit in his right leg and then 'pinked' in his left. Despite his wounds, he remained
on the ship for the next two days, during which time he attended to approximately 750
wounded men. As Admiral de Robeck remarked when recommending him for a DSO,
the doctor was 'in great pain and unable to walk' for much of that grim ordeal.[49] The
doctor was to remain in Gallipoli until the evacuation at the end of the year. He went on
to serve at the Royal Naval College at Osborne during a deadly measles epidemic, before
finally setting up a private practice in London. However, his health rapidly declined on
account of his war injuries and he died on 6 April 1920 while staying at the home of his
brother in Ballitore, County Kildare. He was survived by his wife and one daughter.

From behind the sandbank, Captain Geddes dashed out with seven 'gallant' men in
a bid to clear a path through the barbed wire. Three were killed outright and Geddes
was shot in the shoulder. He and the other three survivors dug themselves in as best
they could while Geddes calculated that he had now lost 140 men, or 70 per cent of his
company, including his Sergeant Major, who was killed, and two second lieutenants,
who were wounded. With the aid of a semaphore, he established contact with Colonel

Tizard and explained that he could no longer achieve his objective 'because I had no men left'. And then, with blood pumping from his shoulder, he sank back into the sand.

For the 200 or so men rammed beneath the sandbank, there was nothing to do but wait. As Raymond Lane observed, 'any man who put his head up for an instant was shot dead'. Nearly 1,200 men were still on board the *River Clyde* when the commanders agreed to halt the attack and await the fall of night.

The casualty rate was horrific, no doubt, but it was by no means all one way. On top of the intensive naval bombardment that started the day, the Turks at Seddelbahr were also reeling from the deadly effects of Jos Wedgwood's 11 Maxim guns mounted on the *River Clyde*, which severely depleted their numbers. Moreover, word must by now have reached the Turkish commanders that this was not an isolated attack. All along the south and west coast of Gallipoli, thousands of Allied soldiers were making their way onshore. Three of the four hills at Cape Helles had already been captured. The 29th Division had been greatly delayed, but the invasion had not been stopped. And all that stood between them and the conquest of the cape was the village and fortress of Seddelbahr.

During the pitch-black night that followed, the remaining troops from the *River Clyde* disembarked and, free from accurate sniper fire, they advanced onto V Beach. It was by now perfectly clear that if these men were to accomplish their mission, the wire entanglements on the beach had to go.

The task of destroying the wire fell to Company Sergeant Major Alfred Bennett of the Royal Munster Fusiliers. Born in 1881, he had grown up near the regimental head-quarters in Tralee where his father Alexander was steward of the Blennerhassett estate at Ballyseedy. As dawn broke on 26 April, Sergeant Major Bennett led a company of 50 men up towards the barbed wire. Just moments later, a bullet slammed into his brain and the Kerryman fell.

With Bennett dead, Corporal Willie Cosgrove, the giant from Cork, took command and brought the surviving men on up to the barbed wire entanglements which, as he later remarked, 'ran in every direction and were fixed to stout posts that were more than my own height'. The men set to work with pliers, but it quickly became apparent that the wire was so strong that, to quote Cosgrove, 'you might as well try and snip Cloyne round tower with a scissors'. His head throbbing with the urgency of the situation, Cosgrove did what any giant would do under the circumstances. He wrapped his arm around one of the metal posts and heaved it out of the ground. As it came loose, the men watching from behind the bank and from the *River Clyde* realised what he was up to and began cheering loudly. Cosgrove, who heard nothing but 'the screech of bullets' all around him, advanced to the next post and yanked that one up too. And until his back was peppered with shrapnel, forcing him to withdraw, he just kept on pulling up posts. Dr Burrowes Kelly summed up the feelings of many when he wrote: 'The manner in which the man worked out in the open will never be forgotten by those who were fortunate to witness it.'

Corporal Cosgrove underwent two operations in Malta and survived, but his war was over. He was sent home to Ireland to recuperate, during which time he learned that

During the pitch-black night of 26 April, the remaining troops from the *River Clyde* disembarked and advanced onto V Beach. This illustration entitled 'Night Landing at the Dardanelles' was published in *Les Pays de France* in 1915.

LEVEN &
LEMONIER
15.

he had been awarded the Victoria Cross.[50] 'I did my best and the boys around me were every bit as good as myself,' he said. Almost single-handedly, the butcher from Cork Harbour had created a gap in the wire that was big enough for the men on V Beach to break through and advance on the fortress.

Another deed of considerable daring was then performed by Lieutenant Lawrence Boustead, Royal Dublin Fusiliers, the son of a Ceylonese tea planter. In a lonesome charge, the 22-year-old managed to lodge himself in an opening at the side of the fortress. With his revolver he either killed or wounded enough Turks within the fort to stop them firing for just long enough to enable the British to storm the building and take control. Boustead was shot through the cheek but survived, only to be killed in action at the battle of Gully Ravine eight weeks later.

Inspired by the courage of Cosgrove and Boustead, the Irishmen charged up the hill, bayonets fixed, into the village of Seddelbahr. Among those killed during the charge was Lieutenant Robert Bernard, the 23-year-old son of the Right Rev JH Bernard, Bishop of Ossory.[51] Later that week, Bishop Bernard wrote in his diary '… our dearest boy was killed last Sunday in action. Poor Maud is broken hearted. My darling Robert — it is hard to believe.'

'The village was an awful snag', wrote Captain Guy Nightingale, one of the Munsters, to his sister. 'Every house and corner was full of snipers and you only had to show yourself in the streets to have a bullet at your head. We spent from 9am to 2.30 before we finally cleared them all out. We lost a lot of men and officers in it. I got one swine of a Turk with my revolver when searching a house for snipers but he nearly had me first.'[52]

Among those killed in the final attack on the village was 40-year-old Major Cecil Grimshaw, DSO, whose father had served as both Registrar General of Ireland and President of the Royal College of Physicians of Ireland. During the South African War, Grimshaw had been captured by the Boers and held in the same prison camp as Winston Churchill, then a war correspondent, who noted him as 'a very energetic and clever young officer.'

Having secured the village, Nightingale led his company up the hill that dominated the town and drove the Turks from its slope. 'It was a relief after all that sniping,' he wrote. 'We rushed straight at the top and turned 2,000 Turks off the redoubt and poured lead into them at 1,000 yards'.[53] By mid-afternoon, all of Cape Helles was under British control. At a cost of 3,800 men, or 20 per cent of its force, the 29th Division had completed its first objective. Turkish fatalities were estimated at between 800 and 1,000.

The casualties were particularly high for the Irish regiments at V Beach. Precise figures vary, but of the 26 officers and 900 Munster men who arrived at V Beach on 25 April, approximately 600 had been killed or wounded by the time French reinforcements took over the line on the morning of 27 April.[54] The Dubs suffered equally harshly, with ten officers and 153 men dead and nearly 600 wounded.[55] Indeed, the casualties were so overwhelming that, on 29 April, the surviving men of the two battalions were temporarily amalgamated as one into the 'Dubsters'.

Guy Geddes was exceedingly lucky to survive. Having dressed his shoulder wound, he remained with his men for 13 hours. By the time Dr Burrowes Kelly examined him, he was so gravely infected that his red hair had turned white. However, he made a full recovery, was awarded the DSO and was appointed commander of the 1st Battalion of the Munsters on 19 May. Geddes survived the war and later married and had two sons. He died aged 74 on 24 April 1955, exactly 40 years after his 'shakedown' on the *River Clyde*.

• • •

A scene inside the dismantled fortress of Seddelbahr. An Allied warship is also visible in the Dardanelles Straits in the background.

YOUR PAL
IN THE
TRENCHES
IS WAITING TO
SHAKE HANDS
WITH YOU.

JAMES WALKER (DUBLIN) LTD   30000-H.M.S.O.

A British recruitment poster from 1915 promoting the concept of 'Pals' battalions where friends who enlisted together were promised that they would also serve together.

THE
DUBLIN PALS
AND SUVLA BAY

...

THE BIRTH OF D COMPANY

KIRETCH TEPE, GALLIPOLI, 21 AUGUST 1915. IT WAS MADNESS, OF COURSE, TO CHARGE UP the slope like that with bayonets, knowing that the enemy were waiting there with artillery and machine-guns. But madness and war so often go hand in hand. And charging the Turkish lines had to be a better bet than staying put in that hellhole where the Dublin Pals, increasingly bereft of ammunition, had few options but to try and catch the incoming hand grenades and hurl them back before they exploded. Cricket this was not.

Almost exactly one year earlier, many of the men who charged at Kiretch Tepe that day had assembled on the rugby pitch at Lansdowne Road to participate in a two-hour-long military drill. Just days after the declaration of war on Germany, the Irish Rugby Football Union had invited the sportsmen of Ireland to form a Volunteer Corps 'to defend their country, if the necessity should arise'.[56] Over 100 amateur Irish rugby players showed up for that first drill on 24 August 1914, marching under the austere gaze of the Kilkenny-born Sergeant Major Michael Stacey of the Dublin University Officers' Training Corps.[57] It was a remarkable assemblage of barristers, doctors, solicitors, clerks, engineers, stockbrokers, bankers, civil servants and other professionals, representing the cream of Dublin society.

The men returned to Lansdowne Road the following evening, in greater number, and did it all again. And the next night and the next, so that by the time General Sir Bryan Mahon, commander of the new 10th (Irish) Division, called in for an inspection on 31 August, there were already 250 men in the corps. The General was impressed by the speed at which they learned. As one commentator put it, 'they executed their movements with precision notable for men who had been only a week under training.'[58]

In early September, the IRFU's Volunteer Corps gathered in Lansdowne Road for an address by Frank 'Chicken' Browning, a former Irish international player and President of the Irish Rugby Football Union.[59] Standing alongside Mr Browning was

• • •

Recruits for D Company of the 7th Royal
Dublin Fusiliers assemble at Lansdowne
Road in September 1914. Standing at the
front of the men are Frank 'Chicken'
Browning, President of the Irish Rugby
Football Union, and Sergeant Major
Allen Guest, who went on to the Curragh
as their Company Sergeant Major.

Lieutenant Colonel Geoffrey Downing, a former captain of the Monkstown 1st XV, who was to command the newly formed 7th (Service) Battalion in the Royal Dublin Fusiliers.

Colonel Downing informed the rugby players that the 7th was to be a 'Pals' Battalion so that, as *The Irish Times* put it, 'friends who wish to serve together may enlist by Sections, Platoons, or Companies, and so far as possible, they will be kept together'.[60] Furthermore, D Company within the 7th Battalion was to be exclusively reserved for the IRFU volunteers. By the close of the meeting, every man present had signed up to serve in D Company 'with payment and allowance at army rates'. Most refused the option of an officer's commission, insisting that they wanted to remain on an equal rank with their peers.

Many were intimately connected with Trinity College, Dublin. The Offaly-born barrister Ernest Julian was not only the university's Reid Professor of Criminal Law but also coached the University of Dublin Boat Club.[61] Gerald 'Billie' Bradstreet, the only son and heir of Sir Edward Bradstreet of Clontarf, had captained Trinity's 1st XV during a season in which they were unbeaten.[62] Poole Hickman, a barrister from Kilmore House, near Knock, County Clare, had captained the Wanderers in 1908.[63]

Ernest Hamilton, whose father founded the acclaimed White House department store in Portrush, County Antrim, had proved himself a zippy three-quarter and goal kicker when he studied medicine at Trinity College. Another Trinity medical student was Alex Crichton from Enniscrone, County Sligo, a kinsman of the whiskey-distilling Jamesons. He could boast to his classmates of a medical tradition that went back to his great-grandfather Sir Alexander Crichton, a pioneer in psychiatry who served as personal physician to Tsar Alexander I of Russia in the early 1800s. Also present were two of the Findlater brothers, scions of the Dublin wine merchant firm, namely Charlie, a 44-year-old engineer, and Herbert, a 42-year-old solicitor.[64]

Not everyone who joined D Company was a Trinity graduate. Albert Wilkin was the 31-year-old manager of a boot and shoe shop in Clontarf where he played rugby.[65] His father grew up on a farm in Cavan while his mother's family manufactured corduroy and other textiles in Dublin's Liberties.

Jack Boyd, who also played rugby for Clontarf, had similarly come south from Cavan and worked as a clerk in the Department of Agriculture. Walter Appleyard was a clerk with the Irish Land Commission in Upper Merrion Street. Joe Brady from Naas, County Kildare, ran the billiard rooms at Parkgate Street in Dublin, for which he pocketed a tidy annual salary of £500.[66] Jasper Brett, a solicitor from Dún Laoghaire, had earned his first international cap for Ireland earlier in the year.

No sooner had the 'Dublin Pals' Battalion been formed than it was sent to the Curragh Camp to begin intensive training. On the morning of 16 September, accompanied by the band of the Royal Irish Constabulary, the 7th Battalion marched along Nassau Street, through College Green and down Dame Street all the way to the Curragh-bound trains at Kingsbridge (Heuston) Station. Large crowds cheered them every step of the way, waving handkerchiefs, fluttering makeshift Union Jacks from the windows and belting out verse and chorus of 'It's a Long, Long Way to Tipperary'.

With so many well-known rugby players and society dons in its ranks, D Company instantly became the talk of the crowd. Initially known as 'The Footballers', some wag thought of a pun on the 2nd Battalion's nickname 'Old Toughs' and D Company was rechristened the 'Toffs'.[67]

Over the coming weeks, hundreds of new recruits joined the 7th Battalion. Among those assigned to D Company was 19-year-old Douglas Gunning who was working in a bank in Sligo when he decided to cycle 50 miles to his home in Enniskillen in order to join up alongside his older brother Cecil. The brothers were accomplished swimmers, oarsmen and rugby players.

Hugh Crawford Pollock from Clonskeagh, who had played for Wanderers alongside Poole Hickman, came all the way back from Sumatra where he was an assistant manager with Messrs Harrison & Crossfield's Tea Company.[68]

One of D Company's more unlikely latter-day recruits was Charles Frederick Ball, known as Fred to his friends, who was born in Leicestershire in 1879. The son of an English chemist, he turned his mind to botany and by 1906 he had become a sub-foreman of the Royal Botanic Gardens at Kew in London. That autumn, Sir Frederick Moore, Head Keeper of the Royal Botanic Gardens at Glasnevin informed the curator at Kew that he was looking for an outdoor foreman. The latter recommended Fred Ball as 'an excellent fellow in every way, gentlemanly, quiet, good-looking', and offered to send him over 'if you'd like to sample him'.[69] Sir Frederick duly recruited the chemist's son and within just seven months Fred had been promoted to principal assistant at Glasnevin. Amongst those working alongside him were the artist Rose Barton and Mary Helen Graves, a half-sister of Robert Graves, the soon-to-be war poet.[70] During his annual leave, Fred Ball invariably went to the Alps in Switzerland and northern Italy to study Alpine gems. In 1911, he and fellow Alpine plant enthusiast Herbert Cowley went on a mission to Bulgaria. Sponsored by Pierce O'Mahony, one of Parnell's most loyal supporters, the two men were personal guests of King Ferdinand, later to become one of the Kaiser's allies. As well as looking after the gardens in Glasnevin, Ball was editor of the magazine *Irish Gardening*.[71]

A fine cricketer, golfer and all-round sportsman, Fred Ball's friends generally considered him fearless. However, somebody else thought otherwise. According to Sir Frederick Moore's son, Ball was the recipient of a white feather which was sent to him at the gardens in Glasnevin. He took it seriously although, when he enlisted in late November, even *The Irish Times* acknowledged that 'it came as rather a surprise to hear that Mr C. F. Ball is on the warpath'. In December 1914, shortly after he married his girlfriend Alice, Fred Ball made his way to the Curragh Camp to commence training with D Company.

At the Curragh, the men engaged in endless musketry training, trench digging and route marching. In the middle of October, a correspondent for the *Dublin Evening Mail* called down to see how the 'Toffs' were getting on. 'It was difficult to believe,' he wrote, 'that the majority of the men were civilians like the rest of us only a month ago. They marched and countermarched, and formed fours; and wheeled and counterwheeled, and deployed and performed all the other evolutions of the parade ground with, so far as I could judge, the smartness and certainty of veterans... No cursing, swearing, jack-booted, bullying Prussian non-commissioned officer could have his men in better shape or fit.'[72]

The men did get the occasional break, so that they could concentrate on the more important things in life, namely scrumming down and charging at try lines. On 17 October, Frank Browning refereed a match between D Company and other members of the Volunteer Corps at Lansdowne Road. The crowd that howed up was so big it felt like an international rugby match. Ernest Hamilton and Jasper Brett were among those who lined out for D Company and Hamilton kicked a penalty home in what was ultimately a drawn match at 8 points all.[73] Brett transferred to the Machine-Gun Section of the 7th Battalion's B Company in December 1914.

Another time they marched to Woodbrook, near Bray, the home of Sir Stanley Cochrane, heir to the Cantrell & Cochrane soft drinks fortune. Woodbrook had long been a mecca for sportsmen and artists; Jasper Brett was among those who played on Sir Stanley's highly regarded cricket team. The battalion camped at Woodbrook overnight and then marched back to the Curragh in full battle gear next day.[74]

In early 1915, the Dublin Pals returned to the capital city, where they were stationed at the Royal Barracks (later Collins Barracks). It was not yet clear where they would be sent, but the glum news of the massive fatalities suffered by the Irish regiments in Gallipoli that April must have inclined some to wager that a trip to the Mediterranean was on the cards.

THE INVASION OF SUVLA BAY

On the last day of April 1915, the 7th Battalion marched down the quays to the North Wall — once again 'lustily cheered' all the way — and boarded a troopship bound for Holyhead. From Wales, they made their way to Basingstoke in southern England, where the bulk of the 10th (Irish) Division was by then concentrated. They would remain in Basingstoke for the next ten weeks, engaging in still more training exercises.

On 10 July, the 7th Battalion steamed out of Devonport on the transport ship *Alaunia* and headed south. Captain Arthur Rostron, the *Alaunia*'s skipper, had won widespread praise three years earlier when, as master of the ocean liner *Carpathia*, he led the rescue effort for the survivors of the *Titanic* disaster.

During the two-week voyage, as Douglas Gunning later recalled, the battalion was 'stuck at the bottom of the boat, but good food, salt water baths and sea air had already combined to make us feel fit'. For Gunning, the highlights included swimming races, majestic sunsets, ice-cold oranges from a refrigerator and porpoises gliding in the moonlight. At Alexandria, they stopped for long enough to march around the old harbour and entertain the Egyptians with a loud rendition of 'Tipperary'. Five days later, on 25 July, they disembarked on the island of Lemnos where thousands of Allied soldiers were now gathering in advance of a major new offensive on Gallipoli.

Three months had passed since the costly battle of Seddelbahr had left over 1,000

• • •

British WWI troops at Suvla Bay,
Gallipoli, Turkey, 1915.

Irishmen dead or wounded. Cape Helles may have been captured, but the campaign
was not going well and the Allies were pinned down at both Cape Helles and Anzac
Cove. As General Godley, commander of the New Zealand and Australian Division,
put it in a letter to his cousin in County Leitrim, 'I do not suppose in history, that
anything so utterly mismanaged by the British Government will ever be recorded.'[75]
Put simply, the Allies had completely underestimated the terrain and climate of the
Gallipoli peninsula, as well as the tenacity of the Turkish soldiers who defended it.

The Dublin Pals were to take part in one last push, known as the August Offensive. Under the command of General Sir Frederick Stopford, three divisions of British
soldiers — including the 10th (Irish) — were to land at Suvla Bay on the west coast of
Gallipoli. The game plan was to capture the Sari Bair ridge, the high ground that dominated the centre of the peninsula, and so break the deadlock. If that could be achieved,
as the British War Office blindly hoped, then the Turks could at last be ousted from

Gallipoli, enabling the Royal Navy to sail up the Dardanelles, lay siege to Constantinople and knock the Ottoman Empire out of the contest.

On Friday 6 August 1915, the 6th and 7th Battalions of the Royal Dublin Fusiliers boarded a fleet of four steamers and set off for Suvla Bay. Elsewhere, eight battalions of Royal Inniskilling Fusiliers, Royal Munster Fusiliers, Royal Irish Fusiliers and the Royal Irish Regiment were amongst those boarding other Gallipoli-bound ships.

Shortly after midnight on 7 August, the five officers and 300 men who constituted D Company got their first view of Gallipoli. Through the darkness, Captain Poole Hickman, their company commander, watched the flashes of the big guns and listened to the rattle of distant musketry. It was, he wrote, 'the first indication to us that we were within the war zone'.

At 5.30am, two companies — A and C — began landing men on shore at Suvla Bay. The newcomers were greeted by a barrage of shrapnel from the Turkish guns mounted on the towering heights above, killing one — their first casualty — and wounding 11 more.

Captain Hickman landed D Company soon afterwards. Douglas Gunning described the scene. 'We could hear the boom boom and see the flash from Turkish guns coming from the big ridge of mountains, shells bursting, our men landing from the lighters and stretcher bearers bringing down and collecting wounded on the beach. The whole bay was quivering with the vibration… Somehow, we got on to the beach safely. It was remarkable how quickly you got used to it and soon we never bothered ducking unless the shell was quite close. I must say the discipline stood to us marvellously… for we were more or less stupefied.'[76]

At 8am, the Dublin Pals were ordered to advance. Their objective was to take control of a hill three and a half miles from where they had landed. Their load was lighter than it should have been. In one of those bureaucratic botch-ups that was to be a hallmark of the Dardanelles campaign, the bulk of their artillery pieces had been sent to France instead of Gallipoli.

'We had not advanced 100 yards,' wrote Poole Hickman, 'when we were greeted with a perfect hail of shrapnel. And shrapnel is not a pleasant thing. You hear a whistle through the air, then a burst, and everything within a space of 200 yards by 100 yards from where the shrapnel burst is liable to be hit. The wounds inflicted are dreadful — deep, big, irregular gashes, faces battered out of recognition, limbs torn away.'[77]

Having initially taken cover, Hickman realised he had little option but to urge his company on. In intense heat, and under constant attack from snipers and artillery, the Irishmen gradually worked their way eastwards through a landscape of ploughed fields, dry salt lakes and dense hedgerows. Major Richard Harrison, an aspiring pilot, led the way, waving a green flag tied to a stick.[78]

By the time they reached the Turkish trenches at the bottom of the hill, Major Harrison's line comprised A and D Companies, along with some of the Inniskillings. The Turks assigned to defend the hill had retreated to the summit. The Dublin Pals fixed bayonets and, roaring at full volume, charged upwards. The surviving Turks skedaddled and the hill was taken. Poole Hickman described it as 'a magnificent performance' and Colonel

. . .

Preparing for the advance on
Chocolate Hill from Suvla Bay.

Downing, commander of the 7th Battalion, likewise declared to his wife, 'they did splendidly, and I am so proud of them.'[79] Initially christened 'Fort Dublin', the newly conquered mount of dark, rich brown earth was soon to become known as Chocolate Hill.

The Pals had achieved their objective, but such elation was much tempered by the human cost. The 7th Battalion suffered over 100 casualties on the first day, including 22 from D Company. Lieutenant Ernest Julian, the 36-year-old Trinity professor, was shot in the back during the final assault and died of his injuries the following day on the hospital ship *Valdivia*. Buried at sea, he was one of 25 Irish barristers killed in the Great War.

On the summit of Chocolate Hill, the Pals awaited the arrival of much-needed water to quench their fierce thirst. Each man carried two days' rations, consisting of a tin of bully beef, tea, sugar, biscuits and a few Oxo tablets. When Poole Hickman tucked into a biscuit at 1.30am on the Sunday morning, it occurred to him that it was the first thing he'd eaten since their arrival on Gallipoli 24 hours earlier.[80] As they awaited the dawn, Private Walter Appleyard was counting his lucky stars that he had not been hit when a bullet passed through the leg of his trousers. As it happened, he didn't have many lucky stars left to count.

Turkish high command was by now completely aware of the Allied invasion and dispatched two divisions to forestall any further British advance. The Turks were not in great shape — three months of incessant fighting had taken its toll and, like the Allies, their rank and file were plagued with disease — but, in their vast favour, it transpired that the British invaders had almost no understanding of the landscape in which they now found themselves. Inaccurate maps served to break up any form of organisation, so that by dawn on Sunday 8 August, the exhausted soldiers were scattered in isolated pockets, separated from one another by a maze of tangled gullies and gorse-covered foothills.

The grand advance fizzled out. And then the Turks launched their counter-attack. Unable to provide a cohesive defence, the Allies were slowly but assuredly pushed backwards.

Chocolate Hill was by no means secure. On Monday 9 August, less than 48 hours after the hill was captured, Lieutenant Colonel FAR Greer, commander of the 6th Royal Irish Fusiliers, was standing near the summit talking with his 35-year-old adjutant, Captain James Cecil Johnston. Captain Johnston lived at Magheramenagh Castle, near Belleek, County Cavan, and was a close confidant of the Earl of Aberdeen, the Lord Lieutenant of Ireland. As the two men spoke, a Turkish shell screamed in upon them, smashing the Colonel's arm to pulp before landing on Captain Johnston who was, as one witness put it, blown 'literally to pieces'.[81] By 12 August, the Turks had swept back onto Chocolate Hill.

THE CHARGE AT KIRETCH TEPE

The Allies now switched their focus to the Kiretch Tepe Ridge that dominated the north of Suvla Bay.[82] Under the overall command of Sir Bryan Mahon, five battalions from the 10th (Irish) Division attacked the high ridge at 7.30am on 9 August. The 7th and 8th Battalions of the Royal Munster Fusiliers had also advanced along the ridge the previous day and were already entrenched. The Dubs now pushed as far as they could before a combination of thirst and fatigue brought them to a standstill. The initial high was rapidly wearing off as the Irishmen combated the blazing hot sun and the hostile alien landscape.

While the Generals pondered the options, the men were ordered to dig in on the ridge and await further orders. Digging in was no easy feat. Most of Kiretch Tepe was rock and even the earthy parts were characterised by a thick mesh of plant roots, much to the curiosity of the botanist Fred Ball.

As Turkish snipers were all around them, randomly pinging limbs and faces, some form of defensive wall was urgently required. The Pals began to gather up rocks, breaking up the ground where they could, and constructed stone walls not dissimilar to those found on the Aran Islands.

D Company was in the thick of it. Four days had passed since their arrival but, Poole Hickman wrote, 'all this time we never had even our boots off, a shave, or a wash, as even the dirtiest water was greedily drunk on the hill, where the sun's rays beat piti-lessly down all day long, and where the rotting corpses of the Turks created a damnably offensive smell. That is one of the worst features here — unburied bodies and flies — but the details are more gruesome than my pen could depict.'[83]

For five long days the men held their ground on Kiretch Tepe and waited. Scorched by the sun, their thirst was worsened by the hot air that drew the salt from the nearby salt lake and blew it into their faces, so that every man had white scum around his lips. A human chain attempted to pass buckets of water up and down the slopes but, subject to continuous sniping and shellfire, such supplies were exceedingly limited. In the midst of it all, a mailbag stuffed with memories from home arrived.

On the sixth day — Sunday 15 August — the 7th Battalion was ordered to renew their advance.[84] As they clambered along the ridge, a Turkish sniper fired three shots at Colonel Downing, catching him in the foot with the third. While the Colonel was stretchered off to hospital, Major Harrison assumed command. They took up positions beneath the crest of the ridge and entrenched themselves as best they could.

There was fresh horror come the dawn on Monday 16 August when the Turks began a ferocious assault, lobbing hand grenades into their lines. The Dubliners had nothing to retaliate with but the stones around them. Some tried heaving large boulders over the crest to roll upon the Turkish lines. Others endeavoured to catch the grenades before they exploded, and throw them back. Albert Wilkin, the shoe shop manager from Clontarf, caught four grenades as if they were cricket balls and flung them back over the crest. The fifth one exploded as he caught it and blew him to shreds.[85] Seven days after his miracle on Chocolate Hill, Walter Appleyard was also engaged in that blackest of games when a sniper shot him through the heart.[86]

In the meantime, Major Harrison decided that, in order to win Kiretch Tepe, his men must charge the Turkish bombers on the ridge. Nobody can have fancied their chances, but orders were orders. With a guttural roar from the depths of his soul, Captain Poole Hickman, the former Wanderers skipper, led his men forward, with fixed bayonets at the ready.

The chargers had barely covered five yards when a Turkish bomb exploded in the middle of them and blew Poole Hickman apart.[87] Nearly every man with him was either killed or wounded. The Sumatra tea trader Hugh Pollock died alongside his old Wanderers captain.[88] So too did Herbert Findlater, solicitor, yachtsman, actor, sportsman and father of two small boys. Alex Crichton, the doctor's son from Sligo, also fell; his nephew and namesake would later become managing director of Jameson. Jack Boyd, the rugby player from Cavan, died of his wounds the following day. The by now capless Major Harrison was still waving his green flag above his head and urging the men forward when a grenade struck him and exploded on contact.

Eleven D Company officers and 54 men were killed or wounded during the charge, and a further 13 were missing. Only four men managed to crawl back unhurt. 'It was a mad-man's charge, but on the other side a very brave one,' remarked one of those who witnessed it.[89]

To his shock, Ernest Hamilton discovered he was now the only D Company officer still alive. The medical student from County Antrim had been badly wounded by a hand grenade during the charge but made it back to the relative safety of the ridge.

As darkness fell, the surviving Irishmen maintained their position beneath the crest of Kiretch Tepe. Their ammunition supply was dangerously low and they were engaged in sporadic but constant bayonet skirmishes with the Turks. As one survivor put it, 'the only thing to keep our spirits up was an odd song and a smoke from a Woodbine'.[90] When reinforcements arrived, Lieutenant Hamilton was ordered to evacuate his men to the safety of the Allied dug-outs a mile back. Morale was not helped that evening when two shells landed on the men as they ate their dinner, killing one and taking the leg off another.[91]

On Tuesday morning, Lieutenant Hamilton took a roll-call and counted over 100 members of D Company absent. 'That evening', recalled Douglas Gunning, 'we looked at the sun setting in the west and thought of home. Although we couldn't, I'm sure a "blub" would have made us feel better.'

As he made his way to a hospital ship, Hamilton handed command to Company Sergeant Major William Kee from Meenagrove, Ballybofey, County Donegal. He later penned a letter home, published in *The Irish Times* on 16 September, in which he detailed the events leading up to the fateful charge. 'If you were ever proud of D Company, you should have seen them in this action', he wrote. 'Every one of them were heroes… Dublin should be proud to own such men.'[92]

When the news of D Company's virtual extermination reached Dublin, complete shock set in. Nobody had imagined that men like Ernest Julian and Poole Hickman could ever die in war. These men were, after all, not professional soldiers. They were rugby players, students, barristers and cyclists. Yet die they did and, as the writer Katherine Tynan recalled, 'blow after blow fell day after day on one's heart… For the first time came bitterness, for we felt that their lives had been thrown away and that their heroism had gone unrecognised.' By the end of August, the Irish capital seemed to be 'full of mourning' with black-veiled widows and mothers at every turn.

• • •

This is the landscape where the Dublin
Pals took on the Ottomans. The view
looks north across Suvla Bay, with the line
of Kiretch Tepe Sirt in the distance and
the Salt Lake in front of it.

THE BATTLE OF SCIMITAR HILL

On the afternoon of Saturday 21 August, five days after the charge at Kiretch Tepe, those members of D Company still fit for service were summoned to take part in what would be the last hurrah of the Gallipoli campaign.

Their destination was Scimitar Hill, a prominent rise overlooking Suvla Bay, midway between Chocolate Hill and the Anafarta Ridge. The 6th Battalion of the Royal Dublin Fusiliers had actually captured it on the day they landed two weeks earlier but, as with Chocolate Hill, the Allies subsequently relinquished control to the Turks.[93]

Over 14,000 Allied soldiers were involved in the battle, including most of the 29th Division and the veterans of Seddelbahr.[94] The plan was to capture Scimitar Hill, as well as some other hills, and so forge a direct connection with the ANZAC forces to the south.

Another massive bombardment by the Allied fleet and land batteries was unleashed and the Turks appeared to have been quietened as D Company advanced nervously across the open plains. And then the Turks opened fire.

'Good Lord!' recalled one survivor. 'They didn't half plop the shells into us — shrapnel, high-explosive and lyddite shells were bursting in absolute hundreds in front, above, and behind us, and now and then, to add intensity to their fire, numerous land mines blew up, throwing men and rocks into the air and blinding us with sand.'[95]

Those who survived the onslaught ran through the smoke to the end of the plain and flung themselves onto the ground. Heavy rifle fire picked off man after man as they ran. Charlie Findlater was shot in the leg, but amongst those still in the fight were Fred Ball, Jasper Brett, Douglas Gunning and Billie Bradstreet.

Meanwhile, sensing yet another Gallipoli disaster, the Allied commanders whistled up the five brigades of the 2nd Mounted Division from the safety of their reserve position at Lala Baba on the south of Suvla Bay. On foot, these 5,000 men were ordered to march in formation almost two miles across the dry salt lake into the billowing smoke. The Turkish artillerymen could not believe their eyes and showered them with high-explosive shells. The initial objective for the Mounted Division had been to take Chocolate Hill. However, when it became clear that the battle for Scimitar Hill was not going the Allies' way, the five brigadiers were instructed to finish the job.

One of these brigadiers was Thomas Pakenham, 5th Earl of Longford. Born in Dublin in 1864, Lord Longford succeeded to the earldom at the age of 23. During the Anglo-Boer War, he led the ill-fated Imperial Yeomanry, otherwise known as the Dublin Hunt Squadron, whom the Boers managed to trap outside the town of Lindley in 1900. Four hundred of Britain and Ireland's hunting elite were captured in an instant, including Lords Longford, Ennismore, Donoughmore, Leitrim and the future Lord Craigavon. The whiskey baronet Sir John Power was among 21 fatalities in the same action.

Fifteen years later, Lord Longford grimaced at the prospect of another military failure being notched up against him. As Brigadier General of the 2nd South Midland Mounted Brigade, he led his men through the haze, stormed Scimitar Hill and seized control of the hillcrest. However, the Turks had mounted heavy-duty artillery on a nearby hill, and rapidly began shelling Lord Longford and his men. Realising the end was nigh, his lordship apparently turned to one of his officers and said, 'Don't keep ducking, Fred. It upsets the men and it doesn't do any good.' When one of his ancestors was killed in battle against the Americans in 1812, the Royal Navy preserved his corpse in brandy and shipped his body home to be buried with his Pakenham kinsmen in Ireland. The 5th Earl would not be afforded such a gallant finale; his body was never found.[96]

The 1st Battalion of the Royal Inniskilling Fusiliers also made several bold attempts to take Scimitar Hill but in each instance they were driven back. One of these assaults was led by Captain Gerald 'Micky' O'Sullivan of Kingstown (Dún Laoghaire), County Dublin, who had just been awarded a Victoria Cross for showing immense courage in an earlier battle. He rallied 50 men behind him for the charge; a solitary sergeant limped home alive. Like Lord Longford, Micky O'Sullivan's body would not be found. Nor would the Allies ever regain control of Scimitar Hill.

The madness continued elsewhere. As darkness fell, Sir John Milbanke, Colonel of the Sherwood Rangers, dryly informed his junior officers that he had received his orders from brigade headquarters. 'We are to take a redoubt but I don't know where it is and don't think anyone else knows either, but in any case we are to go ahead and attack any Turks we meet.' Sir John was married to Amelia Crichton, a niece of the Earl of Erne, and spent much of his time at Mullaboden near Naas, County Kildare, from where he regularly hunted with the Kildare and Meath Hounds. He had won a Victoria Cross in the Anglo-Boer War when, under heavy fire, he about-turned his horse, scooped a fallen comrade onto his mount and galloped to safety. In the battle of Scimitar Hill, he advanced into the night, as ordered, and died at the head of his men.[97]

It was not until after midnight that the Allied commanders finally agreed that enough was enough and called off the attack. Over 5,000 men had been killed or wounded for almost no territorial gain.[98] Many succumbed to flames as gorse fire, ignited by bursting shells, tore through the landscape. Aside from exhausting the Turks, who suffered 2,300 casualties, not a single objective had been achieved. It simply underlined the fact that the Gallipoli campaign had been a near-total disaster. Over a quarter of a million Allied soldiers were dead, wounded or missing, and yet the Allies had never got much further than the beaches on which they landed.

It spelled the end of Sir Ian Hamilton's military career.[99] Winston Churchill also lost his job as First Sea Lord and, apparently in penance for his failure, spent six months commanding a battalion on the Western Front. Ever resourceful, he set out with a portable bathtub and a water-boiler.

The only undeniable success of the campaign was the evacuation at its conclusion whereby, with the aid of Admiral de Robeck's fleet, 90,000 troops and over 200 guns left Gallipoli without a single loss of life.

The 7th Battalion's campaign concluded shortly after midnight on 30 September when the 10th (Irish) Division left Gallipoli for Lemnos. After seven gruesome weeks, just 79 of the original members of D Company were still available for active service. A third of the battalion had been killed outright or died of their injuries. Many more fell victim to the extremes of heat and cold, contracting the deadly diseases that flourished amid the decomposing corpses, insect plagues and putrid waters.

WALTER D'ANCIE APPLEYARD

CF BALL

JOHN BOYD

LIEUTENANT COLONEL
GEOFFREY DOWNING

HERBERT FINDLATER

CHARLES FINDLATER

POOLE HICKMAN

ERNEST JULIAN

GERALD 'BILLIE' BRADSTREET

FRANK BROWNING

ALEX G CRICHTON

DOUGLAS GUNNING

CECIL GUNNING

ERNEST HAMILTON

WILLIAM KEE

Ernest Hamilton survived his wounded leg and the dysentery that followed but, traumatised by what he had seen, he became a chronic alcoholic. In April 1917, he was court-martialled for unspecified misconduct on the Western Front and dismissed from the army.[100] He was among 55 former members of D Company who attended a series of reunion dinners in Jury's Hotel, Dublin, in the mid-1930s.[101] During the Second World War, he worked with the American Red Cross in Northern Ireland. He died at the Royal Victoria Hospital in Belfast in 1946, aged 51.

Sergeant Major William Kee, the 26-year-old from Donegal who briefly commanded D Company, later became a hero on the Western Front, winning a Military Cross shortly before he was killed at the Somme in March 1918.[102]

The Somme also claimed the life of Douglas Gunning. The former banker sailed home from Gallipoli after the debacle of Scimitar Hill, riddled with dysentery.[103] His father died just weeks after his return to Enniskillen; Douglas helped carry his coffin. In June 1916, he rejoined the army as a sub-lieutenant in the 6th Inniskillings. On 1 July he was leading his platoon forward at the Somme when a shell exploded directly on top of him.[104]

Charlie Findlater, engineer and cyclist, was one of over 100 Royal Dublin Fusiliers killed in the battle of the Ancre at the end of the Somme campaign. His oldest brother Alex, who served with the Royal Army Medical Corps, earned the DSO at Chocolate Hill on 29 September 1915 when he crossed over 200 yards of open ground under intense shellfire to help two wounded men. One of them was beyond help but he saved the other man's life. After the war, the doctor returned to a hero's welcome at his home in England.

Joe Brady, the renowned billiard player, had excelled as a stretcher-bearer during the first part of the campaign, but contracted enteric fever and was sent home on 20 August. Promoted to the rank of Sergeant, he transferred to the 11th (Reserve) Battalion in Dublin and was placed in command of the guardroom at Wellington Barracks. In November 1916, a court-martial prisoner under his custody escaped and Sergeant Brady was himself court-martialled for negligence. He was found not guilty but transferred to the 1st Battalion and went to France where he was killed on 1 March 1917.[105]

For reasons unknown, Billie Bradstreet, who had captained the Trinity rugby team, stayed on at Gallipoli after his fellow Pals departed. During the August offensive, he earned considerable respect when he rallied the despondent men after the loss of Poole Hickman and the other officers. He was killed at Sulajik Farm in the Suvla Plain on 7 December 1915. Ironically, he was gazetted a Captain on the very same day, but that can have been scant consolation to Sir Edward Bradstreet who, having lost his only son and heir, was to be the last of the Bradstreet baronets.[106]

Not everyone died a hero. Second Lieutenant Jasper Brett, who played rugby for Ireland before the war, went on from Gallipoli to fight the Bulgarians in Serbia. Suffering from severe shell-shock and rampant enteritis, he was dispatched back to England where he was diagnosed insane and sent to Latchmere Hospital, an institution in Richmond, Surrey, specifically designated for shell-shocked officers. Discharged as 'medically unfit,' he returned to Ireland with his father and moved back to the family home in Dún Laoghaire. On 4 February 1917, the young man made his way into the Khyber Pass tunnel just east of Dalkey Station in County Dublin, lay down on the line and awaited the coming train.[107]

Fred Ball did not survive. Between the bombs and the bayonet charges, he spent much of his first four weeks examining the peninsula's flora. He sent a number of seeds back to the Botanic Gardens in Glasnevin for cultivation, including some acorns from the Gallipoli oaks. Numerous seedlings continue to grow at Glasnevin from the seeds he gathered in the vicinity of Suvla Bay. He was killed on 13 September 1915. A friend saw him just before he died, sheltering behind a rock, digging up weeds with his bayonet. His botanical colleagues would honour him by affixing his name to the *Escallonia C. F. Ball*, a hybrid that he himself created, which was characterised by dark green leaves, rich red flowers and a propensity to attract bumble bees.

WOMEN OF BRITAIN SAY – "GO!"

Published by the PARLIAMENTARY RECRUITING COMMITTEE, London. Poster No. 75   Printed by HILL, SIFFKEN & Co. (L.P.A. Ltd.), Grafton Works, London, N.   W. 3689 50 M. 5/15.

ROUGH FITZGERALD

AND THE ORDER OF THE

WHITE FEATHER

...

IT IS SAID THAT FRED BALL JOINED THE ARMY IN RESPONSE TO A WHITE FEATHER WHICH arrived at the Royal Botanic Gardens in Glasnevin addressed to him. This dark gesture meant that somebody had directly accused him of either being a coward or otherwise shirking his duty to defend the Empire with his physical being. The concept was based on the old cock-fighting lore that a cockerel with a white feather in its tail is a coward because 'it is a proof he is not of the true game breed'.[108]

The idea received a huge boost in 1902 with the publication of AE Mason's best-selling redemptory novel *The Four Feathers* about Lieutenant Harry Faversham, a British officer who resigns from the army on the eve of the 1882 Mahdist War in Sudan, only to be presented with four white feathers by his three best pals and his fiancée.

It was with Mason's book in mind that Admiral Charles Uniacke-Penrose-Fitzgerald founded the Order of the White Feather in August 1914. Born in 1851, 'Rough' Fitzgerald, as his naval colleagues called him, was descended from the Knights of Glin and Kerry, and grew up in Corkbeg, County Cork. The castle, town and lands of Corkbeg had been granted to a Geraldine ancestor in the late 17th century. The Admiral's maternal grandfather was the Rev Robert Austin, prebendary of St Colman's Cathedral in Cloyne, County Cork.

Rough Fitzgerald's naval career got off to a promising start when, having just joined the Royal Navy, he boarded HMS *Victory* at Portsmouth in 1854 at the age of 13. He became one of the most highly regarded sea commanders of his generation and made many astute predictions, including that the Americans would be the first people to reach the moon.[109] However, he earned the wrath of some traditionalists when he launched a successful campaign to modernise Her Majesty's fleet, calling for the abolition of sails and masts.

In 1882, Rough married Henrietta Hewson, a clergyman's daughter from Dunganstown near Kilbride in County Wicklow.[110] Meanwhile, his older brother, Sir Robert Uniacke-Penrose-Fitzgerald, who owned over 6,000 acres in counties Cork and Laois, had become a director of the Property Defence Association in Ireland. A celebrated rower in the 1860s, Sir Robert served as Conservative MP for Cambridge for 21 years and, in 1896, he was created 1st Baronet of Corkbeg and Lisquinlan in County Cork.[111]

Rough's career floundered when he sided with Admiral Sir George Tryon, commander of the Mediterranean fleet, who advocated that there should be no need for quite so much signalling between ships if captains would simply use more initiative. Their campaign fell apart in 1887 following one of the most astonishing cock-ups in naval history. As his entire fleet steamed in two parallel columns off the coast of Lebanon, Admiral Tryon inexplicably ordered the leading ships to turn inwards. With perfect precision the *Victoria* and the *Camperdown* did just that and struck each other with the enormous rams affixed to their bows. Admiral Tryon was one of 358 men on the *Victoria* who drowned in the disaster. 'It is all my fault' were his unquestionably accurate last words. Among the *Victoria*'s few survivors was John Jellicoe, later Commander in Chief of the British Grand Fleet at the battle of Jutland.

During the early 20th century, Admiral Rough Fitzgerald — by now retired but as fit as ever — continued to be outspoken on naval policy and was a frequent critic of the reforms introduced by Jacky Fisher, the First Sea Lord.

When he founded the Order of the White Feather, he did so with support from Baroness Orczy, the British-Hungarian author of *The Scarlet Pimpernel*, and the antisuffrage campaigner Mary Ward. The Order also managed to gather the backing of prominent suffragists such as Emmeline Pankhurst and her daughter Christabel.[112] Collectively, the game plan was to bring shame on all 'slackers' and 'loafers', as Fitzgerald described young men who had not joined the armed services. When a man was espied not wearing a military uniform, a woman — often a pretty one — would present him with a white feather.

The campaign had the desired effect. Hundreds, if not thousands, of unfortunate young men were duly humiliated into service by these zealous 'feather girls'. The Irish got a taste of them when a group of emigrants boarding an America-bound ship at Liverpool found themselves subject to a large crowd who jeered them as 'cowards' and 'traitors' and showered them with white feathers.[113]

The situation got out of hand. The government found that so many public servants and state employees were being cajoled into enlisting that Reginald McKenna, Britain's Home Secretary, had to commission thousands of badges marked 'King and Country' to show that such men were off-limits for the white feather brigade. More badges had to be manufactured for war veterans who had returned from the front lines sick or wounded.

But there were still plenty of awkward moments when soldiers home on leave were given white feathers. Seaman George Samson was given one as he made his way, dressed in civvies, to pick up a Victoria Cross he'd won for helping Commander Unwin secure the barges at V Beach while the Munsters and the Dubs were being annihilated at Gallipoli.

The writer Compton Mackenzie, author of *Whisky Galore*, who served with the Royal Marines and founded the Aegean Intelligence Service, objected to these 'idiotic young women… using white feathers to get rid of boyfriends of whom they were tired'. Wilfred Owen also slammed the campaign in the final lines of his magnificent but grizzly poem 'Dulce et Decorum Est'. But perhaps the perfect response came from the pacifist Archibald Fenner Brockway who received so many white feathers that he turned them into a fan.

• • •

Women in the east end of London hoist the 'white feather' flag deriding those not enlisting in a time of war with the message 'Serve your country or wear this'.

• • •

James Cecil Parke was probably Ireland's
greatest all-round sportsman when he
arrived into Anzac Cove in August 1915.

CECIL PARKE –

THE

ORIGINAL CLONES CYCLONE

...

CECIL PARKE WAS IN HIS TRENCH ON THE ROCKY SLOPES OF CHUNUK BAIR WHEN THE Turkish bombardment began early on the morning of 10 August 1915. Moments later, a shrapnel shell exploded nearby and several chunks of metal shot into him. One went straight through his wrist. As his blood pumped out, Cecil Parke was entitled to fret about his wounded wrist. This was not any old wrist. It was a wrist that had helped make him the greatest all-round sportsman in Irish history.

The Parkes were of Presbyterian stock. William Parke, Cecil's father, was born in 1824 and grew up at Longfield Lodge near Carrigallen on the Cavan-Leitrim border. His wife, Mary Pringle, hailed from an esteemed County Monaghan family who lived at Ballinahone near Emyvale.[114] Her relatives included James Pringle, Ulster Unionist MP for Tyrone and Fermanagh from 1924 to 1929, and Victoria Cross winner, Dr John Alexander Sinton.[115]

By the 1870s, the Parkes were living at The Hill in Clones, County Monaghan, where William served as the local magistrate. James Cecil Parke, their youngest son, was born in Clones on 26 July 1881.[116] He showed a hint of his future brilliance at the age of nine when he was selected to play on the Clones chess team.

He studied law at Trinity College, Dublin, later becoming an Irish Law Society gold medallist. At Trinity he proved himself a top-class track and field sprinter, an impressive tennis player (of which more to come), a very useful cricketer and a fine scratch golfer, which he played to a handicap of four. He also liked to dabble in table tennis, croquet, hockey, billiards, badminton and squash. It's hard to imagine he had a moment to study.[117]

However, it was international rugby that first brought him such wide acclaim throughout his Irish homeland. A superb centre, he was still a student at Trinity when he made his green jersey debut in 1903.[118] Over the next five seasons, he played for Ireland 20 times — a huge tally in those days — twice as captain.

The crowds who flocked to see this 'football genius' were frequently rewarded with a 'brilliant performance'. In 1906, he was one of 13 Irish players left on the pitch when both halfbacks were carried off with injuries during a match against a powerful Welsh team; the Irish rallied and held out to win 11-6. One of his fortes was as a place kicker and his score of five penalty goals in one international remained an Irish record until 1927. In the last game he played for Ireland on 20 March 1909, he scored five points — a drop goal and a conversion — in an epic 19–8 victory over France at Lansdowne Road.

He then retired from rugby to focus on tennis, becoming probably the best player Ireland has ever fielded. Once upon a time the Irish were very good at tennis. During a Golden Age that ran from the 1890s up to the start of the Great War, Ireland's players racked up nine Wimbledon titles, as well as two Olympic Golds, the Australian Open, the US Open and, effectively, the Davis Cup.

Cecil Parke was 19 years old when he won his first trophy at the Clones Lawn Tennis Club in 1900. He went on to win eight Irish singles championships, but it was as an international player that he sparkled. By the end of 1907, the year his aged father died, he was the Singles Champion of Europe. The following year, he added a silver medal to his collection when he reached the Men's Doubles Final at the London Olympics.

Contemporaries described him variously as 'very sound and dour', 'brilliant but erratic'. S Powell Blackmore, lawn tennis correspondent at the *Daily Express*, was an avid fan. 'James Cecil Parke has a slight Irish brogue and a big Irish heart,' he wrote. 'His shots are rather pushed out at you if he is standing still, but once Parke gets on the run, he hurls himself at the ball and you get a hot return, and Parke will go on hurling himself at the ball even at a time when things seen hopeless.'

In 1912, Cecil Parke sailed for Hastings on New Zealand's North Island to compete in what was then called the Australasia Open. He smashed his way into the record books by winning both the singles and doubles titles. In the singles, his opponent was Alfred Beamish, an illegitimate scion of the brewing dynasty from Macroom, County Cork. With the pace of a Clones puma, Parke defeated Beamish in five sets to take his first and only Grand Slam title.

From New Zealand, he voyaged directly to Melbourne where he led the British team that lifted the 1912 Davis Cup. Now ranked World No 3, Parke was asked for the secret of his success. 'My four-leafed shamrock', he replied. He offered some rather more practical advice in later life. 'As soon as I find I am getting particularly fond of a stroke, I try to forget all about it for a week.'[119]

Parke's extraordinary roll continued through 1913 as he defeated the reigning champions of Australia, England and the USA. His five-set victory over Maurice McLoughlin, the US No 1, is regarded as one of the finest matches ever played at Wimbledon. The *Daily Chronicle*'s sports correspondent was by no means alone when he proposed to his readers that Cecil Parke was now 'the world's best player'.[120]

Although he reached the semi-finals in 1910 and 1913, the Wimbledon Men's Singles title eluded Parke. He did gain the compensation of a Wimbledon title when he part-

• • •

JC Parke in action at the Lawn Tennis
Championships at Wimbledon. At his
peak, he was ranked as the World No 3.

nered Ethel Larcombe, the Ladies Singles champion, to win the mixed doubles in 1914. Parke was duly selected for the Davis Cup team once again and sailed for America soon after Wimbledon. He was defeated in Boston by Australia's Norman Brookes on 5 August.[121] Both players may have had other things on their mind during the game. Every newspaper in the city that day carried the news of Britain's declaration of war on Germany.

When not playing tennis, Cecil Parke was a practising solicitor in Clones with his brother William. However, when he returned from the US after the Davis Cup, the Monaghan man — then ranked as the World No 6 — was commissioned into the Prince of Wales's Leinster Regiment (Royal Canadians).

On 6 August 1915, Captain JC Parke was among the thousands of men who landed at Anzac Cove. After just three days of intense fighting, the Leinsters were sent to relieve Colonel Malone's beleaguered New Zealand troops holding the summit of Chunuk Bair. As they advanced up the hill at daybreak, a New Zealander ran down, shouting, 'Fix your bayonets, boys — they're coming.' Lieutenant Colonel Craske, commander of the Leinsters, charged up the slope at the head of his men and drove the Turks back. Three Leinster officers died and several more were wounded, including Colonel Craske. This was the action in which the aforesaid shrapnel shell exploded beside Captain JC Parke and shot into his wrist.[122]

Parke not only survived Chunuk Bair but his wrist made a complete recovery.[123] Miraculously, the bullet that went through it did so without breaking a bone or tearing a tendon. After a few weeks in a Maltese hospital, Parke was sent home to Clones and that autumn he was strong enough to make a cameo appearance in a rugby match at Lansdowne Road.[124]

On 18 December 1916, Cecil was promoted to Major and transferred to the Essex Regiment as second in command of the 10th Battalion.[125] He then went to the Western Front but on 18 March 1918, he managed to nip back to Wales where he married a woman called Sybil Smith in the popular seaside resort of Llandudno.[126] On his return to France, he took command of the 10th Battalion but, during his first action, he was wounded while on a reconnaissance mission in September 1918. He resigned his commission on 5 May 1920 and left the army with the rank of captain.[127]

Amazingly, he had recovered sufficiently from his injuries to resume his position on the international tennis circuit just over a month later. In June 1920, he had another crack at Wimbledon and promptly inflicted a shock defeat on the reigning US singles champion Bill Johnston in the second round.[128] Parke subsequently fell to Bill Tilden, the ultimate winner, but he finished as runner-up in the Men's Doubles and, by the end of 1920, the 39-year-old war veteran was ranked as the World No 4.[129]

S Powell Blackmore felt compelled to update his thoughts. 'Parke is one of the world's greatest fighters, not on account of his cunning, but because of his daring strokes when cornered. Parke is most dangerous when his opponent thinks a shot has beaten him. It is not tactics, it is sinew, superlative nerve and the heart of a big sportsman.'[130]

In the autumn of 1920, Cecil Parke moved to his wife's home in Llandudno and joined the legal practice of Messrs Chamberlain and Johnson. He retired from the tennis circuit in 1925 when he became a partner in the firm.[131] He also published *How to Play Lawn Tennis*, described as 'a book of practical instruction containing 47 specially-taken photographs'.

He retained his love of sport, setting up Llandudno's municipal tennis courts, overseeing the local scouts and serving as chairman of the North Wales Golf Club. He died suddenly in Llandudno on 27 February 1946 at the age of 64. The *Llandudno Advertiser* mourned 'the loss of one who often played the part of the Good Samaritan, with unfailing kindness and a distinctive charm of manner'. He was survived by his wife Sybil, an early animal rights campaigner, and their only son Arthur Patrick Parke, who worked alongside Cecil in the legal firm.

· · ·

Wounded in the battle of Chunuk Bair,
Hurst subsequently spent 23 days recuperating from jaundice in a hospital tent
in Cairo. The matron christened him 'the
Daffodil of B. 11'.

BRIAN DESMOND HURST — THE EMPRESS OF GALLIPOLI

...

'I WOULD FIGHT FOR ENGLAND AGAINST ANYBODY EXCEPT IRELAND.'

Why for England?

'Because an Englishman is worth twenty foreigners.'

Why not against Ireland?

'Because an Irishman is worth fifty Englishmen.'

So ran an interview in *Punch* in 1969 with Brian Desmond Hurst, aka 'the Empress of Ireland', Belfast's first bona fide Bohemian and Ireland's most prolific 20th century film director, who was amongst the more unlikely men to have served at Gallipoli.

He was born in 1895 in Ribble Street in East Belfast, a doggedly Protestant neighbourhood where most people, his father included, worked at the Harland and Wolff shipyard in the great age when the *Titanic* was constructed. Following the death of both parents in his early childhood, he was raised by his stepmother who treated him harshly. At the age of 13, he left school to work at the city's Bloomfield Linen Factory. He was still based there in September 1912 when he was amongst nearly half a million people to sign the Ulster Covenant.

Christened Hans Moore Hawthorn Hurst, he changed his name to Brian after the outbreak of the First World War. He enlisted at the age of 19, along with his best friend Bobby McKenzie, and the two teenagers became privates in the 6th Battalion of the Royal Irish Rifles.

The 6th Battalion was remarkably diverse in terms of religion, with men from Protestant and Catholic 'districts' of Belfast, as well as Dubliners and others from the Irish countryside.

Having trained at the Curragh, Brian and his fellow men set off from Liverpool for Gallipoli on 7 July 1915. Two weeks later they landed on the volcanic island of Lemnos in the north Aegean Sea. In Greek mythology, this was where Hephaestus, god of metallurgy, fell when hurled from Olympus by Zeus. In the summer of 1915, it was hot, desolate and plagued with flies.

On 5 August, the 6th Battalion were part of the massive invasion force that stormed Anzac Cove, landing shortly before midnight. They spent their first night bivouacked amid what Brian called 'the mucus and dysentery fluid' of Shrapnel Gully, a narrow cleft that ran down to the shore and served as the main route to the front line throughout the campaign. The regiment were still 'battle virgins' when the Turks began shelling the gully the following night. As the first Irishmen fell dead and wounded, the battalion retreated to another valley.

On 8 August they marched all day across the Sari Bair plateau, a soul-draining trek through wild scrub and rocky gorges, with the Gallipoli sun burning high above. Ahead of them marched the 10th Hampshires. Ahead of them lay the heights of Chunuk Bair, which a New Zealand group, under Colonel William Malone, had just managed to seize from the Turks. The Royal Irish Rifles were part of the force sent to provide the Kiwis with vital backup.

Plans went awry when darkness descended and, working off their useless maps, the advancing column became comprehensively lost amid the folds of Gallipoli. Dawn was breaking by the time they regained their bearings and the battle for Chunuk Bair was raging with gusto.

At 8am, Private Hurst was with the 6th Battalion when, as ordered, they charged a ridge on Chunuk Bair. Pummelled by Turkish machine-guns, they were driven to the ground almost 280 yards short of their target. With their comrades wounded and dying all around them, the dehydrated Irishmen entrenched for a terrifying, sleepless night. At 4.30am, the Turkish artillery began another mighty bombardment. And then came Mustafa Kemal Atatürk's troops, wave after wave, a ghastly wall of gleaming bayonets and screaming Turks that exploded into red as the Riflemen's bullets struck home.[132]

The 6th Battalion stood their ground for an hour and a half until it became apparent that they were being overpowered and massacred. They withdrew 800 yards until three or four men stopped and rallied them to form a new line, which they held until they were relieved at dawn. Of the 21 officers and 700 Riflemen who started the day, 357 were casualties by nightfall.

Private Hurst was very nearly amongst the slain. In his memoirs, he recorded: 'During one of the uphill charges with fixed bayonets, a huge Turk made for me. I wasn't too frightened, but very excited. He lunged with his bayonet at my guts and I went by my instinct to the "on guard" position. His rifle slid along mine and his bayonet went into my arm. Something rushed by my head. Sergeant Bradley near me had swung his gun, held by the barrel and smashed the Turk's skull. He had run out of bullets.'

Forty-five of the battalions' officers and riflemen lay dead on the slopes. 'We buried as many as we could,' wrote Hurst. 'In the torrential rains that came later, they were washed out of their shallow graves and we had to rebury them… it was an awful job.'[133]

By the time Hurst reached the hospital in Cairo, he was suffering from chronic dysentery, malignant malaria and yellow jaundice, as well as an arm on the cusp of gangrene. 'Lying in bed, having the saline treatment because the wound had begun to fester, I was dangerously ill for 23 days. Because of the jaundice, the matron promptly christened me "the Daffodil of B. 11".'

What Hurst saw at Chunuk Bair would remain with him for ever. As he sagely put it, 'Rupert Brooke has written of "some corner of a foreign field that is for ever England". The earth at Gallipoli is stuffed with Irish, Scots, Gurkas, Welsh, Indians and Pakistanis as well'. The only positivity to be found, he later maintained, was that 'Catholic-Protestant antagonism vanished in this holocaust'.[134]

After the war, Hurst returned to Belfast where his brother Robert had succumbed to the Spanish Flu in 1917. Finding the city of his birth rather too angry for his liking, he secured a government grant that enabled him to emigrate to Canada in 1921.

He studied art in Toronto and then, after two years at the École des Beaux-Arts in Paris, he fetched up in Hollywood, where he became John Ford's assistant. The two men claimed to be cousins or, as Hurst said, 'better than that, we're Irish cousins'. The Belfast man not only introduced Ford to the Aran Islands novelist Liam O'Flaherty, but also played a key role in producing O'Flaherty's War of Independence masterpiece *The Informer*. The film won Ford his first Academy Award for Best Director in 1935. When Ford decided to film *The Quiet Man* in Ireland nearly two decades later, Brian Desmond Hurst was again by his side.

Hurst also directed several of his own movies in Ireland, kicking off with two low-budget films in 1933, *Tell Tale Heart* and an adaptation of JM Synge's *Riders to the Sea*. For the latter, a 40-minute black-and-white movie set in the wilds of Connemara, he employed a number of Abbey Theatre actors.

The following year he directed what many consider to be Ireland's first feature-length 'talkie', *Irish Hearts* (or *Norah O'Neale*). He is also credited with one of Britain's first films noir, *On the Night of the Fire*, with Ralph Richardson, released just before the Second World War.

In all, he directed 27 films, including such gems as *A Christmas Carol* (with Alistair Sim peerless as Scrooge), *Malta Story*, *Tom Brown's Schooldays*, the romantic melodrama *Dangerous Moonlight* and *The Shadow of the Glen*. Others did poorly, including the 1962 comedy *His and Hers* and, his last film, *The Playboy of the Western World*.

One of his greatest box office hits was *Theirs Is the Glory* which, released in 1946, followed the doomed attempt by the British 1st Airborne Division to capture Arnhem Bridge in 1944. The film starred real veterans of the battle and clearly echoed what Hurst had seen at Gallipoli 30 years earlier. Hurst was not alone when he declared: 'I say without modesty it is one of the best war films ever made.'[135] The British Prime Minister Clement Atlee attended the premier, George VI requested a private showing at Balmoral and the film became the highest-grossing war film in a decade.

Hurst was now an icon of Britain's thespian community, mingling with Noël Coward, Cecil Beaton, Michael Redgrave, Peter Ustinov and such like. Full of laughter and mischief, he was not inclined to take a wife. 'Some people have asked me over the years whether I'm bisexual,' he said. 'In fact, I am tri-sexual. The Army, the Navy and the Household Cavalry.' On another occasion, he gasped at a lady friend: 'My dear, they've opened a new box of policemen and they look delicious.'

Amongst actors who owe their breakthrough to him are Roger Moore, Vanessa Redgrave and Richard Attenborough. The writer Christopher Robbins penned an acclaimed memoir about his friendship with the film director titled *Empress of Ireland*. Hurst occasionally returned to Belfast for what he called 'a spiritual bath', sometimes donning the costume of Santa Claus, always astounding his devoted young nephews and nieces with Hollywood gossip.

In his latter years, this most flamboyant Gallipoli veteran and child of Protestant Belfast went to a monastery in Kent where he converted to Catholicism. His new religion offered a timely distraction from his considerably depleted wealth. He died in good spirits in 1986 at the age of 91.

• • •

Hurst, pictured arriving at London
Airport in 1952, was Ireland's most
prolific 20th century film director.

Sir Alexander Godley relaxing at Killegar, the family home in County Leitrim.

GENERAL GODLEY

AND THE

ANZACS

...

General Sir Alexander Godley never really recovered his reputation after what happened at the Nek on 7 August 1915. For generations to come he would be held responsible for the debacle. Godley's Abattoir, they called it. There were no excuses. He made the wrong call. Twice.

Firstly, he ordered the Australians to proceed with the charge despite the arrival of fresh information that strongly suggested such a move would be disastrous. And then, to seal his horrible blunder, he failed to halt the charge when disaster became reality.

Instead, from the safety of his binoculars, he watched 600 men advance to their doom.

They ran at the Turks in four waves, 120 seconds between them, bayonets fixed. When the Maxims and rifles opened fire, the Australians were scythed like sheaves of corn. Two-thirds fell in less than 15 minutes, and 234 of them never got up again.

The Nek was one of several low points during General Godley's wartime career. Combined, they would utterly eclipse all the years of good, competent, innovative service he put in during the three decades before the war began.

When the time came for him to write his memoirs, the General would unflinchingly entitle them *Life of an Irish Soldier*. Although born and educated in England, Alexander 'Alick' Godley always considered himself an Irishman. His family had been in Ireland since the 17th century. John Godley, the founding father of the dynasty, was Sheriff of Dublin in 1706. John's son married the heiress to the Killegar estate in County Leitrim where the General's father grew up.

The General's military career began in 1886 when, aged 19, he was commissioned as a lieutenant in the Royal Dublin Fusiliers. Lanky but agile, he excelled as a horseman and frequently hunted with the Kildare and Meath hunts. In 1896 he rode out against

APRIL 25th ANZAC

a rather more dramatic quarry than foxes when dispatched to Rhodesia (present-day Zimbabwe) to help the British South Africa Company suppress a rebellion by the Shona tribesmen. In the Anglo-Boer War, he served as adjutant to Colonel Robert Baden-Powell during the 217-day Siege of Mafeking, which was finally lifted when Bryan Mahon, the future commander of the 10th (Irish) Division, galloped his men through the Boer lines.

Godley's primary talent was his ability to train both men and horses. During the first decade of the 20th century, he trained and commanded a number of different mounted infantry units in England. As well as his officer's pay, he earned some useful money training polo ponies. In 1908, he was one of the four British officers who played for England in the first international polo game ever played in Argentina. They won 4-1.[136]

In December 1910, life changed considerably for him when he was sent to faraway New Zealand, with orders from Lord Kitchener to reform and modernise the British

JVE 19165

During the night of 25 April 1915, 16,000 men, primarily from the Australian and New Zealand Army Corps (ANZAC), landed at night on the western (Aegean Sea) side of the Gallipoli peninsula. This photo shows the landing craft moored at a pontoon with other small vessels in the background and soldiers gathered on the beach, which later became known as ANZAC Cove.

colony's lacklustre military forces. Godley is said to have been reluctant to take the job, but perhaps he felt compelled by family connections; his Dublin-born uncle John Robert Godley founded the New Zealand city of Christchurch.

Alick Godley threw himself into his new role with single-minded aplomb. By 1914, he had created a Territorial Force of 30,000 men whose smartness, efficiency and ability to handle artillery and machine-guns impressed the War Office in London.

However, while few could doubt his organisational prowess, Godley failed to endear himself to his Kiwi soldiers. They not only found him pompous and detached but also resented the manner in which, when appointing new officers, he consistently snubbed them in favour of officers seconded from the British Army. His popularity wasn't helped when his redoubtable wife Louisa — eldest daughter of Robert Fowler of Rahinston, County Meath — allegedly showed up during a parade and hollered out, 'Make 'em run, Alick!'[137]

As early as 1912, Godley had regarded war with Germany as inevitable. Logic dictated that the Kaiser's forces would seek to forge an alliance with the Ottoman Turks in order to take control of the Suez Canal which, as Godley and his contemporaries well knew, was the lifeline of the British Empire. He calculated that the New Zealanders under his command were highly likely to be sent to the Middle East in the event of a war. To this end, he rather ingeniously devised the New Zealand Expeditionary Force. His men, he vowed, would be ready for rapid deployment as and when required.

He was, of course, quite right. In October 1914, he set sail from Wellington at the head of 8,500 men. Initially destined for the Western Front, the fleet was diverted to Egypt when, as Godley had predicted, Turkey came into the war on Germany's side.

In Egypt, General Godley began training his men for combat in the Middle Eastern climate. With one eye on the extra-curricular activities of his Kiwi soldiers, he also rather tactfully opened a number of bars and venereal disease treatment centres. Louisa Godley simultaneously established a convalescent home for soldiers on Alexandria's shore.[138]

Early in the morning of 25 April 1915, the first troops of the Australian and New Zealand Army Corps (ANZAC) landed on the west coast of the Gallipoli Peninsula. By the end of the day, some 16,000 soldiers had come ashore at what was to become known as Anzac Cove. It is not known how many of the ANZAC invaders were Irish. Possibly hundreds, perhaps more. At least 6,600 Irish-born men and women served in the Australian Imperial Force (AIF) during the First World War, of whom 970 died.[139] And the Australian Imperial Force (AIF) was just one part, albeit the largest, of the force who landed at Anzac Cove.

On the eve of the invasion, Sir Alexander Godley was appointed commander of the New Zealand and Australian Division. His superiors were General William Birdwood, commander of the ANZACs, and Sir Ian Hamilton, commander of the entire campaign. Between them they decided that the immediate objective for Godley's division was to capture a hill called Maltepe, which they believed was the key to the all-important Sari Bair Ridge.

When Godley's officers studied their maps of Gallipoli, it looked as though Maltepe was bang in front of them and that its capture would thus be relatively straightforward. What the maps failed to show was that the distance between the men and the hill was such a twisted landscape of dense bushes, jagged turns and tangled ravines that even an agile mountain goat would have baulked at it. Unaware of this massive cartographical oversight, the ANZACs advanced. By dawn, the terrain had utterly fragmented their line into pocket after pocket of small groups of confounded men.

One such group was commanded by Captain Joe Lalor of the AIF's 12th Battalion. He was a grandson of Peter Lalor, the revolutionary from County Laois who led the Australian gold miners during the Eureka Rebellion of 1854. Against all regulations, Captain Lalor had carried his family sword all the way to Gallipoli. By early afternoon, Lalor and his company were feeling the brunt of a Turkish counter-attack as more and more Ottoman reinforcements piled onto the peninsula under the command of Mustafa Kemal Atatürk and Sami Bey. Sensing trouble ahead, Lalor ordered his men to dig in while they tried to work out where to go. It was not long before the Turkish army was sweeping down upon them. Joe Lalor stood up to lead his men in a charge and managed to shout 'Come on, the 12th' just before he was shot dead.[140]

All along their broken line, the ANZACs were driven backwards by an enemy who knew the landscape infinitely better than they did. The Turks regained control of so many key locations that by the time Godley himself arrived on shore at noon, it was already too late. Not only was there no chance of achieving their objective but his men were in great danger of being utterly wiped out by the Turkish counter-attack. To their great dismay, Hamilton and Birdwood found themselves contemplating an evacuation. In the meantime, Hamilton counselled, 'there is nothing for it but to dig yourself right in and stick it out'.[141] The ANZACs did just that.

Elsewhere on the Gallipoli Peninsula that very same night, Guy Geddes, Willie Cosgrove and hundreds of other Irishmen were huddled beneath the sandbank at Seddelbahr.

From their coastal entrenchments, the ANZACs waited and waited. Hours turned to weeks. Every day Turkish snipers, camouflaged in the rocks, would pick off some of the men. Others were soon stricken with utterly debilitating dysentery as the army latrines became ever filthier. Godley remained with his division throughout this gruelling period. Every time the six feet two inch General visited a trench, someone cracked a joke about how they should have dug a little deeper to accommodate his height.[142] Crummy jokes were important in times like this, but Godley rarely responded with camaraderie. The coldness he consistently showed to his men in the face of their ongoing misery began to cause anger and dismay.

In the meantime, he focused on trying to hold onto the few outposts the ANZACs still possessed. One of these was Quinn's Post on the lower slopes of Monash Gully. It was named for Major Hugh Quinn, a boxing champion from Charters Towers, Queensland, whose father came from Ireland. Quinn had commanded the company that took the post on 26 April and, despite the fact that it was exposed to the Turks on two sides, he managed to hold onto it. On 7 May, the Turks tried to retake Quinn's Post; Godley personally organised the successful defence. Hugh Quinn died defending his post three weeks later but, while the Allies remained in Gallipoli, it was never taken by the enemy.[143]

On 19 May, the Turks launched a massive offensive, sending the best part of four divisions to push the ANZACs back into the sea. It was an utter disaster for the Ottomans, who lost 3,500 men killed and 6,500 wounded, mostly by the ANZACs' rifles and machine-guns. By contrast, the ANZAC losses totalled 160 dead and 468 wounded. The bodies of those who died lay sprawled on No Man's Land until 24 May when the stench became so ghastly that the two sides agreed to a brief armistice to bury the dead.

And then the waiting game resumed until 6 August, the day that the Dublin Pals, Cecil Parke and tens of thousands of other troops began coming ashore at Suvla Bay. That evening, Godley and Birdwood kicked off the ANZACs' contribution to the August offensive with a diversionary assault on Lone Pine, named for a soon-to-be-exterminated solitary pine tree that stood beyond the ANZAC trenches. As ever, the attack began with an artillery bombardment designed to blow the Turkish defences to bits and shred the barbed wire entanglements. And, as ever, the bombardment failed. Three battalions of Godley's Australian troops ran forward to find the wire still intact. As they hesitated, the Turkish machine-guns opened fire. It took the Australians many

Quinn's Post was named for the Irish-Australian boxing champion who captured the strategic outpost. Godley personally organised its successful defence and Quinn's Post remained in Allied hands until the evacuation.

long hours of vicious fighting before they won the ground at Lone Pine. By the time it was theirs, they had suffered over 2,200 casualties. Among the dead was Second Lieutenant Everard Digges La Touche, an Anglican clergyman from Newcastle, County Down, who moved to Australia before the war. Inevitably, this suicidal attack would also be chalked up against General Godley's plummeting reputation.

And then, less than 24 hours later, came the calamitous Australian charge at the Nek. Redemption nearly came Godley's way early on 8 August when he received news that 56-year-old Colonel William Malone and the Wellington Infantry Battalion had unexpectedly captured the vital summit of Chunuk Bair. If Malone could hold on, perhaps Godley could salvage his reputation. However, the furious Turks were soon unleashing such an intensive bombardment on Malone's men that the exhausted Colonel sent word requesting urgent backup. Godley didn't have any troops to spare. Somehow the parched and starving Kiwis held on until the following evening, but at an appalling cost. By the time a battalion of 700 Loyal North Lancashires relieved them, all but 49 of the 760 infantrymen who set out with Malone were dead or wounded.

Colonel Malone was killed in his trench by misdirected friendly fire from behind their own lines. Also dead was the New Zealand rugby player Hami Grace, one of 50 Maoris to die in Gallipoli. When the first Native Contingent of Maoris arrived at Anzac Cove in early July, it prompted Godley to have some fun with the General Headquarter Staff. As he wrote to his cousin, Lord Kilbracken: 'Before the Maoris arrived, they asked us what was their strength and did they require any special diet? I replied that there were 500 of them but that the question of their diet should offer no difficulty as I trusted that, during their stay with the Division, enough Turks would be killed or taken prisoner to go round. Sir Ian was much amused.'[144]

The Lancashires were soon joined in their attack by the 5th (Service) Battalion of Wiltshires, the Prince of Wales's Leinster Regiment, including Cecil Parke, and the 6th Battalion of the Royal Irish Rifles, with the future film director Brian Desmond Hurst in its ranks.

The Allied battalions met their match when a determined Mustafa Kemal Atatürk ordered the No 8 Division to sweep them away. The first two waves of the Turkish assault were mown down, but the third strike succeeded. Chunuk Bair was back in Turkish hands and Godley's chance for redemption expired. Amongst nearly 2,500 who died in the battle was Lieutenant Colonel Harry Levinge, the 51-year-old Commanding Officer of the Lancashires, who grew up at Knockdrin Castle in County Westmeath.

The failure of the August offensive marked the end of the Gallipoli campaign. That said, six weeks were to pass before Lord Kitchener finally came to view the situation with his own eyes. He gave London the nod that withdrawal was the only sensible option. Known as the Silent Ruse, the ensuing evacuation over the course of 19–20 December was a remarkable success. That can have been little recompense to the families of the 3,500 Irish, over 2,700 New Zealanders and nearly 9,000 Australians who died in Gallipoli.[145]

General Godley did not lose his command. Neither did he seem to have felt in any way culpable for what happened in the campaign. On 12 January 1916, he wrote to Lord Kilbracken: 'The politicians seem grateful to us for having got them out of their Gallipoli muddle.'[146]

• • •

Charles Gwynn, a surveyor from County
Donegal, served as Godley's Chief of Staff
both in Gallipoli and on the Western
Front.

He was made a Knight Commander of the Order of the Bath for his services in the campaign. Initially reassigned to defend the Suez Canal, he was then given a new command in February 1916 — to take charge of II ANZAC Corps, formed from two new Australian divisions, the 4th and 5th, along with the ANZAC Mounted Division.

Godley was blessed with a brilliant new Chief of Staff in the shape of surveyor Charles Gwynn. Born in Ramelton, County Donegal in 1870, Gwynn was the son of a Trinity College divinity professor. His older brother Stephen Gwynn, a well-known journalist, had been elected MP for Galway City in 1906 and was one of the five Irish MPs now serving in the army. Like Godley, Charles Gwynn learned much of his craft in Africa, winning considerable praise for his survey of the wild Sudan-Abyssinian frontier. In 1911, he was appointed director of military art at the Royal Military College in Duntroon near Canberra, the Australian Army's equivalent of Sandhurst. Some of his fellow officers tended to dismiss Gwynn, perhaps because of his slight stammer, which, as one contemporary recalled, 'intensified after the third glass of port'. However, he proved enormously popular with the cadets and was a masterful teacher in strategy, tactics and military history. Overlooked during the first year of the war, Gwynn was sent to Gallipoli during the August offensive to command the 5th and 6th Brigades of the 2nd Australian Division. His men spent a relatively calm 12 weeks in Gallipoli, holding a quiet part of the line, before the evacuation began.

After intense training in Egypt, Godley, Gwynn and the men of II ANZAC Corps made their way to the Western Front. On 19 July 1916, the 5th Division saw its first action during the battle of Fromelles. It transpired to be the most deadly 24 hours in Australian history. A disastrously planned attack on the Bavarians resulted in 5,533 Australian casualties in one night, more than Australia lost in the Anglo-Boer War, Korean War and Vietnam War combined.

'Stammering scores of German machine-guns spluttered violently,' observed a survivor, WH Downing. 'The air was thick with bullets, swishing in a flat criss-crossed lattice of death. Hundreds were mown down in the flicker of an eyelid, like great rows of teeth knocked from a comb.'

Godley was not to blame for Fromelles, but it did nothing to improve the confidence of the Australians and New Zealanders under his command. He did receive something of a bounce just under a year later when, largely thanks to Charles Gwynn's meticulous planning, II ANZAC Corps scored a rare triumph at the battle of Messines in June 1917. Godley regarded it as 'the greatest success of the war so far'. However, he then blew it during the Passchendaele offensive when, overriding advice that the appalling weather had converted the ground into a mudbath, he ordered his men to advance on the Passchendaele ridge. It was Lone Pine and the Nek all over again. The German defence held steady, despite formidable losses, and nearly 3,000 men from Godley's New Zealand Division lay dead in the mud.

James Allen, the New Zealand Minister of Defence — whose son died in Gallipoli — began to seriously question Godley's leadership. While Godley would remain commander of the New Zealand Expeditionary Force until its disbandment in November 1919, he was thereafter placed in charge of the distinctly less antipodean British XXII Corps.

Bedecked in medals, he spent much of the early 1920s in Germany, commanding the British Army of the Rhine, and served as Governor of Gibraltar from 1928 to 1933. He was also in the running to become Governor of New South Wales, although the enormous loss of Australian lives on his watch put paid to that. When he offered his services to the New Zealand Government at the outbreak of World War Two, they responded with a deafening silence. Undaunted, Alick Godley published his memoirs in 1939. He died in Oxford in 1957 aged 90.

Charles Gwynn was promoted to the rank of Major General in 1925. The following year he became commandant of the Staff College in Camberley; his students and fellow instructors included future field marshals Wilson, Brooke, Montgomery and Alexander. Knighted after his retirement in 1931, he died in Dublin in 1963.

ARTHUR CORRIE LEWIN, DSO — AVIATOR EXTRAORDINAIRE

...

IN OCTOBER 1937, THERE WAS A COLLECTIVE GULP THROUGHOUT THE WORLD OF AVIATION WHEN IT was reported that Brigadier General Arthur Corrie Lewin, DSO, and his wife had gone missing in north-east Africa. The couple were last seen flying down the valley of the White Nile in their Miles Whitney two-seater. Less than four weeks earlier, the 63-year-old Irish aviator had astonished his contemporaries when, on his debut attempt, he came second in the prestigious King's Cup Air Race.[147]

Born in 1874, Arthur Lewin grew up at Castlegrove, one of the west of Ireland's finest mansions, which stood near Tuam on the Galway-Mayo border. Educated at Cheltenham and Cambridge, he won a DSO while serving with the Mounted Infantry during the Anglo-Boer War (1899-1902).

In 1913, he was given command of the 3rd Battalion of the Connaught Rangers. One of his officers was his younger brother Fred, who was to die tragically in November 1915 when a bomb unexpectedly exploded during trench practice at the Preghane rifle range in Kinsale, County Cork.[148]

Arthur Lewin was dispatched to Gallipoli during the Dardanelles campaign and, in September 1915, he assumed command of the 5th (Service) Battalion of the Wiltshire Regiment, which had been practically annihilated in the battle for Chunuk Bair. The following month he was promoted to Brigadier General and given the 40th Infantry Brigade. The dismal campaign was largely over by then, but with dysentery and jaundice spreading rapidly amongst his men, General Lewin played a key role in the successful evacuation of Gallipoli, keeping a close eye on operations in both Cape Helles and Suvla Bay.

He spent the rest of the war in Mesopotamia and Persia (present-day Iraq and Iran), taking part in the relief of Kut in 1916 and the advance on Baghdad in March 1917. During August 1918, he commanded all British troops in north-west Persia on behalf of General Marshall. Two months later, he witnessed the final overthrow of the Ottoman forces on the Tigris at the battle of Sharqat.

After the war, the General returned to Ireland and, along with his wife Norah and their two sons, he settled at Cloghans Castle, which one of his ancestors had purchased in 1663, and which had remained a Lewin stronghold ever since. The castle was close to his childhood home of Castlegrove, where his older brother now lived.

Shortly after his move to Cloghans Castle, the political temperature in Ireland became unbearable, not least when anti-Treaty forces looted and burned Castlegrove to the ground on 25 July 1922. Lewin relocated to the British colony of Kenya, where he took up farming. Nonetheless, he maintained his connections to Ireland, attending the annual Connaught Rangers dinner in Restaurant Jammet in Dublin's Nassau Street in 1929 and 1931.

General Lewin was 57 years old when he discovered his true passion in life. 'Flying is full of surprises', he remarked. 'It keeps you young. It is the finest game in the world.'[149] He was also astonishingly good at it. At the end of 1931, the same year that he learned how to fly, he covered the 6,300-mile journey from England to Kenya in a solo run that took over 50 hours. He was to repeat the journey many times.

It was thus no surprise when newspapers around the world began to panic when the Lewins and their monoplane disappeared over the Nile on their return from the 1937 King's Cup. But fortune smiled on the couple when a flying boat pilot on the London to Cape Town route spotted them waving frantically from a Sudanese swamp. The General and his wife had been compelled to force-land and were subsequently marooned. The flying boat dropped food supplies and led an RAF convoy out to find them. Ten days after their plane went down, the Lewins were rescued, scathed, bruised and hungry, but very much alive.[150]

Fifteen years later, the irrepressible Galway man cemented his reputation as an icon of aviation when he piloted a Tiger Moth to victory in the East African Aerial Derby in March 1952. He died of heart failure six months later at the age of 78.

. . .

Arthur Corrie Lewin from County Mayo
commanded the 5th (Service) Battalion of
the Wiltshire Regiment during the latter
phases of the Gallipoli campaign.

THE DAILY MIRROR, Wednesday, July 29, 1914.

AUSTRIA DECLARES WAR ON SERVIA.

The Daily Mirror

LATEST CERTIFIED CIRCULATION MORE THAN 1,000,000 COPIES PER DAY

No. 3,358. | Registered at the G.P.O. as a Newspaper. | WEDNESDAY, JULY 29, 1914 | One Halfpenny.

AUSTRIA-HUNGARY DECLARES WAR ON SERVIA : ARE WE ON THE EVE OF A TERRIBLE EUROPEAN CONFLICT?

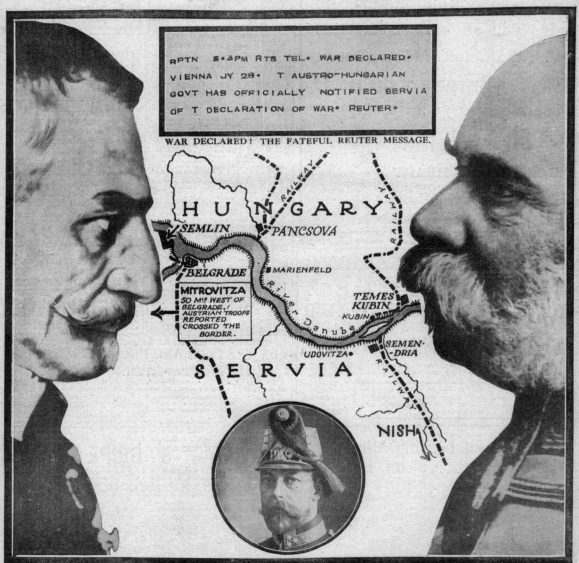

RPTN 5·5PM RTS TEL· WAR DECLARED· VIENNA JY 28· T AUSTRO-HUNGARIAN GOVT HAS OFFICIALLY NOTIFIED SERVIA OF T DECLARATION OF WAR· REUTER·

WAR DECLARED! THE FATEFUL REUTER MESSAGE.

MITROVITZA 50 M.S WEST OF BELGRADE. AUSTRIAN TROOPS REPORTED CROSSED THE BORDER.

King Peter of Servia.　　How the River Danube—　　King George as Austrian colonel.　　—divides the two countries.　　The Emperor Francis Joseph.

The war cloud which has been hanging over Europe has burst; and "Austria-Hungary finds it necessary to safeguard its rights and interests and to have recourse for this purpose to force of arms." The gravity of the news cannot easily be exaggerated, as it may involve the Great Powers of Europe in the most terrible conflict of modern times. The whole Continent is, indeed, preparing for the worst, and mobilisation is going on everywhere. The most interesting figure at the moment is Austria's aged Emperor, the murder of whose heir is the immediate cause of the war. King Peter abdicated quite recently, and the Regent is Prince Alexandre.

···

PART THREE

···

FORGOTTEN

FRONTS

···

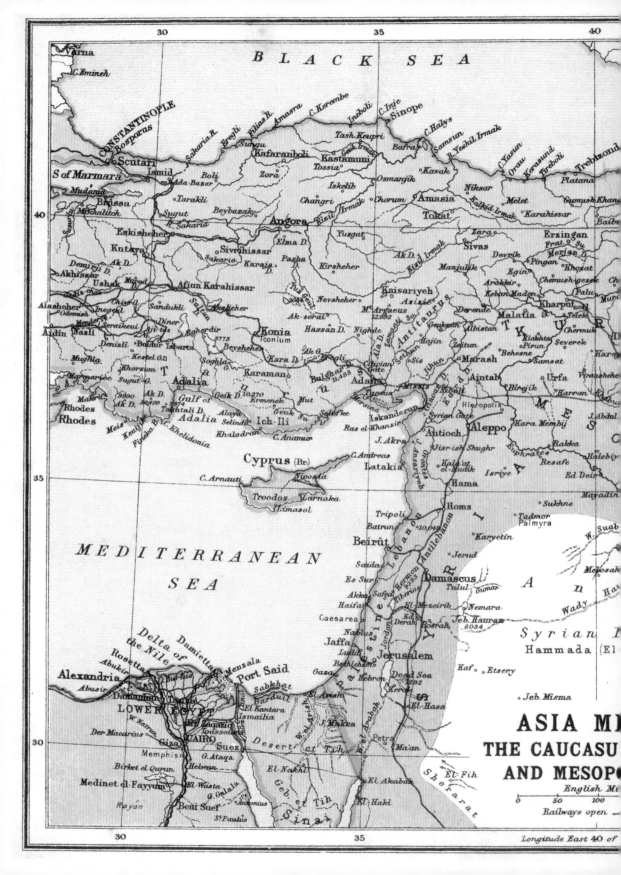

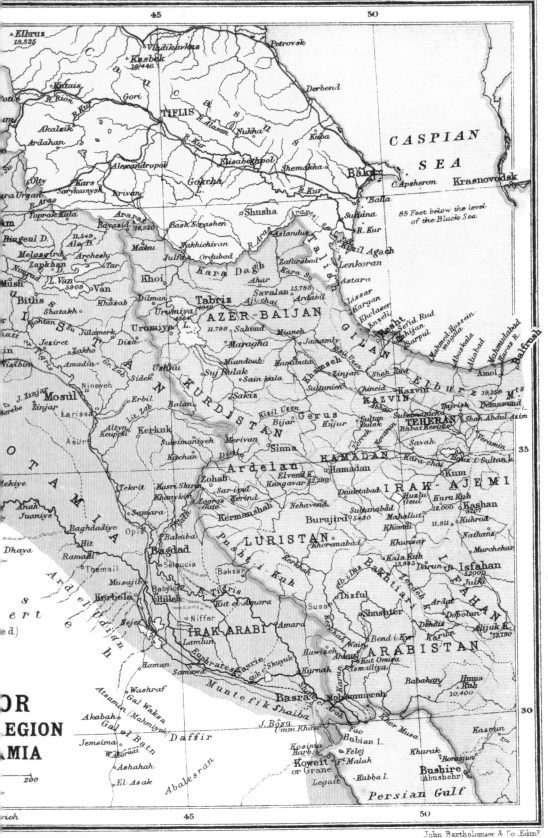

△Elbruz
18,525

Vladikavkaz
Petrovsk

Kotais
△Kasbek
16,446
Gori
R. Rion
R. Kur
TIFLIS
R. Alazan
Nukha
Derbend

C

Akalzik
Ardahan
Elisabethpol
Shemakha
Kuba

Olty
Kars
Sarykamysh
Alexandropol
Gokcha L.
R. Kur
Baku

CASPIAN
SEA

Ara Urgan
R. Aras
Krivan
R. Aras
Balla
C. Apsheron
Krasnovodsk

Am
Toprak Kala
Ararat
16,920
Bayazid
Bash Norashen
Aslandus
Salian
R. Kur
85 feet below the level
of the Black Sea

Bingeul D.
11,549
Ala D.
Archesly
Makeu
Nakhichivan
Julfa
Ordubad
Zafarabad
Kizil Agach

Melazgird
Zapkhan D.
Tar
Khoi
Kara Dagh
Ahar
Kara Su
Lenkoran
Astara

Nimrud
L. Van
5909
Van
Dilman
Savalan 15,788
Ardabil
Jissar
Kargan

Mush
Bitlis
Shatakh
Khasab
Urumiya
4964
Tabriz
Aji-chai
Kheloser
Enzeli
Resht
Sefid Rud

Bohtan
Julamerk
Disa
Urumiya L.
AZER-BAIJAN
11,798
Sahend
Mianeh
Shah Rud
Sarpul
Mahmed Hussein
magala

Jeziret
Zakho
Amadin
Gr. Zab
Ushnu
Suj Bulak
Sain Kala
Khamseh
Zinjan
Chineid
Kazvin
19,256
Amol
Mahmudabad
Balfrush

Nisibin
Tigris
Sidek
Nineveh
Maragha
Janamly
Sultanieh
KAZVIN
Taghsh
Demavend
Shah Abdul Azim

Mosul
Erbil
Balan
Lit. Zab
Sakiz
Kizil Uzen
Bijar
Gerus
Kujur
Sultan Bulak
Subamadick
TEHERAN
Rabat Kerim

Larissa
Zinjar
Altyn Keupri
Suleimaniyeh
Merivan
Kochan
Diala
Sinna
Kara-chai
Savah
Veramin

Asur
KURDISTAN
Ardelan
HAMADAN
Kum
35

Mehiye
Tekrit
Kasri Shirin
Zohab
Elvend K.
12,290
Kangavar
Hamadan
Daulatabad
Huzlu Neul
Kura Kun
12,000
Kashan
320

Anah
Juaniye
Khanykin
Zaagros Gate
Kerind
Sar-i-pul
Nehavend
Sultanabad 5480
Mahallat
Khomia
Kuhrud
Nathanz

Dhaya
Baghdadiye
Hit
Opis
Kermanshah
Burujird
Khonsar
11,811
Murchehar

Ramadi
Themail
Bakuba
Baghdad
Pushti-Kuh
Khoremabad
LURISTAN
Khunsar
Isfahan
5200
Julfa

Musajib
Seleucia
Baksan
Kerkhah
Kala Kuh
13,845
Darun
Zendeh
Ardat
Dopolan

Kerbela
Hillah
Babylon
Tigris
Dizful
Shushter
Bakhtiari
Dehdia
Alijuk K.
13,780

Nejef
Niffer
Kut el Amara
Susa
Kerkhah
Naia
Karun

IRAK-ARABI
Amara
Hawizeh
Ahwaz
ARABISTAN
Babahan
Huma Kuh
10,400

Lamlun
Euphrates
Nasrie
Silk el Shuyuk
Kurnah
Kut Omara
Ismailiya

OR
REGION
AMIA

Washraf
Gal Waksa
Atsaman (Mahmiyeh)
Akabah
Gal el Batn
Muntefik
Shaiba
Basra
Shatt el Arab
Mohammerah
Shor Musa
30

Jemeima
Daffir
J. Bosa
Umm Khasr
Tao
Bubian I.
Khurak
Kazrun

W. Absruat
Ashahah
Abalesran
Kosima Harb
Felej
Ft Malah
Koweit or Grane
Legait
Kubba I.
Bushire
(Abushehr)
Borasjun

El-Asak

200

Persian Gulf

45
50

EN MÉSOPOTAMIE -- Cavalerie britannique assaillie par le « Sam » ou tempête du désert

FORGOTTEN FRONTS

. . .

MANY THEATRES OF WAR IN WHICH THE IRISH SERVED HAVE BEEN OBSCURED by the better-known campaigns at the Western Front and Gallipoli. And yet, for thousands of Irish, men and women, their battlegrounds were in Western Asia where their principal foe was "Johnny Turk", the forces of the Ottoman Empire, the world's most powerful Islamic state since the 16th century.

Present-day Iran (formerly Persia) and Iraq (Mesopotamia) were embroiled in the conflict early on. Indeed it is arguable that the Allied victory was predetermined by the tycoon Knox D'Arcy who gambled his fortune on drilling for all-important oil in the wilds of Persia long before the first shot was even fired. Certainly, oil would be the fundamental reason why the future guerrilla leader Tom Barry spent two years fighting along the banks of the River Tigris, locked in a bitter struggle to oust the Turks from Mesopotamia.

Further to the south, Erskine Childers, the hero of the Howth gun-run in 1914, had a bird's eye view of the Middle East campaign when he flew spotter planes over Palestine and the Sinai Peninsula. John Alexander Howard, a former Dublin draper, pioneered an ingenious way to extract water from the Palestinian desert. Untold numbers of Irish helped General Allenby's army seize Jerusalem in the epic battle for the Holy Land.

For thousands more Irishmen, the Balkans was the battleground and the enemy was "Johnny Bulgar", aka the army of Ferdinand I, Tsar of Bulgaria. Indeed, for close on two years, the Bulgarians were Enemy No 1 for the 10th (Irish) Division. They fought one another along the Salonika or Macedonian Front, pitted against the elements of Albania, Bulgaria and Greece. Serbia was another land in which the Irish fought, few with more vigour than Flora Sandes who, with the blood of her Kerry forefathers coursing through her veins, became a sergeant in the Serbian Army.

• • •

Erskine Childers is often hailed as the world's
first spy novelist. In 1920, the year this photograph was taken, he published 'Military Rule in
Ireland', a scathing attack on British policy.

SKY PATROL

WITH

ERSKINE CHILDERS

...

AT SEVEN O'CLOCK ON A COLD NOVEMBER MORNING IN 1922, A THIN, WHITE-HAIRED MAN
with a hacking cough was led to the yard of Beggarsbush Barracks in Dublin to face a
firing squad. He had been found guilty by a military tribunal of possessing a prohibited
firearm, an ivory-handled Spanish automatic, which was said to have been a gift from
Michael Collins during happier times. Collins was now dead, shot down at Béal na
Bláth eight weeks earlier. And it was the soldiers who had served under Collins who
were now preparing to execute the man with the cough.[1]

The condemned man was Erskine Childers, one of the most curious figures to
emerge during the fight for Irish independence. For many in Ireland the Englishman
became an 'Irish' hero the moment he sailed a cargo of guns into Howth for the Irish
Volunteers in 1914. He was also widely regarded as one of the best novelists of his day.
His 1903 thriller *The Riddle of the Sands* is considered the world's first spy novel. In
1920, he served as Chief Secretary to Collins and the other four men sent to London to
negotiate the Treaty that ended the Anglo-Irish War. Steadfastly opposed to the terms
of that Treaty, he subsequently became principal spin doctor for de Valera and the Anti-
Treaty forces. His decision to turn against the Free State Government ultimately led to
his arrest and execution.

Winston Churchill was thrilled when he heard Childers had been shot. 'No man,'
he declared, 'has done more harm or more genuine malice, or endeavoured to bring a
greater curse upon the common people of Ireland than this strange being, actuated by a
deadly and malignant hatred for the land of his birth'.

Some of Churchill's bitterness undoubtedly stemmed from the fact that Childers
was not only an Englishman but a decorated war hero. Just over five years earlier, he
had been awarded a DSO (Distinguished Service Order) for his outstanding reconnaissance skills over the North Sea, Gallipoli and Palestine.

Born in London in 1870, Robert Erskine Childers was the son of an English professor of Oriental languages. His Irish connection came through his mother's family, the Bartons of Glendalough, County Wicklow, kinsmen of the family who owned the Barton vineyards in France, as well as Straffan House, now the K Club, in County Kildare. Erskine was just six years old when his parents succumbed to tuberculosis — his father died almost at once and his mother, to whom he was devoted, was packed off to a sanatorium, never to be seen again.

Together with his four siblings and his Barton cousins, he spent the remainder of his childhood in the care of an uncle and aunt, secreted amid the lush, 15,000-acre Glendalough estate.

His formative years were typical of his class. He went from an English public school to Cambridge to a desk job at Westminster. Full of jingoistic zest, he joined the British Army in 1899 and marched off to South Africa to clobber the dastardly Boers.

And then he started to change.

His experiences of the Anglo-Boer War — of villages in flames, of women and children incarcerated in disease-riddled concentration camps — led him to seriously question the merits of British imperialism.

Erskine's passion had always been sailing. During his twenties, he and his brother frequently sailed around the rocky coastline of the North Sea, keeping an eye on Germany's ever-growing naval might. In 1903, the 33-year-old converted his knowledge into *The Riddle of the Sands*, the bestseller that made him a household name. Shortly after the book was published, he attended a dinner party in Boston where he met Molly Osgood, the daughter of Dr Hamilton Osgood, a prominent American physician credited with introducing the first rabies antibodies to the US. Molly had fractured both hips as a child and spent 12 years on her back. She could walk, with difficulty, supported by walking sticks but her favourite mode of transport was by boat and, like Erskine, she was an accomplished helmsman.

The couple were married in 1904. His first cousin Bob Barton stood as best man. One of their wedding presents was the *Asgard*, an elegant 50-foot yacht, paid for by Dr and Mrs Osgood.

The newlyweds then settled in London where their first son Erskine Hamilton Childers was born in 1905. Their social life was relatively low-key in the ensuing years and involved much sailing around the North Sea and the Baltic on the *Asgard*.

In 1908, Erskine joined Bob Barton and Horace Plunkett on a motor tour of southern Ireland. The experience convinced the cousins that colonialism was fundamentally wrong and they became open supporters of Home Rule and, from 1913, of the Irish Volunteers.

In April 1914, the Childers learned that Sir Edward Carson's Ulster Volunteers, who were utterly opposed to Home Rule, had successfully landed a shipment of 35,000 German rifles at Larne. The British authorities had seemingly watched the whole thing unfurl and done nothing to intervene.

Appalled by this sudden imbalance in Ulster's favour, Erskine and Molly joined a committee of well-to-do Republican sympathisers who began to look at ways of arming

• • •

Erskine Childers with his American wife
Molly aboard the *Asgard*, circa 1910.

the Irish Volunteers in a like manner. As Patrick Pearse reputedly remarked, 'the only thing more ridiculous than an Ulsterman with a rifle is a Nationalist without one'.

On 3 July 1914, Erskine and Molly casually sailed the *Asgard* out from the Welsh coast towards the North Sea. Also on board was a British aviator, two Donegal fishermen and Mary Spring Rice, a cousin of the British Ambassador in Washington. Nine days later, the *Asgard* and another Irish yacht called *Kelpie* rendezvoused with the German tugboat *Gladiator* at the mouth of the Scheldt River, just off the Belgian coast. The *Gladiator* duly unloaded its cargo and about-turned for Hamburg.

On 26 July, the *Asgard* completed her journey when she sailed into Howth Harbour in north County Dublin. Standing in neat formation along the pier were 800 members of the Irish Volunteers and Fianna Éireann, headed up by Bulmer Hobson, Eoin MacNeill and Michael O'Rahilly. As Molly disembarked, MacNeill gallantly kissed her hand, saying, 'You're the greatest soldier here, Ma'am, indeed ye are.' The *Asgard*'s cargo of 900 Mauser rifles and 29,000 rounds of black powder were quickly dispersed amongst the Volunteers.

When the authorities got wind, they hastily dispatched a force of the Dublin Metropolitan Police, but they were too late to disarm the Volunteers. The day was to end on an ominous note when, in the wake of the landing, a detachment from the King's Own Scottish Borderers opened fire on an angry crowd who were pelting them with rotten fruit on Bachelors Walk, leaving three civilians dead and 32 wounded, including young Luke Kelly, the father and namesake of the Dubliners singer.

Two days later, the Austro-Hungarian Empire declared war on Serbia. When Britain entered the war on 4 August, 44-year-old Erskine Childers put his thoughts of Ireland on hold and threw himself behind the Allied cause. He donned the dark blue uniform of a lieutenant in the Royal Naval Volunteer Reserve.

On account of his nautical genius, he spent the first six months of the war as an Intelligence Officer on board HMS *Engadine*, a seaplane carrier operating in the North Sea. Having become so intimately acquainted with the region through his pre-war yachting excursions, his intelligence was greatly prized. During his time on the *Engadine* he also took part in several flights as an aerial observer.

One of Britain's greatest fears in the early days of the war was an aerial bombardment by German Zeppelins, many of which were housed in sheds at Cuxhaven on the coast of Lower Saxony. Childers managed to whip up such a detailed picture of what the Cuxhaven area looked like that, on Christmas Day 1914, the Royal Navy launched the first combined sea and air strike in history. The mission was commanded by Cecil L'Estrange Malone, captain of the *Engadine,* and a cousin of the Hamiltons of Hamwood, County Meath. Malone, another Anglo-Irish oddity, would one day join the Communist Party of Great Britain and become the first communist to be elected a Member of Parliament.

The Cuxhaven Raid began when seven of nine seaplanes managed to take off from the *Engadine*, including one in which Childers gamely sat as an observer. Poor weather and alert German anti-aircraft gunners prevented the Yuletide raiders from reaching their target, but important lessons were learned about the possibilities of air attacks launched from ships like the *Engadine*. As Childers wrote in his diary, 'it marks a new

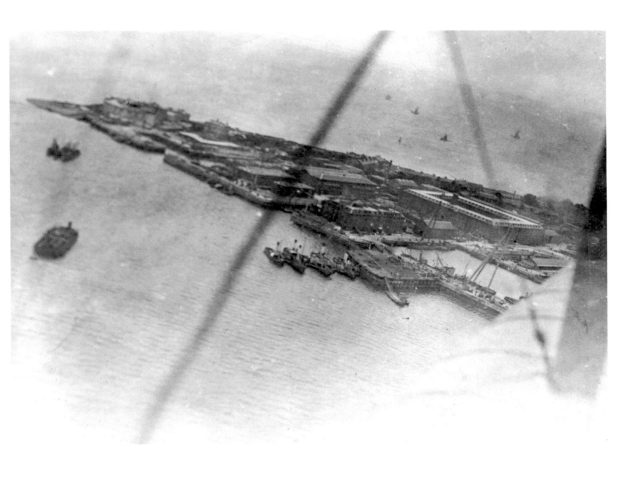

• • •

It is thought that Childers photographed
this aerial view of the German naval base
at Cuxhaven while participating in an
aerial raid on Christmas Day 1914.

era in war; the first regular battle between the ships of the sea and the ships of the air'. The Admiralty was certainly impressed to learn that, following the raid, the Germans had relocated the bulk of their High Seas Fleet from Cuxhaven to the distant Kiel Canal in the Baltic Sea. If nothing else, such raids could scare the enemy into a retreat.

Three months after the Cuxhaven Raid, Childers was transferred to HMS *Ben-My-Chree*. The name is Manx for "woman of my heart"; the ship had been an Isle of Man steamer before its conversion into a seaplane carrier. His friend Cecil Malone was installed as its captain. The two men were headed for a place where experience, initiative and modern thinking were desperately needed: Gallipoli.

The *Ben-My-Chree* dropped anchor off Mytilene on the island of Lesbos on 12 July 1915. It was a timely arrival for the ship and its complement of eight aircraft. For several months, Admiral de Robeck's fleet had faced relatively little threat from enemy vessels in the Aegean Sea, but German submarines had lately been spotted and everyone was fearful of a torpedo attack. Childers was one of the *Ben-My-Chree*'s eagle-eyed observers and he excelled at spotting enemy submarines in those crystal clear, blue waters. He was also highly adept at communicating the precise locations of such submarines to the Royal Navy's gunners.

In the first week of August 1915, when the Dublin Pals and thousands of other fresh Allied troops were landed at Anzac Cove and Suvla Bay, the *Ben-My-Chree*'s seaplanes were engaged in a diversionary attack on the port of Sığacık on Turkey's Aegean coast. However, while the grim battles raged on the Gallipoli Peninsula over the ensuing weeks, the planes were relatively powerless to do anything. If they came too close to land, Turkish artillery would have felled them in a flash.

Childers was never quite sure why he'd been sent to the Mediterranean, given that his expertise was the North Sea and, a few yachting jaunts aside, he knew little of the terrain. Perhaps, after such a long period in the dark, cold north, he relished such warm climes but the weather had many downsides. Seaplane engines were constantly in danger of being choked by wind-blown sands, and the woodwork was prone to warp in the intense heat. Furthermore, the German submarines may have dived deeper since the spotter planes arrived, but they hadn't gone away. On 2 September 1915, a torpedo struck the *Southland*, a transport ship from Egypt carrying nearly 700 Australian troops. The *Ben-My-Chree* was just ten miles north of the stricken ship. Upon picking up the mayday distress call, Cecil Malone steered to the rescue, and his crew gathered up most of the troops and crew from the rafts and lifeboats. But 40 men had died; a pertinent reminder that the enemy was afoot.

During the course of September, Childers continued to engage in reconnaissance missions over the Turkish lines. There was also the occasional, generally futile bombing expedition, such as an attempt to destroy the flour mill in Gallipoli from which the Turkish troops obtained their bread.

September was also the month in which Bulgaria declared war on the Allies. During the last weeks of 1915, Childers flew as navigator in a series of attacks on a crucial Bulgarian railway bridge that carried the Berlin to Constantinople line over the Maritza River. They only managed to close it for a few weeks, but this modest success was nonetheless saluted in newspapers from New York to New Zealand.

When the long-necessary evacuation of Gallipoli finally began in December 1915, it did so in secret — for fear of what the Ottomans and the Germans might unleash if they learned of such an operation. Childers and his fellow crew were instructed to intensify their search for enemy activity in the Aegean waters. As the evacuation got under way, Childers described in his diary the sense of 'melancholy' he felt when he considered 'the prodigious amount of time, money, labour and the like wasted over the attempt to force the Dardanelles'.[2] He was also despondent about the lack of 'enterprise and dash' of the Allied leaders entrusted with ongoing operations against the Turks.

Almost as soon as the last troops were evacuated from Gallipoli, Lieutenant Commander Malone received fresh orders from the Admiralty. The *Ben-My-Chree* was to make its way to Port Said on the north-east coast of British-occupied Egypt, where she was to become the flagship of the new East Indies and Egypt Seaplane Squadron. Her primary role was henceforth to protect the Suez Canal from Turkish attack. Once again, Childers and his squadron had the immense advantage of uncontested control of the air, so they could virtually do as they pleased.

Over the next three months, Childers flew on numerous patrol missions over southern Palestine and the Sinai Peninsula. As an observer, his brief was to monitor human activity, just as a present-day drone might do: keeping a look-out for moving vehicles and camel convoys, taking note of any geographical or infrastructural features that might be relevant, such as a broken bridge or the foundation of a new railway line. This was precisely the sort of vital intelligence that had been so lacking in the Gallipoli campaign. Moreover, he now had a new tool at his disposal: a camera with which he quickly became highly proficient.

Childers felt greatly privileged to get such a close insight into Palestine, the setting for so many of the Bible stories he read in his childhood. That didn't stop him bombing the place if there was an opportunity to play havoc with the Turks. He particularly enjoyed dropping bombs on the railway line that ran from Syria through Palestine, terminating at Beersheba, where the Australian cavalry would make their epic charge a year later.

However, underneath it all, Childers was starting to feel restless. There was nothing he could really sink his teeth into and he felt that his talents were being wasted on menial, if not fruitless, missions.[3]

Colonel Frederick Sykes, his commanding officer, concurred and while he hailed Childers as a 'brilliant officer and utterly fearless', Sykes noted the novelist's tendency to seek out action when he was supposed to stay put.

Childers must have briefly perked up in March 1916 when it became apparent that the Turks had finally established an air base at Beersheba. At least there would now be the possibility of dogfights with the Ottomans to liven things up. However, for him, it was not to be. That same month, he was summoned back to London to take up a mundane desk job at the Admiralty's Air Department.

On 10 March 1916, Lieutenant Erskine Childers said goodbye to the men with whom he had lived and flown over the skies of Gallipoli, Egypt, Palestine and the Sinai Penin-

The Imperial Camel Corps
Brigade at Beersheba, 1915.

sula for the previous year. As he left the ship, his fellow officers formed a line along the gangway. Childers shook hands with each man before clambering down to the waiting motorboat. 'The motorboat shoved off,' he recalled, 'and three cheers were given by the whole ship's company standing on the upper deck. It was utterly unexpected and I felt quite overcome. I cheered back and waved my cap. We rounded the bow of a French carrier, and I saw the last of *Ben My Chree*.'[4] Turkish artillery shells sank the seaplane carrier off the south-west coast of Turkey ten months later.

Childers cannot have been long back in London when the Easter Rising erupted in Dublin at the end of April. Many of the Irish Volunteers who fought did so with

the antiquated but effective Mauser rifles he had sailed into Howth 20 months earlier. He was not involved with the Rising per se but his shock at the execution of its leaders intensified his feelings that Ireland must be free from British rule.

For the rest of 1916 until July 1917, Lieutenant Commander Erskine Childers, as he now was, worked as an Intelligence Officer with the Coastal Motor Boats at Queenborough off the coast of Kent. It was drab work until April 1917 when, operating out of Dunkirk, he served on one of the motorboats that patrolled the sea, by day and night, keeping tabs on the minefields strewn along the coast between Zeebrugge and Ostend. Enemy seaplanes and shore batteries frequently fired at the boats — one received a

• • •

HMS *Ben-My-Chree*, the Royal Navy seaplane carrier on
which Childers served as an intelligence officer in 1915
and 1916, primarily in Gallipoli, Palestine, the Sinai
Peninsula and Egypt.

direct hit at short range — and Childers' boat narrowly missed being sunk by a submarine. He was also in the observer's hot seat when a Handley Page bomber embarked
upon a bombing raid on the Gotha airfields at Sint-Denijs-Westrem. On 21 April, he
was awarded the DSO in recognition of his services in the Mediterranean.

The Irish question became of paramount importance for Childers again in July
1917 when he took his place on the Secretariat of the Irish Convention alongside Bob
Barton and Diarmuid Coffey, who had sailed on the *Kelpie* in 1914. Summoned by
Lloyd George, the nine-month convention took place at Trinity College, Dublin and,
with representatives from all Irish parties and backgrounds, it sought to hammer out
a solution to the ongoing deadlock. Childers advanced his arguments for Dominion
Home Rule but it soon became apparent that the convention could drag on intermi-
nably without any resolutions.

The Irish Convention was ultimately a casualty of the German Spring Offensive
launched along the Western Front on 21 March 1918. Within six weeks Britain had lost
nearly 300,000 men. Desperate to shore up the Allied defence line, the British Government offered immediate Home Rule, but only on condition that enforced conscrip-

tion be introduced into Ireland. Infuriated by such political intrigues, Childers quit the convention and, like many others, transferred his allegiance to the Sinn Féin party.

However, before he returned to the Irish political scene, there was still a war to be fought in Europe. On 24 April, two weeks after he left the Irish Convention, Childers resumed his role as an Intelligence Officer with the RAF. He was subsequently sent to the RAF station at Bircham Newton in Norfolk, where he was one of the brains who masterminded a major air raid — the first of its kind — to take place on Berlin. Scheduled for 10 November 1918, the attack was postponed for 24 hours on account of bad weather. Berlin was not to have an easy ride in the coming years, but the city was at least spared from Childers' aerial bombardment because at 11am the following morning, the Armistice was signed and the Great War stuttered to a close.

Childers was promptly sent on a six-week assignment to Flanders to assess the impact of five years of bombing on the landscape. He was still in Belgium when, a few days before Christmas, he became seriously ill, having most probably contracted the deadly influenza known as the Spanish Flu. Hospitalised for over three months, he then returned to Glendalough to recuperate. He now came under the influence of his cousin Bob Barton, who persuaded him to abandon his quest for Home Rule and to become a committed Republican.

Much admired by de Valera, Childers became de facto Director of Propaganda for the underground Dáil cabinet in 1920. When the British authorities raided his house in March 1920, it prompted Lieutenant Colonel Malone, his old friend from the *Ben-My-Chree* and now an MP, to ask the House of Commons, 'Was it necessary, in order to carry out the raid, to ransack the nursery, and to wake up the children?' *The Irish Times* noted that his question received no reply.[5]

Having served as Chief Secretary for the delegation that negotiated the Anglo-Irish Treaty, Childers became one of the linchpins of the Anti-Treaty campaign. In November 1922, the 'damned Englishman' — as Arthur Griffith referred to him — was arrested by Irish Free State soldiers at his beloved Glendalough. He was charged with possession of a pistol, which de Valera described as 'a tiny automatic, little better than a toy and in no sense a war weapon'. But the Free State government under WT Cosgrave had found a legal excuse to eliminate Childers from the plot. He was one of 77 republicans to be executed by the Free State between November 1922 and the end of the Civil War in May 1923.[6]

At six o'clock on the morning of his execution, he wrote to Molly, 'It all seems perfectly simple and inevitable, like lying down after a long day's work.' When the firing squad took their positions in Beggarsbush Barracks later that morning, he called out to them, 'Take a step closer, boys. It will be easier that way.'

Bob Barton mourned Childers' execution as 'the wreck of all our hopes'. De Valera maintained that 'of all the men I ever met I would say he was the noblest.' But the story of the Childers family was by no means over. His son, Erskine Hamilton Childers, became fourth President of Ireland in 1973. His grandson, Erskine Barton Childers, served as Secretary General of the World Federation of United Nation Associations. His granddaughter, Nessa Childers, has been a Member of the European Parliament in Europe since 2009.

THE BARTON BROTHERS

All three of Erskine Childers' male Barton cousins served in Britain's armed forces during the Great War. Robert 'Bob' Barton, the eldest, initially trained as a private in the Inns of Court Officers' Training Corps. When the Easter Rising broke out in 1916, he was sent to Dublin and gazetted as a second lieutenant to the 10th (Commercial) Battalion of the Royal Dublin Fusiliers. He arrived in the city the following Wednesday but, ostensibly because he did not have the right uniform, he was quickly packed off to Glan (Glendalough House) where he spent the rest of the week. He later assumed he had been sidelined because of his probable sympathies with the rebels. It is often stated that he was so appalled by the heavy-handed British response to the Rising that he immediately resigned his commission and joined the Republican movement. It is true that he did later become a Sinn Féin MP and a Minister in the Irish Free State cabinet, as well as one of the key negotiators of the Anglo-Irish Treaty. However, he did not resign his officer's commission, as claimed.

After the Rising, he was posted to Richmond Barracks in Inchicore, Dublin, where his principal duty was to look after the personal effects of rebel prisoners, 3,000 of whom were held at the barracks before they were either released or transported to prison camps in Northern Ireland, England and Wales. He was evidently so good at his job that when the 10th Battalion left Ireland in August, the British military headquarters in Parkgate Street refused to let him go with them. He was instead transferred to the newly formed 11th Battalion and instructed to complete his work sorting out the prisoners' belongings. Meanwhile, his comrades from the 10th were hurled into the carnage of the Ancre, where the battalion suffered appalling casualties of over 50 per cent; 81 died on 13 November alone.

Bob's two brothers were less fortunate than him. Less than three months after the Easter Rising, his youngest brother Thomas, a second lieutenant with the Inniskillings and a veteran of Gallipoli, was killed leading a charge at the Somme. In the summer of 1918, his only surviving brother Ernie, a captain in the Royal Irish Rifles, was badly gassed while marooned in a trench in France. The 36-year-old was rushed to hospital where he died on 23 August.[7] It is not known whether he was aware that their mother Agnes Barton had passed away less than two weeks earlier. Ernie was married as a young man but had no children.

Following the collapse of the Irish Convention in 1917, Robert Barton, the Master of Glendalough, became a committed nationalist. In December 1918, he was elected Sinn Féin MP for West Wicklow. He was simultaneously appointed Chairman of Wicklow County Council. Two months later he was arrested for making seditious speeches and imprisoned in Mountjoy. In a letter to the Capuchin Friar Albert Bibby, he stated that 'prison life is no affliction to me. I much prefer the rest, seclusion and study of a cell to discoursing in public platforms'. Certainly his sense of humour was not dampened by his time in Mountjoy. When Michael Collins helped him escape, he left a courteous note for the Governor explaining that he could no longer stay, as the service was unsatisfactory. Moreover, he wondered, would they mind looking after his luggage until he sent for it?

In April 1919 Éamon de Valera appointed him Director of Agriculture in the First Dáil, an office he retained until August 1921. During this time he co-founded the National Land Bank, with Erskine Childers as one of its five directors. Re-arrested in January 1920, Bob was sentenced to a further three years in England's Portland Prison, but he was released on the signing of the Truce in 1921.

He was serving as the Second Dáil's Secretary of State for Economic Affairs when de Valera selected him as one of the five delegates who were sent to London to negotiate the Anglo-Irish Treaty in the latter months of 1921. He was the Treaty's last and most reluctant signatory, regarding it as 'the lesser of two outrages forced upon me'. In January 1922 he was among the cabinet members who, led by de Valera, resigned in protest at the ratification of the Treaty.

In later life, Bob Barton served as Chairman of both the Agricultural Credit Corporation and Bord na Móna. In the summer of 1950, the 69-year-old finally took a wife, Rachel Lothrop Warren, an American niece of Erskine's wife Molly who, as a child, was painted by John Singer Sargent. He died peacefully at Glan aged 95 in August 1975.

• • •

Members of the Irish delegation at the signing of the Anglo-Irish Treaty between Great Britain and Ireland in London on 6 December 1921. Childers is standing on the left with lawyer George Gavan Duffy, and fellow secretary John Chartres on the right. Seated from left, Arthur Griffith, Eamonn Duggan, Michael Collins and Childers' cousin Robert 'Bob' Barton.

HOLYHEAD HARBOUR & STATION HOTEL.
S.S."HIBERNIA" LEAVING FOR DUBLIN.

• • •

SS *Hibernia*, a twin-screw steamer passenger vessel operated by the London and North Western Railway, is
pictured leaving Holyhead for Dublin. During the war
she was requisitioned by the Admiralty, renamed HMS
Tara and sunk in action off the coast of north Africa.

HIBERNIA

AND THE SENUSSI

OF LIBYA

...

ON 5 NOVEMBER 1915, THE GERMAN U-BOAT U.35, COMMANDED BY WALDEMAR KOPHAMEL, was hiding outside Sallum Bay off the coast of Egypt when she fired a torpedo at an incoming 1,800-ton British armed boarding steamer. The ship, which sank with the loss of 12 lives, was HMS *Tara*. She was rather better known in Ireland by her former name of *Hibernia*, having served as the Holyhead-Kingstown (Dún Laoghaire) passenger ship for the London and North Western Railway Company in Dublin from 1900 until 1914.

As the ship sank, the submarine rose to the surface, enabling the 93 surviving passengers and crew to cling to her deck. Captain Kophamel then towed his captives to Port Suliman on the east Libyan coast where they were handed over to the Senussi, a Muslim sect in league with the Ottoman Turks. The Senussi had recently raised jihad and were in the throes of attacking British Egypt from the west. Things had become so heated on the north African coast that, on 23 November, Admiral de Robeck had to provide the sloop *Clematis* and six trawlers from the Dardanelles fleet to evacuate the British troops guarding the port at Sallum.

A counter-offensive against the Senussi commenced in December and, by March 1916, the British had regained Sallum. One of the most epic events to take place in North Africa during the Great War then followed when the flamboyant Duke of Westminster led a fleet of 40 armoured vehicles, cars and ambulances across the Libyan desert to rescue the *Tara* survivors from a remote oasis where they had been held captive for several months.

The Duke, whose lovers included Coco Chanel, later married Nancy Sullivan of Glanmire, County Cork. As Duchess of Westminster, Nancy became world famous as the owner of the outstanding Irish thoroughbred racehorse Arkle, winner of three consecutive Cheltenham Gold Cups and the King George VI Chase.

• • •

Gottfried Freiherr von Banfield, pictured on the right, was
the Austro-Hungarian Empire's leading naval air ace in the
Great War. His grandfather was a British Army accountant from Bandon, County Cork. This photograph was
published by *Berliner Illustrirte Zeitung* circa 1916.

THE
EAGLE OF TRIESTE

...

IRELAND HAS A CURIOUS LINK TO GOTTFRIED FREIHERR VON BANFIELD (1890–1986), THE most successful Austro-Hungarian naval pilot of the war. Known as the 'Eagle of Trieste', he descended from the Banfields, a Quaker merchant family from Clonmel, County Tipperary. His grandfather Thomas Collins Banfield (1799–1855) was born in Bandon, County Cork, and served as an accountant with the British Army. In 1853, Thomas was married in Vienna to Josephine von Frech, an Austrian aristocrat. Their son Richard — Gottfried's father — became an Austrian citizen and was commissioned as a gunnery officer with the Austro-Hungarian Navy (the k.u.k. Kriegsmarine). Born in Montenegro in 1890, Gottfried racked up nine confirmed air kills (and 11 unconfirmed) over the Adriatic between 1915 and 1918. After the war, he moved to Newcastle-upon-Tyne in England and married the Contessa Maria Tripcovich. Their son Raffaello de Banfield became a celebrated composer and was a close friend of Herbert von Karajan, the Austrian conductor of the Berlin Philharmonic.

. . .

Having made his first fortune from Australian gold, William Knox D'Arcy was destined to repeat his success with Persian oil, paving the way for the birth of BP.

KNOX D'ARCY —
THE MAN WHO OILED THE
ROYAL NAVY

...

ON 21 NOVEMBER 1918, TEN DAYS AFTER THE ARMISTICE ENDED THE WAR, LORD CURZON, a leading member of Britain's wartime cabinet, attended a euphoric dinner at the Inter-Allied Petroleum Conference in London. To tremendous applause, he declared that the Allies had 'floated to victory on a wave of oil'. He was referring to the fact that Britain's unimpeded access to oil had enabled the Allies to run such an efficient fleet of motor trucks that they had ultimately triumphed over Germany's coal-fired railway.

He was also giving a nod to a decision taken in 1911 by Winston Churchill, then First Lord of the Admiralty, to convert the driving systems of every vessel in the Royal Navy from coal to oil. Churchill's monumental decision came just a few months after the British Government had purchased a 51 per cent stake in the Anglo-Persian Oil Company, thereby becoming majority shareholders in Masjed Soleyman in south-western Persia (now Iran), the largest oilfield in the world.

When the Persian oil was first discovered, Churchill declared it 'a prize from Fairy-land beyond our wildest dreams'. He was also quick to acknowledge Knox D'Arcy, the Irish multi-millionaire who bankrolled the project.

Knox D'Arcy hailed from a family that had been in Ireland since at least the 14th century. William Francis D'Arcy, his father, was born and raised on a farm in Gorteen, a boggy townland just west of Charlestown in north-east Mayo. In the wake of the Great Famine of the 1840s, WF D'Arcy made his way to Newton Abbott in England, where he became a solicitor and married the local Rector's daughter. William Knox D'Arcy was the sixth of their seven children — and their only son.

In 1865, WF D'Arcy was declared bankrupt and fled to Australia with his family, including 16-year-old Knox. He reopened his solicitor's practice in Rockhampton, Queensland, but died less than five years later. Young Knox took over the practice, married a Mexican-born blonde beauty nine years his senior and rapidly established himself as one of Rockhampton's most influential citizens.

In 1882, he formed a syndicate with the Morgan brothers, who held the mining lease on Ironstone Mountain (later renamed Mount Morgan) outside the town. It turned out that the mountain was stuffed with so much gold that by 1890 Knox D'Arcy was one of the wealthiest men in the British Empire, with a fortune equivalent to that of Bill Gates today.

An inexorable capitalist, he purchased two large mansions in England, town houses in Paris and Brussels, and a substantial chunk of Grosvenor Square in London. He commissioned the Holy Grail tapestries from William Morris for his dining room, thus financing one of the supreme achievements of the Arts and Crafts movement. He commissioned Frank Dicksee to paint a portrait of his wife. He hosted dinners at his private enclosure at the Epsom Racecourse, held long shooting weekend parties on his Norfolk estate and threw wild parties in London where guests twirled to the voices of Nellie Melba and Enrico Caruso.

His marriage collapsed, with his wife, the mother of his five children, stating that all the 'flattery and success has turned his head'. Two years later, he was married again to Nina Boucicault, daughter of Irish-Australian newspaper boss Arthur L Boucicault and a niece of the acclaimed Dublin dramatist Dion Boucicault.

By 1900, Knox's knuckles were crunching restlessly. Gold was all very well, but wasn't there a way to make even more money? That same year, this moustachioed lion of London society received a visit from Sir Henry Drummond Wolff, who served as Britain's foremost diplomat in Tehran for several years. Sir Henry explained that he had lately met some high-ranking Persians who believed Persia possessed vast, untapped oil reserves. The region was, in the words of one geologist who had surveyed its terrain, 'unquestionably petroliferous territory'. All the Persians needed was a financial backer.

With the prospect of a major European war never far away, D'Arcy understood that the world's increasingly mechanised armies would need to be fuelled by oil. Lots of oil. He recognised that internal combustion engines would soon revolutionise every aspect of human life. Whoever controlled oil would hold the key to world power.

He also realised that, when it came to oil supplies, the British Empire was shockingly deficient. Oil had been discovered in the Caspian Sea, in the Dutch East Indies, and in the United States, but there was no sign of it in either Britain or any of its colonies. If the British could not find oil, they would no longer be able to rule the waves and the empire would almost certainly collapse.

Whether such imperial concerns preyed upon Knox D'Arcy's mind is unknown, but in 1901 he made the Shah of Persia an offer he could not refuse, namely £30,000 in cash and a large stake in his new oil-drilling venture. The D'Arcy Concession, as this rather scurrilous deal became known, gave D'Arcy 60 years' worth of exclusive rights to explore and exploit petroleum resources through 490,000 square miles of the Persian Empire, a territory larger than Texas and California combined. It was the most lucrative deal in the short but ever-frantic history of the petroleum industry.

Deal done, D'Arcy recruited a gung-ho engineer and self-taught geologist called George Reynolds to start drilling. Over the next seven years, Reynolds and his team moved across Persia in pursuit of oil. The costs of equipping and maintaining this drilling party, including 900 mules, were astronomical. Month after month, year after year, D'Arcy wrote cheques to support the venture. His spirits soared in January 1904 when Reynolds struck oil near the present-day Iraqi border, but crashed a few months later when the well ran dry. Bit by bit, D'Arcy's fortune slipped away. His patience and resources were sorely tested.

'Good news from Persia would be very acceptable now', he dryly advised Reynolds in May 1905. No such news came and in 1908, with his coffers approaching rock bottom, he sent a telegram to Reynolds ordering him to 'cease work, dismiss the staff, dismantle anything worth the cost of transporting to the coast for reshipment, and come home'.

Reynolds considered the options. After seven years of exceptionally trying conditions, he was not prepared to give in. Legend has it that, even as he read the telegram, an old-timer told him, 'I can feel a strike in my bones'. Reynolds advised his men that in such a remote region, telegrams could not be trusted. They must continue working until the message was confirmed by post.

Three weeks later, Knox D'Arcy received a telegram from Persia to say that Reynolds's team had struck oil at Masjed Soleyman in Khuzestan province. Today, a large signpost at the entrance to this prosperous town proudly announces that this was the site of the first commercial oil well in the Middle East.

The D'Arcy Concession was reborn as the Anglo-Persian Oil Company in 1909, and was later to evolve into British Petroleum, aka BP. D'Arcy had recouped his fortune and lived out his final years at his country mansion in England, passing away in 1917. Without his money or his perseverance, the British are highly unlikely to have discovered oil in Persia. And without oil, they could not have triumphed over Germany.

• • •

This is believed to be the 'discovery well' at Masjed Soleymán in Khuzestan province shortly after the first oil strike on 26 May 1908. The strike heralded the dawn of the Middle East's oil and gas industry.

The iconic Irish guerrilla fighter
Tom Barry learned much of his
military expertise while serving as a
gunner with the Royal Field Artillery in Mesopotamia.

GUNNER TOM BARRY

AND THE

SIEGE OF KUT

...

On 9 April 1916, Gordon King and Bertie Tierney lifted themselves up from the roasting hot Mesopotamian earth and charged for a third time at the Turkish trenches. The Kerryman and the barrister from County Clare had only been in the region for six weeks but, as veterans of the Gallipoli campaign, the two young officers knew as much as anyone about how tough and appalling war could be. Some of the men who lay alongside them also managed to stumble to their feet and join the last charge. But most were too exhausted to go any further and simply watched despondently as the Irishmen vanished into the Turkish smoke.

Mesopotamia is one of the least-known fronts of the Great War, largely because the campaign was such a debacle for the British. Irishmen were involved at every level and many would die out there in the land that we know today as Iraq. Among those who survived was Tom Barry, later to become an iconic guerrilla fighter in West Cork during the Irish War of Independence. He was to spend two years in a region that he described in his memoirs as 'that land of Biblical names and history, of vast deserts and date groves, scorching suns and hot winds, the land of Babylon, Baghdad and the Garden of Eden, where the rushing Euphrates and the mighty Tigris converge and flow down to the Persian Gulf.'

Tom Barry's life was destined to be dramatic from the moment his father Thomas, a Roman Catholic officer in the Royal Irish Constabulary (RIC), first clapped eyes on Margaret O'Donovan, the pretty daughter of a businessman from Liscarroll, County Cork.

The elder Barry grew up on a small farm near Rosscarbery, a loyalist stronghold on the coast of West Cork. Having joined the RIC in 1893, Thomas was based in Liscarroll when he first met Margaret. Her father was not prepared to accept a policeman as a son-in-law, but when Thomas was transferred to Killorglin, County Kerry, Margaret eloped with him. Duly disowned by her father, Margaret married Thomas and they

British soldiers trudge through the dust beneath the Hamrin mountains in north-east Iraq during the Mesopotamian campaign. In ancient times, the ridge behind them formed the border between Babylonia to the south and Assyria to the north.

settled at Chubbs Corner in Killorglin where Thomas Bernardine Barry, the second of 14 children, was born on 1 July 1897.

Known as 'Bernie' during his boyhood, Tom Barry spent his first decade living the life of a policeman's son. In 1907, his father resigned from the service and moved back to Rosscarbery where he helped his aunt Hannah (née Barry) and her husband Jerh Collins run a pub-shop called The Arcade. It was one of those classic Irish pubs where the customer could purchase groceries or hardware, or be sized up for a suit by an in-house tailor while supping on a pint of stout at the bar. Jerh Collins was a first cousin of the iconic patriot Michael Collins.[8]

From The Arcade, Tom Barry walked to the Boys' National School in Ardagh, where he quickly became a favourite of his Irish-speaking schoolmaster John McCarthy, a rousing storyteller and ardent nationalist. The youngster proved so bright that McCarthy not only gave him extra tuition after class and lent him books, but also instructed him on how to use his sporting rifle, with which he shot rabbits, pigeons and woodcock. 'Not alone did I give Tom Barry his formal education,' McCarthy remarked, 'but I took him one day when he was quite young and showed him how to hold, carry, load and fire the gun.'[9] As well as mastering Gaelic football during this era, Barry also learned how to Swim very suddenly when some older boys shoved him over a 12-foot drop into water, leaving him no option but to sink or swim.

Tom Barry's sense of mischief came to the fore when a friend challenged him to ride the family cow through Rosscarbery. As his girlfriend Kathy Hayes recalled, 'No sooner said than done, he jumped on the cow's back and headed for the town. The dogs went mad, barking, jumping and pulling the cow's tail. Naturally, people came to the doors to see what was causing the racket. Through the town, round the corner, hell for leather! Bernie [i.e. Tom] clung on. At the stall door he threw himself on a heap of manure just in time to save his head.' He received a considerable telling-off from his family for the embarrassment it caused, not least when it was revealed that the cow was in calf.

Kathy Hayes also remembered the restless youngster leading a gang who must have been the scourge of Rosscarbery at the time. Their party trick was to await the arrival of the country folk who came into town for Mass on their pony and traps. And then, while they were engaged in prayer, Barry and his pals would untie the ponies for a little devilment. 'They would race them up and down the hill and around the fields,' recalled Miss Hayes. 'When the owners would come out from Mass, the horses would be in a lather of sweat. He [Barry] was a terror!'

Perhaps eager to tame the boy and aware of his superior intelligence, Tom's wealthy O'Donovan aunts offered to pay for his education at Mungret College, a Jesuit-run boarding school near Limerick. He lasted a year before his expulsion in September 1912 for running home 'without knowledge of superiors'.[10]

Meanwhile, his parents were struggling to make enough money from The Arcade to support such a large family. Shortly before the war they sold their home on Fair Lane and relocated to Upper Convent Hill in Bandon, a largely pro-British garrison town where, as local wags put it, even the pigs were Protestant. As a former policeman, the elder Barry may have fitted in quite well, although he was a supporter of John

Redmond's Home Rule campaign while Margaret was increasingly sympathetic to the cause of Irish nationalism.

Young Tom became a clerk in Emerson's, a Protestant merchant's shop on MacSwiney's Quay, where he sold machinery, coal, manure, oil, timber and general provisions. Every Sunday he cycled the 20 miles back to his beloved Rosscarbery to hang out with his girlfriend Kathy Hayes and their friends.

With the outbreak of the Great War, Bandon was unsurprisingly jingoistic. When Tom Barry expressed a desire to join up, he was offered a commission in the Royal Munster Fusiliers.[11] However, ever the pyromaniac, he instead fastened his eyes on the Royal Field Artillery (RFA).[12] On 30 June 1915, the 17-year-old and his friend Frank McMurrough enlisted in the RFA in Cork. The recruitment officer who sized him up noted that he was five feet ten inches tall, brown haired, clean-shaven, smartly dressed and adorned with a large mole on his left thigh.

Barry described his motives for joining up in his memoirs:

'In June, in my seventeenth year, I had decided to see what this Great War was like. I cannot plead I went on the advice of John Redmond or any other politician, that if we fought for the British we would secure Home Rule for Ireland, nor can I say I understood what Home Rule meant. I was not influenced by the lurid appeal to fight to save Belgium or small nations. I knew nothing about nations, large or small. I went to the war for no other reason than that I wanted to see what war was like, to get a gun, to see new countries and to feel a grown man. Above all I went because I knew no Irish history and had no national consciousness. I had never been told of Wolfe Tone or Robert Emmet, though I did know all about the kings of England and when they had come to the British throne. I had never heard of the victory over the Sassenach at Benburb, but I could tell the dates of Waterloo and Trafalgar. I did not know of the spread of Christianity throughout Europe by Irish missionaries and scholars, but did I not know of the blessings of civilisation which Clive and the East India Company had brought to dark and heathen India?'[13]

Two days after he joined up, he was posted to the Royal Field Artillery depot at Athlone from where he went on to train in Woolwich. His loyalist neighbours in Bandon were apparently so optimistic about his prospects that they composed the following verse:

> And what of Gunner Barry,
> A fearless son is he;
> We hope he will return
> With the shining bronze V.C.[14]

Barry was assigned as a gunner to the RFA's 4th Brigade, working with the 14th Battery. The brigade initially served with the 7th (Meerut) Division on the Western Front. It is thought his first action was at the battle of La Bassée in October 1914 where he was gassed.[15] He was taken back to Boulogne and then to the Royal Hospital in Woolwich. It is not clear when he rejoined his battery, but the 4th Brigade was to serve in the battles of Neuve-Chapelle, Aubers Ridge, Festubert and Loos in 1915.

Barry was destined to become a brilliant fighter, but he was by no means naturally inclined to obedience. On 28 October 1915, he was reprimanded for being 20 minutes late for a 6am parade 'when on active service' and also for 'not complying with an order'.

Shortly after Christmas 1915, he was with the 4th Brigade when it sailed from Marseilles to Mesopotamia, where everything was beginning to go horribly wrong for the Allies.

And it had all started so promisingly. During 1914 and most of 1915, the Ottoman government who ruled Mesopotamia didn't seem wildly interested in defending the land, preferring to focus their armies on the other battlegrounds in the Caucasus, the Sinai and, latterly, the Dardanelles. Eager to protect the oil refinery of Abadan Island at the head of the Persian Gulf, as well as the oilfields of the Anglo-Persian Oil Company, the British had authorised the army in British India to form Indian Expeditionary Force D, which was to take on the Turks in Mesopotamia. The bulk of this force initially comprised the 6th (Poona) Division under the command of General Sir Charles Vere Ferrers Townshend whose great-great-grandfather had been Lord Lieutenant of Ireland in the late 18th century.[16]

Commencing in November 1914, Townshend's force enjoyed a good deal of success against the under-equipped Turks, securing the city of Basra on the River Tigris which, along with the Euphrates, marked one of the main communication channels through the wide plains of Mesopotamia. One of their greatest victories took place in April 1915 at Shaiba near Basra, and culminated in the distraught Turkish commander shooting himself. Meanwhile, the British were left to lionise the efforts of Major George Massy Wheeler, a 42-year-old cavalry officer from a well-known Dublin family, who was last seen spurring his horse onwards, far in advance of his squadron, in an attempt to seize a Turkish flag.[17] Major Wheeler was awarded a posthumous Victoria Cross.[18]

Shortly after the battle of Shaiba, a new man arrived to take command of the entire Mesopotamian campaign. General Sir John Eccles Nixon was born in 1857 to a family who had been based at Drumcrow on the southern shore of Lower Lough Erne, County Fermanagh, since the 1690s and traced their ancestry to the Rev Adam Nixon, Vicar General of Clogher.[19] Sir John's father, an officer in the Bombay Army, had been Consul General and Political Agent for Turkish Arabia during the 1870s. Sir John had been with the British Indian Army since 1878, campaigning in the mountainous regions of present-day Afghanistan and Pakistan, as well as leading a cavalry brigade in South Africa during the Anglo-Boer War. Prior to his Mesopotamian appointment, he had commanded British India's Southern Army for five years.

Sir John's ADC during the Mesopotamian campaign was another Nixon from Ireland, although it is unclear if or how Captain Ernest John Nixon was related. Born in County Kilkenny in 1885, Captain Nixon grew up at Cloone House, the family home near Ballyragget. Major General Arundel Nixon, his father, commanded the Royal Artillery in Gibraltar from 1906 to 1910 and was a leading patron of the Red Cross, particularly in Dublin Castle, as well as a Justice of the Peace for County Kilkenny. Educated at Cheltenham College and the Royal Military Academy, Woolwich, Ernest became Nixon's ADC in 1915.

• • •

Pitched on the left bank of the River Tigris, Kut-al-Amara was once a prosperous town, equally prized for its carpets and its cereal. Occupied by General
Townsend's forces on 3 December 1915, it was surrendered to the Turks on 29
April 1916, the same day the Irish rebels surrendered in Dublin. Kut was recaptured by allied troops under General Sir Stanley Maude in 1917 but much of the
old town was left in ruins.

General Nixon's game plan was relatively straightforward. General Townshend
was to bring the 6th (Poona) Division up the River Tigris from Basra and capture the
Mesopotamian capital of Baghdad. With a certain amount of misgivings about the plan,
Townshend duly worked his way up, keeping his army supplied by a convoy of river-
boats and hastily improvised donkey and camel transports. By the end of September
1915, they had captured Kut-al-Amara, a town approximately 100 miles south of
Baghdad, set within a loop of the Tigris.

Recognising Kut's superior defensive characteristics, Townshend sent word to
General Nixon proposing that he and his men stay put in Kut rather than risking an
advance on Baghdad. However, Nixon was under pressure from London to capture
Baghdad in order to restore flagging morale resulting from the failure of the Dardanelles campaign.

On 22 November 1915, Townshend's 11,000-strong amphibious army reached the town of Ctesiphon, just 26 miles south-east of Baghdad. However, things were about to change dramatically for the British. Finally realising the strategic importance of Baghdad, Enver Pasha, the Ottoman Minister of War, had brought in thousands of troops to defend the city. The 18,000-strong Turkish Army was placed under the temporary command of Nureddin Ibrahim Pasha, Governor of both Basra and Baghdad Provinces, who duly engaged Townshend's force at Ctesiphon and crucially halted the British advance, albeit with a severe loss of life.

After three days of heavy fighting, the two armies had taken such a hammering that the two commanders simultaneously began to withdraw their exhausted troops. From Townshend's viewpoint, his division was so badly depleted that it couldn't possibly capture Baghdad on its own. Logic dictated that he should bring the division back down the river, at least as far as Kut and then, as he initially proposed, dig in.

When Nureddin got wind of a British retreat, he promptly whistled up fresh troops from Baghdad and sent them in hot pursuit. The Turks chased Townshend's isolated force all the way back to Kut, so that by the time the 6th (Poona) Division was safely within the city, its numbers had been whittled down by 4,600 men. Not surprisingly, the British Indians who fought at Ctesiphon thereafter referred to the town as "Pistupon".

In the midst of all this, Sir John Nixon got a personal taste of defeat when the paddle-steamer on which he voyaged up the Tigris to oversee the campaign was attacked from both sides and ran aground. At length, the vessel had no option but to run up a white flag and invite their assailants on board for negotiations. The attackers turned out to be Arabs who apparently compelled Nixon to pay them a large sum of money before allowing him to continue back to Basra.[20]

While some felt Townshend should have continued on down the Tigris to Basra, Townshend reckoned he could hold steady at Kut. He just managed to get his cavalry out before 11,000 Turks surrounded the town and trapped the remainder of his force inside. The Turks were now commanded by Baron Colmar von der Goltz, an elderly German general and military historian who knew how to keep his enemy hemmed in.

Although the failure to capture Baghdad was a massive dent to British morale, damage limitation enthusiasts felt there was some merit in tying down so many Turks into a siege situation, not least because Kut had enough supplies to keep Townshend's men going for several months. However, Townshend was clearly eager to move on. In January 1915, he dispatched a message to Nixon suggesting they try to break out. Nixon rejected the plan but when Townshend erroneously claimed their supplies were running low, Nixon hastily summoned a force of 19,000 men to break the siege.

Command of the relief expedition was assigned to Lieutenant General Fenton Aylmer, scion of a family active in County Kildare since at least the 15th century when, at the height of the Wars of the Roses, Richard Aylmer of Lyons was appointed Sovereign of the Borough of Tassagard (present-day Saggart), with orders to protect its English settler community from attacks by the neighbouring septs of O'Toole and O'Byrne. Sir Gerald Aylmer served as Chief Justice of Ireland under Henry VIII, while his elder brother Richard was awarded the lucrative manor house of Donadea for his help in suppressing Silken Thomas Fitzgerald's abortive rebellion. Another ancestor narrowly survived the 1798 Rebellion to become a founding father of the Kildare Hunt.

Fenton Aylmer became a household name in 1891 when he took part in the storming of Nilt, a powerful enemy fortress in the North-West frontier (present-day Pakistan), during the Hunza-Nagar campaign. The 29-year-old forced its inner gates open by laying explosive gun-cotton slabs directly beneath them, under intense fire. Despite being shot in the leg, he managed to ignite the explosives and loosed off 19 shots with his revolver, killing several of his opponents. He continued fighting until, severely wounded, he fainted from loss of blood. Carried to safety, he awoke a hero and was subsequently awarded the Victoria Cross.

A quarter of a century later, Aylmer was sent to relieve Townshend, a fellow veteran of the Hunza-Nagar campaign. At his disposal was the Tigris Corps, consisting of the 7th (Meerut) Division, the 12th Indian Division, and a number of smaller military units.[21] And among the brigades that came with the 7th (Meerut) Division was the 14th Battery of the Royal Field Artillery's 4th Brigade, with 18-year-old Gunner Tom Barry from West Cork to the fore. Barry and his division had sailed from Marseilles for Egypt shortly after Christmas 1915, just as General Aylmer's force left Basra in late December.

Tom Barry arrived in Mesopotamia just in time to do battle with the Turks at Sheikh Sa'ad on 6–8 January in the first of many attempts to break the siege of Kut. Amid strong winds and heavy rains, the British forced the Turks back to the Suwaikiya Marshes, but Aylmer lost nearly 4,000 men, killed or wounded, in the process. Many succumbed to illness and it was blatantly obvious that the medical resources available were completely insufficient.

When another 1,600 men were knocked out of Aylmer's force at the battle of Wadi on 13 January, Sir John Nixon sent him more British Indian reinforcements in the shape of the 3rd (Lahore) Division. These newcomers were mauled during a catastrophic attack on the Ottoman trenches at Hanna on 21 January in which Tom Barry's battery of six 18-pounder field guns also participated. Another 2,700 British were killed or wounded and yet the Ottoman line remained unbroken.[22]

General Townshend took the news glumly but directed a communiqué to his besieged men on 26 January that concluded defiantly: 'We will succeed — mark my words! But save your ammunition as if it were gold!'[23] However, Aylmer's failure spelled the end for General Nixon who, allegedly suffering from ill health, was replaced by General Sir Percy Lake. Nixon would ultimately be held responsible for the shambles of Kut and he died in disgrace on the Côte d'Azur in France in 1921, aged 64.

On 1 March, Gunner Barry was raised to the rank of bombardier (equivalent to corporal). Seven days later, he was back in the deep end when General Aylmer launched his third attempt to break the siege of Kut. It was another colossal failure, racking up a further 4,000 British casualties. Aylmer was given the boot. His days as a battle commander were over although, unlike Nixon, he was not disgraced. In fact, he served as Commandant of the Royal Engineers from 1922 until his death in 1935. In 1928, he succeeded his older brother to become 13th Baronet of Donadea, County Kildare.

Following Aylmer's failure, Townshend addressed another communiqué to his troops on 10 March, acknowledging 'three months of cruel uncertainty' and expressing his determination to 'hold out'. In order to do this, he explained, 'I am killing a large number of horses so as to reduce the quantity of grain eaten every day, and I have had to reduce your ration. It is necessary to do this in order to keep our flag flying.'[24] However, as March turned into April, things became ever more desperate for Townshend's beleaguered force. Disease was spreading. Food supplies really were running low. And so too was patience.

On 5 April, George Gorringe, Aylmer's successor, united with Sir Stanley Maude's newly arrived 13th (Western) Division for one last attempt to break the siege of Kut. One of the battalions in Maude's ranks was the 8th Battalion of the Cheshire Regiment, which numbered two close Irish friends amongst its officers.

Herbert Stanislaus Tierney, the 26-year-old son of a Dublin bank manager, was born in County Clare and educated by the Jesuits at Belvedere College in Dublin.[25] Known to his friends as 'Bertie', he had been practising as a barrister on the Munster circuit since 1910. He initially served with the Dublin Pals in Gallipoli before voyaging to Mesopotamia with the Cheshires where he was assigned the rank of Temporary Captain. From Basra he wrote to his mother that he was now 'on the bank of the Euphrates, not far from the Garden of Eden, but oh! How it has changed'.[26]

Serving alongside Tierney was Second Lieutenant Gordon Ulick King, the 23-year-old son of the Rev William John King, Rector of Kilcolman, near Milltown, County Kerry. Educated at King's Hospital, which was in Blackhall Place in Dublin at the time, Gordon had gone on to read Classics at Trinity College. He too had fought in Gallipoli, where both his older brother William and his brother-in-law, the Rev Everard Digges La Touche, were killed during the battle of Lone Pine.[27]

Another man serving in Maude's division was 22-year-old Captain Lewis William Murphy from Cork.[28] Following his father's premature death, Lewis's mother Eileen was remarried in 1897 to Robert May Wetherell, an officer in the Duke of Cornwall's Light Infantry.[29] By 1916, Wetherell was a lieutenant colonel in the regiment, and young Lewis joined the ranks direct from school in 1912. Wounded twice during service in Europe, he joined the Mediterranean Expeditionary Force in November 1915 and was attached to the 5th (Service) Battalion of the (Duke of Edinburgh's) Wiltshire Regiment which came north to Amarah from Kuwait in March.[30]

The combined force of 30,000 men was virtually a man-for-man match to the numbers now drawn up by the Turks under General Halil Pasha and Baron von der Goltz. The British force, including Tom Barry's battery, attacked the Ottoman trench lines at Fallahiyeh and Sannaiyat, but they were repeatedly repulsed and were again unable to break through.

The Cheshires endured a particularly hellish time on 9 April when they were assigned to attack the trenches at Sannaiyat. Having been in Basra since the end of February, they had spent a month training for this moment, practising with full-scale dummy trenches. Unfortunately, the preparatory reconnaissance proved fatally inept. When they launched their first charge, the men ran as fast as they could towards the Turkish trenches only for it to become apparent that the trenches weren't where they were supposed to be. As Turkish fire began to increase all around them, the bewildered

• • •

Tom Barry would have been highly adept
at using guns such as this 18-pounder,
pictured here near the French village of
Meteren in April 1918.

men regrouped and charged onwards. Once again, there were no trenches to conquer and as they hit the ground, the exhausted soldiers could do nothing more than lie down and breathe heavily between the blistering sunshine and the Turkish artillery fire.

It fell to Bertie Tierney and Gordon King to lead a small group of men in a third charge. This time they reached the Ottoman trenches but, utterly outnumbered, they were rapidly cut to shreds by the Turks and not one of the men who participated in that final charge came back alive. Bertie Tierney is recalled on the Barristers' Memorial at the Four Courts in Dublin. Gordon King's name can be found in the War Memorial Reading Room at Trinity College, Dublin.[31]

Lewis Murphy also died at Sannaiyat, similarly leading his men onwards. Just four days earlier, his courage at Fallahiyeh had earned him a recommendation for the Military Cross. 'No more gallant officer ever led men into action,' wrote his brigadier, 'and his loss is felt by all throughout the brigade.'

Captain Ernest Nixon, ADC to Sir John Nixon, was awarded a Military Cross for his actions during the battle and was mentioned in dispatches by both Generals Gorringe and Townshend. He survived to win a DSO and a Croix de Guerre. He was more fortunate than his younger brother Gerrard, a keen sportsman and well-known follower of the Kilkenny Hounds, who was killed in a night attack near Neuve-Chapelle. Their father sold their Kilkenny home at Cloone House in 1917 and moved to England. Ernest served in Upper Burma and Egypt after the war, and passed away aged 84 in 1969.

After the failure of General Gorringe's attack, the British forces fell back, stunned by the loss of so many men and the relentlessly cold weather conditions. Cholera and typhoid were now becoming epidemic within Kut itself, where some 1,750 men would die during the course of the siege, including Brigadier General Frederick Hoghton who apparently succumbed when he ate some poisonous herbs. Nor were the Turks spared the ravages of disease with the most high-profile victim being Baron von der Goltz who died on 19 April.

Nonetheless, it was clear the Turks had won the siege of Kut. A last-ditch attempt was made when Aubrey Herbert, a former Irish Guardsman, and TE Lawrence (aka Lawrence of Arabia), the son of a Westmeath landlord, tried to negotiate a deal with Halil Pasha, offering £2 million and a promise to withdraw Townshend's troops from the region. The offer was rejected and on 28 April, Townshend sent a final communiqué to his men. 'Whatever has happened, my comrades, you can only be proud of yourselves. We have done our duty to King and Empire; the whole world knows that we have done our duty.'

The following day, the 147-day siege came to an end when Townshend surrendered his army of 2,700 British and 6,500 Indian soldiers to Halil Pasha who would ever after be known as Halil Kut, the Hero of Kut. The loss of so many men after such a prolonged siege was a major blow to British prestige in the region and was swiftly chalked up as yet another failure by Prime Minister Asquith and his flailing cabinet.

Generals Lake and Gorringe were recalled after the surrender. The Ottomans banished Townshend to the island of Heybeliada (Halki) in the Sea of Marmara where

. . .

Knowing that their trenches were about to be captured by Royal Munster Fusiliers, the Germans helpfully left two handwritten signs informing the Irishmen about the Easter Rising in Dublin and the simultaneous capture of over 9,000 British and Indian soldiers at Kut-al-Amara by Turkish forces. The left-hand sign reads 'Interesting War News of April 29th 1916[.] Kut el Amara has been taken in by the Turcs [sic] and the whole English [sic] army theirin [sic] — 13000men — maken [sic] prisoners'. The right-hand sign reads: 'Irishmen! Heavy uproa[r] in Ireland [.] English guns are firing at your wifes [sic] and children! 1st May 1916.'

he sat out the remainder of the war, enjoying the use of a Turkish navy yacht. Elected to the House of Commons in 1920, Townshend later fell from grace when it emerged that nearly half the men he surrendered had subsequently died. He was further castigated for failing to win the battle of Ctesiphon and for his dubious claims over the quantity of food supplies at Kut. He died in May 1924, just over eight years after his inglorious surrender.

The Turkish treatment of the prisoners of Kut was certainly shocking with approximately 40 per cent dying before the end of the war. Many succumbed to exposure, fatigue, mistreatment and starvation during the nightmare 700-mile desert march to the prison camps at Anatolia in Turkey. In scenes that were to be replicated in Burma and Thailand during the Second World War, the survivors were forced to work on the railway through the Taurus Mountains. Amongst them was David Curran, a 39-year-old carpenter from Downpatrick who had moved to Melbourne in 1907. Curran was serving as an air mechanic in the Australian Flying Corps when taken prisoner at Kut. He survived the march but died 'a horrible death' at Nusaybin on 16 June 1917.

Two weeks after the surrender of Kut, Bombardier Barry and his battery were encamped in a nullah some 12 miles away when he caught sight of a war communiqué that was to completely alter his life. 'REBELLION IN DUBLIN' roared the headline. He then read of the doomed Easter Rising, the destruction of central Dublin, Pearse's surrender on 29 April (the same day Townshend surrendered Kut), the mass arrest of the Irish Volunteers and the execution of the rebel leaders. When he finished reading it, he read it again. And then he read it again and again.

'It was a rude awakening,' he recalled. 'Guns being fired at the people of my own race by soldiers of the same army with which I was serving. The echo of these guns in Dublin was to drown into insignificance the clamour of all other guns during the remaining two and a half years of war... Walking down the nullah my mind was torn with questionings. What was this Republic of which I now heard for the first time? Who were these leaders the British had executed after taking them prisoners: Tom Clarke, Padraic Pearse, James Connolly and all the others, none of whose names I had ever heard? What did it all mean?... It put me thinking. What the hell am I doing with the British army? It's with the Irish I should be!'

Presumably in protest at the British response to the Rising, Tom Barry chose to drop rank on 26 May, reverting from bombardier to gunner, the rank he held until the end of the war. The following day the West Cork man was reprimanded for 'irregular conduct'.

He was to remain in Mesopotamia for another two years, during which time he did much to perfect the skills that would make him arguably the greatest guerrilla fighter of his generation. Operating a gun battery in such a climate was excellent training. They had to learn how to synchronise their movements with both infantry and cavalry, to move with speed and in silence, to communicate effectively, to plan every step, yet also to be able to rapidly adapt to the constantly changing battle environment, to counteract the challenges of hunger and extreme heat, as well as disease and the intensity of the fighting itself.

In January 1917 his battery was in action during the capture of the Hai salient, south of Kut, where they supported a massive assault on the Turkish trenches. Kut was retaken by the Mesopotamian Expeditionary Force under General Maude at the end of February, paving the way for the conquest and occupation of Baghdad just a week later. Barry's unit was with Maude's army when they seized Baghdad's agricultural hinterlands, capturing Fallujah and Baquba, before continuing up the Tigris valley to attack the town of Samarrah and force the Turks back to Tikrit.

By December 1917, Gunner Barry was serving in Palestine where his battery supported General Allenby's advance on Jaffa and Jerusalem. On 20 May 1918, the 33rd (Lahore) Division was sent to Egypt. Barry's attitude was clearly hardening at all times.

On 7 June, he was found guilty of being late for parade, 'stating a falsehood' and 'diso-bedience of battery orders'. Whatever he did was enough to warrant 'field punishment No 2' which meant that he was shackled in irons for 'up to two hours a day'.

He was to find himself back in shackles for a further seven days shortly before Christmas when Major Reynolds of the Royal Field Artillery charged him with 'creating a disturbance and improper reply to an NCO'.[32] Nevertheless, when Barry was officially discharged from the army on 7 April 1919 he was described as sober and 'a good hard-working man'. He was later awarded a small pension for 66 weeks in compensation for suffering malaria and DAH (Disordered Action of the Heart).

Tom Barry arrived back in Ireland on 4 March 1919, returned to Bandon and enrolled at Skerry's College in Cork to study Law, English and Business Affairs. In Bandon he found himself in the awkward position of trying to get onside with the Irish Volunteers, or the Irish Republican Army as they were about to become, whilst maintaining friendship with the British Army personnel garrisoning the town, as well as other ex-servicemen of His Majesty's army living locally. The Volunteers inevi-tably suspected him of being a spy, not least when this war veteran son of a Royal Irish Constable raised the Union Jack in Bandon on Armistice Day 1919.

However, in July 1920, the capture and brutal torture of Tom Hales and Pat Harte, the commander and quartermaster of the 3rd (West) Cork Brigade of the Irish Volun-teers, appalled Barry to such an extent that he persuaded some of his cousins to vouch for him. The 23-year-old was finally accepted as an intelligence officer in the late summer of 1920. He then became a training officer, teaching the Volunteers how to shoot straight, and went on to command the brigade's virtually invincible flying column, overseeing the legendary ambushes at Kilmichael and Crossbarry. 'They said I was ruthless, daring, savage, bloodthirsty, even heartless,' he wrote. 'The clergy called me and my comrades murderers; but the British were met with their own weapons. They had gone in the mire to destroy us and our nation and down after them we had to go.'

Opposed to the Treaty, he was incarcerated at Gormanston, County Meath, during the Civil War, but escaped to command the 2nd Southern Division for the anti-Treaty forces, capturing several towns in Munster, including Carrick-on-Suir, Thomastown and Mullinavat. He became Chief of Staff of the Irish Republican Army in 1937, but left the organisation three years later amid controversial circumstances relating to both the assassination of Admiral Somerville and ongoing negotiations between the IRA and Nazi Germany.

His 1949 book *Guerrilla Days in Ireland* became something of a bible for budding guerrilla fighters, while both Che Guevara and Menachem Begin requested his assist-ance in training the young men and women of Cuba and Israel, respectively. He declined, but Guevara had a copy of his book while Mao Zedong, Vo Nguyen Giap, Georgios Grivas and Fidel Castro are all said to have closely studied the Irish method of guerrilla warfare.[33] Tom Barry passed away in 1980 and was survived by his wife, Leslie de Barra (née Price), a former President of the Irish Red Cross society and director of organization for Cumann na mBan.

. . .

Born in Derry and trained in Omagh and Dublin, Nurse
Annie Colhoun was matron of a small hospital on Canada's
west coast when this photograph was taken in 1913.

NURSE COLHOUN

AND THE

BOMBING OF VERTEKOP

...

IT WAS NOT THE FIRST TIME THE GERMAN BOMBERS HAD STRUCK. THE PREVIOUS SUMMER, when the nurses first arrived in Vertekop, there had been three separate air raids. But this one was so much worse. Seventeen bombs fell on the Red Cross hospital that horrible morning and, when the dust settled, two nurses and four orderlies lay dead.

For Nurse Annie Rebecca Colhoun, Macedonia must have made an extraordinary contrast to her Irish childhood. Born in Londonderry in 1876, she was the third daughter of Robert Colhoun, a building contractor, and his wife Anne Walker, the daughter of a leather dealer from the Diamond on the west bank of the Foyle.

According to family tradition the Colhouns were Presbyterians who settled on Doagh Island off the Inishowen Peninsula of County Donegal in the late 17th century. In the 1860s, Robert and his brother Joseph moved to the townland of Elagh More which formed part of the Derry county border, with County Donegal to its west. As Colhoun Bros., they became one of the biggest contractors in the north-west, building Londonderry's Guildhall, completed in 1890, as well as the Methodist Church on Carlisle Road and a good deal of the Bogside. They also built the barracks and the Roman Catholic Church in Omagh, and added a new wing to the Lough Swilly Hotel in Buncrana.

Annie was 16 when her father and uncle dissolved their partnership in 1892. Joseph subsequently took over the Londonderry Saw Mills on Strand Road while Annie's brother Robert took on the building firm.[34]

One of seven children, Annie grew up on Strand Road and was educated at the nearby Strand House School. Her sister Ida married William Jack, a timber merchant who had come to work for the Colhoun business. He was in his forties when he was commissioned as a second lieutenant in the 12th Battalion of the Royal Inniskilling Fusiliers in June 1915. Later transferred to the Royal Irish Regiment, he was in Egypt when Allenby's troops defeated the Turks in Palestine, but he appears to have been stricken with malaria and confined to the British military hospital in Cairo for most of this time. William and Ida's daughter Ivy later married Billy Trimble and was mother of the Nobel Peace Prize winner David Trimble, the first First Minister of Northern Ireland from 1998 to 2002.[35]

From school Annie went to train as a nurse in Tyrone County Hospital in Omagh when it opened in 1899. She was living in Omagh with 12 other nurses at the time of the 1901 Census. She then went to work at the Rotunda Hospital in Dublin before taking the massive decision to emigrate to Western Canada in about 1911.

In 1913, Annie Colhoun became first matron of a small hospital established earlier that year on Salt Spring Island, one of the Gulf Islands in the Georgia Strait between Vancouver Island and the mainland of British Columbia, Canada.[36] Annie was not only the matron but was also, for some time, practically the only nurse, and consequently spent many long hours nursing and caring for the patients on her own. As well as her medical duties, she was constantly to be found washing dishes, cooking meals for the patients, scrubbing floors, keeping both the kitchen stove and the hospital furnace lit, trimming wicks and cleaning oil lamps.

Upon the outbreak of the war, Annie returned to Europe and, by June 1916, she had joined Queen Alexandra's Imperial Military Nursing Service. She was then sent to Macedonia to serve as Staff Nurse to the 37th General Hospital in Vertekop (now Skydra) on the Monastir Road, about 40 miles west of Salonika. The hospital, a tented village with approximately 1,600 beds, was one of five British hospitals on the Salonika Front assigned to Britain's Serbian allies. Most of its patients were wounded men who arrived in by rail to the train station which stood just over a mile away. The ground outside the hospital was distinctively marked with large red crosses in order to alert any passing enemy aircraft that the 37th was a hospital and that it was therefore off-limits.

On the morning of Monday 12 March 1917, a squadron of German aeroplanes bombarded the railway station at Vertekop. A section of the squadron then broke away from the main body and flew towards the 37th General Hospital.[37] When the three aeroplanes first appeared overhead, the nurses must have felt a degree of security on account of the prominently displayed red crosses, but then the horror began and the first bombs fell on the tented commune.

Nurse Mary Marshall was the first to die, pulverised when a bomb landed in the operating theatre where she was based. Chaos reigned for the next 30 minutes, during which the medical officers pleaded with the nurses to take cover. However, the nurses were not willing to leave their bedridden patients unattended during such an appalling time. One of Nurse Margaret Dewar's patients was in particular agony, so she ran to adjust his pillow and bring him some relief. It did the trick, but as she bent over him, another explosion rocked the hospital and a fragment of the bomb's casing smashed into her chest.

Somebody — probably Annie Colhoun and Ethel Garrett — managed to carry Nurse Dewar to a bed, but moments later the Glaswegian succumbed to her wound. Annie Colhoun cradled the woman in her arms and offered the 'last gentle ministrations' as she slipped away.[38]

• • •

The nurses who survived the Vertekop bombing were
personally awarded Serbian Gold Medals by Crown
Prince Alexander of Serbia. He later reigned over the
Kingdom of Serbs, Croats and Slovenes (aka Yugoslavia)
from 1921 until his assassination in 1934.

During a subsequent blast, a splinter from a bomb hit Annie Colhoun. Despite the immense shock, she and Nurse Garrett remained at their posts, looking after their helpless patients while fresh bombs continued to fall. The tent where they were based was by now full of smoke and acrid fumes. When a bomb blast fractured the skull of a nearby soldier, Nurse Garrett sprang to his aid and successfully administered life-saving first aid while fourteen more bombs fell within 60 to 80 yards of her.[39] The consequent fire raged for several hours before they brought it under control. Despite their intense exhaustion, Nurses Colhoun and Garrett insisted on carrying out heavy duties in what remained of the operating theatre.

Four orderlies from the Royal Army Medical Corps were also killed during the Vertekop bombing.

On 12 May 1917, Annie and Ethel were summoned before the Crown Prince of Serbia who awarded them the Serbian Gold Medal 'for conspicuous bravery in a most trying situation'. They were the first women to win the award.[40]

Two weeks later, *The London Gazette* announced that they had been awarded the Military Medal.[41] Approximately 91 of the 128 Military Medals awarded to women went to nurses. As women could not have official status as officers, it was the only bravery award open to them. Maud McCarthy, Matron in Chief to the Army in France, later remarked, 'The Nursing Service, as a whole, have considered it a great honour to be given a medal which is awarded solely for bravery in the field.'

The two nurses were also awarded the French Croix de Guerre (bronze star) and Annie fetched up with nine blue service chevrons.

In July 1917, one year after she first went to Macedonia, Annie sailed for England where she went to work in the Military Hospital at Husley Camp near Winchester. On 24 July, she was married in Wimbledon to 34-year-old Private Frank Lowther Crofton of the Canadian Army Service Corps. He was the fourth and youngest son of Captain the Hon FG Crofton, a Royal Navy officer. He also had strong Irish roots through his grandfather, Edward Crofton, 2nd Baron Crofton of Mote, County Roscommon, who was one of Ireland's Representative Peers. The following day, Annie attended the Investiture at Aldershot where she was presented to the Queen and decorated with her Military Medal by King George V.[42]

Annie retired from the service following her marriage. Shortly after the birth of her only son, Francis David Crofton, on 26 January 1919, she and Frank moved back to Salt Spring Island. They settled on Ganges Hill from where Frank operated a taxi service. Annie Crofton died in 1954.[43]

FATHER KAVANAGH

AND THE

SINAI-PALESTINE

CAMPAIGN

...

As the battle raged beneath the walls of Jerusalem in the days before Christmas 1917, Father Bernard Kavanagh watched yet another fellow Irishman fall victim to the incessant Turkish fusillade. He hobbled to the dying man's side and stooped low to hear the final confession, just as he had done countless times before. When he had finished giving him absolution, the 53-year-old Limerick padre calmly stood up. A sniper's bullet smashed into him and he crumpled to the ground unconscious.

Bernard Kavanagh, Acting Chaplain to the Forces, was born in Limerick in 1864, the son of one of the city's most eminent physicians. Educated at Crescent College, Limerick, he became a Redemptorist novice at the age of 18. A man of considerable eloquence, he made his way to London where he was variously based amongst the working-class communities of Kensal Green and Edmonton. Father Kavanagh was frail and suffered badly from sciatica, but that did not stop his Provincial from submitting his name to the War Office as a suitable chaplain when the Great War broke out.

And so, aged 50, he made his way to Purfleet, a military training encampment on the banks of the Thames, where he celebrated his first Mass for Kitchener's new recruits on 27 September 1914. His hopes of being sent to the Western Front were dashed when the medical authorities refused to give him the required travel permit because of his chronic rheumatism.

In October 1915, he sailed for the British Protectorate of Egypt where he spent the next 16 months performing hospital duties in Alexandria and Ismaïlia. From the latter city, on the banks of the Suez Canal, he wrote to his sister, a Notre Dame nun: 'We are very comfortable here in our tents on the hot sands, not very far from where Abraham pitched his tent, and Moses crossed the Red Sea.' For company, he had 'a black battalion from the West Indies, cheery, chatty negroes, all Christians of various sorts who speak English perfectly, are intensely loyal, and describe themselves as "English gentlemen" [and] an Anzac Depot, some 2,000 vigorous and restive bushmen, who swagger and boast and guess they are going "to pull the old country out of the hole".'

Father Kavanagh was determined to get to the front lines 'as I have not yet seen the realities'. His superiors were reluctant, fearful that the long marches and sleeping rough in the rains would be too much for him. He persisted, until he was eventually attached to the Royal West Kent Regiment. As part of Britain's Egyptian Expeditionary Force, he duly found himself marching towards the Sinai Peninsula in order to take on the Fourth Army of the Ottoman Empire in an epic bid to oust the Turks from the Holy Land.

Now part of Egypt, the triangular Sinai Peninsula is about the same size as Ireland without the province of Munster. Sandwiched between the Mediterranean and the Red Sea, it was extensively mined for turquoise by the Pharaohs of Ancient Egypt while, in Jewish lore, this was the land through which Moses led the Israelites en route to the Promised Land. The peninsula had been under British control since 1906 and formed a thick and vital boundary between the Ottoman-controlled Middle East and the 102-mile long Suez Canal, one of the British Empire's most vital waterways.[44] Command of Sinai became all the more critical from November 1914, when the Ottoman Empire entered the war on the side of Germany, the Austro-Hungarian Empire and, in due course, Bulgaria.

At the end of January 1915, a German-led Ottoman force invaded Sinai in a bid to capture the Suez Canal. The raid was unsuccessful, but Turkish morale soared during the ensuing months as the Ottoman Army not only crushed the Allied attempt to invade the Gallipoli Peninsula but also made a mockery of the British attempt to capture Baghdad by forcing the surrender of General Townshend's besieged army at Kut.

By June 1916, the Allies had considerably improved their game. From his spotter plane over Palestine, Erskine Childers was dispatching vital intelligence to the War Office. Across the Gulf of Aqaba, TE Lawrence and Sir Henry McMahon had persuaded the Arab tribesmen to rise up against the Ottomans. And now the campaign for control of the Holy Land began.

The Allies completely outnumbered the Ottoman Turks and, by early January 1917, they had recaptured Sinai. Two months later, they almost managed to capture southern Palestine via the Mediterranean coastal town of Gaza, but made an ill-judged retreat on the brink of victory. A second attempt to seize Gaza in April 1917 proved an unqualified disaster for the Allies, who suffered heavy casualties, while Turkish morale soared anew and large numbers of Ottomans arrived to reinforce their front line from Gaza to the town of Beersheba in the Negev desert. Situated 40 miles south-west of Jerusalem, Beersheba was the town Erskine Childers had so much enjoyed trying to bomb a year earlier.

Riddled with septic ulcers all over his legs and hands, Father Kavanagh marched alongside his battalion throughout the campaign. Those who knew him spoke of his 'cheerfulness of spirit' and immense courage. 'He was as brave as a lion,' remarked one. During the second battle for Gaza, he helped the doctor attend to the wounded men with their shattered limbs, until the doctor himself was hit by a bullet in the chest and had to be carried off by stretcher. Father Kavanagh then ventured out into the battleground. In part, this was to boost morale — 'for I knew that the chaplain's presence does much to encourage the men', as he explained to his sister — but, inevitably, it was also to offer absolution to the dying. The West Kents took a terrible hit at Gaza, with at least four officers and almost 50 men killed, and hundreds disabled. When he found four dead men, 'I tried to compose their scattered limbs, then placed their helmets over their faces.'[45]

After the battle, he helped gather up the wounded, heaving the worst of the injured into carts, strapping others onto camels, maintaining his pace until two o'clock in the morning. 'These are great days, and I am delighted to feel that I have at last reached the realities', he wrote to his sister.

The failure to capture Gaza resulted in a long stalemate in Palestine that the Allies could endeavour to resolve only by bringing in more men. Amongst the tens of thousands of soldiers who now poured into this theatre of war were the 10th (Irish) Division. Most arrived directly from Macedonia where so many had been riddled with malaria in the Struma Valley that Sir Edward Allenby, the new Commander in Chief of the Egyptian Expeditionary Force, was advised to give them all three months off to recuperate.

The 7th Battalion of the Royal Dublin Fusiliers arrived in Egypt from Salonika on 12 September 1917 and proceeded to Palestine. One of their officers was Captain William Victor Edwards, D Company, a cabinet-maker's son from Belfast. A chartered accountant by day, the 30-year-old Ulsterman had been rather better known before the war for his sporting prowess. Twice capped for the Irish rugby team, Billy Edwards was hailed in an *Irish Times* feature titled 'Popular Belfast Sportsmen' as 'one of the most consistent forwards in the north of Ireland' whose 'footwork is invariably excellent'.[46] A formidable swimmer, he was also Ireland's 220 yards swimming champion and played water polo for the country. Perhaps his most remarkable achievement came in August 1913 when he swam across Belfast Lough, covering just under five miles between Bangor and Whitehead in precisely four hours. He is believed to have been the first person to have swum across the lough.[47] Prior to his arrival in Palestine, Billy Edwards had served on the Western Front. He fought at the capture of Ginchy on 9 September 1916, during which a bullet from a German machine-gun clipped the right side of his head. He survived with a four-inch scar and what we would now regard as considerable physical and psychological damage in the form of dizziness, headaches and insomnia.

Also in D Company were George and Teddy Hare, the sons of a Church of Ireland clergyman, who grew up at 18 North Frederick Street, Dublin.[48] Their grandfather, the Rev George Hare, had been Chaplain to the Royal Hospital in Kilmainham in Dublin. Born in County Fermanagh in 1886, George was the older brother by 12 years. Educated at Dublin's Mountjoy School, he had worked as a Land Registry clerk and played forward for Wanderers rugby team before the war.

As a sergeant in D Company, he must have been wise to the truth when 15-year-old Teddy lied about his age to join the battalion in 1915.[49] That same summer, the Hare brothers had been with the Dublin Pals when they landed into Suvla Bay, serving through the ensuing Gallipoli nightmare.[50] Now, nearly two years later, they were marching on the Holy Land together.

Arrival of General Folkenhayn.

• • •

German General Erich von Falkenhayn and the
Ottoman military ruler General Djemal Pasha
walk past the Turkish honorary battalion during
Falkenhayn's visit to Jerusalem in October 1917.

Awaiting a British attack at Beersheba.

• • •

Ottoman forces awaiting a British attack at
Beersheba in the Negev desert, 1917.

Amongst other Irish regiments entering the fray were the Royal Inniskilling Fusiliers, whose 6th Battalion included James Duffy, a 28-year-old stretcher-bearer from Crolly in the Gweedore parish of north-west Donegal.

On 31 October 1917, the Palestinian stalemate came to an exceptionally dramatic end when 800 Australian cavalry, armed with bayonets, charged the Turkish lines and captured the desert town of Beersheba. Their success was undoubtedly fuelled by a zeal to avenge those who fell in the Dardanelles; their Turkish opponents were the same hardy veterans of III Corps who had been their foe at Gallipoli. Many men from the 10th (Irish) Division were also closely involved with the conquest of Beersheba.

Two days after Beersheba fell, Captain Billy Edwards and the Hare brothers were in the thick of it when the Allies finally captured Gaza. The Turks were now caught on the hop, considerably weakened by their disastrous campaign against the Russians in the Caucasus. On 6 November, the 10th (Irish) Division helped oust the esteemed Yıldırım Army Group from the Sheria Position, securing another vital cog of the rapidly fragmenting Turkish line. While 12 Irish battalions were involved in the capture of Sheria, Billy Edwards and the Hares were fast becoming a rare thing in the 10th (Irish), namely Irishmen. The much-battered division was by now being steadily strengthened and 'Indianised' with the introduction of recruits from British India.

The weeks before Christmas 1917 introduced intensive fighting to the Judean mountains as the Allies and Turks combated one another along the Mediterranean coast. Father Kavanagh vividly described his experiences of the third and final battle of Gaza to his sister: 'As you know, I never looked to join the Army at my time of life — being in it I have never prayed that I might outlive this war and carnage where so many younger and better men are falling. But I have prayed the good God earnestly for grace to do my bit and not to flinch. I have seen men fall upon the ground hysterical under a persistent fusillade, others become insane. I have stumbled at night over some dead comrade, who, a few hours before, was full of life and laughter. I have jammed dozens into the ground by night and scraped a little earth on top of them before the battle was renewed at day-break. More than once as I went my rounds a machine-gun was turned on me and the ground ploughed up with bullets a few yards in front. I have lain about in holes and crawled through gullies, or hidden like one of those lizards under a rock when movement was impossible, and was fully conscious that the next movement might be my last. Yet strange to say, by God's mercy — for it is not I — I have never experienced one moment of dismay. And I assure you, I attribute this and many other graces to your prayers. May God bless you and reward you.'

Lloyd George had asked General Allenby if he could take Jerusalem 'as a Christmas present for the British people' to compensate for another bad year on the Western Front with the heavy tolls at Arras, Cambrai and Passchendaele. Allenby did as requested, and so the Allies marched on the Holy City, playing music as they went. Father Kavanagh wrote of his joy at seeing places such as Jacob's Well ('the clearest and most delicious water I have ever tasted out here'), Bethlehem ('white, radiant and beautiful') and Hebron ('a stronghold of Moslem fanaticism… the people turned out to see us, silent and sullen').

• • •

General Edmund Allenby enters
Jerusalem on foot out of respect
to the Holy City on 11 December
1917. Two decades earlier, Kaiser
Wilhelm II insisted on entering the
city mounted on his white horse,
causing considerable insult locally.

On 11 December, the Allies took Jerusalem. As a mark of respect, General Allenby entered the Old City through the Jaffa Gate as a pilgrim on foot. He was the first Christian to have control of Jerusalem in over 600 years. 'The wars of the Crusaders are now complete,' he said. Such words must have struck home with Father Kavanagh, completely absorbed as he was in this extraordinary trek across the Holy Land.

Father Kavanagh was to die in Jerusalem. The bullet that struck him beneath the city walls proved fatal and he passed away eight hours after he was hit on 21 December. He was laid to rest in the British War Cemetery on the Mount of Olives. A friend wrote: 'He was not young in years when he donned the khaki he coveted, but he was young in spirit, and his energy was young, and so we mourn him as one taken in his youth.'

On the same day that Father Kavanagh died, Lloyd George got a Christmas bonus when the Allies captured the ancient port city of Jaffa (now part of Tel Aviv). Appalled to have yielded such prizes to their enemy, the Turks launched a series of counter-attacks in the last days of December. The 10th (Irish) Division was to the fore in the ensuing defence of Jerusalem, which was accompanied by a massive effort to drive the Ottoman Army north, so that the Holy City was no longer within range of their artillery. The 10th (Irish) was instructed to sweep around Ramallah from the west and push the Ottoman line back.

Two battalions from the Royal Irish Fusiliers, nicknamed the 'Faughs', had the job of clearing the Turks from the extremely precipitous terrain of the Kereina Ridge outside Jerusalem. It was here that James Duffy, the stretcher-bearer from Gweedore, came as close as you can get to meeting your maker. Utterly exposed to Turkish fire, he was stretchering a wounded comrade to safety when his fellow stretcher-bearer was hit and fell. Private Duffy found a replacement bearer, only for the new man to be killed almost straight away. Seeing little alternative, Private Duffy then headed back out to the danger zone and, with shells and bullets pouring down all around him, he hauled not one but both of the injured men to safety. All three men survived and, in due course, Private Duffy was invited to Buckingham Palace where King George V pinned a Victoria Cross on his chest.[51]

George Hare, the former Wanderers forward, was killed near Ramallah on 27 December. Billy Edwards, the man who swam across Belfast Lough, fell two days later just east of the village of Deir Ibzi.[52] Like Father Kavanagh, the two Dublin Pals were laid to rest in the Jerusalem War Cemetery.

The defence of Jerusalem was that rare thing, an Allied success, and when it was over, the Sinai-Palestine campaign was also over. The British had suffered over 550,000 casualties, primarily due to the intense heat and disease. The number of Turkish casualties is unknown but it is assumed to be even greater. General Allenby's army continued to surge into Ottoman territory through the first months of 1918, despite the withdrawal of so many men, including most of the 10th (Irish) Division, to plug the gaps on the Western Front created by the Germans' Spring Offensive.

The Ottoman Empire never really recovered from the loss of the Holy Land. On 1 October 1918, Prince Faisal, son of the Grand Sharif of Mecca, commanded a force that, with extensive Allied support, captured the Syrian city of Damascus.[53] Just over three weeks later, Faisal's army took Aleppo. And on 30 October, almost a year to the day since the Australian charge at Beersheba, the Turks announced a cessation of hostilities and signed the Armistice of Moudros. They conceded control of both the Dardanelles and the Bosphorus to the Allies, as well as all ports, railways and other strategic points. The Ottoman Army and air force were dismantled. Churchill's dream of occupying Constantinople was finally realised and, after six extraordinary centuries, the Ottoman Empire was broken up.

Born in Rathgar, Dublin, John Howard Alexander worked as a draper and interior designer in the city before venturing to South Africa to reinvent himself as an engineer.

COLONEL ALEXANDER

AND THE

SPEAR-POINT PUMP

...

ONE OF THE GREATEST CHALLENGES THAT THE ALLIES FACED DURING THE SINAI-PALESTINE campaign was how to provide enough water for tens of thousands of troops, as well as vast numbers of horses, mules and camels. Without an adequate water supply, the British could not mount an effective offensive against the Turks. Even the possibility of sending water wagons into the desert was redundant because the terrain was impassable in so many places. The traditional solution was to send Tommy in with a pick and shovel to dig and dig until he struck the water table. However, in the Sinai Desert, this too was almost pointless because the loose sands kept filling the holes.

Step forward Major John Howard Alexander. The Dublin-born engineer introduced a system of spear-point pumps by which, using sledgehammers and monkey-pulley bars, the Allied army was able to penetrate the desert sands and extract water as and when required.

The importance of Major Alexander's spear-point pumps cannot be overstated. They gave the Allies the mobility they needed to traverse the Sinai Peninsula with speed. The consequence of this was a string of victorious attacks on the fixed Turkish lines, culminating in the fall of Jerusalem. Ultimately, this led to the collapse of the Ottoman Empire, which freed up enough men from the desert war to finally defeat the Germans on the Western Front.

David Alexander, John's grandfather, hailed from Carrickfergus, County Antrim, and is thought to have served in the Royal Navy. His sons David and Charles were born in Malta in the late 1840s and, by 1851, they were living with their mother Anne in Woolwich, Kent.[54]

During the 1880s, the Alexander brothers set up business as lithographic artists in south Dublin. David and his Limerick-born wife Emily (née Gahagan) lived at 71 Frankfort Avenue in Rathgar where John, the fourth of ten children, was born in 1880.[55]

John Howard Alexander was a 15-year-old pupil at High School, Rathgar, when he received a baptism of fire on a Sunday evening in June 1895. He was accosted on his way home by a neighbour called John Kenny who, having accused him of swearing at his children, beat the boy up. When David Alexander, John's father, called on Kenny to demand an explanation, the latter replied that he was 'sorry he had not a dog whip' at the time. David Alexander duly called the police and Kenny was hauled before the Northern Divisional Police Court, where John Alexander vehemently denied Kenny's accusation and David Alexander insisted it was a case of 'mistaken identity'. The judge fined Mr Kenny £50.[56]

At the time of this unfortunate incident, John was working part-time for Messrs Ferrier and Pollock, a wholesale silk and haberdashery firm based in the present-day Powerscourt Townhouse in South William Street in Dublin. In 1896, he went to work for Anderson, Stanford and Ridgeway, a new company that specialised in carpets, curtains and interior furnishing, whose warehouse stood at 28 and 29 Grafton Street.

In March 1900, he joined the 2nd Dublin Company of the 61st (South Irish) Company, which formed part of the Imperial Yeomanry. He served with them as a trooper right through the Anglo-Boer War.[57] He was still with them when they marched through the yard at Dublin Castle to Ship Street Barracks in June 1901.[58] Like so many veterans of that war, he fell under South Africa's spell, and in August 1903 his colleagues at Anderson, Stanford and Ridgeway presented him with a purse of sovereigns before he embarked on a new career as an inspector of buildings for the Zululand Railway.[59] By the end of the year, he was working with the Public Works Department of the British colony of Natal, where he remained until 1910.

During his time in Natal, he worked as an engineer with the Dundee Coal Company at Talana and established a farm near Maritzburg.[60] He was also profoundly involved with a lesser-known event from the annals of South Africa's 20th century history. In 1906, verging on bankruptcy, Natal's colonial government imposed a poll tax of £1 per hut on all men over the age of 18. Hand in hand with this, the Natal Police sent a force of 150 men to arrest the Zulu chief Bambatha Zondi, in order to preclude him from leading resistance to the tax. Bambatha's men ambushed the police force en route, killing four white men, and thereby launched a serious rebellion against the authorities. John Henry Alexander, who was fluent in the isiZulu language, was one of the hundreds of colonial troops drafted in to suppress the revolt. However, his role would seem to have been considerably more intimate than most. Bambatha was apparently one of 3,500 killed during the rebellion, although there is an ongoing claim by the Zondi clan that he secretly escaped to Mozambique and lived to be an old man. Many years later, a trunk was found in the attic of Ashorne Hill, Alexander's home in Warwickshire. Inside was a typed report detailing the nature of Bambatha's death in June 1906. The report stated that he was shot twice and then stabbed with an assegai blade. Alongside the report was an envelope containing what purports to be a lock of the Zulu chief's hair.[61]

In October 1909, JH Alexander was elected an Associate of the Institute of Mining Engineers.[62] The following year he was given command of a force of 50 men in the short-lived Natal Engineer Corps. In 1912, General Jan Smuts created South Africa's

Union Defence Force (UDF) and Alexander was entrusted with a unit of mounted field engineers. When the Great War broke out, South Africa declared for the British Empire. Alexander's engineers played a key role in persuading German forces in South-West Africa (present-day Namibia) to surrender to the UDF on 9 July 1915. At the time, this was regarded as the Allies' first major victory of the war.

Although Alexander would ostensibly remain with the UDF throughout the war, he was with the Royal Engineers in January 1916 when he called home to visit his family in Dublin. Shortly afterwards he made his way to Egypt and onwards to Palestine, where the Allies were in a quandary about how to proceed against the Turks without a decent water supply. In March 1916, the ANZAC Mounted Division was formed from three brigades of Australian Light Horse along with the New Zealand Mounted Rifles Brigade. Major Alexander was assigned to command a squadron of field engineers within the division. Their role would be to construct or demolish bridges, roads, communication lines and observation posts as and when required.

The division engaged in continuous guerrilla warfare with the Turks throughout the Sinai-Palestine campaign. Both riders and mounts had to survive extreme heat, harsh terrain and water shortages. One particularly suffocating dust storm lasted 16 hours while temperatures sometimes soared to 46 degrees Celsius. Such weather wreaked carnage on the unfortunate horses, with approximately 640 horses and mules dying every single week.

It was during this time that Major Alexander came up with his ingenious spear-point pump system. It is thought that the concept may have originated in the Queensland outback in Australia in the late 19th century but, operating from workshops in Cairo, Alexander's engineers made the device so effective that it changed the course of global history. Once his sappers had driven the spear down to the water table, a pump was screwed on to extract the water. Sometimes the water lay in depressions less than six feet underground. Occasionally, they found an existing well constructed by the Romans nearly 2,000 years earlier and subsequently buried beneath the sands. On one happy occasion, a spear point was inserted into the base of an apparently dry well, which then pumped out a strong and continuous stream of water for eight hours straight, filling up the ANZAC's large canvas reservoirs.

The equipment required by Alexander's spear-point pumps was relatively minimal, freeing up the pressure on the transport. Showing yet more gumption, Alexander also invented a system of 'racks and carriers' so that the pumps and driving gear could be carried on packhorses, or pulled on sleighs, rather than relying on slow, clumsy camel trains. In his diary, he allowed himself a pat on the back. 'This method I may say is working with excellent results.'

By the summer of 1916, spear-point pumps were being extensively used, with comparative ease, by the Australian Light Horse all across the Sinai Peninsula from Romani to El Arish. On 26 June 1916, Alexander was awarded the Military Cross. He was to be mentioned in despatches on four occasions and was honoured with the Distinguished Service Order on 4 January 1919.[63]

• • •

Some of the water pumps and spear pumps devised by Major Alexander for carriage on 'horse pack saddles' during the Sinai campaign.

• • •

Photographed by Major JH Alexander, the horse is saddled with a rack and some of the equipment invented by him which the Anzac Mounted Engineers were to use to establish and maintain water supplies during the Sinai campaign.

In May 1917, Alexander's engineers teamed up with the 1st Light Horse Brigade for a daring raid on the Beersheba to Hafir el Auja railway. Under the Dubliner's guidance, they demolished 14 miles of the Ottoman railway line, including three bridges.

The following month, Alexander learned of the death of his younger brother Charles, a well-known rower and footballer in Dublin before the war. Charles had moved to Australia where he was Mathematical Master at Knox College in north Sydney. In December 1916, the 33-year-old enlisted in the 9th Australian Light Trench Mortar Battery with whom he went to the Western Front. Charles was acting commander of the battery during the battle of Messines when he was shot in the head by a sniper while peeking out from a trench in Ploegsteert Wood.[64]

It is assumed that Alexander was still with the Australian Mounted Division when they stormed the Turkish lines at Beersheba in October 1917, when Jerusalem fell that Christmas, when they invaded Moab across the Jordan River in the spring of 1918, and when the division became the first of the Allied troops to enter Damascus in October 1918.

In 1918, Lieutenant Colonel John Howard Alexander, MC, was appointed Deputy Controller of Baghdad Railway, serving as its Military Director from the Armistice until 1920. The railway was the brainchild of a group of German businessmen from

Deutsche Bank, Siemens and other leading companies of the German Empire who had joined forces a decade before the war to fund the construction of a line to connect Berlin to the Ottoman city of Baghdad. The Germans wanted direct access from Berlin to a port on the Persian Gulf, ideally Basra, as well as to several oilfields which they had secured control of. For their part, the Ottoman Turks wanted to expand their influence into Europe and to reduce British dominance of the Red Sea.

Over 990 miles of railway line had been laid through present-day Turkey, Syria and Iraq by the time the war broke out. Crucially, it was still 300 miles shy of completion and, during the war, the completed section of the Hejaz railway was to be continually harried by guerrilla forces led by Lawrence of Arabia, as well as Colonel Alexander's own raid of May 1917. The Irishman was still Deputy Controller when the railway line between Basra and Baghdad opened on 15 January 1920. Less than three months later, Germany's rights to the Baghdad Railway were cancelled and the British military authorities transferred the line to a British civilian administration, Mesopotamian Railways.

By 1923, Alexander was working for British Thomson-Houston, a subsidiary of General Electric Company, serving as head representative on the contract to electrify the Natal Railway in South Africa. However, the following year he was obliged to return to England for family reasons. His engineering expertise was not in much demand in post-war England and, over the next ten years, he worked as a golf club secretary. In 1933, he was installed as manager of an ailing margarine and cheese factory in Mitcham, London. His efforts to save it from bankruptcy came to nothing when the chief debenture holder died, and his executors foreclosed.

In 1934, Colonel Alexander married Frances Marie Callow, a talented harpist from Hempstead, New York, who had studied in France with the great French harpist Henriette Reine. Five years later, on the eve of the Second World War, the Alexanders became joint managers of Ashorne Hill, near Leamington Spa, Warwickshire, on behalf of the British Iron and Steel Confederation.[65] For the remainder of the war, the building served as a hideout for over 600 men and women who, working for the Ministry of Supply, coordinated the production of iron and steel with such secrecy that the house was dubbed 'the Bletchley Park of the steel industry'. Mrs Alexander oversaw the catering and housekeeping, and continued to do so after the war, when the house became a residential conference centre controlled by the Iron and Steel Board.[66]

During this period, Colonel Alexander commanded the 1st Warwickshire (Warwick) Battalion, Home Guard. He had his own wartime sorrows to deal with. One of the early civilian casualties was his younger sister Winifred Wade, who died along with her two teenage daughters, when a U-Boat torpedoed the SS Yorkshire, a cruise liner 'subbing' for a hospital ship, in October 1939.[67]

In 1956, after 17 years at Ashorne Hill, the Alexanders retired to live at Field Head near Calgarth on Lake Windermere, in England's Lake District.[68] John Alexander's collection of Zulu spears, once mounted on the wall of the Great Hall at Ashorne Hill, is now to be found in the University of KwaZulu-Natal's Campbell Collection at the Killie Campbell Museum in Durban, South Africa.[69]

Sergeant Major Flora Sandes, whose family hailed from County Kerry,
talks with an officer from the Serbian Army while recovering from
injuries sustained during her battles against the Bulgarians.

SERGEANT MAJOR FLORA SANDES, SERBIAN ARMY

...

THE REV SAMUEL DICKSON SANDES MUST HAVE PREDICTED IT. OKAY, MAYBE NOT THE
Serbian Army, but still, some form of military career. Even as a child, the youngest of
his eight children had prayed each night that she might wake up as a boy. The last time
the elderly Irish clergyman saw his daughter, she was headed for Serbia with the Red
Cross. He was over two years dead by the time the Bulgarian soldier hurled his hand
grenade at Sergeant Flora Sandes of the Serbian Army.

The Sandes family had been in Ireland since the 17th century when Flora's ancestor,
Lancelot Sandes, served as Member of Parliament for Kerry in 1662. He lived at Carria-
gafoyle, near Ballylongford, County Kerry, an area that was to remain the family headquarters throughout the 18th century and much of the 19th century. Stephen Creaghe
Sandes, Flora's grandfather, was born at Sallow Glen near Tarbert, County Kerry, and
became Bishop of Cashel in 1839.

The Rev Samuel Sandes, Flora's father, was born at 4 Fitzwilliam Square, Dublin,
in 1822 and studied at Trinity College. Having been called to the Irish Bar, he changed
direction, returned to Trinity for four more years to read Theology and became Rector
of Whitechurch, County Cork, in 1855. The following year, Samuel married Sophia
Julia Besnard, a 23-three-year old from Cork. The Sandes family lived in Cork until
1872, when they upped sticks with their seven children to begin a new life in England.

Flora, their eighth and last child, was born in Yorkshire on 22 January 1876.[70] Like
many a clergyman's daughter, she had a somewhat unsettled childhood, moving between
parishes in Yorkshire, Suffolk and Surrey, coupled with long visits to her relatives in
Ireland. Educated by governesses, she developed into the ultimate tomboy, becoming
a passionate horsewoman and a keen shot. Inspired by Tennyson's 'The Charge of the
Light Brigade', she dreamed of charging on horseback through the Crimea. She enjoyed
drinking and smoking and was also a formidable driver, powering down country roads
in her Sizaire-Naudin, a French single-cylinder racing car.

Flora trained as a stenographer in London before heading off on a tour of the world, aided by the 'considerable legacy' of a wealthy uncle. Having worked as a secretary in Cairo for a year, she made her way across North America to stay with her brother Samuel on Texada Island off the west coast of Canada, arriving in January 1905. During her trip she allegedly shot a guardsman on a goods train in self-defence. When she was later asked if she had really shot the man, she said she 'couldn't remember'.[71]

In 1907, the 31-year-old signed up with the First Aid Nursing Yeomanry Corps (FANY), a newly formed all-women mounted paramilitary organisation where she mastered first aid, signalling and drill, as well as further improving her horsemanship skills.

Two years later, she broke away from FANY and, in conjunction with Mabel St Clair Stobart, she joined the Women's Sick and Wounded Convoy. During the First Balkan War of 1912, Mabel led the convoy to the Balkans where Serbia, Greece, Montenegro and Bulgaria had united in war against the Ottoman Empire. For reasons unknown, Flora was not involved with this Balkan assignment but she was soon to become very familiar with the region.

When the Great War broke out in 1914, Flora offered her services as a nurse to the Volunteer Aid Detachment, but she was rejected because of her lack of qualifications. Instead, she joined a unit of St John Ambulance which was raised by Mabel Grouitch (née Dunlop), a surgical nurse from West Virginia who had married a Serbian doctor called Slavko Grouitch.

On 12 August 1914, Flora was with 'Madame Grouch', as she called her, and 35 other Red Cross nurses when they left Victoria Station in London bound for Serbia. Ten days later, they embarked on a nightmarish 36-hour voyage on the deck of a cattle ship that took them from the Greek port of Piraeus to Salonika in Macedonia, while a powerful thunderstorm lashed the seas around them. A train journey through the Vardar valley then brought them to the Serbian city of Kragujevac where Flora was handed a sombre telegram. It stated that her beloved father, with whom she had lived right up until her hasty departure, had died on 23 August.

Serbia was already in the throes of a humanitarian crisis, with wounded soldiers pouring back from the front lines where they were intensely engaged in trying to stop the superior forces of the Austro-Hungarian Empire from crossing the Danube. Flora and six other nurses were immediately put to work in Kragujevac's desperately under-equipped First Reserve Hospital. She spent the next three months helping the Serbian doctors attend to over 1,000 sick and wounded soldiers. The seven nurses took turns sleeping on straw mattresses, sharing a single blanket between them.

By the time Flora returned to England shortly before Christmas 1914, she was wholly dedicated to the Serbian cause. She soon befriended Elsie Inglis, the Scottish doctor and suffragist, who had brought a similar spirit of innovation to the Rotunda maternity hospital in Dublin when she was based there in the 1890s.[72] Since the outbreak of the war, Elsie had been instrumental in sending ready-made all-female relief hospitals to assist Britain's allies in Russia and France. With Elsie's support, Flora launched a huge fund-raising campaign in order to buy anaesthetic, cotton, gauze and other medical supplies for Serbia.[73] Within six weeks, she had raised £2,000 , close to £170,000 in modern terms.

Mabel Grouitch (née Dunlop), or 'Madame Grouch' as Flora nicknamed her, raised the St John Ambulance unit with which Flora went to Serbia in 1914. Originally from Clarksburg, West Virginia, Mabel Grouitch became acquainted with the Balkans when she went to study archaeology in Athens in 1901.

For much of the journey back to Serbia, Flora and her friend Emily Simmonds, a graduate of the Roosevelt Hospital, sat on packing crates containing 120 tons of the sorely needed supplies. Upon their arrival in early 1915, Flora was one of 16 nurses who volunteered to go into the camp at Valjevo. The huge naval hospital was known as Serbia's 'death trap' after it became the epicentre of a horrific typhoid epidemic that was killing an average of 200 people a day. Serbia lost 126 doctors at the hospital. Flora

Bulgarian infantry in action against the Serbs near Kaymakchalan in the mountains of Monastir, September 1916.

1222

and her fellow nurses desperately tried to rid the afflicted of lice by running endless hot baths and sterilising clothes with steam. All 16 nurses were struck down by the disease. Eight of them died, but Flora survived and she remained at the camp long after the epidemic was finally brought under control.

In October 1915 she volunteered for service with a field ambulance unit attached to the Serbian Army's Second ('Iron') Infantry Regiment. That same month, an army of 300,000 Austrians, Germans and Bulgarians swooped into Serbia, forcing the Serbian Army south. On 20 November, Flora set off on horseback with a group headed by Colonel Dimitrije Milić, the Iron Regiment's commanding officer, to assess the enemy strength. 'The Commandant seems awfully bucked that I can ride,' she wrote in her diary, 'and declares they have a small sort of cavalry detachment of 30 of the best riders in the Reg. And that I'd better belong to that. They seem bent on turning me into a soldier, and I expect I'll find myself in the trenches next battle!'[74]

Sure enough, as the Iron Regiment prepared to pull back to within a few miles of Monastir (present-day Bitola), the capital of Serbian Macedonia, Colonel Milić asked Flora if she would like to stay on with them. It was by no means unknown for women to serve in the Serbian Army and Flora's ability to shoot and ride had greatly impressed the Colonel. And so it was that Flora put on the uniform of a dead Serbian soldier and enlisted in the regiment's 4th Company.[75] Colonel Milić took the small brass regimental badges from his own epaulettes and fastened them onto her shoulder.

Flora was with the Iron Regiment that devastating, ice-cold winter when the Serbian Army marched on the Great Retreat through the Albanian mountains to Durazzo on the Adriatic Coast. She did what she could to find food and clothing for her fellow soldiers, many of whom were crippled with frostbite. If necessary, she amputated their toes with a pair of blunt scissors. Mabel Grouitch, who was also on 'that terrible retreat', recalled how 'hundreds of men suffered amputations because they had no socks, mittens… or sweaters'. She reckoned she was spared the amputation of one foot simply because 'although frostbitten, I was protected by a single pair of knitted stockings given me by an American friend'.[76]

On 1 January 1916, Flora was promoted to Corporal. Nine weeks later, she was elevated to the rank of Sergeant in recognition of 'her gallantry in the field and services rendered to the wounded and sick during the retreat'. Shortly after this she returned to England on another fund-raising tour. She teamed up with the Scottish suffragist Evelina Haverfield who, once arrested for punching a policeman in the mouth, retorted, 'It was not hard enough. Next time I will bring a revolver.' Together they established the Hon Evelina Haverfield's and Sergeant Major Flora Sandes' Fund for Promoting Comforts for Serbian Soldiers and Prisoners.

Flora was fast becoming a celebrity. 'Serbia's Joan of Arc' boasted the English press. 'The model of the modern girl', applauded the *Glasgow Herald*. *The New York Times* opted for her roots when it ran a story in August 1916 captioned 'WOMAN FIGHTS FOR SERBS — Irish Nurse Reaches Toulon on Way Back to Service'. The accompanying article explained that 'Miss Flora Sandes, an Irish woman, who is a Sergeant in the Serbian Army [was] on the way to rejoin her regiment after a holiday in Ireland.'[77]

Such publicity did no harm to her fund-raising coffers, not least when she gathered her front-line letters and diaries into a best-selling autobiography. Published in 1916, she used a chunk of the proceeds to purchase more medical supplies, as well as clothing, tea, lemonade and cigarettes, for her Serbian comrades.[78]

By the autumn of 1916 she was back with her regiment once again as the Bulgarians launched another attack on Monastir. At seven o'clock on 3 November, Sergeant Flora Sandes was in the Serbian trenches just north of the city when her company was ordered over the top. The Bulgarians were entrenched on a steep, snow-bound hill directly opposite. Flora was one of the first out and she charged up the slope with all her might. As she reached the Bulgarian trench, a soldier threw a grenade at her. The explosion knocked her out, broke her arm and shredded her back and right side from her shoulder down to her knee.[79] A lieutenant from her company managed to drag her back into the trench before the Bulgarians finished her off. 'The next day,' she recalled some years later, 'when our troops attacked and occupied the Bulgarian trenches, they found a number of our men who had been taken prisoner. Each one lay dead in the trench with the throat cut from ear to ear. That is the Bulgar way of dealing with prisoners.'[80]

She spent the next two months in hospital and convalesced in Bizerta, Tunisia, during which time she took her ambition to be 'one of the men' to such an extreme that she accompanied her Serbian comrades to a brothel. When one of the young women planted herself on Flora's knees and began cooing about how shy the soldier was, Flora 'kept it up for a while', as she put it, but was compelled to reveal her sex when the young woman tried to kiss her.

She then returned home to visit her relatives in England and Ireland. Oh, and to pick up some essentials. When she rejoined her regiment in May 1917, she came equipped with enough underwear, socks and other necessities to fit every soldier of the 2nd Regiment and all the soldiers of the Morava Division.

Wounded again in the scorching hot July, she returned to hospital where she was awarded the Order of the Star of Karađorđe, the highest decoration of the Serbian Military, and promoted to the rank of Sergeant Major. Three months later she took part in the last drive on the Salonika Front, which completely broke the Bulgarian Army. They pushed the Bulgarians out of Monastir, although the ancient city was subject to daily bombardments from aeroplanes and batteries right through until Bulgaria's surrender in the late autumn of 1918.[81]

In June 1919, Flora was commissioned as a Second Lieutenant in the Serbian Army in acknowledgement of her 'personal bravery on the battlefield'. A special Act of Parliament was required to give her the commission. One of Serbia's senior military men hailed her as 'an example of courage and self-sacrifice in every engagement [who] had a great influence on the men in her platoon, company and battalion being a woman, and a foreigner — and advancing with them in the first line, rifle in hand.'[82] As *The Irish Times* noted, this was 'possibly the first instance in history of a woman being honoured with a commission as a combatant officer in a European army.'

She was demobilised in October 1922 but was on stand-by for active service should Serbia return to war. 'I never loved anything so much in my life', she lamented when asked about army life. 'I felt neither fish nor flesh when I came out of the army. The first time I put on women's clothes I slunk through the streets.' Out of uniform, she discovered that her former comrades were rather less comfortable in her presence. 'Though still quite friendly, they were now quite different. Never again could it be quite the same. As long as I had occasion to notice, men are never quite so naturally themselves when there are women present, as when among themselves.'

Her visit to Colonel Milić was a case in point. He was so shocked by the sight of his former sergeant in a new dress and hat that he threw his hands in the air and ordered her to put on a uniform without delay. 'He didn't know where he was with me, nor how to talk with me,' explained Flora.[83]

In May 1927, she married Colonel Yuri Vladimovich Yudenich, a White Russian from Belarus who was 12 years her junior. Yuri had commanded a corps of artillery and transport horses in Tsar Nicholas II's army before the Bolshevik Revolution in October 1917, and had served as one of Flora's sergeants during the last part of the war. They briefly lived in Paris where Flora found work as chaperone to a troupe of pretty young Folies Bergère cabaret singers. She became a highly sought-after speaker and, sporting her Serbian Army uniform, she delivered lectures in North America, Europe, Australia and New Zealand.

Flora and Yuri later settled in the Serbian capital of Belgrade where Flora taught English and apparently drove the city's first taxi. They both fought for Yugoslavia during its ten-day resistance to the German invasion of 1941.[84] Flora was captured, escaped, recaptured by the Gestapo and then released on parole. One of her fellow prisoners described how she 'possessed a wonderful fund of Serbian swear words, which she launched at the guards with such devastating effect that they behaved almost respectfully'. Internment took its toll on Yuri who was taken ill and died in September 1941.

Flora subsequently went to live with a nephew in Jerusalem before moving to Bulawayo in Rhodesia (present-day Zimbabwe) in July 1945. True to form, she caused consternation amongst her white peers when she took to drinking soghum beer and puffing cigarettes with Bulawayo's Ndebele population. She later returned to Suffolk, where she whizzed around in an electric chair until her death in Ipswich, aged 80, in November 1956. On account of her services during the two world wars, she was entitled to wear seven decorations.[85]

As for her wartime colleagues, 'Mrs Grouch' became a major fund-raiser for Serbians in America, while her husband Dr Slavko Grouitch was appointed first Ambassador to the US from the new Jugoslav Kingdom.[86] Elsie Inglis was stricken with cancer and died in November 1917. Evelina Haverfield went to work in a Serbian orphanage in September 1919, but contracted pneumonia and died in March 1920, aged 53.

SERVIAN TROOPS

Serbian troops prepare to tackle the Austrian invaders upon the outbreak of war in 1914. Although outnumbered, the Serbs fended off three separate invasions by the Austrians during the war. It came at a heavy cost: by 1919, Serbia had lost about 850,000 people, a quarter of its pre-war population.

NOTES

PART ONE: THE WESTERN FRONT (1–137)

The Irish Dames of Ypres (pp 7–18)

1. Dame Mary Joseph Butler of Callan, Co Kilkenny, was a sister of Francis Butler of Gray's Inn and a cousin of the Duke of Ormond. In 1687, the newly crowned Catholic monarch James II persuaded Dame Butler to found a Benedictine abbey in Great Ship Street in Dublin. The Irish abbey received the Royal Patent in 1689 and formally became 'His Majesty's Chief Royal Abbey'. Following its plunder by Williamite soldiers during the Jacobite Wars, Dame Butler and her sister nuns returned to Flanders.
2. *The Sacred Heart Review* (Boston College), Volume 32, Number 9, 27 August 1904.
3. Dame Placid and Sister Romana were already in Poperinghe, having been sent ahead some days earlier to check on the Lady Abbess.
4. The identity of this regiment is a mystery. Dame Columban described how 'every man wore the harp and shamrock on his collar and cap'. The shamrock on the cap badge suggests the Royal Munster Fusiliers, but the harp and the fact that they sang 'Tipperary' points to the Connaught Rangers. Both regiments were in the area at the time, as were the Royal Irish Rifles who also had a harp.
5. The story of the flag is the subject of some debate. According to an article in *The New York Times* in 1915, Dame Teresa rescued a portion of this flag from the choir in Ypres, where it hung, and brought it back to England for safekeeping from the German troops. However, the late John Martin Brennan relates the following in his 2011 thesis 'Irish Catholic Chaplains in the First World War', p. 62:
   'Fr Henry Gill searched for [the flag of Clare's Dragoons] amongst the rubble of the Benedictine convent of Les Dames Irlandaises on three occasions during the war. On the last occasion, he reported "it must be remembered that during all this period shells were falling in the town and at least on one occasion when I was in the cellar shells actually struck the building". Even after that experience, he wrote to the Mother Abbess (now living with her congregation in England) asking about the flag and she wrote back detailing exactly where it was hidden along with other treasures including an "old English martyrologie given by Thomas Moore with his signature on the first page. This book is small and very old". Gill did not find the flag and, after a long investigation, he concluded it had been destroyed in the shelling.'
   The 19th century Nationalist poet Thomas Davis mentions the flags in his poem 'Clare's Dragoons' —
   'The flags we captured in the fray
   Look lone in Ypres Choir they say.'
   And again in 'The Flower of Finae' —
   'In the Cloisters of Ypres a banner is swaying.
   And by it a pale weeping maiden is praying;
   That flag's the sole trophy of Ramillies fray;
   This nun is poor Eily, the Flower of Finae.'
6. Obituary of Lady Abbess Ostyn, *Catholic Herald*, 22 November 1940.

Jack Judge — the man who wrote 'Tipperary' (pp 21–6)

7. *Daily Mail*, 18 August 1914.
8. Griffith's Valuations recorded three Gilbert Judges, all in Annagh parish, at Carrow Beg, Corraun and Derrylea.
9. Thomas Maguire, a bricklayer, and his wife Jane McGuire are sometimes said to have been from Tipperary, but this is, as yet, unproven. They arrived in Oldbury from Ireland in the early 1850s and lived in Low Town, near Oldbury's Malt Shovel public house. John Judge Jnr married their eldest daughter, Mary McGuire. In 1875, his younger brother, James Judge, married Mary McGuire's younger sister, Ann.

10. John Thomas Judge, known as Jack, was born on 3 December 1872. In 1877, his father was laid off by Bromford Iron Works and, in pursuit of work, he moved his family to Wolverhampton, and then to Moseley in Birmingham. Most of Jack's education took place at St Patrick's School, Wolverhampton, and St Anne's School, Moseley. When the Bromford Iron Works reopened in 1883, both John and Jack (who was by now a strapping 12-year-old) were employed by the company.

11. The four children were John ('Jackie') in 1897, Jane Anne ('Cissie') in 1900, Thomas in 1902, and James Patrick ('Jimmy') in 1905.

12. As part of HC Lovell's company, he performed in a 'musical comedy phantasy' called 'The Queen of Sheba' at the Tivoli Theatre in Dublin in January 1911. *The Irish Times* (p. 7) of 24 January 1911 applauded Jack's performance as 'very amusing'.

13. 'Tipperary' first appeared on a gramophone record bearing the label of 'The Winner' (no manufacturer's name given) British Patent 1912 in which Ted Yorke delivered the song as an old-fashioned music hall ballad, singing the verse in a near-Irish accent but breaking into unmistakable Cockney for the chorus.

14. Jack toured Ireland with a group called the London Comedy Four, co-starring the dancers Doris Hunter, Syd Sydney, Pop Carson, Mabel & Malfer and the Three Charringtons. *The Irish Times*, 27 August 1914.

15. Jack also recorded 'The Place Where I Was Born' in 1915, written before the war, which focused on the mutual compassion of working-class families during hard times.

16. Harry Williams later settled in California and was well known for other lyrics such as 'In the Shade of the Old Apple Tree', 'Cheyenne' and 'I'm Afraid to Go Home in the Dark'. In May 1922, he was taken seriously ill with tuberculosis and died in a hospital in Oakland. Feldman reputedly gave him a weekly pension of £1 during his latter years.

17. 'He must have made a fortune out of a tune which, though it cannot be described like the "Marseillaise" and "John Brown's Body" as a tune that made history, is certainly a tune that has achieved historical fame... the refrain of "Tipperary" can still recall more immediately than anything else the spirit and excitement of the early days of the War.' (*The Times*, 29 July 1938, p. 12).

Hoppy Hardy — the multiple escaper (pp 29–35)

18. It seems likely that Hoppy Hardy was a direct descendant of Obediah Hardy and Mary Antesil (Entwisell?). Their son William Joseph Hardy (1755–1828) married Sarah North and was the father of Freeman Hardy (1797–1863) who seems to have established the High Street business and married Mary Gardiner (1800–1866) from Bath in Somerset, England. It is thought that Freeman's son Thomas was born in 1830 and that he was a resident of Holywood, County Down by 1852. He was almost certainly father to Howard Hardy, born 1854, the father of Hoppy.

19. Howard Hardy lived at 31 Edwardes Square in Kensington, London. His wife Katherine, 18 years his junior, grew up in London. Katherine's brother Hugh died in the Great War and was buried in Dar es Salaam. At some point before the Great War, Howard and Katherine moved to Hillsbrook, Berkhamsted, in the Chiltern Hills of west Hertfordshire.

20. Jocelyn Lee Hardy was born in London on 10 June 1894. He was commissioned into the Connaught Rangers on 24 January 1914. He probably secured the commission through his father's Ulster connections. Although their principal barracks and recruiting depot was at King House in Boyle, County Roscommon, the 2nd Battalion was stationed in Aldershot at this time. On 21 September 1914, while held as a German captive, JL Hardy was promoted to lieutenant.

21. Before Halle, he was briefly transferred from Targau to Burg, near the city of Magdeburg.

22. Also imprisoned at Augustabad was the artist and mountaineer Conrad Thomond O'Brien-ffrench, second son of the Marquis de Castelthomond.

23. On 5 March 1918, Hoppy boarded a ship at Rotterdam. It did not sail for a week, but when it did, his three-and-a-half year period of captivity was over. Hoppy and Loder-Symonds were presented to the King at Buckingham Palace on the morning of 18 March, along with Henry Strother Cautley MP. Two days later, the Director of Military Intelligence forwarded his application for a 1914 ribbon.

24. He is thought to have rejoined the Connaughts at 'L' Infantry Base Depot at Beaumaris, Rouen. Just days later, on 22 April, he transferred from the Connaughts to the 2nd Inniskillings with whom he appears to have spent the rest of his war service.

25. *Guerrilla Warfare in the Irish War of Independence*, 1919–1921, by Joseph McKenna, p. 89.

26. Tony Woods, Staff Captain, IRA. Interviewed in *Survivors Related to Uinseann Mac Eoin*. Argenta Publications, Dublin. 1980.

27. A witness statement made by Joseph Dolan, member of A Company, 1st Battalion, Dublin Brigade, G.H.Q. Intelligence. 'We were looking for a British Intelligence Officer named Hardy for months. He had an artificial leg and was very vicious.'

28. I am unsure when this took place. There may have been a second attempt at Dún Laoghaire. Generally, he is said to have always been accompanied by a well-armed bodyguard.
29. He bought a large farm at Washpit Farm near King's Lynn, Norfolk.
30. His publications were: *Escape!* (1927); *Everything Is Thunder*; *The Key*, a play with Robert Gore-Browne; *Never in Vain* (1936); *Recoil* (1936); *The Stroke of Eight* (1938) and *Pawn in the Game* (1939).
31. On 1 November 1919 he was married in All Souls Church, Marleybone, London, to Kathleen Isabel Hutton-Potts, the 22-year-old daughter of Hong Kong stockbroker Alec Hutton-Potts.

Lord Desmond FitzGerald and the Micks (pp 39–55)

32. The family connection to Taplow stretched back centuries. In 1747, the first Duke of Leinster, then Earl of Kildare, married one of the famous Lennox sisters, daughters of the Duke of Richmond, and was given the subsidiary title of Viscount Leinster of Taplow in the County of Buckingham.
33. Desmond was also the subject of the unrequited love of his cousin Marian Beckett, daughter of Hermione's niece Mabel Duncombe.
34. *The New York Times*, 1 March 1908. 'SETTING TRAPS FOR A DUKE: London Mammas Fear American Girl May Capture Leinster. Special Cable.'
35 Before Eton he spent three years at Mr Tabor's school in Cheam, Surrey.
36. *Evening Post*, Rōrahi Putanga 20, 23 July 1914, Page 7; *The Mercury* (Hobart, Tasmania), Sunday 25 July 1914, p. 5.
37. 'Catastrophe 1914: Europe Goes to War', Max Hastings.
38. 'BRIGHT ARMOUR — MEMORIES OF FOUR YEARS OF WAR' by Monica Grenfell. *The British Journal of Nursing*, October 1935, Vol. 83, p. 272.
39. 'Sgt Gallacher (of Donegal) told me he saw Col George Morris riding in the woods, and the only way he knew he had been wounded was when he spotted blood coming from his field boot. A pencil drawing of Col Morris is in the Commanding Officer's office to this day. Gallacher saw it at Windsor in 1977, and recognised it at once.' Private correspondence with Sir William Mahon, February 2014.
40. The four missing officers were Lieutenant Lord Robert Inns-Ker, Second Lieutenant Viscount Castlerosse, Lieutenant the Hon Aubrey Herbert, MP (the interpreter, later to become a close friend of Mark Sykes and the only Irish Guards officer to go to Gallipoli other than General Godley) and Lieutenant Shields, RAMC (the medical officer). They were captured by the Germans but later released in the wake of the French counter-attack on 12 September.
41. *The Irish Times*, Saturday 19 September 1914, p. 3.
    'The Guards Grave in the woods at Villers Cotterts was paid for by the Comrades Graves fund of the Foot Guards. It was seen by Kipling who was conducting Asquith's wife in a search for her missing Grenadier son in the woods some weeks after the battle. By this time many regiments had scattered graves all over northern France and Belgium, and the Guards Grave at V-C became the inspiration for the Imperial War Graves Commission of which Kipling with Fabian Ware was an early initiator. This was of course before the loss of John Kipling.' Private correspondence with Sir William Mahon, February 2014.
42. 'BRIGHT ARMOUR — MEMORIES OF FOUR YEARS OF WAR' by Monica Grenfell. *The British Journal of Nursing*, October 1935, Vol. 83, p. 272.
43. 'Until after WW1 the Foot Guards continued to spell Serjeant like that, although it was standardised throughout the army after that.' Private correspondence with Sir William Mahon, February 2014.
44. The only son of Sir Henry Singer Keating, a former Solicitor General for England, educated at Trinity College, Dublin, connected to Bansha, County Tipperary.
45. It is not clear what role Desmond FitzGerald played in these bloody events. Did he charge alongside his men? Was he there when the two sides agreed to hold fire while the stretcher-bearers ran out to gather up a wounded soldier? Did he watch when a sword-wielding German officer once charged over the top with 50 men, all to be mown down by the Guardsmen's guns?
46. Charles John Stewart lived at Rockill House, Letterkenny, County Donegal.
47. While talking with Battalion Machine-gun Officer, Lieutenant Straker, a beam fell and crushed Captain Brabazon to death. Straker's foot was pinned into the crumpled dug-out so badly that it took an hour to extricate him.
48. *The Man Who Wouldn't Be King: King Edward VIII*: A Biography By Philip Ziegler (Alfred A Knopf, 1991). The Prince clearly enjoyed his time so much that he joined Desmond and the other officers for dinner in Béthune a few days later.
49. On 27 September, Jack Trefusis, now the 20th Brigade's commanding officer, managed to wade back through the trenches to lunch with his old battalion. He even found time for a haircut. Jack Trefusis

was shot through the forehead by a sniper four weeks later. At the time of his death he was the youngest Brigadier General in the British Army.

50. Terence Dooley, p. 179; 'In memoriam of Major Lord Desmond FitzGerald' by Lord D'Abernon in JCKAS, 8, 1915–17, p. 424.
51. 'Fr John Gwynn' by Richard Stewart via The Sacred Heart Church (Caterham, Whyteleafe & Godstone) website at www.sacred-heart.co.uk.
52. Claude Hanbury, whose mother was a Handcock, was killed at Ypres on 9 October 1917. His father had lost their family fortune before the war.
53. Desmond FitzGerald is buried in Calais Southern Cemetery, Plot A, Row Officers, Grave 5.
54. According to Rudyard Kipling, Lord Desmond FitzGerald 'was so severely wounded that he died within an hour… Lieutenant TEG Nugent was dangerously wounded at the same time through the liver, though he did not realise this at the time, and stayed coolly in charge of a party till help came. Lieutenant Hanbury, who was conducting the practice, was wounded in the hand and leg, and Father Lane-Fox lost an eye and some fingers. Lord Desmond FitzGerald was buried in the public cemetery at Calais on the 5th. As he himself had expressly desired, there was no formal parade, but the whole Battalion, of which he was next for the command, lined the road to his grave. His passion and his loyalty had been given to the Battalion without thought of self, and among many sad things few are sadder than to see the record of his unceasing activities and care since he had been second in command cut across by the curt announcement of his death.
    'It was a little thing that his name had been at the time submitted for a well-deserved D.S.O.' See also: 'Bomb Kills Duke's Heir: Lord Desmond Fitzgerald Was Experimenting with New Missile', *The New York Times*, 8 March 1916. The article states that FitzGerald 'was experimenting with a new kind of bomb, when it exploded and a fragment struck him in the head. He was taken to a hospital and died an hour later.'
55. *Ettie: The Intimate Life and Dauntless Spirit of Lady Desborough* by Richard Davenport-Hines.
56. *Mons, Anzac and Kut* (1919) by Aubrey Herbert.
57. 'Copy W. H. L. McCarthy to Lord de Vesci, 2 April 1916' (in private possession).

Captain DD Sheehan, MP for Mid-Cork (pp 61–73)
58. 'In the Front Trenches', *Daily Express* (London), Daniel Desmond Sheehan, 9 February 1916.
59. The other four MPs were JL Esmonde, Stephen Gwynn, Willie Redmond and William Redmond, while former MP Tom Kettle also joined up.
60. *Ireland Since Parnell* by Captain DD Sheehan (London: Daniel O'Connor, 1921), 'Chapter II — A Leader Is Dethroned!'
61. Sheehan was briefly allied to Redmond's party in 1906, but was expelled for steadfastly refusing to allow the ILLA to play second fiddle to the IPP's aims.
62. DD Sheehan built his campaign on a promise to pursue 'the great democratic principle of the government of the people, by the people and for the people'. As well as cottage building, the young MP was instrumental in pushing through schemes for land reclamation, drainage and road building throughout Munster. He also established a Model Irish Village at Tower near Blarney, complete with 17 cottages, a school, a laundry and a community hall.
63. At the Mansion House in February 1909, 'Little Joe' Devlin ordered his army of 400 militant 'Mollies' to use their batons to bludgeon anyone with a 'Cork accent' who tried to address the gathering. Sheehan was amongst those bloodied during the ensuing mêlée, which became known as the 'Baton Convention'. Sheehan and O'Brien regarded themselves as the true heirs of Parnell's conciliatory legacy, believing nationalists and unionists alike could agree upon a 'form of self-government for the island of Ireland as a whole.'
64. While Sir Edward Carson, leader of the Ulster Unionists, applauded the AFIL's attempts to include Ulster in an All-Ireland Home Rule settlement, the proposal was fatally hampered by the IPP's refusal to allow any concessions to Ulster.
65. William O'Brien, Cork Town Hall, 2 September 1914.
66. *Ireland Since Parnell* by Captain DD Sheehan (London: Daniel O'Connor, 1921).
67. 'Why I joined the Army', DD Sheehan, *Daily Express*, 1 February 1916.
68. 'And so early last year saw me enrolled as a fighting soldier in Kitchener's Army. I learnt my trade in the barrack square of Buttevant, Co. Cork. I tumbled out of bed at six o'clock every morning—and I was by no means an early riser before—I went through my hour's physical drill with the youngest and the best and it gives me a rare pleasure to say that Mr. Stephen Gwynne, M.P., over whom I possess some advantage in age, did likewise. He and Mr Kettle, from the Redmondite side, I from the O'Brienite camp, others

of every varying hue of political thought, and some of no political bias at all, forgot everything save that we were soldiers in a common cause, and that it was "up to Us" in the least possible time so to get trained ourselves that we may be able to train others to take their place in the military organization of the Empire. We have already been in the trenches. We know what trench warfare means. We have suffered our share of casualties, but we are out here for the glory of Ireland and to maintain the prestige of British arms, and we mean to leave our mark on the battlefields of France before this dreadful carnage comes to an end.' Extracted from *The Tablet. The International Catholic News Weekly*, on 5 February 1916, p. 10.

69. *The Irish Times*, 15 April 1916. On 14 April, the Cork City and County Recruiting Committee resolved that for recruitment in Ireland to succeed, a policy of 'preferential treatment' should be adapted to those who served, or had served, as well as their families, when it came to the redistribution of lands by the Estates Commissioners and the Congested District Boards

70. In 1925, Michael Sheehan married Lilian Taylor, with whom he had three children: Barbara, Christopher and Patricia (aka Ms Frank Johnson). Having been raised between India and England, Barbara later moved to Switzerland and married Guido Bischofberger. Their daughter Cilla married Robert Patton of the Monaghan firm David Patton Ltd., one of the oldest and largest private animal feed compounders in Ireland.

71. See for instance DD Sheehan, 'How a Trench-Raid VC was Won'; 'In the Front Trenches'; 'Father Gleeson and his Altar Boy', all online.

72. *The Irish Times*, Friday 19 May 1916, p. 5.

73. The Royal Munster Fusiliers' Reserve depot in County Cork was initially at Aghada, and then at Ballincollig Barracks.

74. The bulletin published in *The London Gazette* stated that he 'relinquished his commission on account of ill-health contracted on active service, and is granted the honorary rank of Captain, 13 Jan. 1918.' In addition to the honorary captaincy, he was awarded three campaign medals, as well as the Silver War Badge. His three WWI campaign medals were the 1914–15 Star, the British War Medal and the Allied Victory Medal. All seven Sheehan-O'Connor family members were awarded the medals, with Eileen being awarded the latter two. (The National Archives, Kew, London, Medal Card Records.)

75. Sergeant Robert O'Connor is recalled on the Menin Gate Wall, Panel 44, Ypres, Belgium. His son Robert O'Connor later became an Irish Army sergeant at Collins Barracks in Cork.

76. Extract from a declaration by DD Sheehan made in 1926 in an unrelated matter, to his personal circumstances in 1918–19, describing how he and his wife had to leave Ireland. From private correspondence papers held by Niall Ó Síocháin.

77. *Ireland Since Parnell* by Captain DD Sheehan (London: Daniel O'Connor, 1921).

78. 'Citizenship & Loyalty', *Dublin Chronicle* editorial, Saturday 16 November 1929, by Captain DD Sheehan BL, editor and publisher, late MP for Mid-Cork and ex-Royal Munster Fusiliers.

79. *DD Sheehan, BL, MP, His Life and Times* by John Dillon. Foilsiúcháin Éireann Nua, Templemore, Co Tipperary (2013), p.39, ISBN 978-0-9576456-1-5.

80. DD Sheehan, 'A Tribute and a Claim'.

81. From original letter with address: Lt. M.J. Sheehan, 13 Squadron, R.A.F., B.E.F., France, dated 10 July, in Sheehan family possession. Letter can be viewed on www.europeana1914-1918.eu under "Sheehan O'Connor family from Cork – seven served on the Western Front."

82. Three days later, Richthofen was wounded in the hip by anti-aircraft fire and crash-landed; his injuries kept him out of combat for five months. He was killed in a commercial plane crash in July 1922. Also on board were the silent movie star Fern Andra and her director Georg Bluen. Bluen died the following day, but Andra survived, spending a year recovering from her injuries.

The short army career of Private Kit Conway (p. 74)

83. 'Letter of 19 January 2005' by Seán Ua Cearnaigh quoted at http://irelandscw.com/ibvol-KitConway.htm.

Major General Louis Lipsett (pp 75–81)

84. This information came by courtesy of Jennifer Lipsett, a distant cousin of the family, who lives at Cashel, Rossnowlagh, County Donegal. When I spoke to her in January 2014, she told me that the shop sold everything from grocery to china and that the Lipsett brothers were also well-known auctioneers. Richard and Robert were the sons of Louis Lipsett. Robert's son William Lipsett, a barrister, was killed at Ypres in 1915.

85. Louis Lipsett's entry by Desmond Morton from *Dictionary of Canadian Biography, Volume XIV* (1911–1920).

86. Arthur Hill McBride and Mary D'Arcy were from counties Down and Limerick, respectively. Sir Richard McBride's entry by Patricia E Roy, from *Dictionary of Canadian Biography, Volume XIV* (1911–1920).

87. *No Place to Run: The Canadian Corps and Gas Warfare in the First World War* by Tim Cook (UBC Press, 2011), p. 22–8.
88. One of his men later wrote: 'I think that if they had a man of less calibre than Lipsett, we would probably have been all taken because he stood firm. He was a wonderful soldier and a wonderful man.' *Hell in Flanders Fields: Canadians at the Second Battle of Ypres*, by George H Cassar (Dundurn, 2010), p. 322.
89. As well as being made a Companion of the Order of the Bath, and winning numerous other medals, Louis Lipsett was posthumously awarded the Croix d'Officier de la Legion d'Honneur and the Croix de Guerre by the French Government.
90. Citation published in *The London Gazette*, 8 November 1917.

Woodbine Willie – the soldiers' poet (pp 83–91)
91. William Studdert Kennedy married, as his second wife, Jeannette Kerr Anketell in 1868 in County Monaghan. See *Memoir of the Family of Anketell* (1885) by Anketell Henry Kennedy.
92. 'The School of Courage: Chapter X' from *Now It Can Be Told* (1920) by Philip Gibbs.
93. He did not win over everyone. The right wing regarded him as a rabid socialist. The left dissed him as a lackey of the industrialists, especially during the General Strike of 1926 when he endeavoured to liaise between the miners and the colliery owners, even presenting £200 of his own limited funds to the Miners' Distress Fund.
94. A memorial plaque on the cathedral wall reads: 'GEOFFREY ANKETELL STUDDERT KENNEDY — A POET: A PROPHET: A PASSIONATE SEEKER AFTER TRUTH: AN ARDENT ADVOCATE OF CHRISTIAN FELLOWSHIP.' He even got a mention in *Finnegans Wake* by Irish author James Joyce: '...tsingirillies' zyngarettes, while Woodbine Willie, so popiular with the poppyrossies...'
95. *The Irish Times*, Monday 6 May 1929. Backed by Trinity College, the Studdert Kennedy Memorial Fund was established to look after his wife and children.

Hill 16 — legends of the rubble (pp 93–4)
96. *The Irish Times*, Friday 8 June 1917, p. 4.
97. Quoted in Neville Lytton's *The Press and the General Staff* (1920), p. 97.

Tom Kettle and Emmet Dalton (pp 99–115)
98. Quoted in *War Letters of Fallen Englishmen* by Laurence Housman (University of Pennsylvania Press, 1930).
99. A compendium of Tom Kettle's war journalism was published as *The Ways of War* in 1917 and edited by his wife, Mary Kettle. She also compiled the aphorisms of *An Irishman's Calendar* (1938). His letter to Joe Devlin, written shortly before he died, was quoted in *The Ways of War*, p. 34: 'I hope to come back. If not, I believe that to sleep here in the France that I have loved is no harsh fate, and that so passing out into silence, I shall help towards the Irish settlement. Give my love to my colleagues — the Irish people have no need of it.'
100. William Hatchell Boyd was the second son of Rev Samuel T Boyd, Methodist, of Dublin.
101. Emmet Dalton was born on 4 March 1898.
102. The gold medal is mentioned in *The Irish Times*, Thursday 15 November 1900, p. 6.
103. Adrian Gregory, Senia Paseta, *Ireland and the Great War: A War to Unite Us All?* Manchester University Press, 2002, p. 8–12.
104. He could also be wicked, describing Tim Healy as 'a brilliant calamity', and a new book aimed at Yuletide shoppers as 'very suitable for the Christmas fire'.
105. *The Enigma of Tom Kettle: Irish Patriot, Essayist, Poet, British Soldier, 1880–1916*, John Benignus Lyons (Glendale Press, 1983), p. 93. See also *The New York Times* article 'Money for a Free Ireland' of 22 October 1906.
106. 'Ireland' in *The Ways of War*, p. 4.
107. Adrian Gregory, Senia Paseta, *Ireland and the Great War: A War to Unite Us All?* Manchester University Press, 2002, p. 9.
108. *German Atrocities, 1914: A History of Denial* by John Horne and Alan Kramer (Yale University Press, 2001) provides detailed research on German atrocities perpetrated on the Belgian and French civilian population in the Autumn of 1914.
109. *The Rise and Fall of Imperial Ireland: Redmondism in the Context of Britain's Conquest of South Africa and Its Great War on Germany 1899–1916*, by Pat Walsh, p. 404.
110. His first attempt to enlist was apparently rejected on the grounds of his poor health, possibly connected to his drinking.
111. Extracted from 'NEWS FROM IRELAND — An Appeal to Irishmen', *The Tablet*, 7 August 1915.

112. Desmond Ryan, *The Singing Flame* (Anvil Books, 1978).
113. Ó Broin, Leon, *Protestant Nationalists: The Stopford Connection* (Dublin: Gill & Macmillan 1985), p. 117.
114. PRONI, D.3809/67/2, McLaughlin papers, letter, TM Kettle to Sir Henry McLaughlin, 7 August 1916. Quoted in *Irish Regiments in the Great War — Discipline and Morale* by Timothy Bowman, p. 128.
115. Housman, p. 166.
116. Housman, p. 166.
117. Letter from Willie Redmond to Arthur Conan Doyle, dated 18 December 1916, quoted in *Memories and Adventures* by Arthur Conan Doyle (Hodder & Stoughton, London, 1924)
118. Patrick Moylett later recalled, 'Emmet Dalton told me that John Redmond was getting him a commission in the British Army. Emmet Dalton was wearing a Christian Brothers cap at the time; he told me he was 18 years of age. His statement made me sad, because it cut straight across what he was then doing. I tried to persuade him not to join, but I was not successful.' Bureau of Military History (WS 767).
119. At some point he revoked the copyright in his works in favour of his wife.
120. *The Ways of War*, p. 36–39.
121. Quoted in 'In Memory of Lieutenant Tom Kettle, 'B' Company, 9th Royal Dublin Fusiliers', by Tom Burke, *Dublin Historical Record*, Vol. 57, No 2 (Autumn, 2004), pp. 164–173. Published by Old Dublin Society.
    Letter to Mary Kettle from Emmet Dalton c/o Liverpool Merchants Hospital at Etaples, France, dated 14 October 1916. It begins: 'Dear Mrs Kettle, I presume by now that you are utterly disgusted with me for failing to reply to your letter, but I assure you that if I had been in a fit condition I would I have....' It is quoted in full in Tom Burke's article in *Dublin Historical Record*.
    Dalton's version of events is rather different from those given by an unnamed staff captain to Mrs Kettle, which were published in both *The Irish Times* (Saturday 23 September 1916) and in *The Ways of War*, p. 36–39. Why was this so? Did Mrs Kettle prefer the idea of her husband leading his men, even as he lay dying on the ground? Here is what the staff captain said:
    "In the Guillemont fighting I caught a glimpse of him for a brief spell. He was in the thick of a hard struggle, which had for its object the dislodgment of the enemy from a redoubt they held close to the village. He was temporarily in command of the company, and he was directing operations with a coolness and daring that marked him out as a born leader of men. He seemed always to know what was the right thing to do, and he was always on the right spot to order the doing of the right thing at the right moment. The men under his command on that occasion fought with a heroism worthy of their leader. They were assailed furiously on both flanks by the foe. They resisted all attempts to force them back, and at the right moment they pressed home a vigorous counter-attack that swept the enemy off the field. The next time I saw him his men were again in a tight corner. They were advancing against the strongest part of the enemy's position in that region. Kettle kept them together wonderfully in spite of the terrible ordeal they had to go through, and they carried the enemy's position in record time. It was in the hottest corner of the Ginchy fighting that he went down. He was leading his men with a gallantry and judgment that would almost certainly have won him official recognition had he lived, and may do so yet. His beloved Fusiliers were facing a deadly fire and were dashing forward irresistibly to grapple with the foe. Their ranks were smitten by a tempest of fire. Men went down right and left some never to rise again. Kettle was among the latter. He dropped to earth and made an effort to get up. I think he must have been hit again. Anyhow, he collapsed completely. A wail of anguish went up from his men as soon as they saw that their officer was down. He turned to them and urged them forward to where the Huns were entrenched. They did not need his injunction. They swept forward with a rush. With levelled bayonets they crashed into the foe. There was deadly work, indeed, and the Huns paid dearly for the loss of Kettle.'
122. In Tullow, County Carlow, Captain WJ Murphy's devastated mother gifted a house and garden to the people of the parish in his memory; this is now known as the Captain Murphy Memorial Hall. To my considerable surprise, it transpired that the Murphys also briefly lived at Kill, a former Bunbury house, and owned a substantial chunk of the Square in Tullow including the building where I have my office. Captain Murphy's portrait is in the museum in Tullow.
123. Dalton's Military Cross citation: 'At the capture of Ginchy, on the 9th of September, 1916, he displayed great bravery and leadership in action. When, owing to the loss of officers, the men of two companies were left without leaders, he took command and led these companies to their final objective. After the withdrawal of another brigade and the right flank of his battalion was in the rear, he carried out the protection of the flank, under intense fire, by the employment of machine-guns in selected commanding and successive positions. After dark, whilst going about supervising the consolidation of the position, he, with only one sergeant escorting, found himself confronted by a party of the enemy, consisting of one

officer and twenty men. By his prompt determination the party were overawed and, after a few shots, threw up their arms and surrendered.'

124. *Poems & Parodies*, by TM Kettle (Dublin: Talbot Press, 1916). William Dawson wrote under the pen name 'Avis', primarily for the *Leader*, and was a cousin and close friend of the politician Arthur Clery.

125. Andrew Kettle died on 22 September 1916 at St Margaret's, Finglas, aged 83.

126. As a member of General Headquarters Staff, Emmet Dalton both conceived and took part in the daring plan to rescue the IRA's flying column leader Seán Mac Eoin from Mountjoy prison in May 1921. All went well until it emerged that Mac Eoin was not where they expected him to be, and so the would-be rescuers made a hasty retreat.

Sir William Orpen (pp 117–19)

127. They lived in Oriel House in Grove Avenue, Stillorgan, County Dublin. Sir William's brother Richard Orpen (1863–1939) was a prominent architect.

128. When Orpen and Yvonne parted ways in the late 1920s, he gifted her his Rolls-Royce along with William Grover-Williams, his chauffeur. Yvonne then married Grover-Williams, who became a Grand Prix racing driver but was later captured and executed by the Nazis.

129. Keith Jeffery, 'Ireland and the Great War', p. 85–91.

The Irish air aces (pp 127–37)

130. The calm and quiet Flight Commander Captain Gwilym Lewis, DFC, nicknamed 'Noisy' by 'Mick' Mannock, downed 12 planes during his tour of duty. He returned to England, where he lived until his death in 1996. He was the next to last surviving British ace from the war.

131. George's father Samuel McElroy, BA, was the son of farmer George McElroy (1828–1909) and his wife Kittie (Katherine) (1836–1905) of Kiltycreighton, just outside Boyle, County Roscommon. At least three of Samuel's siblings emigrated to the USA, and some of the McElroys ended up in Montana. Samuel's Westmeath-born wife Ellen Synnott, described in 1901 as a 'work mistress' was the daughter of farmer Edward Synnott of 38 Glengariffe Parade. They were wed in St George on 18 July 1892. The McElroy family headstone is in Mount Jerome Cemetery, Harold's Cross, Dublin.

132. Mountjoy School, a boarding school in Mountjoy Square, Dublin, was in the same building as the Incorporated Society for Promoting Protestant Schools.

According to Scott Addington in *For Conspicuous Gallantry: Winners of the Military Cross and Bar During the Great War*, McElroy initially joined the Royal Engineers as a Corporal with the regimental number 28292.

133. Initial training was completed at Reading and basic flying training at Nos 14, 6 and 54 Training Squadrons.

134. McElroy would go on to become the highest scoring ace of the unit

135. 'On my return from leave, the gap in the flight caused by Kennedy's death had been filled by a sturdy, curly-headed young Irishman, McElroy. To differentiate between the two "Macs" in his flight, Mick [Mannock] called McElroy "McIrish" and me "McScottish", names which stuck to us until I left the squadron. Unlike the majority of new pilots we had had, McElroy immediately fitted into the working of the flight. A new pilot was nearly always a danger to himself and to the others; if he was too cautious he was liable to be left behind to be sniped off by an astute enemy when the flight attacked; or, if he were courageous, he was just as liable to be "downed" in his first scrap because of his ignorance of what was going on around him. In either case, his misdemeanours were likely to incur special dangers for the rest of the flight. McElroy never caused us any anxiety. His attitude towards the war was that of a terrier let loose in a rat-infested barn. Both in the mess and the rugger field, his sturdy scrapping was a source of great pleasure to the flight.' Quoted in George McLanachan, *Fighter Pilot*.

136. Designed and built at the RAF Factory in Farnborough, the SE5a was, along with the Sopwith Camel, pivotal in ensuring that the Allies regained control of the west-European skies after the horrors of 'Bloody April' 1917.

137. The greatest air ace of World War One was Manfred von Richtofen, with 80 victories.

138. 'The other fellows all laugh at me for carrying a revolver. They think I'm going to shoot down a machine with it, but they're wrong. The reason I bought it was to finish myself as soon as I see the first signs of flames.' — Quoted in George McLanachan, *Fighter Pilot*.

He was greatly disturbed when Henry Dolan was shot down in flames by Raven Freiherr von Barnekow on 12 May. Dolan had been amongst Mannock's best pupils and had shot down seven enemy planes by the time of his death.

139. Traditionally, the British preferred to praise the team rather than the individual and, in contrast to the

way the German media had elevated the Red Baron to superhero status, Britain's air aces were rarely acknowledged unless they died. However, Lord Northcliffe, the Dublin-born newspaper tycoon, changed all that in January 1918 by splashing an illustrated feature on McCudden across the pages of the *Daily Mail*.

140. Sergeant Major William H McCudden was born in Carlow. See www.rootsweb.ancestry.com/~irlcar2/McCuddens.htm

141. Quoted in *In Clouds of Glory: American Airmen who Flew with the British During the Great War* by James J Hudson (University of Arkansas Press, 1990), p. 78.

142. On 26 March 1918, McElroy was awarded the Military Cross, for showing 'a splendid offensive spirit in dealing with enemy aircraft' and for destroying 'at least two enemy machines, and has always set a magnificent example of courage and initiative.' By 26 March 1918, when he was awarded the Military Cross, he had upped his scalp collection to 18 'kills'. His tally would ultimately include four enemy planes sent down in flames, with a further 23 planes and three balloons destroyed. Nicknamed 'Deadeye' by some of his colleagues, he also sent at least 16 enemy craft spinning 'out of control' and thereby out of the fight.

143. The Bar to his Military Cross was given on 22 April 1918 with the following citation: 'When on an offensive patrol, observing a hostile scout diving on one of our aeroplanes, he opened fire, and sent down the enemy machine in an irregular spin out of control, when it finally crashed completely. Later in the same day, he sent down another enemy machine in flames. On another occasion, when on offensive patrol, he singled one out of four enemy machines, and sent it down crashing to earth. On the same day he attacked another enemy machine, and, after firing 200 rounds, it burst into flames. On a later occasion, he opened fire on an enemy scout at 400 yards range, and finally sent it down in a slow spin out of control. In addition, this officer has brought down two other enemy machines completely out of control, his skill and determination being most praiseworthy.'

144. This was at Conteville, the aerodrome to which 'Forty' squadron were obliged to retreat on account of German advances on the ground.

145. *An Incomplete History of World War I* by Edwin Kiester (Barnes & Noble, 2007), p. 117.

146. McElroy's citation of 26 July read: 'While flying at a height of 2,000 feet, he observed a patrol of five enemy aircraft patrolling behind the lines. After climbing into the clouds, he dived to the attack, shot down and crashed one of them. Later, observing a two-seater, he engaged and shot it down out of control. On another occasion he shot down an enemy scout which was attacking our positions with machine-gun fire. He has carried out most enterprising work in attacking enemy troops and transport and in the course of a month has shot down six enemy aircraft, which were seen to crash, and five others out of control.'

147. The two-seater, a Hannover CL, would be chalked up on some accounts as his 47th and certainly final victory. There is a theory that he was shot down by a novice, Unteroffizier Gullmann of Jasta 56, who claimed to have shot down an SE5 south-west of Armentières at 10.15. No other SE5 was shot down that day. See 'Who Downed the Aces in WW1?' by Norman Franks (Barnes & Noble, 1998).

148. 'McElroy of "Forty"' by FT Gilbert, with a foreword by John Simon. From a private manuscript by courtesy of Rob McElroy.

149. His posthumous Distinguished Flying Cross citation on 3 August read: 'A brilliant fighting pilot who has destroyed thirty-five machines and three kite balloons to date. He has led many offensive patrols with marked success, never hesitating to engage the enemy regardless of their being, on many occasions, in superior numbers. Under his dashing and skilful leadership his flight has largely contributed to the excellent record obtained by the squadron.'

150. The citation for his Bar arrived on 21 September and read: 'In the recent battles on various army fronts this officer has carried out numerous patrols, and flying at low altitudes, has inflicted heavy casualties on massed enemy troops, transport, artillery teams, etc., both with machine-gun fire and bombs. He has destroyed three enemy kite balloons and forty-three machines, accounting for eight of the latter in eight consecutive days. His brilliant achievements, keenness and dash have at all times set a fine example and inspired all who came in contact with him.'

PART TWO: THE DARDANELLES (PP 139–229)

Sackville Carden and the naval attack on the Dardanelles (pp 145–55)

1. Fisher to Jellicoe, 16 March 1915, Jellicoe mss., British Library Additional Manuscripts 49006. 'Who expected Carden to be in Command of a big Fleet! He was made Adl. Supt. of Malta to shelve him!'

2. There was a second branch of Cardens in nearby Templemore. Two sons of Sir John Craven Carden, 4th Baronet, also died in the war, namely Major Henry Charles Carden, DSO (1855–1915) and Derrick Alfred

Carden (1875–1915), commander of the 7th Argyll and Sutherland Highlanders.

3. Woodcock was sentenced to hard labour, but this part of his punishment was not imposed.

4. Receipt addressed to A. Carden, Esq from school frigate 'Conway', Liverpool, for £20 half-year's fees and £8.10.0 extras for S. H. Carden as pupil on board 'Conway' for season beginning 1 Aug 1869. (Sackville Carden's personal papers).

5. *Straits: British policy towards the Ottoman Empire and the Origins of the Dardanelles campaign*, Geoffrey Miller (University of Hull Press, 1997), Chapter 19.

6. Sackville Carden was subsequently angry with Churchill for stating in the House of Commons in November 1915 that he had said the Dardanelles operation '*could*' be undertaken when he actually wrote '*might*'. Having received an unsatisfactory reply from the Naval Secretary, Carden wrote to Balfour, then First Lord of the Admiralty, whose reply dated 2 December 1915, said:

'Admiral Carden, I am much obliged for your letter enclosing a correction of Mr Churchill's quotation from your telegram. I am not quite clear … whether, when you used the word "might", you intended to convey that in your opinion the operation was one which could be undertaken with prospects of success. Yrs v truly (autograph).'

Sackville's reply, of which a draft exists, apparently said '… naturally been thinking the matter out since my arrival at Dardanelles the previous Sept. and intended by my reply to convey that in my opinion its complete success was uncertain — though I considered it worth trying for several reasons …' (Sackville Carden's personal papers).

Presumably, that is what he said in due course in his evidence to the Dardanelles Commission.

7. *The Immortal Gamble and the Part Played in It by H.M.S. "Cornwallis"* by AT Stewart (A. & C. Black, Ltd., 1917).

8. In the middle of February, Admiral Sir Henry Jackson of the Admiralty War Group raised an objection to Carden's 'ships only' plan. He believed that forcing battleships through the Narrows into the Sea of Marmara would be utterly pointless unless 'strong military landing parties with strong covering forces' were on hand to take control of the Gallipoli Peninsula.

9. *The Naval Annual — 1913* (David & Charles; J. Griffin & Co.), p. 192.

10. Every battleship was to be fitted with mine bumpers.

11. Aside from the two dreadnoughts, the fleet was largely surplus to requirements. For Fisher, the positive aspect of this was that if the operation failed, then the Navy could save face by pointing out that these were not their best ships.

12. During the battle of 18 March, de Robeck told how several shells burst prematurely in several older guns, putting them out of action at critical moments. De Robeck's telegram 282, p. 36 of Admiralty Telegrams 3 January–29 May 1915 (Dardanelles Commission, September 1916).

13. The obvious answer was to bring down some of the stronger planes from the Western Front but, again, this was overlooked.

14. Sackville Carden's signal following the bombardment on 19 February included 'Fire was opened… by *Vengeance*, *Cornwallis*, *Triumph*, *Suffren*, *Gaulois*, *Bouvet* at ranges from 4,000 to 10,000 yards, supported at 13,000 yards by *Agamemnon* and *Inflexible*.' (Sackville Carden's personal papers).

15. Letter from Keys to Carden, HMS *Queen Elizabeth*, 31 March 1915. (Sackville Carden's personal papers).

16. De Robeck's telegram 282, p. 35, Admiralty Telegrams, 3 January–29 May 1915 (Dardanelles Commission, September 1916).

17. The demolition parties were supported by Royal Marines and the Royal Navy Division's Plymouth Battalion, of whom 22 men died.

18. Sackville Carden's personal papers include a complete contemporary set of telegrams for the whole period. Admiralty Telegrams 3 January–29 May 1915 (Dardanelles Commission, September 1916) includes telegram 154 dated 4 March, and is stated to include the words: 'My latest estimate of number of days required to enter Marmora is fourteen.' This is a paraphrase of 153 — his words were actually 'Your 77 — 14 days,' in reply to No 77 dated 28 February from Churchill asking 'What is your latest estimate of number of days required excluding bad weather days, to the Sea of Marmora.' There was no mention of Constantinople by Carden, though Constantinople was mentioned by the Admiralty in their reply dated the same day. (Sackville Carden's personal papers).

19. In *The End of the Myth*, Robin Prior convincingly proposes that Carden was having serious doubts about the feasibility of the whole operation, that he was playing for time and 'going through the motions', hoping the War Council would quickly revert to an alternative plan and send in ground troops instead.

20. The accident on Sunday 9 March left both Arnold and his wife in serious shock. *The Irish Times*, Tuesday 9 March 1915, p. 6.

NOTES TO PP 154-65

21. The *Inflexible* was initially detailed to confront The *Goeben* when they reached the Sea of Marmara. This would no longer be possible.
22. When Sir John Maxwell, GOC of Egypt, visited Carden on 5 March, he opined that a strong force would be necessary; Maxwell would later order the execution of the Easter Rebellion leaders in Dublin.
23. For ships to pass safely through the Dardanelles, de Robeck advised on 27 March, 'it would be vital… for the peninsula to be occupied by the army, as the guns on the Asiatic side can be commanded from the European shore sufficiently to permit ships to pass through'. De Robeck's telegram 282, p. 36 of Admiralty Telegrams 3 January–29 May 1915 (Dardanelles Commission, September 1916).
24. From Admiral Superintendent Malta to Admiralty, London (undated copy), 775. 'Admiral Carden has been admitted to Bighi Hospital for observation and treatment. Deputy Surgeon General is of opinion that he will require at least seven days complete rest and proposes to report further in two days' time. He states Admiral Carden appears to be suffering from atonic dyspepsia with painful acerbations and is much run down but has improved since leaving the Dardanelles. "Minerva" leaves to rejoin Flag of V.A.E.M.S. at noon Sunday 21ˢᵗ. When she leaves I am at Admiral Carden's request, transferring his FLAG from Minerva to Cruiser.'
    From Admiralty to A. S. Malta, 27 March 1915 11.30 pm. 599. 'Your 866. Inform Admiral Carden that Admiralty sympathises with his desire to resume command of the operations at earliest possible moment but this is a matter that must be governed by medical advice. He should therefore return to England for survey.' (Sackville Carden's Personal Papers).
25. The letter from Churchill dated 16 April was addressed to 57 Rutland Gate, SW. Roger Keys wrote on 31 March: 'My dear Admiral, I must tell you how sorry we all are to hear that you are going home.' (Sackville Carden's personal papers).
26. Sackville's youngest brother, James Rutter Carden, died of wounds received at Ypres on 30 April 1915, six weeks after the disastrous naval attack on the Dardanelles.

Admiral Jack de Robeck (pp 157–9)
27. *A Naval History of World War I* by Paul G. Halpern, p. 95.
28. As Admiral Carden's second-in-command, de Robeck had submitted a report as early as 3 March 1915 stating his belief that the invasion of the Dardanelles could not succeed unless ground troops were landed on one or both shores of the straits to destroy the Turkish howitzers that were preventing the minesweepers from performing their task.

The battle of Seddelbahr (pp 163–79)
29. 'South African War 1899–1902. 24 January, the 1st Battalion RMF evacuated Rhenoster Kop and proceeded to Balmoral. While there 2nd Lieuts. G.W Geddes, H.C.H O'Brien and E.L.H. Henderson joined the 1st battalion during the month.' Extract from p. 29 of *The History of the Royal Munster Fusiliers* by Capt. S. McCance, Volume 2 (1860–1922). Reprinted by Naval and Military Press.
30. 'The East India Company maintained its own army, composed of a few "European" regiments - white men, mostly Irish - and a growing number of "native" regiments. From 'Queen Victoria's Little Wars' by Byron Farwell. The East India Company had a recruiting office in Watling Street in Dublin
31. Born on 8 August 1880, GW Geddes was the only son of Charles Turner Geddes of Selborne, Hampshire, and Hastings Street, Upper Wood Street, Calcutta.
    Eric Lockhard Hume Henderson was born on 31 July 1881, just weeks after the death of his grandfather General Hume Henderson in Quetta (now Pakistan) on 27 June 1881. Colonel William George Hume Henderson, his father, joined the Indian Medical Service in 1876 and remained until 1908.
32. Raymond Henderson, a lieutenant in the 2nd Battalion Connaught Rangers, was killed on the Western Front while defending the trenches near La Cour de Soupier on the Aisne Heights on the evening of 19 September 1914.
33. 'Sergeant William Cosgrove V.C. — October 1888–July 1936' via www.royalmunsterfusiliers.org
34. *Press*, Volume LI, Issue 15265, 29 April 1915, p. 6.
35. Many of Hamilton's advisers actually told him to steer clear of the 'hazardous' peninsula. Sir John Maxwell warned that the landscape was so cramped he would be 'very liable to be held up and have a sort of miniature Flanders to fight'. De Robeck warned that any Allied attempt to land troops at Morto Bay or Seddelbahr would be 'extremely costly'. General Aylmer Hunter-Weston, commander of the 29th Division, urged a complete abandonment of the project on the grounds that its failure would be 'a disaster for the Empire'. However, Kitchener had advised that 'there can be no idea of abandoning the scheme'. 'The

passage of the Dardanelles must be forced', he wrote. Nobody, not even Prime Minister Asquith, was ever called upon to formally authorise the invasion.

36. They were part of a grand fleet, commanded by Admiral de Robeck, comprising 22 warships, 20 destroyers, miscellaneous craft and 60,000 men.

37. *The Weekly Irish Times*, 17 April 1915, p. 10.

38. 'A first hand report of the Landing from The River Clyde at V. Beach April 25th 1915' by Captain GW Geddes, X Company Commander, 1st Royal Munster Fusiliers.

39. *Gallipoli: A Turning Point* by Mustafa Askın published by Gallipoli Peace Park, Çanakkale.

40. When the *Albion*'s gunners later attempted to renew their bombardment of the trenches at Seddelbahr, they were informed that their firing was so wide of the mark that some of the shells were falling on the British troops at Y Beach.

41. *Remember Father William Finn* by Martin Coyle, Mayo Peace Park, London. William Finn was born in Hull on 27 December 1875. Local research and the 1881 census for England show that his father, Austin, and mother, Catherine, came from Aghamore, Ballyhaunis, County Mayo. In the 1881 and 1901 censuses Austin gave his occupation as 'General Dealer'. *Bulmer's Gazette*, Hull (1892) shows him as a rope, metal and zinc dealer (61 Church Street), owner of a wood yard (9 Hendon Road) and a general dealer (33 Hendon Road). Austin and Catherine had nine children, all born in Hull. The children were John, Sarah, James, Kate, Austin, Mary, William, Agnes and Francis. In 1889, William entered the seminary at Ushaw, Durham; the 1891 census shows him, aged 15, as a Student of Rudiments. On 5 August 1900, he was ordained at Middlesborough Cathedral. From 1900 to 1908 he was curate at the Cathedral Church of St Mary's, Middlesborough, and from 1908 to 1909 at St Hilda's, Whitby, Yorkshire. From 1909 to 1913 he was Parish Priest at All Saints, Thirsk, Yorkshire. At the outbreak of war he was serving at the Holy Family Church, Houghton Hall.

42. Dr Burrowes Kelly's letter to his father Gilbert Kelly at Ballintubbert, Co. Laois, is quoted in S Parnell Kerr's book, *What the Irish Regiments Have Done: With a Diary of a Visit to the Front by John E. Redmond*.

43. The Mallaghan brothers inspired Margaret Whittock's novel *Ghost of Gallipoli*.

44. William Harris of Shrewleen Lane, Athy, County Kildare. Letter to his mother Ellen, published in the *Leinster Leader*, 7 August 1915.

45. *The Civil & Military Gazette*, Wednesday 23 June 1915.

46. The 86th or 'Fusilier' Brigade comprised the 2nd Royal Fusiliers, 1st Lancashire Fusiliers, 1st Royal Munster Fusiliers and 1st Royal Dublin Fusiliers.

47. Eric Henderson died of his wounds in Alexandria on 20 May. Surgeon Henderson, his father, died in London seven weeks later. See The Loreto Register 1825–2000; *British Medical Journal* 24 July 1915; 2 (2847): 163.

48. *The History of the Royal Munster Fusiliers* by Capt. S. McCance, Volume 2 (1860–1922), p. 49.

49. 'Dr Peter Burrowes Kelly, D.S.O' (*British Medical Journal* 22 May 1920; 1(3099): 724). According to a report by Vice Admiral de Robeck in *The Naval Who's Who 1917*, he 'remained in *River Clyde* until morning of 27th during which time he attended 750 wounded men, although in great pain and unable to walk during the last twenty-four hours.'

50. *VCs of the First World War: Gallipoli* by Stephen Snelling (The History Press).

51. *The Civil & Military Gazette*, Wednesday 23 June 1915.

52. Letter from GW Nightingale to his sister, 1 May 1915, in PRO WO 30/71/3 and IWM. Quoted in Martin Staunton's 'The Royal Munster Fusiliers (1914–1919)', MA thesis UCD (1986).

53. Letter from GW Nightingale to his sister, 1 May 1915, in PRO WO 30/71/3 and IWM. Quoted in Martin Staunton's 'The Royal Munster Fusiliers (1914–1919)', MA thesis UCD (1986).

54. Only seven officers and 372 men of the original RMF arrivals were still available for service when roll-call was taken on 11 May. Almost 700 of those who died were buried in V Beach Cemetery.

55. Of the 25 officers and 987 other ranks who had left Mudros, only one young officer and 374 others were still with the battalion by 30 April.

The Dublin Pals and Suvla Bay (pp 181–99)

56. *The Irish Times*, Tuesday 1 September 1914, p.6.

57. *The Irish Times*, 9 August 1914, p.7; *The Irish Times*, 24 August 1914, p.3; *Weekly Irish Times*, Saturday 12 September 1914, p.5.

58. *The Irish Times*, 1 September 1914, p.6.

59. *Weekly Irish Times*, Saturday 12 September 1914, p. 5. In *The Irish Times* of 11 September 1914, an advertisement expressed dismay at the slowness of the Irish response to Kitchener's call, warning that

Scotsmen and Englishmen could now be drafted into the Irish Division, which would be 'a discredit to Ireland'. Clearly not everyone was as enthusiastic for war as Ireland's rugby players.

Frank Browning was mortally wounded in an ambush near Beggarsbush Barracks in Haddington Road during the Easter Rebellion and died two days later. At the time, he was at the head of a group of unarmed veterans, clad in civvies, sporting rifles but no ammunition. Nicknamed the 'Gorgeous Wrecks' after the 'Georgius Rex' motto on their armbands, the Irish Rugby Union Football Corps were returning to the Barracks from their Easter Monday parade when they were ambushed. Seven members of the corps were shot; four died. Frank Browning was buried in Deansgrange Cemetery, County Dublin. A headstone was erected by the Irish Rugby Football Union Volunteer Corps in memory of 'an honourable comrade and true and distinguished sportsman'.

60. *The Irish Times*, 11 September 1914. Entrance into D Company was open to anyone between 19 and 35 years of age, or, for ex-soldiers, those up to 45. Anyone older than that, or otherwise deemed 'unfit', was invited to remain in Dublin as a 'home guard'.

61. Educated at Charterhouse and Trinity College, Dublin, Ernest Julian was the only son of the late John and Margaret Julian, of Drumbane, Birr, King's County (County Offaly). Presidents Mary Robinson and Mary McAleese both held the same Chair in the 1970s.

62. GE Bradstreet also captained the Portora XV who won the Ulster Cup in 1908. 'An Irishman's Diary' in *The Irish Times* of Saturday 16 December 1950 refers to both his dramatic and his sporting prowess and gives his nickname 'Billie'.

63. Poole Henry Gore Hickman was born on 8 June 1880 to Francis William Gore Hickman of Tyredagh Castle and Elizabeth Brown O Brien.

64. *Findlaters: The Story of a Dublin Merchant Family 1774–2001*, Chapter 8, Gallipoli.

65. *The Weekly Irish Times*, 2 October 1915.

66. Quoted in *A Pal on Trial*, via www.royaldublinfusiliers.com.

67. *Alexander's East India and Colonial Magazine*, Volume 10, p. 429 refers to 'the light company of the Bombay European regiment (the old Toughs)'. By 1843 the unit had expanded to two battalions and they were known as the 1st Madras Fusiliers and the 1st Bombay Fusiliers until 1862. They later evolved into the 1st and 2nd Battalions of the Royal Dublin Fusiliers, with their depot at Naas, Co Kildare.

68. Hugh Crawford Pollock was a son of Hugh Percy and Helen C Pollock, of 4, Vergemount Hall, Clonskeagh, Dublin.

69. *The Brightest Jewel: A History of the National Botanic Gardens, Glasnevin, Dublin*, Charles Nelson, Eileen McCracken (Boethius, 1987), p. 205, 215.

70. *From Lady Pupil to Lady Gardener* (VM Ingram and M Forrest, Glasra (*Contributions from the National Botanic Gardens, Glasnevin*) 3(1), 1997).

71. 'Born in Loughborough in 1879, CF Ball was the son of Alfred Bramley Ball (a pharmaceutical chemist) and Mary Bowerly Ball (a British subject born in Ohio, USA).

72. Hanna, pp 24–27.

73. *The Irish Times*, Monday 19 October 1914, p. 10.

74. *Findlaters: The Story of a Dublin Merchant Family 1774–2001*, Chapter 8.

75. Letters of Arthur, Lord Kilbracken, and General Sir Alexander Godley (1932).

76. 'The Gunning Family', Marion Maxwell, BBC Northern Ireland's 'Your Place and Mine'.

77. Letter from Captain Poole Hickman, published in *The Irish Times*, Tuesday 31 August 1915.

78. Richard Scorer Molyneaux Harrison was born in 1883 and previously served in Peshawar, India, as a Captain with the 51st Sikh Regiment.

79. 'It was a magnificent performance, and we have been personally congratulated on it, and we have called the hill fort Dublin.' From a letter from Captain Poole Hickman, published in *The Irish Times*, Tuesday 31 August 1915.

80. Letter from Captain Poole Hickman, published in *The Irish Times*, Tuesday 31 August 1915.

81. p. 87, *The Irish at the Front* by Michael MacDonagh. Captain James Cecil Johnston grew up between Magheramena Castle, near Belleek, and Glencore House in County Fermanagh, and was educated at Charterhouse. He served in the Anglo-Boer War as a young man. Since 1910, he had been a close confidant of the Earl of Aberdeen, Lord Lieutenant of Ireland, serving as both his Private Secretary and Master of the Horse at the time of his departure for Gallipoli. From 1910 to 1912 he was also Deputy Ranger of the Curragh. Johnston, who offered his services on the outbreak of war, was made Adjutant of the 6th (Service) Battalion of the Royal Irish Fusiliers in October 1914. He left a widow and three daughters, all under the age of six. One of them grew up to become the novelist Myrtle Johnston. The Johnstons abandoned Magheramena after his death and the castle was demolished in the 1950s.

See *The Roll of Honour: A Biographical Record of All Members of His Majesty's Naval and Military Forces Who Have Fallen in the War*, Vol. 1, p. 221.

82. Kiretch Tepe is an Anglicised spelling of Kireçtepe, part of the Kizlar Dagh hills.

83. Letter from Captain Poole Hickman, published in *The Irish Times*, Tuesday 31 August 1915.

84. Initially held back, D Company was dispatched to support the 5th Inniskillings who were being annihilated by heavy-duty shellfire and machine-gun fire near Kidney Hill.

85. Captain RG Kelly, a HQ Lieutenant with the 7th RDF, recalled how during the fighting at Kireçtepe Sirt, he saw the Turks lobbing bombs over the trench at the 7th Dublins and the Dubs catching them and hurling them back again. 'The Irish troops resisted gallantly although the few bombs they had were far inferior… Couple of dozen hurriedly made Jam Tins. Turkish bombs were caught and thrown back again. One private (Wilkins by name) caught four but fifth unfortunately blew him to pieces. PS. I hold a copy of recommendation for this particular Private to whom no recognition was ever given, which of course was nothing out of the ordinary on Gallipoli.' This information came from a letter written on 11 May 1931 by Captain RG Kelly of Rathmines, Dublin, to General Aspinall-Oglander, the official historian of the Great War.

Hanna, p. 110. 'The sights I saw going along that place I shall never forget. Some of our fellows throwing back the bombs which the Turks threw over and which had not exploded. One fellow caught them like catching a cricket ball. Wounded and dead lying everywhere. The sun streaming down and not a drop of water to be had. Neither had we bombs to reply to the Turks and drive them out.'

86. Private Walter Appleyard was buried in Gallipoli at the foot of Dublin Hill.

87. This account comes from an unpublished letter in Alex Findlater's possession, which is thought to have been sent to Willie Findlater in Dublin. It was written from Chichester and dated Saturday 18 September, but has no name at the end.

88 At least 33 Wanderers rugby players were killed in the war.

89. Unpublished anonymous letter in Alex Findlater's possession.

90. Unpublished anonymous letter in Alex Findlater's possession.

91. 'We went back to our dug-outs about a mile back. Just as we were getting our dinner… two shells came along… and one fellow got his head blow off…and another lost his leg.' (H. Hanna).

92. Ernest Hamilton, 'The 7th Dublins in Gallipoli — Desperate Days Fighting', letter published in *The Irish Times*, Thursday 16 September 1915, p. 4.

93. Amongst those who died capturing Scimitar Hill was Second Lieutenant Bob Stanton, a solicitor from Cork. A few years before the war, Bob had fallen out badly with his father, with whom he worked, when the latter refused to permit him to marry the woman he loved because her family were riddled with tuberculosis. Bob abandoned the Stanton practice and in 1912 he moved to Clones, County Monaghan, where he was the only Catholic solicitor in the era. His body was never found because the shelling set fire to the bush.

94. As Robin Prior put it, the 29th was 'brought north from Helles for its final martyrdom'.

95. Quoted by Henry Hanna in *The Pals at Suvla Bay*.

96. Eliza Pakenham, *Soldier Sailor: An Intimate Portrait of an Irish Family*, p. 217. The oaks at the end of the avenue at Tullynally were planted by the 5th earl's mother, to mark the event of his return from the Boer War.

97. Lady Milbanke, Sir John's widow, would marry Sir Bryan Mahon after the war.

98. Winston Churchill summed up this battle thus: 'The British losses were heavy and fruitless… On this dark battlefield of fog and flame Brigadier General Lord Longford, Brigadier General Kenna VC, Colonel Sir John Milbanke VC, and other paladins fell. This was the largest action fought on the Peninsula, and it was destined to be the last.'

99. Sir Ian Hamilton, the commander of the British at Gallipoli, failed to refer to the Irish when he later wrote, 'So I bid them all farewell, with a special God speed to the campaigners who have served with me through from the terrible yet most glorious earlier days — the incomparable 29th Division; the young veterans of the Naval Division; the ever victorious Australians and New Zealanders; the stout East Lancs, and my own brave fellow-countrymen of the Lowland Division of Scotland'.

100. 'An Irishman's Diary', *The Irish Times*, Kevin Myers, Saturday 9 November 1991, p. 11.

101. *Weekly Irish Times*, Saturday 3 February 1934, p. 13.

102. William Kee won a Military Cross (plus posthumous Bar) for his valour at the Somme, but died three days later on 24 March 1918. He is recalled by a monument at Stranorlar (St Anne) Church of Ireland, County Donegal.

103. He sailed on board the *Alaunia*, a hospital ship for 2,000 people. There were 68 burials at sea on the voyage home.

104. His brother Cecil Gunning survived the war and became a bank manager in Belfast.
105. 'Joseph Brady — A Pal on Trial' via www.royaldublinfusiliers.com.
106. Lieutenant Gerald Bradstreet, only son and heir of Sir Edward Bradstreet of Clontarf, was born in Algiers in 1891 and studied engineering at Trinity. In August 1915, a party of infantry advancing to the Turkish trenches lost all the officers leading the attack. The men wavered and seemed inclined to turn back. 'He did a plucky thing. The infantry had been drawn from some trenches and being tired and having only junior officers with them they were not able to advance. Lieut. Bradstreet was sent up by the General to tell them they must advance, and he rallied them, cheering them on, and was almost at once hit in the leg. The trenches were retaken. He crawled back to Brigade Headquarters, refusing assistance, and was from there helped onto the ship.' Source: Marquis de Ruvigny's Roll of Honour, Part 2, p. 37
107. Brett served as a machine-gunner with B Company, 7th RDF, at Gallipoli, until evacuated with enteritis.

Rough Fitzgerald and the Order of the White Feather (pp 201–3)
108. *A Classical Dictionary of the Vulgar Tongue*, 1785.
109. Andrew Gordon, *The Rules of the Game: Jutland and British Naval Command* (Naval Institute Press, 2013), p. 221.
110. Henrietta Elizabeth Hewson was the daughter of the Rev Francis Hewson of Dunganstown, Brittas Bay, County Wicklow. Two sons and two daughters followed. Their son John Uniacke Penrose Fitzgerald, who also joined the navy, was killed on active service in World War II on 11 December 1940, aged 52.
111. The baronetcy became extinct upon his death in July 1919.
112. *Sticklers, Sideburns and Bikinis: The Military Origins of Everyday Words and Phrases* by Graeme Donald. (Osprey, 2013).
113. *Limerick's Fighting Story 1916–21: Told by the Men Who Made It*, edited by Ruán O'Donnell (Mercier Press, 2009), p. 88.

Cecil Parke — the original Clones Cyclone (pp 205–9)
114. The Pringles lived at Ballinahone, Emyvale, from 1696 to the 1960s.
115. John Alexander Sinton was Cecil Parke's first cousin once removed on his mother's side.
116. Cecil's sister, Maud Pedlow of Lurgan, was grandmother of Cecil Pedlow, an Irish rugby international who played for the British Lions in 1955.
117. At the time of the 1901 Census, he shared a flat with his Pringle cousins Robert, a barrister, and Seton, a medical student. Seton Sydney Pringle later served as president of the Royal College of Surgeons in Ireland from 1934 to 1936.
118. Playing in the three-quarter line, he captained the university team for the 1904–1905 season.
119. *Weekly Irish Times*, Saturday 9 June 1923, p. 4.
120. *Daily Chronicle*, 26 July 1913; 29 July 1913.
121. *The Irish Times*, Saturday 8 August 1914.
122. *British Regiments at Gallipoli* by Ray Westlake (Leo Cooper, 2004); *The Tenth (Irish) Division in Gallipoli* by Bryan Cooper (Irish Academic Press, 1993), p. 84–85.
123. *The Irish Times*, August 1915.
124. Details of his wounds in *The Irish Times*, Friday 8 October 1915, p. 7.
125. *The London Gazette* (1917), p. 509.
126. *Lisburn Standard*, Friday 22 March 1918. 'At St George's Church, Llandudno, N.W., by the Rev K. Hughes, M.A., Rector, J. Cecil Parke, Captain, Essex Regiment, youngest son of the late William Parke, J.P., Clones, County Monaghan, to Sibyl, only child of Harry Smith, Morwenna, Llandudno.'
127. *The London Gazette*, 4 May 1920, p. 14.
128. Parke stole the contest in what *The New York Times* hailed as 'one of the greatest matches ever played on the historic Wimbledon court.'
129. He reached the Wimbledon Men's doubles final with Algernon Kingscote in 1920, but the pair lost to their American opponents, Chuck Garland and Richard Norris Williams II. In the singles, he reached the fifth round, but then lost to Tilden, the ultimate winner. His last major win was the 1920 singles title at Hythe.
130. *Lawn Tennis Up-to-Date 1921* by S Powell Blackmore.
131. A plaque outside the offices of Swayne Johnston solicitors in Llandudno commemorates the achievements of this extraordinary man.

Brian Desmond Hurst — the Empress of Gallipoli (pp 211–14)

132. *Records of the Great War*, Vol. III, ed. Charles F Horne, National Alumni 1923.

133. *Field of Bones: An Irish Division at Gallipoli* by Phillip Orr, Lilliput Press, 2006, p. 44.

134. Wilfred De'ath, *Punch*, 8 October 1969, p. 575, 576.

135. Smith, Allan Esler, 'Theirs is the Glory — 65th anniversary of the filming of the movie', Ministory No 106. (Friends of the Airborne Museum Oosterbeek, November 2010).

General Godley and ANZACs (pp 217–26)

136. *The Evolution of Polo* by Horace A Laffaye, p. 71–72.

137. Quoted on page 23 of *Sorry, Lads, But the Order Is to Go: The August Offensive, Gallipoli: 1915*, by David W. Cameron (UNSW Press, 2009).

138. *All the World, Volume 36* (Salvationist Publishing and Supplies, 1915), p. 539; Parliamentary Debates: Legislative Council and House of Representatives, Volume 172, p. 536–538.

139. Jeff Kildea, 'Irish Anzacs: the contribution of the Australian Irish to the Anzac tradition' (jeffkildea.com, 2013).

140. Captain Lalor's sword was found but then lost again and is rumoured to have made a recent but brief cameo in a Turkish museum. See *Gallipoli: The Battlefield Guide* by Mat McLachlan (Hachette UK, 2010). See LM Newton, *The story of the Twelfth, a Record of the 12th Battalion, AIF, During the Great War of 1914–1918*, Hobart, 1925, p. 73.

141. Prior, p. 121.

142. Les Carlyon's 'Gallipoli' (Macmillan, 2001) p. 126.

143. Hugh Quinn was the elder son of John Quinn, a mounted police constable from Ireland, and his Australian-born wife Mary Jane, née Irwin.

144. Letters of Arthur, Lord Kilbracken, and General Sir Alexander Godley (1932).

145. The evacuation was masterminded by Godley's Australian-born Chief of Staff, Brudenell White.

146. Letters of Arthur, Lord Kilbracken, and General Sir Alexander Godley (1932).

Arthur Corrie Lewin, DSO — aviator extraordinaire (pp 227–8)

147. *The Sydney Morning Herald*, 12 October 1937; *The Irish Times*, 25 February 1939.

148. 'Captain Frederick Henry Lewin', *Journal of the Connaught Rangers Association*. No 1. Vol 1. July 2003.

149. *The Irish Times*, Tuesday 9 October 1934, p. 7.

150. *Flight and Aircraft Engineer* (26 September 1952), p. 405.

PART THREE: FORGOTTEN FRONTS (PP 231–303)

Sky patrol with Erskine Childers (pp 237–49)

1. Jim Ring, *Erskine Childers* (Faber & Faber, 2011).

2. Erskine Childers War Diary, December 1915, Imperial War Museum, quoted in *Erskine Childers* by Jim Ring.

3. In February 1916 the *Ben-My-Chree* was instructed to confront the Senussi tribesmen who were causing trouble along the Egyptian border posts in the Western Desert.

4. Jim Ring, *Erskine Childers* (Faber & Faber, 2011).

5. *The Irish Times*, Friday 19 March 1920, p. 5.

6. Diarmuid Coffey, his colleague from the Irish Convention, visited him with an offer to spare his life if he, presumably, transferred his allegiance to the Free State. Childers refused.

7. *The Irish Times*, Monday 26 August 1918, p. 5.

Gunner Tom Barry and the Siege of Kut (pp 259–73)

8. The *Southern Star*, 21 January 1922: Obituary of Mrs Julia Hayes.

9. Meda Ryan, *Tom Barry, IRA Freedom Fighter* (Cork, 2003).

10. Irish Jesuit Archives, School Register of Apostolic School, Mungret College, p. 66.

11. *The Cork Examiner,* 10 November 1915

12. Peter Hart, *The I.R.A. and Its Enemies: Violence and Community in Cork, 1916–1923*.

13. Tom Barry, *Guerrilla Days in Ireland* (Anvil Books, 1949, 1981).

14. Ibid.

15. Ibid.
16. Field Marshal Viscount George Townsend was Lord Lieutenant of Ireland from 1767 to 1772.
17. *Weekly Irish Times*, Saturday 11 September 1915, p. 6.
18. Major Massy Wheeler's wife Nellie was a daughter of Dr Ferdinand Purcell, surgeon to the Cancer Hospital, Brompton, and the first surgeon in Great Britain or Ireland to perform vaginal hysterectomy for cancer of the uterus. Dr Ferdinand A Purcell obituary, *British Medical Journal*, 13 April 1907; 1(2415): 904.
19. Rev Adam Nixon, Vicar General of Clogher, purchased the lands at Drumcrow in 1709. See *The Families of French of Belturbet and Nixon of Fermanagh, and Their Descendants* (Alex. Thomas & Co. Ltd., 1908).
20. Everyone on board the steamer is said to have been sworn to secrecy on pain of death. This was the eyewitness testimony of Albert Maynard, who apparently still feared that he would be shot for telling the tale when he was in his eighties.
21. In August 1915, Sir John Nixon requested that one of the Indian divisions be sent from France to Mesopotamia. Austen Chamberlain, the Secretary of State for India, was more than happy to comply, as the Indians had found the European winter of 1914–15 extremely hard going.
22. The 13th (Western) Division was also added to Aylmer's corps, but likewise failed to unseat the Turks.
23. Sir Charles Townshend's Communiqué on the Siege of Kut, 26 January 1916. *Source Records of the Great War, Vol. IV*, ed. Charles F. Horne, *National Alumni 1923*.
24. Sir Charles Townshend's Communiqué on the Siege of Kut, 10 March 1916. Source: Horne (1923).
25. Herbert Stanislaus Tierney was a son of Dublin bank manager Christopher Tierney and his wife Frances. They lived at 14 Rostrevor Terrace, Rathgar, Co. Dublin. The National Library of Ireland contains typescript copies of letters he sent to his mother from Gallipoli and Egypt which were written between 30 June 1915 and 16 March 1916.
26. *Irish-American Diaspora Nationalism: The Friends of Irish Freedom, 1916–1935* by Michael Doorley, Kevin Kenny, p. 410; *Irish Historical Studies*, Vol. 35, No 139 (May 2007), pp. 410–412.
27. Gordon Ulick King was born in 1893 in Gortmore, Dunurlin, County Kerry. His father, educated at Trinity College, Dublin, was ordained the year before his birth and was Rector of Kilcolman from 1898 to 1925. Gordon's mother Kate was a daughter of Thomas and Catherine Ferry of Milltown. Gordon's older sister Eva was the wife of Rev Everard Digges La Touche, the Anglican clergyman killed at Lone Pine, Gallipoli. Gordon's older brother William went to Gallipoli with the Australian Imperial Forces and also died at Lone Pine.
28. Lewis William Murphy was the only son of HL Murphy of Sans-Souci, Blackrock Road, County Cork.
29. *Weekly Irish Times*, 17 July 1897, p. 7.
30. *The Tablet*, 21 October 1916. Obituary of Lewis William Murphy.
31. On 31 January 1921, Gordon King's sister Alice and her husband Captain Will King, County Inspector of the Royal Irish Constabulary, were ambushed at Mallow Railway station. Both were wounded but Mrs King died the following morning. Another sister Eileen worked with the Volunteer Aid Detachment in Plymouth and later went to Jamaica to help her brother Marshall King, ADC to the Governor of Jamaica, when his ship was torpedoed with the loss of all his belongings.
32. On 19 December 1918 Tom Barry was given seven days' field punishment No 2 by Major Reynolds RFA.
33. Joseph McKenna, *Guerrilla Warfare in the Irish War of Independence, 1919–1921* (McFarland, 2011).

Nurse Colhoun and the bombing of Vertekop (pp 275–8)

34. *The Dictionary of Irish Architects 1720–1940*, Irish Architectural Archive.
35. Dean Godson, *Himself Alone: David Trimble and the Ordeal of Unionism* (HarperCollins UK, 2014).
36. The hospital on Salt Spring Island was one of 43 hospitals, mostly rural, built in Canada at this time and funded by Lady Minto, wife of Canada's Governor General.
37. 'Aviators Kill Two Nurses', *The New York Times*, 15 March 1917. The German official statement of 13 March merely reported on an attack by a German squadron on 'the railroad station at Vertekop'.
38. *The British Journal of Nursing*, 28 April 1917, p. 291.
39. Details via 'Military Medal Awards to QA Nurses' c/o www.qaranc.co.uk
40. *The British Journal of Nursing*, 12 May 1917, p. 323, noted: 'Nurse Colhoun, who has received a gold medal from the Crown Prince of Serbia "for conspicuous bravery in a most trying situation," and has been nursing at Salonica for some time, is an Irish nurse.'
41. *The London Gazette*, No 30095, page 5190, of 26 May 1917: 'For conspicuous bravery and devotion to duty during an enemy air raid. She attended to, and provided for the safety of, helpless patients. She was assisting Staff Nurse Dewar when the latter was fatally wounded, and although the tent was full of smoke and acrid fumes, and she had been struck by a fragment of bomb, she attended to Staff Nurse Dewar and also to the case of a helpless patient.'

42. *The British Journal of Nursing*, 11 August 1917, p. 91.
43. Salt Spring Archives, 14 May 1964.

Father Kavanagh and the Sinai-Palestine campaign (pp 279–87)

44. The Ottoman Turks ruled Sinai from 1517 until 1906, when it was formally handed over to the Egyptian Government which, since 1882, had been a British Protectorate.
45. 'Chaplains in the Great War — Father Bernard Kavanagh, C.SS.R.' (*The Dublin Review*, July–September 1919), is an excellent account of his life which includes his letters to his sister and his Provincial, as well as some diary extracts.
46. *The Irish Times*, Saturday 4 November 1911, p. 6; Saturday 29 January 1966.
47. *The Irish Times*, Saturday 23 August 1913, p. 20.
48. Lieutenant George Hare of D Company was born in County Fermanagh in 1886, the eldest son of the Rev Henry and Helen Hare. By 1901, the family lived at 18, North Frederick Street, Dublin, but his father appears to have died or vanished by then and his County Meath-born mother was head of the house. In 1911, the family were at the same address.
    George's headstone states that his parents lived at 'Fernside', a detached house on the corner of Home Farm Road and Upper Drumcondra Road in Dublin. This was the setting for an epic gun battle in 1920 that left up to 12 people dead, including, ultimately, Dan Breen.
49. Edward 'Teddy' Henry Hare, one of innumerable underage soldiers in the army, was 13 at the time of the 1911 Census. Commissioned a lieutenant in September 1917, he was killed in Afghanistan while serving with the Yorkshire Regiment on 23 July 1919, aged 21. He is commemorated on Face 23, Delhi Memorial India Gate. See *The Irish Times*, 24 July 1922, p. 1.
50. George Hare was commissioned as a lieutenant in September 1915.
51. In September 1918, Private James Duffy was briefly engaged in the recruiting campaign in north-west Ireland, touring with Sergeant Daniel Gillen, another of the Inniskillings, who was a well-known ventriloquist. Private Duffy, the only one of the Inniskillings VC winners not to die in the war, passed away in Letterkenny in 1969 at the age of 77. See *Weekly Irish Times*, Saturday 7 September 1918, p. 1.
52. Captain Edwards assumed command of D Company on 26 December.
53. Sir Richard Butler of Ballintemple, County Carlow, serving with the 60th Rifles (later the Green Jackets), was one of the first to reach Damascus in the wake of the city's fall to General Allenby. It was at this time that he heard news from Ireland that Ballintemple, his ancestral home, had been destroyed in an accidental fire.

Colonel Alexander and the spear-point pump (pp 289–93)

54. The younger David was David McGowan Alexander. The Carrickfergus reference is contained in *The Irish Times*, Saturday 8 February 1913, p. 24, which refers to JH Alexander's uncle, Charles, and his grandfather, David Alexander, of Carrickfergus.
55. Emily Alexander, who was ten years younger than her husband, was a daughter of Francis Power Gahagan of County Limerick.
56. *The Irish Times*, Wednesday 12 June 1895, p. 7. John Kenny lived at 47 Rathgar Road.
57. Also known as the 'Millionaires' Own', the Imperial Irish Yeomanry included the 47th (Duke of Cambridge's Own) and was raised from rich 'men-about-town' in London by the Earl of Donoughmore. The battalion officers included the Earl of Leitrim, Sir John Power (of the Power's whiskey family) and James Craig (later Lord Craigavon).
58. *Weekly Irish Times*, Saturday 15 June 1901, p. 23.
59. *The Irish Times*, Friday 28 August 1903, p. 8.
60. His older brother, Alfred Gahagan Alexander, a Trinity College graduate, was also in Africa. In 1910, Alfred was Medical Superintendent of the Freed Slaves Home at the Sudan United Mission. That same year he was married in Umaisha, northern Nigeria, to Isabel Milne of Dundee. See *Weekly Irish Times*, Saturday 5 March 1910, p. 24.
61. Gillings, Ken, 'The 'Death' of Bhambatha Zondi — Recent Discovery' (*Military History Journal* Vol 12 No 4, December 2002).
62. *The Irish Times*, Thursday 14 October 1909, p. 11.
63. *The London Gazette*, 26 June 1916; *The Irish Times*, Tuesday 27 June 1916, p. 6. He was mentioned in despatches on four occasions — on 31 May 1916, 29 September 1916, 6 July 1917 and 12 January 1918. A keen amateur photographer, many of his photographs from this period are now held by the West Sussex Record Office.

64. 'We were all very proud of your gallant son,' wrote Charles Alexander's Colonel to his parents, 'for on many occasions he had distinguished himself by brave, cool action in time of great stress and danger. He had had many narrow escapes, and it was the hope of us all he would be equally fortunate in the big operation in which he was engaged.'

65. The house had been home of the wealthy Tree family. Mrs Ethel Tree was a daughter of Chicago department store founder Marshall Field and married Admiral Beatty of Jutland fame. In July 1939, Mrs George Bryant sold the estate to the British Iron and Steel Confederation.

66. Detail from Ashorne Hill website at www.ashornehill.co.uk

67. Mrs Wade, wife of Lieutenant Colonel EW Wade RAMC, and their two daughters, Doreen Winifred, aged 19, and Betty Aurielle, aged 17, drowned on the SS *Yorkshire*.

68. *The Foundry Trade Journal*, Volume 101 (Cornell University, 1956).

69. Confirmed to Ken Gillings by Mr Vusi Buthelezi, head of the Campbell Collections in Durban, South Africa, in April 2014.

Sergeant Major Flora Sandes, Serbian Army (pp 295–302)

70. Flora Sandes's older brother was the Cork-born journalist, poet and novelist John Sandes (1863–1938). After graduating from Oxford in 1885, he moved to Australia, writing for the *Argus* and then the *Daily Telegraph*. His wife, Clare Louise Berry, was the actor daughter of former Victorian premier Sir Graham Berry. Much of Sandes's writing dealt with the Great War, including his long poem *Anzac Day, Landing in the Dawn* (1916), and the essay 'Australian National Character in the Crucible', both of which helped develop the 'Anzac legend'. In 1919 John Sandes became the *Daily Telegraph*'s London correspondent, in which capacity he attended the Versailles peace conference. He returned to Australasia in 1920 in company with the Prince of Wales, whose tour he covered for the Australian Press Association. He settled in Australia permanently from 1922.

71. Louise Miller, 'A Fine Brother: The Life of Captain Flora Sandes' (Alma Books, 2012) pp. 29–30.

72. Elsie Inglis later did much to improve hygiene and reduce typhus and other epidemics in Serbia's hospitals. Her efforts were noted by the Crown Prince of Serbia, who awarded her the Order of the White Eagle (V class) in April 1916. She was the first woman to be so honoured.

73. Some accounts say she also went to New York in this time. *Black Lambs and Grey Falcons: Women Travellers in the Balkans*, edited by John B. Allcock, Antonia Young, p. 91–92.

74. Extracted from Flora's diary via http://sandesancestry.net.

75. *Weekly Irish Times*, Saturday 6 September 1919, p. 6.

76. *The New York Times*, 5 January 1919.

77. *The New York Times*, 6 August 1916. 'WOMAN FIGHTS FOR SERBS — Irish Nurse Reaches Toulon on Way Back to Service.'

78. *Weekly Irish Times*, Saturday 6 September 1919, p. 6.

79. *Weekly Irish Times*, Saturday 6 September 1919, p. 6.

80. Peter Grant, *Philanthropy and Voluntary Action in the First World War: Mobilizing Charity*, p. 53.

81. *Weekly Irish Times*, Saturday 6 September 1919.

82. Sandesancestry.net.

83. Allcock and Young, *Black Lambs and Grey Falcons: Women Travellers in the Balkans*, p. 96–97.

84. *The Irish Times*, Saturday 8 September 1945, p. 3.

85. *The Irish Times*, Saturday 8 September 1945, p. 3.

86. *The New York Times*, 5 January 1919.

BIBLIOGRAPHY

Thanks to the miracle of the internet, an enormous amount of research for this book was conducted 'at home' using such wonderful resources as the Irish Times Digital Archive, the Irish News Archive, the National Archives of Ireland's 1901 and 1911 censuses, the National Library of Australia's Trove and Google books. I must also give a nod to Wikipedia. Of course it is not to be entirely trusted but nonetheless, with nearly 5 million English-language articles uploaded to date, it certainly puts one on the right track for finding out more.

PART ONE: THE WESTERN FRONT

1. The Irish Dames of Ypres

Brennan, John Martin. 'Irish Catholic Chaplains in the First World War'. MPhil, University of Birmingham, 2011.

Hickey, Máire OSB. 'Ireland's historic and contemporary connections with Belgium — The Irish Dames of Ypres at Kylemore Abbey'. Kylemore Abbey, 2014.

O'Brien, Richard Barry, ed., and Dame Columban. *The Irish Nuns at Ypres: An Episode of the War*, with an introduction by John Redmond. London: Smith, Elder & Co., 1915.

Villiers-Tuthill, Kathleen. *The History of Kylemore Castle & Abbey*. Connemara: Kylemore Abbey Publications, 2002.

2. Jack Judge — the Man who wrote 'Tipperary'

Daniels, Dr Terry. 'Jack Judge — His Life and Music'. Langley Local History Society, 2011.

Gibbons, Verna Hale. *Jack Judge, the Tipperary Man*. West Midlands: Sandwell Community Library Service, 1998.

Pennell, Catriona. *A Kingdom United: Popular Responses to the Outbreak of the First World War in Britain and Ireland*. Oxford University Press, 2012.

3. Hoppy Hardy — the multiple escaper

www.cairogang.com.

Clark, Chris. *The Sleepwalkers: How Europe Went to War in 1914*. London: Allen Lane, 2012.

Durnford, Hugh. *Tunnelling to Freedom and Other Escape Narratives from World War I*. Courier Dover Publications, 2013.

Ferguson, Niall. *The Pity of War*. Penguin, 2009.

Grinnell-Milne, Duncan. 'Inveterate Escapers', in Hugh Durnford's *Tunnelling to Freedom and Other Escape Narratives from World War I*. Courier Dover Publications, 2013.

Hardy, JL. 'A Winter's Tale' in Hugh Durnford's *Tunnelling to Freedom and Other Escape Narratives from World War I*. Courier Dover Publications, 2013.

Hardy, JL. 'Fugitives in Germany' in Hugh Durnford's *Tunnelling to Freedom and Other Escape Narratives from World War I*. Courier Dover Publications, 2013.

Hardy, JL. *I Escape!* John Lane, 1927.

Jeffery, Keith. *Ireland and the Great War*. Cambridge University Press, 2000.

McKenna, Joseph. *Guerrilla Warfare in the Irish War of Independence, 1919–1921*. McFarland, 2011.

4. Lord Desmond FitzGerald and the Micks

Davenport-Hines, Richard. *Ettie: The Intimate Life and Dauntless Spirit of Lady Desborough*. Orion Publishing, 2008.

Dooley, Terence. *The Decline and Fall of the Dukes of Leinster, 1872–1948: Love, War, Debt and Madness*. Four Courts Press, 2014.

Hastings, Max. *Catastrophe 1914: Europe Goes to War*. William Collins, 2013.

Herbert, Aubrey. *Mons, Anzac and Kut*. London: Edward Arnold, 1919.

Kipling, Rudyard. *The Irish Guards in the Great War, Volumes 1 and 2*. Leonaur, 2007.

Newark, Tim. *Fighting Irish: The Story of the Extraordinary Irish Soldier*. Constable & Robinson, 2012.

Stewart, Richard. 'Fr John Gwynn'. Sacred Heart Parish. Caterham, Whyteleafe & Godstone.

Ziegler, Philip. *The Man Who Wouldn't Be King: King Edward VIII*. Alfred A Knopf, 1991.

5. Captain DD Sheehan, MP for Mid-Cork

Dillon, John. *DD Sheehan BL, MP, His Life and Times*. Foilsiúcháin Éireann Nua, 2013.

Maume, Patrick. 'Daniel Desmond ('D. D.') Sheehan (1873–1948)' in James McGuire and James Quinn, eds., *Dictionary of Irish Biography: From the Earliest Times to the Year 2002*. Royal Irish Academy, Vol. 7, pp. 875–78. Cambridge University Press, 2009.

O'Donovan, John, 'The All-for-Ireland League 1909–1918'. www.theirishstory.com, 2012.

O'Donovan, John. 'Daniel Desmond (D. D.) Sheehan and the Rural Labour Question in Cork (1894–1910)' in Brian Casey, ed., *Defying the Law of the Land: Agrarian Radicals in Irish History*. History Press, 2013.

Ó Síocháin, Niall. 'D. D. Sheehan: Why Family Left Cork in 1918' (Supplement to the above). Foilsiúcháin Éireann Nua, Templemore, Co. Tipperary, 2013.

Ó Síocháin, Niall, and Jack Lane. 'D. D. Sheehan: Why He Left Cork in 1918: correspondence from *The Corkman*.' Aubane Historical Society, 2003.

Sheehan, Captain DD. *Ireland Since Parnell*. London: Daniel O'Connor, 1921.

6. Major General Louis Lipsett

Cassar, George H. *Hell in Flanders Fields: Canadians at the Second Battle of Ypres*. Toronto: Dundurn, 2010.

Cook, Tim. *No Place to Run: The Canadian Corps and Gas Warfare in the First World War*. Vancouver: UBC Press, 2011.

Kirwan, John, and Niall Brannigan. *Kilkenny Families in the Great War*. OLL Editions, 2012.

Morton, Desmond. 'Louis Lipsett', in Ramsay Cook, ed., *Dictionary of Canadian Biography*, Volume XIV, 1911 to 1920. University of Toronto Press, 1998.

Roy, Patricia E. 'Sir Richard McBride' in Ramsay Cook, ed., *Dictionary of Canadian Biography*, Volume XIV, 1911 to 1920. University of Toronto Press, 1998.

Roy, Patricia E. *Boundless Optimism: Richard McBride's British Columbia*. Vancouver: UBC Press, 2012.

7. Woodbine Willie — the soldiers' poet

Freeman, Rev Eric. 'Geoffrey Anketell Studdert Kennedy — Woodbine Willie' via Royal Naval Association Cyprus 2010. www.rnacyprus.org.

Gibbs, Philip. *Now It Can Be Told*. Harper & Brothers, 1920.

Holman, Bob. *Woodbine Willie: An Unsung Hero of World War One*. Lion Books, 2013.

Kennedy, Anketell Henry. 'Memoir of the Family of Anketell', family paper, 1885.

Snape, Michael. *God and the British Soldier: Religion and the British Army in the First and Second World Wars*. Routledge, 2007.

Walters, Kerry, ed., 'Woodbine Willie — The Man and His Message' in *Geoffrey Studdert Kennedy — After War, Is Faith Possible? An Anthology'*. Lutterworth Press, 2008.

8. Hill 16 — legends of the rubble

Carey, Tim. *Croke Park, A History*. Collins Press, 2013.

Cave, Nigel. *Hill 60, Ypres — Battleground Europe*. Leo Cooper, 1998.

Lytton, Neville. *The Press and the General Staff*. London: Collins, 1920.

9. Tom MacGreevy — modernist poet

Dawe, Gerald. *Earth Voices Whispering: An Anthology of Irish War Poetry 1914–1945*. Blackstaff Press, 2009.

Schreibman, Susan. 'When we come back from first death — Thomas MacGreevy and the Great War'. *Stand To,* January 1995.

Schreibman Susan, 'Biographical Essay on Thomas MacGreevy'. *Local Ireland*, 1998.

Thomas MacGreevy Archive www.macgreevy.org.

Anonymous. 'In tribute to Thomas MacGreevy, poet and connoisseur of the arts. Tributes by six learned Irish friends'. *Capuchin Annual*, 1968.

10. Tom Kettle and Emmet Dalton

www.facebook.com/MajorGeneralEmmetDalton.

Bowman, Timothy. *The Irish Regiments in the Great War: Discipline and Morale*. Manchester University Press, 2003.

Boyne, Séan. *Emmet Dalton: British Soldier, Irish General*. Merrion, 2014.

Burke, Tom, 'In Memory of Lieutenant Tom Kettle, 'B' Company, 9th Royal Dublin Fusiliers'. *Dublin Historical Record* (Old Dublin Society), Vol. 57, No 2, Autumn 2004.

Burnell, Tom. *The Carlow War Dead: A History of the casualties of the Great War*. History Press Ireland, 2011.

Connolly, Sean. *A Forlorn Hope: The Royal Dublin Fusiliers in the Kaiser's Battle, March 1918*. Royal Dublin Fusiliers Association, 2008.

Doyle, Arthur Conan. *Memories and Adventures*. London: Hodder & Stoughton, 1924.

Dungan, Myles. *They Shall Grow Not Old: Irish Soldiers and the Great War*. Four Courts Press, 1997.

Gregory, Adrian, and Senia Paseta. *Ireland and the Great War: A War to Unite Us All?* Manchester University Press, 2002.

Horne, John, and Alan Kramer. *German Atrocities, 1914: A History of Denial*. Yale University Press, 2001.

Horne, John, ed. *Our War: Ireland and the Great War*. Dublin: Royal Irish Academy, 2008.

Housman, Laurence. *War Letters of Fallen Englishmen*. University of Pennsylvania Press, 1930.

Kettle, TM. *Poems and Parodies*. Talbot Press, 1916.

Kettle, TM, and Mary Kettle, ed. *The Ways of War*. Talbot Press, 1917.

Levine, Joshua. *Forgotten Voices of the Somme: The Most Devastating Battle of the Great War in the Words of Those Who Survived*. Ebury, 2009.

Lynd, Robert. *Galway of the Races*. Lilliput Press, 1990.

Lyons, John Benignus. *The Enigma of Tom Kettle: Irish Patriot, Essayist, Poet, British Soldier, 1880–1916*. Glendale Press, 1983.

MacMillian, Margaret. *The War that Ended Peace: How Europe Abandoned Peace for the First World War*. Profile Books, 2013.

Ó Broin, Leon. *Protestant Nationalists: The Stopford Connection*. Dublin: Gill & Macmillan, 1985.

Osborn, Edward Bolland. 'Tom Kettle' in *The New Elizabethans, a First Selection of the Lives of Young Men Who Have Fallen in the Great War*. London; New York: John Lane, 1919.

Ryan, Desmond. *The Singing Flame*. Anvil Books, 1978.

Walsh, Pat. *The Rise and Fall of Imperial Ireland: Redmondism in the Context of Britain's Conquest of South Africa and Its Great War on Germany 1899–1916*. Belfast: Athol, 2003.

11. Sir William Orpen

Arnold, Bruce. *William Orpen: Mirror to an Age*. Jonathan Cape, 1982.

Orpen, Sir William. *An Onlooker in France 1917–1919*. Williams and Norgate, 1921.

12. The Irish air aces

Addington, Scott. *For Conspicuous Gallantry — Winners of the Military Cross and Bar During the Great War*. Troubador Publishing, 2006.

Barker, Ralph. *A Brief History of The Royal Flying Corps in World War One*. London: Constable & Robinson, 2001.

Berresford Ellis, Peter, 'Mick Mannock: fighter pilot and curious socialist', an essay on www.irishdemocrat.co.uk/features/mannock/.

Carragher, Michael. *San Fairy Ann?: Motorcycles and British Victory 1914–1918*. First Step Press, 2013.

County Carlow, Ireland Genealogical Projects via www.rootsweb.ancestry.com/~irlcar2.

Dudgeon, James M. *Mick — The Story of Major Edward Mannock*. Robert Hale, 1981.

Franks, Norman LR. *Who Downed the Aces in WW1?* Oxford: Grub Street, 1996.

Franks, Norman LR. *SE 5/5a Aces of World War I*. Osprey, 2007.

Gilbert, FT. 'McElroy of "Forty"', *Popular Flying* (1926), with a foreword by John Simon. From private manuscript, by courtesy of Rob McElroy.

Gleeson, Joe C. *Irish Aviators of World War One*. CreateSpace Independent Publishing Platform, 2013.

Hudson, James J. *In Clouds of Glory: American Airmen who Flew with the British During the Great War*. University of Arkansas Press, 1990.

Jones, Ira. *King of Airfighters: The Biography of Major Mick Mannock, VC, DSO MC*. London: Ivor Nicholson and Watson, 1934.

Kiester, Edwin. *An Incomplete History of World War I*. Pier 9, Murdoch Books, 2007.

Lewis, Gwilym. *Wings Over the Somme*. Bridge Books, 1994.

McElroy Senior, Rory. 'George McElroy's Career'. From private manuscript by courtesy of Rob McElroy, written by a first cousin of George EH McElroy.

McLanachan, George. *McScotch — Fighter Pilot*. London: George Routledge, 1936.

O'Connor, Mike. *Airfields and Airmen of Ypres: Battleground Special*. Pen & Sword Books Ltd, 2000.

Simkin, John. 'Mick Mannock' (September 1997). via www.spartacus.schoolnet.co.uk/FWWmannock.htm.

Smith, Adrian. *Mick Mannock, Fighter Pilot — Myths, Lies and Politics*. Palgrave Macmillan, 2000.

PART TWO: THE DARDANELLES

13. Sackville Carden and the naval attack on the Dardanelles

Sackville Carden's personal papers were loaned by his granddaughter, Annette Fernyhough, in 1994 to Arthur Carden, who has made use of them to provide some previously unpublished material for inclusion in this chapter. It is intended that the papers be given in due course to the National Museum of the Royal Navy at Portsmouth.

Carden, Arthur E. *Carden of Barnane: History of the Barnane Estate in County Tipperary, Ireland*. www.lulu. com, 2004.

Keyes, Roger. *The Naval Memoirs of Admiral of the Fleet Sir Roger Keyes: The Narrow Seas to the Dardanelles, 1910–1915*. London: Thornton Butterworth, 1934.

Miller, Geoffrey. *Straits: British Policy Towards the Ottoman Empire and the Origins of the Dardanelles Campaign*. University of Hull Press, 1997.

The Naval Annual — 1913. J. Griffin & Co., 1913.

Prior, Robin. *Gallipoli — The End of the Myth*. Yale, 2009.

Stewart, AT. *The Immortal Gamble and the Part Played in It by H.M.S. "Cornwallis"*. A. & C. Black, 1917.

14. Admiral Jack de Robeck

Bunbury, Turtle. *A History of the Kildare Hunt*. Due for publication, 2015.

Bunbury, Turtle, and Art Kavanagh. *The Landed Gentry & Aristocracy of County Kildare*. Irish Family Names, 2004.

15. The battle of Seddelbahr

www.dublin-fusiliers.com.
www.royalmunsterfusiliers.org.

Askin, Mustafa. *Gallipoli — A Turning Point*. Gallipoli Peace Park, 2002.

Dungan, Myles. *Irish Voices from the Great War*. Irish Academic Press, 1995.

Geddes, GW. 'The Landing from the River Clyde at V. Beach April 25th 1915 by a Company Commander in the 1st Royal Munster Fusiliers' via ww1.osborn.ws/ the-river-clyde.

Grimshaw, Richard G. *The Irish Line — Farmers, Industrialists, Doctors, Soldiers, Missionaries, Administrators and Family Men*. www.createspace.com, 2011.

Lecane, Philip. *Torpedoed! The R.M.S. Leinster Disaster*. Periscope Publishing, 2005.

McCance, S. *The History of the Royal Munster Fusiliers, Vol. 2 (1860–1922)*. Naval and Military Press, reprinted 2009.

McLachlan, Mat. *Gallipoli: The Battlefield Guide*. Hachette UK, 2010.

Moriarty, D. 'The Diary of Sergeant D Moriarty, No 8308, 1st Royal Munster Fusiliers' at http://ww1.osborn.ws/a-gallipoli-diary.

Parnell Kerr, S. *What the Irish Regiments Have Done: With a Diary of a Visit to the Front By John E. Redmond*. T. F. Unwin, 1916.

Prior, Robin. *Gallipoli — The End of the Myth*. Yale, 2009.

Snelling, Stephen. *VCs of the First World War: Gallipoli*. The History Press, 2010.

Staunton, Martin. 'The Royal Munster Fusiliers (1914–1919)', MA thesis, University College, Dublin, 1986.

Steel, Nigel, and Peter Hart. *Defeat at Gallipoli*. Papermac, 1995.

Whittock, Margaret. *Ghost of Gallipoli*. Dark Mourne Press, 2013.

16. The Dublin Pals and Suvla Bay

Belmont, Lord, 'Magheramena Castle', via lordbelmontinnorthernireland.blogspot.ie/2013/11/ magheramena-castle.html.

Desmond, Ray. *A Dictionary of British and Irish Botanists and Horticulturists*. CRC Press, 1994.

Findlater, Alex. *Findlaters. The Story of a Dublin Merchant Family 1774–2001*. A&A Farmar and www. findlaters.com, 2001.

Hamilton, Ernest. 'The 7th Dublins in Gallipoli — Desperate Days Fighting'. *The Irish Times*, Thursday 16 September 1915.

Hanna, Henry. *The Pals at Suvla Bay: Being the Record of "D" Company of the 7th Royal Dublin Fusiliers on Gallipoli*, with a foreword by Lieut. Gen. Sir Bryan T Mahon. Irish Academic Press, 1998.

Hickman, Poole. 'Irish Valour in Gallipoli — The 7th Dublins at Suvla'. *The Irish Times*, Tuesday 31 August 1915.

Kinsella, Ken. *Out of the Dark 1914-1918, South Dubliners who Fell in the Great War*. Irish Academic Press, 2014.

MacDonagh, Michael. *The Irish at the Front*, with a foreword by John Redmond. Reprint: Whitefish, Montana: Kessinger, 2007.

Maxwell, Manning, 'The Gunning family', BBC Northern Ireland, 'Your Place and Mine', November 2005.

Mumby, Frank A (series Ed.). *The Great World War — A History*, Volume IV. London: Gresham Publishing Co, 1916.

Myers, Kevin. 'An Irishman's Diary'. *The Irish Times*, 25 January 2005.

Nelson, E Charles, with Eileen McCracken. *The Brightest Jewel: A History of the National Botanic Gardens, Glasnevin, Dublin*. Boethius, 1987.

Nelson, E Charles, with Wendy Walsh and Ruth Isabel Ross. *An Irish Florilegium: Wild and Garden Plants of Ireland*. Thames & Hudson, 1983.

Pakenham, Eliza. *Soldier Sailor: An Intimate Portrait of an Irish Family*. Weidenfeld & Nicolson, 2007.

Prior, Robin. *Gallipoli — The End of the Myth*. Yale, 2009.

Quinn, Anthony P. *Wigs and Guns. Irish Barristers in the Great War*. Four Courts Press, 2006.

Ruvigny, Marquis de. *The Roll of Honour — A Biographical Record of All Members of His Majesty's Naval and Military Forces Who Have Fallen in the War*, Volumes 1–5. Standard Art Book Company, 1916–1918.

'The Royal Dublin Fusiliers — Trinity College and World War I' (www.tcd.ie/visitors/Fusiliers).

'D Company, 7th Battalion RDF' — www.dublin-fusiliers.com.

17. Rough Fitzgerald and the Order of the White Feather

Donald, Graeme. *Sticklers, Sideburns and Bikinis: The Military Origins of Everyday Words and Phrases*. Osprey, 2013.

Gordon, Andrew. *The Rules of the Game: Jutland and British Naval Command*. Naval Institute Press, 2013.

Lambert, Andrew. 'Fitzgerald, Charles Cooper Penrose (1841–1921)' in *Oxford Dictionary of National Biography*. Oxford University Press, 2004.

Mac Donald, Robin. 'White feather feminism: The recalcitrant progeny of radical suffragist and conservative pro-war Britain'. *Ampersand*, Volume One, Issue One, Fall Semester 1997.

O'Donnell, Ruán. *Limerick's Fighting Story 1916–21: Told by the Men Who Made It*. Mercier Press Ltd, 2009.

18. Cecil Parke — the original Clones Cyclone

Blackmore, S Powell. *Lawn Tennis Up-to-Date*. Methuen, 1921.

Cooper, Bryan. *The Tenth (Irish) Division in Gallipoli*. Irish Academic Press, 1993.

Dutton, James. 'Amazing Story of James Cecil Parke'. *Daily Post* (Conwy, Wales), 6 July 2013.

Gallagher, Brendan. 'Ireland's finest ever sportsman, James Cecil Parke, remembered 100 years on'. *Daily Telegraph*, 5 February 2009.

Westlake, Ray. *British Regiments at Gallipoli*. Leo Cooper, 2004.

Anonymous, 'Ireland's greatest all-round sportsman' (www.irishidentity.com/extras/famousgaels/stories/parke.htm).

19. Brian Desmond Hurst — the empress of Gallipoli

Callow, Simon. 'Queen of the higher schmaltz — A review of 'The Empress of Ireland' by Christopher Robbins. *The Guardian*, 29 May 2004.

Collins, Jude, ed. *Whose Past Is It Anyway? The Ulster Covenant, the Easter Rising & the Battle of the Somme*. The History Press, 2012.

Findlater, Alex. *Findlaters — The Story of a Dublin Merchant Family 1774–2001*, A&A Farmar and www.findlaters.com, 2001.

Hargrave, John. *The Suvla Bay Landing*. London: MacDonald, 1964.

Horne, Charles F, ed. *Records of the Great War*, Vol. III, National Alumni, 1923.

Hurst, Brian Desmond. *Travelling the Road — A Memoir of a Life in Cinema*. Contextualized by Allan Esler Smith and Professor Lance Pettitt. Lagan Press, 2014. Selected extracts reproduced with kind permission of the Brian Desmond Hurst estate. For additional information, see www.briandesmondhurst.org.

Orr, Philip. *Field of Bones: An Irish Division at Gallipoli*. Lilliput, 2006.

Robbins, Christopher. *The Empress of Ireland*. ISIS, 2005.

Smith, Allan Esler. 'An Irishman Chained to the Truth', RTÉ Radio 1's 'Documentary on One' series, 6 August 2011.

Smith, Allan Esler, and Adam Jones-Lloyd, directors of *Brian Desmond Hurst — Belfast's First Bohemian*. A documentary, 2011.

Smith, Allan Esler. 'Theirs is the Glory — 65th Anniversary of the filming of the movie', *Ministory* No 106. Friends of the Airborne Museum Oosterbeek, November 2010.

20. General Godley and the ANZACs

Cameron, David W. *Sorry, Lads, But the Order Is to Go: The August Offensive, Gallipoli: 1915.* University of New South Wales Press, 2009.

Downing, WH. *To the Last Ridge: The World War One Experiences of W.H. Downing.* Oxford: Grub Street, 2002.

Godley, Sir Alexander John. *Life of an Irish Soldier: Reminiscences of General Sir Alexander Godley.* New York: E.P. Dutton and Company, 1939.

Kildea, Jeff. 'Irish Anzacs: the contribution of the Australian Irish to the Anzac tradition'. www.jeffkildea.com, 2013.

Laffaye, Horace A. *The Evolution of Polo.* McFarland, 2009.

Long, Gavin. 'Gwynn, Sir Charles William (1870–1963)' in *Australian Dictionary of Biography*. National Centre of Biography, Australian National University, 1983.

McLachlan, Mat. *Gallipoli: The Battlefield Guide.* Hachette UK, 2010.

McMullin, Ross, *Pompey Elliott.* Scribe Publications, 2008.

Newton, LM. *The story of the Twelfth, a Record of the 12th Battalion, AIF, during the Great War of 1914–1918.* Hobart: 12th Battalion Association, 1925.

Parliamentary Debates: Legislative Council and House of Representatives, Volume 172. New Zealand Parliament, 1915.

21. Arthur Corrie Lewin, DSO — aviator extraordinaire

Journal of the Connaught Rangers Association. No 1. Vol. 1. July 2003.

Perry, Paula. *A History of the 5th (Service) Battalion Wiltshire Regiment 1914–1919.* The Rifles Wardrobe and Museum Trust, 2007.

PART THREE: FORGOTTEN FRONTS

22. Sky patrol with Erskine Childers

Erskine Childers' wartime service papers are held by the Department of Documents at the Imperial War Museum (www.nationalarchives.gov.uk). His other papers are divided between Trinity College, Cambridge, and Trinity College, Dublin.

Bunbury, Turtle. *The Landed Gentry & Aristocracy of County Wicklow.* Irish Family Names, 2005.

Piper, Leonard. *The Tragedy of Erskine Childers.* Continuum, 2006.

Ring, Jim. *Erskine Childers.* Faber & Faber, 2011.

23. *Hibernia* and the Senussi of Libya

Gwatkin-Williams, RS. *Prisoners of the Red Desert, Being a Full and True History of the Men of the Tara.* London: Thornton Butterworth, 1921.

Halpern, Paul G. *A Naval History of World War I.* London: UCL Press, 1994.

24. Knox D'Arcy — the man who oiled the Royal Navy

Bunbury, Turtle. 'Knox D'Arcy — Mayo's Oil Tycoon', in Terry Reilly, ed., *Amazing Mayo Stories*, Vol. 1. Yew Plain Publishing, 2012.

25. Gunner Tom Barry and the Siege of Kut

Barry, Tom. *Guerilla Days in Ireland.* Mercier Press, 1981.

Crookenden, Arthur. *The History of the Cheshire Regiment in the Great War.* W.H. Evans, 1939.

Farndale, Martin. *History of the Royal Regiment of Artillery: The Forgotten Fronts and the Home Base 1914–18.* Woolwich, 1988.

Hart, Peter. *The I.R.A. and Its Enemies: Violence and Community in Cork, 1916–1923.* Clarendon Press, 1998.

Herbert, Aubrey. *Mons, Anzac and Kut.* London: Edward Arnold, 1919.

Horne, Charles F, ed. *Records of the Great War, Vol. IV.* National Alumni, 1923.

McKenna, Joseph. *Guerrilla Warfare in the Irish War of Independence, 1919–1921.* McFarland, 2011.

McLoughlin, Mark. 'Tom Barry: Guerrilla days in Iraq'. *History Ireland*, Issue 5, September/October 2008, Vol. 16.

Quinn, Anthony P. *Wigs and Guns: Irish Barristers in the Great War.* Four Courts Press in association with the Irish Legal History Society, 2006.

Ryan, Meda. *Tom Barry, IRA Freedom Fighter.* Cork: Mercier Press, 2003.

Swanzy, HB. *The Families of French of Belturbet and Nixon of Fermanagh, and Their Descendants.* Dublin: Alexander Thom & Co., 1908.

26. Nurse Colhoun and the bombing of Vertekop

'Amazing Women of Salt Spring Island', Salt Spring Island Historical Society, via p. 38 of saltspringarchives.com/women.pdf.

The British Journal of Nursing, 28 April 1917.

The Dictionary of Irish Architects 1720–1940, Irish Architectural Archive (www.dia.ie).

Godson, Dean. *Himself Alone: David Trimble and the Ordeal of Unionism.* HarperCollins UK, 2014.

Hay, Ian. *The Story of the British Army Nursing Services*

from the time of Florence Nightingale to the Present Day.
Cassell, 1953.

Kahn, Charles, and Sue Mouat. *Lady Minto Gulf Islands Hospital, a Salt Spring Island History.* Mouat's Trading Company, 2007.

McEwen, Yvonne. *It's a Long Way to Tipperary: British and Irish Nurses in the Great War.* Cualann Press, 2006.

'Military Medal Awards to QA Nurses', via www. qaranc.co.uk/militarymedal.php.

Reiss, RA. *The Kingdom of Serbia — Infringements of the Rules and Laws of War Committed by the Austro-Bulgaro-Germans: Letters of a Criminologist on the Serbian Macedonian Front.* London: George Allen, 1919.

27. Father Kavanagh and the Sinai-Palestine campaign

Anonymous. 'Chaplains in the Great War — Father Bernard Kavanagh, C.SS.R.' *The Dublin Review*, July–September 1919.

28. Colonel Alexander and the spear-point pump

Alexander, JH. His papers are held by the West Sussex Record Office, details of which can be found at www. nationalarchives.gov.uk.

Butler, Steve. *John Howard Alexander.* New Zealand Mounted Rifles Association (www.nzmr.org), 2010.

Gillings, Ken. 'The 'Death' of Bhambatha Zondi — Recent Discovery'. *Military History Journal*, Vol. 12 No 4, December 2002.

Hughes, Wilfrid Kent. *Modern Crusaders: An Account of the Campaign in Sinai and Palestine up to the Capture of Jerusalem.* Melbourne: John Lane, 1918.

www.ashornehill.co.uk.

29. Sergeant Major Flora Sandes, Serbian Army

A massive resource of letters, diaries and other records from Arthur Baker, grandson of Flora's elder sister, Sophia Sandes Baker, can be found at http://sandesancestry.net.

Documents given by Adrian Sandes of Bath, including 'Sallow Glen Kin', can be found at http://sandesancestry.net/source/1062-adrian-sandes.

Allcock, John B, ed., and Antonia Young, *Black Lambs and Grey Falcons: Women Travellers in the Balkans.* Berghahn Books, 2000.

Gregory, Adrian, and Senia Paseta, *Ireland and the Great War: A War to Unite Us All?* Manchester University Press, 2002.

Miller, Louise. *A Fine Brother: The Life of Captain Flora Sandes.* Alma Books, 2012.

Sandes, Flora. *An Englishwoman-sergeant in the Serbian Army.* London: Hodder and Stoughton, 1916.

Sandes, Flora. *The Autobiography of a Woman Soldier: a Brief Adventure with the Serbian Army.* H. F. & G. Witherby, 1927.

Wheelwright, Julie. 'Yudenitch, Flora Sandes (1876–1956)'. *Oxford Dictionary of National Biography.* Oxford University Press, 2004.

USEFUL WEBSITES & FORUMS

dublin-fusiliers.com
royalmunsterfusiliers.org
irishgreatwarsociety.com
1914-1918.invisionzone.com
decadeofcentenaries.com
mylesdungan.com
levinehistory.wordpress.com
britishpathe.com

FACEBOOK GROUPS / PAGES

Let Erin Remember
Irish Military History
Irish Regiments of World War One
From the Sea to the Somme
It's Time to Remember 200,000 Brave Irishmen

For regular updates on Turtle Bunbury's projects, visit turtlebunbury.com or follow his Facebook page at Wistorical.

SOME WORDS OF THANKS

Before the writing comes the research. The vast bulk of this was conducted by me and, therefore, I am almost certainly to blame for any of the inevitable faults within these pages. I have done my best to verify the facts but accounts of war are often hazy, spirited and occasionally rather tall. Two equally intelligent eye-witnesses frequently provide two entirely different versions of the same event. Accuracy can never be absolute but if you should spot any factual errors, I would be extremely grateful if you could alert me via www.turtlebunbury.com so that I can rectify it as much as possible.

A huge number of people helped me along the way. A particular personal delight was establishing contact with the descendants and families of so many of the people mentioned in this book. For that I make a bow to Arthur Carden, Carainn Childers, John de Robeck, Margaret Farrington, Annette Fernyhough, Sue, Lady Kilbracken, Bridget Lindsay, Rob McElroy, Donough McGillycuddy, Johnny Madden, Robbie Ryan, Mike Sandes, Allan Esler Smith, Hilary Tulloch and most especially Niall Ó Síocháin. I would also like to thank Annemarie Kalishoek for her dogged determination in tracking down the ancestry of Hoppy Hardy.

Many learned souls were involved with these texts, adding new details, correcting blunders, sending photographs and such like. I would particularly like to thank Sr Máire Hickey OSB of Kylemore Abbey for her assistance with my essay on the Irish Dames of Ypres. I salute Colonel Sir William Mahon, Bt, LVO, for his wisdom on the Micks. I waggle my wings for Joe Gleeson and Philip Lecane who honed my understanding of the fight in the air. I troop my colours for Sean Connolly (Royal Dublin Fusiliers Association), Dr Myles Dungan, Alex Findlater, Ken Gillings, David Grant, Dominic Lee, Steve 'Mad Paddy' Murtagh, Seamus O'Brien, Robin Prior, Colonel (Retired) TCRB Purdon OBE, Meda Ryan and Dr Susan Schriebman. To Sebastian and Ali Barry, my deepest thanks for your contagious zest and generosity. To Andrew Bunbury, Rohan Boyle and Mathew Forde, let us renew our advance forthwith. And to Miriam Moore and Ross O'Drisceoil, I say 'Gloria in excelsis Deo'.

Patrick Hugh Lynch, Picture Detective extraordinaire, was exceptionally generous with his time, wit and wisdom, while David Power at South Dublin Libraries and the counter staff of the National Library, Kildare Street, all went beyond the call of duty to help gather the illustrations for this book.

My father has also been a tremendous inspiration during this project, not least for his performance in 2013 when he single-handedly proved that miracles can happen.

I take my hat off to the team at Gill & Macmillan for their patience and resolve, to Conor Nagle, Deirdre Rennison Kunz, Jen Patton, Teresa Daly, Graham Thew, Brenda O'Hanlon and all those other unseen eyes that have helped bring *The Glorious Madness* into being.

When I was seeking suitable stories for the book, I was inundated with many brilliant suggestions from far and wide. Sadly I was unable to deal with them all in this particular volume. Perhaps another opportunity will arise but I most sincerely thank all those who submitted ideas to me in any case.

And finally, for assistance great and small, I fire 21-gun salutes for the following:

Dr Jerome aan de Wiel
Ann Adamson
Bruce Arnold
Jules Berridge
Meike Blackwell
Alison Bohan
Alice Boyle
Elizabeth Brennan
Herbie & Jacquie Brennan
Michael Brennan
Michelle Burrowes
Steve Butler (New Zealand
    Mounted Rifles)
Elaine Byrne
John Cahalane
Tim Carey
Michael Carragher
Erskine Childers
Patrick Comerford
Charles Cooper
Winkie Corballis
Andrew Cormack (Royal Air
    Force Museum, Hendon)
David Cotter
Alastair Hubert Bao Butler
    Crampton
Tim Creighton Griffiths
Ciaran Crossey
Noel Cuddy
Ger Delaney (South Mayo Family
    Research)
Matthew Dennison
Anna Maria Donaldson
Dr Terence Dooley
Mark Dorman
Sé Merry Doyle
Tommy Doyle
Simon John Draper
Jake Duggan (Military Museum,
    Carlow)
Dr Patrick Dunae
Alexander Durdin-Robertson
Moira Durdin-Robertson
James Dutton
Tom Edlin
Colette Edwards
Dr Sabine Egger (University of
    Limerick)
Phil Evans
Rory Everard
Las Fallon
Oliver Fallon (Connaught Rangers
    Association Boyle)
Jenny Farrell
William Fennell
Trish Fitzpatrick
Allen Foster
Howard Fox
Emily Gailey
Jerry Gardner
Phil Gilson
Justin & Adam Green
Séamus Greene

David Grenfell
John Grenham
Tom Grimshaw
Patrick Guinness
JJ Hackett
Ray Halpin
Yvonne Harrison (SSAFA Branch
    Secretary)
Virginia Hartley
John F. Headen
Carole Hope
Adrian Hughes (curator of Lland-
    udno Home Front Museum)
Bryan Hughes
Aileen Ivory
Neil Jackman
Mary Jacobs
Matthew Jebb (Keeper,
    National Botanic Gardens)
Hugo Jellett
Arthur Johnson
Morgan Kavanagh
Martin Kelly
Peter Kelly
Kevin Keogh
Ken Kinsella
Brian Kirby (Provincial
    Archivist, Irish Capuchin
    Provincial Archives)
John Kirwan
Rory Knight-Bruce
Joshua Levine
Maria Levinge
Jennifer Lipsett
Theresa Loftus (Monaghan
    County Museum)
Major Robin W.B. Maclean
    (Royal Scots Dragoon Guards
    Museum, Edinburgh Castle)
Paul McCormick (Loyal North
    Lancashire Regiment 1914–18)
Karen McDonnell
Sean McElroy
Yvonne McEwen
Pam McFadden (Curator, Talana
    Museum, Dundee, South Africa)
Una McGarrigle (Donegal Historical
    Society)
John McMahon
Norman McMillan
Chris McQuinn
Ed Magan
Tim Mansfield
Paul Patrick Markham
Joan Marsh
George & Susan Miller
Ida Milne
Angus Mitchell
Nicola Morris
Breda Mulligan
Dermot Mulligan (Carlow
    Museum)
Peter Murnaghan

Celestine Murphy
Laz Murphy
Mal Murray
Jane Murray Brown
Eilish Ní Bhrádaigh
Bernie Nixon
Isabella Rose Nolan
Robert O'Byrne
John O'Donovan
Niall O'Flynn
John O'Keeffe
John Onions
Colin O'Reilly
Manus O'Riordan
James O'Sullivan
William Paton
Cilla Patton
Gordon Power
Jean Prendergast (Royal Munster
    Fusiliers Association)
Chas Preston
Ciarán Priestley
R.D.S. Pringle
Michael Purcell
Maggy Pym
Charlie Raben
Ben & Jessica Rathdonnell
Finola Reid
Barnaby Rogerson
Helen Ryan
Liz S.
Nick Shelley
Jessica Slingsby
Catherine Smith (Charterhouse
    Archivist)
Michael Snape
Christopher Steed
Dacre Stoker
Jenne Stoker
Caroline Sutherland
Tom & Sasha Sykes
Lu Thornely
Simon Tierney
Peter Trill
Seán Ua Cearnaigh
Andy Verney
William Wall
Dr Ciaran Wallace
David Watkins
Georgina Webb
Margaret Whittock
Nick Wilkinson
David Williams
Jim Williamson (jkphotoprint)
David Worsfold
Billy Wright (Tullow Museum)

PICTURE CREDITS

For permission to reproduce photographs, the author and publisher gratefully acknowledge the following:

Alamy: © Classic Image 232–3, © Heritage Image Partnership Ltd 126, © INTERFOTO 147, © Nick Scott 87, © Pictorial Press Ltd 125, 127, 132R, © PV Collection 186, © SOTK2011 vi, © World History Archive 138; Alexander Turnbull Library, Wellington, New Zealand: 218–19, 222; Alice Godley: 216; Courtesy Allan Esler Smith collection: 210; © Australian War Memorial: 292, 292; © BP plc/BP Archive: ARC178498 257, ARC99447 254; Bridgeman Images: © Leven & Lemonier/ Bibliothèque des Arts Décoratifs, Paris, France/Archives Charmet/Bridgeman Images 177, © National Army Museum, London/Bridgeman Images 188–9, © Richard Caton Woodville II/Private Collection/The Stapleton Collection/Bridgeman Images 142, © Sir William Orpen/Imperial War Museum, London, UK/Bridgeman Images 116; Courtesy of Bridget Lindsay: 160; City of Vancouver Archives: 294; CORBIS: Bettmann/CORBIS 134, CORBIS 260–61, Hulton-Deutsch Collection/CORBIS 15, 90, 269; Getty Images: © Central Press/Getty Images 175, 271, Finnerty/Hulton Archive/ Getty Images 114, Getty Images 203, 234, © Hulton Archive/Getty Images 144, 239, 298–9, © Print Collector/Getty Images xvi, 79, © Time Life Pictures/Getty Images 122, © Topical Press Agency/Getty Images 236, 249; Hilary Tulloch: 170–71; Picture courtesy Irish Examiner: 66–7; The Irish Guards: 36, 38, 41, 45, 50, 52, 110; John de Robeck: 152, 156, 159, 166–7, 173, 179; Ken Gillings: 288; © Lebrecht Authors: 82; Mary Evans Picture Library: © David Cohen Fine Art/Mary Evans Picture Library 32T, © Illustrated London News Ltd/ Mary Evans Picture Library 19, 22, © John Frost Newspapers/Mary Evans Picture Library 105, 155, 230, © Mary Evans Picture Library 287, © Robert Hunt Library/ Mary Evans Picture Library 92, 241; Library of Congress Prints and Photographs Division: 47, 77, 84, 130, 180, 200, 204, 244–5, 282, 283, 285, 297, 303; Sr Máire Hickey OSB, Kylemore Abbey: 6, 10; National Botanic Gardens/OPW: 196TC; © The National Library of Ireland: 28, 32B; © National Portrait Gallery, London: 224, 229; Patrick Hugh Lynch: 2, 60, 182, 196TL, 196TR, 197TL, 197TC, 197TR, 196CL, 196C, 196CR, 197CL, 197C, 197CR, 196BL, 196BR, 197B; Phil Evans: 250; © REX FEATURES/Everett Collection: 150, 215; Salt Spring Archives: 274; © The Sandhurst Collection: 132L; By kind permission of the Sheehan family: 62, 72; Dr Terry Daniels Collection: 20, 27; TopFoto: © The Print Collector/ Heritage Images/TopFoto 13, © Roger-Viollet/TopFoto 89, © TopFoto 131, 162, 193, 207, 265, © ullsteinbild/TopFoto 252; © Sir William Orpen/Cyfarthfa Castle Museum & Art Gallery, Merthyr Tydfil: 76; Sir William Orpen/Wikipedia: 120–21; State Library of New South Wales: ii, 95, 140–41; Stephen Callaghan: 109; The Thomas MacGreevy estate: 96; Tullow Museum: 101; University of Toronto/The Canadian Annual Review War Series Vol 4 (1918): 56; Wikipedia: 69, 58, 100, 246, 277.

The author and publisher have made every effort to trace all copyright holders, but if any has been inadvertently overlooked we would be pleased to make the necessary arrangement at the first opportunity.

INDEX